Few people can talk about church planting the way Peyton does. He is the quintessentially reflective practitioner who has pretty much tried all the innovative ideas that he articulately proposes in this book. In my opinion, *Church Plantology* is destined to become essential reading for anyone interested in church planting in Western, post-Christian cultural contexts. This book is an expression of who Peyton Jones is—*outstanding!*

Alan Hirsch, author of numerous award-winning books
on missional movement, leadership, and spirituality;
founder of Movement Leaders Collective, Forge
Mission Training Network, and the 5Q Collective

From one of our Exponential family members comes a road map for multiplication that starts with a strong, principle-centered foundation. To accomplish level 5, movements-based multiplication, planters must value and prioritize multiplication from day one. Strategic gurus tell us to "start with the end in mind," and this is what Peyton Jones outlines in this comprehensive book on planting. Like all the books in the Exponential series, *Church Plantology* will help shift the number of churches that multiply for years to come.

Todd Wilson, president and CEO of Exponential

In *Church Plantology*, Peyton Jones provides an incredibly comprehensive resource on all the significant topics surrounding church planting. If you are a church planter or a network leader who works with planters, this book is an absolute must-read. Don't plant a church without first digesting the insights in this book and allowing them to shape the way you plant churches.

Brad Brisco, author of *Missional
Essentials* and *Covocational Church Planting*

Peyton Jones has delivered a master class in the art and science of church planting. *Church Plantology* is packed with light-bulb moments that help planters and their teams recognize their unique wiring and gifting and understand why they do what they do and feel what they feel. But Peyton doesn't leave it at theory; he walks the planter through the all-too-messy but absolutely crucial stages and challenges they'll encounter in the planting process. Thoroughly biblical, imminently practical, and engagingly readable, *Church Plantology* is destined to become the go-to source for both the philosophy and practicality of church planting for this generation.

Tom Bennardo, executive director of the Synergy Church Planting Network,
author of *The Honest Guide to Church Planting*

Peyton Jones brings first-century biblical insights to bear on twenty-first century church planting challenges, illustrated with practical examples and seasoned with wisdom. Recalibrate your church planting compass by reading *Church Plantology*!

Craig Ott, Trinity Evangelical Divinity School,
coauthor of *Global Church Planting*

By returning to the New Testament for the purpose of fierce integration, Peyton has written a book that feels remarkably modern, even new. His best book yet, *Church Plantology* is both fresh and rooted, a gift to the church.

Brian Sanders, founder of the Underground, author
of *Underground Church* and *Microchurches*

Peyton Jones's latest book, *Church Plantology*, is the intersection of biblical truth, best missionary practices, and church history. This book is a church planting textbook with everything you need to know about how to start a new church. If you're considering planting a church, this is a must-read book.

Dave Ferguson, lead pastor of Community Christian
Church, coauthor of *B.L.E.S.S.: 5 Everyday Ways
to Love Your Neighbor and Change the World*

Leaders of church planting organizations often decry how impractical seminary training is for church planters and missionaries. There are few church planting textbooks that encapsulate what it looks like to plant churches in the twenty-first century. Even fewer are the ones that tie together theology with actual theory and practice. But I assure you that none have the candid, creative, and down-to-earth writing style of Peyton Jones. *Church Plantology* is robust for the guild and practical for the field!

Daniel Yang, director of the Send Institute

Many of the books and resources on church planting were written for a different time and a different place in history. If you are looking for a fresh introduction to church planting for today's world, *Church Plantology* is that book!

Winfield Bevins, director of church planting at
Asbury Seminary, author of *Marks of a Movement*

Since I'm a dedicated disciple-maker and church-multiplier, it was nearly impossible to find "family" with church growth ministry peers, until I encountered Exponential, that is. One of my first Exponential friends was Peyton Jones. He is, however, a disruptor. Read this book cautiously because you won't be the same afterward—and that's a good thing!

Ralph Moore, founder of Hope Chapel churches

CHURCH PLANTOLOGY

CHURCH PLANTOLOGY

THE ART AND SCIENCE OF PLANTING CHURCHES

PEYTON JONES

ZONDERVAN REFLECTIVE

Church Plantology
Copyright © 2021 by Peyton Jones

Requests for information should be addressed to:
Zondervan, *3900 Sparks Dr. SE, Grand Rapids, Michigan 49546*

Zondervan titles may be purchased in bulk for educational, business, fundraising, or sales promotional use. For information, please email SpecialMarkets@Zondervan.com.

ISBN 978-0-310-53417-4 (hardcover)

ISBN 978-0-310-12020-9 (audio)

ISBN 978-0-310-53774-8 (ebook)

Cover design: Darren Welch Design
Cover image: K. Woodgyer, Marina Sun, KamimiArt / Shutterstock
Interior design: Kait Lamphere
Interior artwork (atom image): KamimiArt / Shutterstock

Printed in the United States of America

21 22 23 24 25 26 27 28 29 30 31 /TRM/ 15 14 13 12 11 10 9 8 7 6 5 4 3 2 1

To my first and consistent church planting partner through the years, my wife Andrea, who reminds me of something Ginger Rogers said regarding her dancing partnership with Fred Astaire, "Just remember that everything Fred did, I did backwards, and in high heels."

Bilbo Baggins:
You can promise that I will come back?

Gandalf:
No. And if you do, you will not be the same.

CONTENTS

Rediscovering First-Century Participation:
From Solo Performers to Team Mobilizers

Rediscovering the Spirit's Empowering:
From Fake Bravado to Spiritual Power

Rediscovering Church as Mission:
From Scattering on Mission to Gathering on Mission

Rediscovering Reproducible Sustainability:
From Fully Funded to Apostolically Agile

Rediscovering Kingdom Collaboration Networks for Multiplication:
From Building Upward to Spreading Outward

FOREWORD

Ministry has its foundation in theology with Jesus as the cornerstone. Yet the framing of ministry—the beliefs and activities that give shape and formation to how a church will evangelize and disciple in a particular context—involves both science *and* art.

Science be helpful to any church planter. I wrote my PhD dissertation examining 602 church planters and looking at their work over four years, asking questions to determine which factors affected attendance, conversions, becoming self-sufficient, and more. Those findings provided useful insights to develop more effective tools and trainings for church planting.

Here's an example of what I learned. At that time, people debated whether attending church planting boot camps made any difference. The planters surveyed were recent seminary grads—half of whom went to boot camp after finishing their three-year degree. We compared those who went to the boot camp to those who did not, and comparing planters with the same training—minus the three-day boot camp—revealed a clear statistical difference. The churches with planters who attended the boot camps showed significant growth and vitality compared to those without that experience. This suggested that while a seminary degree is important, laying a necessary theological foundation for gospel ministry, those three days of focused training at boot camp answered a number of specific (and practical) questions for the planters that helped them thrive.

Many church planters send out mailers or create Facebook ads. But what's the typical response to a mailer? If I send out fifty thousand, how many people will likely attend or check out my website? What percentage of people will click on my Facebook ads? Research can show you what results to anticipate. These are all examples of how science can help church planters. And the science of research isn't the only science useful to church planters. Social science can help as well. Early in the twentieth century, Arthur Flake taught what was called Flake's Formula, or "Flake's Five." He laid out five simple principles for the Sunday school that helped thousands of churches grow. Later, the church growth movement focused on missiology under Donald McGavran. Over time, as the movement became more westernized, it engaged more of the social sciences. Eventually it led to methodological mania, overemphasizing the science to the point where there was a formula for everything.

Science is an aspect of common grace. It is neither bad nor sinful to utilize science, and formulas and strategies have helped many planters become more effective at ministry. I understand why some believe we shouldn't use such tools, describing it as sheer pragmatism (as if pragmatism was bad in and of itself). But the real problem is when science trumps theology. When churches and church planters rely more on the sciences than the Savior, they worship the created rather than the Creator. That's a problem.

If used correctly, science and research can help us, and in this book you will find some of the most current and helpful science to aid you in church planting. Peyton Jones lays out the facts, and facts are our friends—whether we like what they tell us or not. His handling of the research will help you see both the grim realities we face and the latent opportunities we dare not miss. He uses research to help us better understand how the early church grew exponentially and how that same growth could happen today.

But science will take us only so far. Peyton also unpacks how planting is an art. This book pushes the reader back to the first century, to a time when planting was driven more by the Spirit than science. I've seen people who were effective at planting a church in one location, but when they went to a new place, they struggled. This is where the art––the nonmechanistic, nonscientific aspect of planting––comes into play. And much of the art of planting is about developing our ability to join in what the Spirit of God is sovereignly working. Here Peyton leans on the example of Paul, who awaited divine opportunities in his own church planting work.

Peyton writes, "Plantology involves the overlap of biblical principles, best missionary experience and practice, and church history." Church planting today must recapture both the science and the art of planting. Your dependency on the power of the gospel, the Word, and the work of the Spirit can overcome some of the weaknesses in your strategy. Learning to rely on the Holy Spirit is one of the glaring truths of Acts, and this reliance allows a planter to be molded by the Lord into the person God can use most effectively.

When we overemphasize the science, we risk turning ministry into a trade show: "The Fifty Tools to Plant a Church" or "Here's How to Do a Mailer." Resources can be good and helpful, but "Instachurch: Just Add Water" doesn't work. Cultivating the art of planting––by answering the call, understanding our giftedness, recognizing the wind of the Spirit, and prayerfully depending

on the Spirit's empowerment––means that we are in tune with where God is
moving and what he is doing. Like Isaiah, we exclaim: "Here I am! send me."
We hunger to be part of God's mission in the world.

I'm a researcher who relies on the science. But as you will read in these
pages, effective church planting means trusting the promptings of the Holy
Spirit, walking in obedience, and living in a missional way. As Peyton writes,
"God is more concerned with what he can do in his servants than what he will
ever do through them." He reminds us that God's math is different. We sow
and we reap; God gives the increase. It's easy to get caught up in using the tools
and forget to rely on the Spirit. But we can do both! We can walk and chew
gum at the same time!

Jesus said we are to be wise as serpents and innocent as doves. In wisdom
we use the best resources and information available to us while innocently, like
a child, depending by faith on the Lord to guide and bless our service to him.
And this book will help you do that.

Ed Stetzer

INTRODUCTION

A few years ago, Exponential, the largest library of multiplication resources in the world, gathered the heads of the biggest church planting networks and denominations to discuss the current crisis of the American church as reflected in two independent studies conducted on church growth. Eighty percent of churches in America are plateaued or in decline. Out of the 20% left, only 7% grew by planting new congregations to carry the torch into the future. So 93% of the church is no longer reproducing itself. The church in America is in trouble.

The youth have already leaked out of the 16% of attractional churches that grow by adding numbers to the megachurch. However, that's not the most disturbing statistic. Although 4% were reproducing churches (meaning they'd planted a church or a handful of churches), they could only locate one example of a church operating at an exponential *level-5 multiplication*. Exponential has introduced the paradigm of church multiplication on a scale of 1 to 5.[1] Level 5 is the level of multiplication. Level 5 churches are multiplying on multiple strands out to at least the fourth generation, meaning you plant a church that plants a church, that plants a church, that plants a church. Level 1 churches are subtracting (or shrinking), level 2 churches have plateaued, and level 3 churches are growing by addition.

Level 1—A church that is in decline (symbolized by a − sign)

Level 2—A church that has plateaued (symbolized by an = sign)

Level 3—A church that is growing by addition, or merely increasing in size (symbolized by + sign)

Level 4—A church that has reproduced by planting a campus or church (symbolized by a / sign)

---

1. Todd Wilson, *Multipliers: Leading Beyond Addition* (Centerville, VA: Exponential, 2019), 21–23.

Level 5—A church that has multiplied to the fourth generation
(symbolized by a x sign)

Sadly, 80% of the churches in America are at level 1 and 2, either shrinking
or plateaued. At the moment, 16% of the churches in America are growing
by addition. Level 3 churches reached a zenith during the church growth
movement but have also experienced self-limiting growth barriers due to the
model itself. Level 4 churches reproduce either by multisite or church planting,
but their growth is not yet multiplication. Only 7% of US churches currently
reproduce.

At levels 1 and 2 the message is *Please stay.*
At levels 3 and 4 the message is *Please come.*
At level 5 the faith community is a launchpad saying *Please GO!*

Levels 1, 2, 3, 4 and 5

Jerusalem qualified as a multiplying church, just as Antioch, Ephesus, and
Rome eventually would in the first century. In forty years, the early church
turned the world upside down, so why does the number of multiplying churches
now register at one?

In order to have kingdom expansion on the level of the first century, you
need multiplying churches, but to have those, you need multiplying leaders.
That's where the whole thing bottlenecks. The solution to the problem facing the Western church was to identify level-5 multiplying leaders in order to
observe what they did and pass down that knowledge to the next generation.

The problem was that when the Exponential team sent out scouts to locate
as many level-5 churches as they could, they returned empty handed. They
then lowered their expectations to finding only twenty-five level-5 multiplying leaders. When that turned out to be a fruitless endeavor, they searched for
ten. After not being able to locate even five level-5 multipliers after scouring
American churches, they found only one.

His name was Ralph Moore, and he'd planted a number of churches from California to Hawaii over a long and fruitful ministry. So far, after discipling three leaders at a time for over fifty years, the current tally of church plants going back to Ralph is 2,730 churches at the time of this writing. The number continues to increase.

The most shocking thing was not how many churches Ralph multiplied, but that in the entire US, there was only one contender. The majority of church structures do not allow for the development of level-5 leaders. For all the leadership development information planters read in book after book, they're missing what made the first-century church planters excel. For somebody who is devoted to the advancement of the church, the next part is hard to say, but for someone devoted to the preservation of the status quo, it is even harder to hear. Today's model of church aims at building upward, whereas the first-century church was wired to expand outward. As form follows function, today's leaders graduate seminary proficient in discoursing upon what the apostles did thousands of years ago as chronicled in the pages of Acts, but they are unable to *do* nearly any of it.

How was the greatest church planter able to plant at breakneck speed so that he could boast "I have fulfilled the ministry of the gospel" from Jerusalem to Macedonia (Rom. 15:19 ESV)? How can we recapture that momentum and make sure that there isn't just one movement of multiplication in America, but an army of movement makers? The answers to these questions are simple, but we cannot accomplish the goal by continuing to engage in ministry as usual. The types of leaders who will catalyze movements must detonate their cushy ministries, and hit the self-destruct button on the status quo if they are to become the type of movements we frequently talk about yet rarely see. Few are willing to pay the price that Paul, Wesley, or Zinzendorf did, and therefore, we fail to put into practice what we desire. Church planting is costly. Level-5 multiplication is costlier still.

I have trained church planters for over fifteen years, and I have grown along the way. I would like to apologize to my first trainees. I didn't know then what I know now. To those reading this book, I'm sorry that I still don't know everything planters need to learn, for my journey has not yet come to an end. Michelangelo is rumored to have signed a sketch he was working on at age eighty-seven with the inscription *"Ancora Imparo,"* translated into English as "I'm still learning."

Therefore,

Ancora Imparo,

PEYTON JONES

WHAT IS CHURCH PLANTOLOGY?

1

Rip it out!
—JOHN KEATING

In the classic film *Dead Poets Society*, Robin Williams plays Mr. John Keating, a first-year literature teacher at Welton Academy, a hundred-year-old Ivy League prep school for young men. The four pillars of Welton are chanted in unison at their first assembly, "Tradition! Honor! Discipline! Excellence!"

On the second day of class, Mr. Keating asks one of the students to read an excerpt from their textbook *Understanding Poetry* by Dr. J. Evans Pritchard, Ph.D. explaining meter, rhyme, and figures of speech. Pritchard suggests a system for plotting "a poem's score for perfection" using horizontal and vertical graphs to reveal whether the poem is "truly great."

Mr. Keating interrupts the student, shocking the class with the following monologue:

> Excrement.
> That's what I think of Mr. J. Evans Pritchard.
> We're not laying pipe.
> We're talking about poetry.
> How can you describe poetry like American Bandstand?
> "Oh, I like Byron. I give him a 42, but I can't dance to it."
> Now, I want you to rip out that page.

The students look up at him in disbelief, then look around at each other to gauge the appropriate reaction. Keating continues:

Go on!
Rip out the entire page.
You heard me. Rip it out.
[He raises his voice] Rip it out! Go on.
Rip it out!

As you read this textbook, I want to hear the sound of ripping. Much of what has passed as church planting instruction doesn't make the grade when boots hit the ground. Much of what is taught on planting in seminaries and classrooms could be likened to studying poetry with J. Evans Pritchard's metric versus being carried away by the passion of the apostles when planting churches.

Mr. Keating urges the students to keep ripping straight through the entire introduction:

"Keep ripping, gentlemen! This is a battle. A war. And the casualties could be your hearts and souls. . . . Be gone Mr. J. Evans Pritchard!"

I would like to see much of the church planting curriculum that has been taught to planters move to the history department to be studied as what church planters used to do. Keating assures the students, "It's not the Bible. You're not gonna go to hell for this."

Finally, he looks at them with that gleam in his eyes, "Now, my class, you will learn to think for yourselves again."[1] Much of what we believe about church planting is because we've inherited a system that is built on something that no longer works: the church growth movement. Even as the church is sinking in the West, it continues to cling to this failed movement like a lifesaving ring made of iron. Much of what is called church planting is really church growth packaged as an ecclesial business startup.

According to data from Pew Research studies conducted in 2012 to 2019, only 65% of people polled in America identify as Christians. In 1990, 85% identified as Christian; this statistic marks a 20% decline in thirty years. Perhaps even more concerning is that from 1990 to 2001, the number dropped 4% in eleven years, maintaining a similar drop of 3% from 2001 to 2012, but plummeting by a drastic 12% during the last seven years. If this trend continues, the Christian population of 167 million in this country will continue to drop drastically.[2]

1. *Dead Poets Society*, produced by Steven Haft, directed by Peter Weir (Touchstone, 1989).

2. "American Religious Identification Survey," CUNY Graduate Center, https://web.archive.org /web/20110709082644/http:/www.gc.cuny.edu/faculty/research_briefs/aris/key_findings.htm; "In U.S., Decline of Christianity Continues at Rapid Pace: An update on America's changing religious

Against this backdrop, Lifeway Research conducted a study in 2014 concluding, "More than 4,000 new churches opened their doors in 2014, outpacing the 3,700 that closed, according to estimates from the Nashville-based research organization based on input from 34 denominational statisticians."[3] Although I don't question the quantitative figures they received, I question whether the qualitative data ruled out the possibility of multiple denominations claiming the same church plants in reporting their data. Every year, networks and denominations report that they've planted a certain number of churches, but many of these new church plants may be a part of multiple denominations. When multiple denominations fund the same planter, they slap their sponsorship sticker on the church plant like a NASCAR race car. If more than one network or denomination reports the same church plant, the figures of churches planted become skewed and unreliable.

Despite Paul stating, "Neither do we go beyond our limits by boasting of work done by others" (2 Corinthians 10:15), it is still standard practice to throw money at a planter boasting credit for their work. Church history, however, demonstrates that the church often thrives when it appears to be failing. In *Transforming Mission*, David Bosch summarized Kraemer, who claimed that the church was born in crisis and in danger of being swallowed up, and that, in this tension, it "has always needed apparent failure and suffering in order to become fully alive to its real nature and mission." The problem, Bosch says, is that the church is so seldom aware of the danger under which it lives, "And for many centuries the church has suffered very little and has been led to believe that it is a success." Any "success" that the church has seemed to enjoy in any century has been an abnormal period for it, and therefore provided an illusion

---

landscape," Pew Research Center: Religion and Public Life, October 17, 2019, https://www.pewforum.org/2019/10/17/in-u-s-decline-of-christianity-continues-at-rapid-pace; "'Nones' On the Rise," Pew Research Center: Religion and Public Life, October 9, 2012, https://www.pewforum.org/2012/10/09/nones-on-the-rise.

3. Lisa Cannon Green, "New Churches Draw Those Who Previously Didn't Attend," Lifeway Research, December 8, 2015, https://lifewayresearch.com/2015/12/08/new-churches-draw-those-who-previously-didnt-attend. This is part of a continuing downward spiral that has been continuing since the 1950s in America. Ed Stetzer reports that 80–85 percent of American churches are on the downside of their life cycle, 3,500 to 4,000 churches close each year, and the number of unchurched has almost doubled from 1990 to 2004. He reported that in 1900, there were twenty-eight churches for every 10,000 Americans. In 1950, there were seventeen churches for every 10,000 Americans. In 2000, there were twelve churches for every 10,000 Americans. In 2011, there were eleven churches for every 10,000 Americans. The research also showed that in the hundred years between 1900 and 2000, "the number of churches increased just over 50 percent while the population of the country has almost quadrupled." Ed Stetzer, *Planting Missional Churches* (Nashville: Broadman & Holman, 2016), 9.

of what success was, but in the current post-modern crisis, Bosch exclaims, "Now, at long last, we are 'back to normal' . . . and we know it!"[4]

CHURCH PLANTING VERSUS CHURCH STARTING

Much of what we call church planting in North America is actually church starting. The first difference between starting a church and planting one is that church starting begins with the church itself as its goal. This goal of starting a church can be translated to renting a large space, gathering a large crowd into it, and reaching "critical mass" so that the church can sustain financial stability and provide a paycheck. When boiled down to basics, what has been accomplished is a "pop-up" church that appears on Sundays and disappears the other six days of the week. In other words, church starting amounts to little more than starting a Sunday service.

Here are the six crucial steps to church starting:

1. Raise funds (usually hundreds of thousands of dollars).
2. Recruit enough people to ensure critical mass.
3. Brainstorm a catchy church name (branding is crucial).
4. Design a sexy logo (branding is everything).
5. Rent a building.
6. Advertise, blast, and promote on social media and hope it's enough to fill the building on launch day.

---

4. David Jacobus Bosch, *Transforming Mission: Paradigm Shifts in Theology of Mission* (New York: Orbis Books, 2011), 2.

The full quote:

It is, rather, normal for Christians to live in a situation of crisis. It should never have been different. In a volume written in preparation for the 1938 Tambaram conference of the International Missionary Council (IMC), Kraemer (1947:24) formulated this as follows, "Strictly speaking, one ought to say that the Church is always in a state of crisis and that its greatest shortcoming is that it is only occasionally aware of it." This ought to be the case, Kraemer argued, because of "the abiding tension between (the church's) essential nature and its empirical condition" (:24f). Why is it, then, that we are so seldom aware of this element of crisis and tension in the church? Because, Kraemer added, the church "has always needed apparent failure and suffering in order to become fully alive to its real nature and mission" (:26). And for many centuries the church has suffered very little and has been led to believe that it is a success. Like its Lord, the church—if it is faithful to its being—will, however, always be controversial, a "sign that will be spoken against" (Lk 2:34). That there were so many centuries of crisis-free existence "for the church was therefore an abnormality." Now, at long last, we are "back to normal" . . . and we know it! And if the atmosphere of crisislessness still lingers on in many parts of the West, this is simply the result of a dangerous delusion. Let us also know that to encounter crisis is to encounter the possibility of truly being the church. The Japanese character for "crisis" is a combination of the characters for "danger" and "opportunity" (or "promise"); crisis is therefore not the end of opportunity but in reality only its beginning (Koyama 1980:4), the point where danger and opportunity meet, where the future is in the balance and where events can go either way.

Renting a building, creating a website, designing a logo, and inviting people to a phantom church that exists only in our minds is an unusual practice. I'm not against raising funds or recruiting launch teams. Both can be helpful if your goal is church starting, but they aren't as necessary in church planting as we've been taught by our own ranks of "J. Evans Pritchard" experts. Much of our fundraising and attempts at reaching critical mass mask the truth that we have attempted to strip all risk out of the endeavor in order to ensure "success." But if "success" is measured by filling a room, we aren't defining it the way Jesus or Paul did. Jesus emptied them on purpose and sent the crowds packing. Church starters may have "success" in filling a room, but at the cost of even greater loss.

- What if gathering crowds occurs at the cost of mission?
- What if the large amount of expense it takes to start a church comes at the expense of making disciples?

If we invest everything in a Sunday service at the expense of mission, then everyone loses, particularly those outside the church. The church is in its current rut because we've learned to "do church" in a way that ensures no one ever really has to engage with the gospel at all.

This is more than mere semantics. Church starts have stripped out the need to make disciples who, in turn, make disciples. At its very foundation, church starting undermines the very thing that makes church planting successful.

Further, I would contend that church starting is what is failing today, whereas church planting will continue to thrive for years to come. The amount of investment one must put into church starting is both financially excessive and heavy in terms of human resources with very little ROI. Church planting, on the other hand, can be cheap or even free.

Compare the field practices of church starting today with effective missionary church planting throughout history:

Church Starting	Church Planting
Choose a sexy church name.	Begin with intense prayer.
Design a sexy church logo.	Focus on bringing the gospel to the lost.
Gather a group of Christians together.	Enter the rhythms of the community.
Create a leadership team.	Make disciples.
Market like mad.	Pick a fight with something.
Attain critical mass.	Move on and await divine opportunities.

REFORMISSION

Why does this church starting model look so different from what Paul did? Paul never rolled up on a community with his hip church name, sexy logo, rental agreement, and flashy website and called it church planting. Nor could anyone remotely conceive of him participating in that method of operation. In that case, why would we?

In *Church Planting in the Secular West*, Stefan Paas identifies the church growth movement as the scientific stream in evangelical church planting theory that comes from the Western emphasis on "empirically tested methods and developing research programs" that view numerical growth pragmatically.[5] If it produced results (i.e., church growth success), it should be adopted. The founders and advocates of this movement were largely concerned with church growth as produced by evangelism, and they unhitched church structure from the rig. As a consequence, discipleship all but vanished; unlike generations before that had gone to "community churches" that were small, yet intimate, a new generation emerged that preferred large, impersonal church systems that enabled mass attendance but not disciple making.

In *Jurassic Park*, chaos theorist Dr. Malcolm observed that, often, innovation in form overtakes sustainability in function, remarking, "Your scientists were so preoccupied with whether or not they could, they didn't stop to think if they should."[6] Ever the realist, Malcolm also quipped, "Change is like death. You don't know what it looks like until you're standing at the gates." Proven by church history, what was produced from this shifting of gears was a church that exhibited, according to Jim Packard, "a faith 3,000 miles wide, but 1 inch deep."[7]

Science only establishes the veracity of a theory after experimentation demonstrates it to be reproducible and predictable. Statistics demonstrate that our "scientific theory" of church planting based on results no longer produces the results from the church growth movement of the '80s and '90s. In any scientific experiment the environmental conditions must be right, and what worked during the age of modernism petered out over the advent of postmodernism. Churches operating in the church growth paradigm are reported by denominational leaders to be over 90 percent in decline. Rather than attempting to reproduce the effects of the church growth movement, leaders should be seeking

5. Stefan Paas discusses the church growth movement as a scientific approach to church planting in *Church Planting in the Secular West* (Grand Rapids: Eerdmans, 2016), 37–39.

6. *Jurassic Park*, produced by Kathleen Kennedy, directed by Steven Spielberg (Universal Pictures, 1983).

7. James Houston, Bruce Hindmarsh, and Steve L. Porter, "A Faith 3,000 Miles Wide, But 1 Inch Deep," Biola University Center for Christian Thought: The Table, November 25, 2013, https://cct.biola.edu/a-faith-3-000-miles-wide-but-1-inch-deep-james-houston-and-bruce-hindmarsh/.

to reproduce the predictable results of implementing first-century practices. Without first-century practices, we will never witness first-century results.

In modern times, church planting practices have largely been calibrated to the metrics of the church growth movement, and the mission of the church is in dire need of reformation. The dictionary defines "reformation" as "to shape again." It is a return to the principles established when the revolution first happened. In ages past, there have been periods of reformation when some of the apostolic roles revived and the methods of the early church re-emerged. God raised up dreamers like Zinzendorf, Wesley, and others who embodied the spirit of innovation Thomas Edison had displayed as he invented the light bulb after he repeatedly exhorted his crew, "There's a better way, boys, find it!"[8]

The need for a reformation in mission has been consistently noted by missionaries who've returned from the field after many years immersed in it. Roland Allen, an Anglican missionary to China, returned home to England and published his groundbreaking work *Missionary Methods: St. Paul's or Ours?*[9] Over one hundred years later, the book remains in print, appreciated as a standard missionary text by today's leading missiologists. Allen believed that we in the church had "shut our eyes to the profound teaching and practical wisdom of the Pauline method."[10]

While many are careful to ensure orthodoxy in accordance with the doctrinal message of Paul, few are concerned with the actual practices Paul modeled in his missional orthopraxis that was born out of his theology. Lesslie Newbigin, another returning missionary, sought to connect the two.

Missionaries like Allen, Newbigin, and others returned to the West as changed individuals but, more important, as individuals convinced that the church needed to change—specifically, to re-embrace the principles of the first century. When I wrote my first book, *Church Zero*, I quickly realized, through the help of my editor, that I was not alone among those who returned from the field convinced that the church's only way to advance again was to return to New Testament principles. My editor had also worked on Jim Peterson's book *Church Without Walls* thirty years earlier and told me that reading my book was like experiencing editorial déjà-vu.[11] We were mission practitioners, and we returned to the West with the same message: The church must reform and recover its first-century revolutionary principles of mission. Only then can we advance again, instead of retreating.

---

8. Advertisement for McGraw-Edison Company, *Newsweek* vol. 50 (December 23, 1957), 28.

9. Michael Pocock, "Paul's Strategy: Determinative for Today?" in *Paul's Missionary Methods: In His Time and Ours*, ed. Robert L. Plummer and John Mark Terry (Downers Grove, IL: InterVarsity Press, 2012), 147.

10. Roland Allen, *Missionary Methods: St. Paul's or Ours?* (Cambridge: The Lutterworth Press, 2006), 119.

11. Jim Peterson, *Church Without Walls: Moving Beyond Traditional Boundaries* (Colorado Springs: NavPress, 1992).

Why the connection to the New Testament from all of these missionary practitioners? The answer is simple, yet commonly overlooked. The entire New Testament was written exclusively by missionary practitioners. Therefore, the New Testament is a missionary book. When missionaries read the New Testament, their practitioner lenses bring missional practices into focus. Practitioners seem to read a different Bible than theorists. Ben Franklin said, "An ounce of experience is worth a ton of theory."

New Testament scholar of Pauline mission Eckhart Schnabel responds to the tendency by missiologists to ignore the New Testament model of mission: "The skepticism regarding information in the book of Acts seems, at least occasionally, to find an explanation in the fact that the university theologians are not familiar with missionary realities from personal experience; they have not seen antagonistic or indifferent people being converted to the Christian faith, or they have not been part of a team that planted a new local church. And it seems that often they have not attempted to at least gather relevant information on such matters."[12] Perhaps one cannot properly understand the nuances and subtleties of the New Testament in context unless engaged on mission.[13]

Allen and the aforementioned missiologists were right: Each generation must examine the practices of mission during their generation to determine whether they've drifted from the methods and practices, and therefore the spirit, of the early church.

Therefore, in order to get an accurate definition of church planting, we must turn to the actions of the early church to get a baseline. Alan Hirsch opens his book *The Forgotten Ways* by probing the secret of exponential growth from 25,000 Christians in AD 100 to 20 million Christians by AD 310.[14] Entire civilizations have lost certain technologies instead of advancing in them, just as the modern church has forgotten the ancient tactics of kingdom advancement employed by the apostles. As Roland Allen challenged, "Either we must drag down Paul from his pedestal as the great missionary, or we must acknowledge that there is that quality of universality in his work."[15] If his work contains "that quality of universality," then there are principles and practices that can be applied to—and

---

12. Eckhard J. Schnabel, *Early Christian Mission: Jesus and the Twelve* (Downers Grove, IL: InterVarsity Press, 2004), 24.

13. This has been the encouraging thing about the resurgence of young people who delved deeply into theology yet also combined it with missional practice. Groups such as Acts 29, Tim Challies's blog, John Piper's *Don't Waste Your Life* address to a crowd of young people numbering 40,000, and the work of South Eastern Seminary have been well documented in Collin Hansen's book *Young, Restless, and Reformed* (Wheaton, IL: Crossway, 2008).

14. Alan Hirsch, *The Forgotten Ways: Reactivating Apostolic Movements* (Grand Rapids: Brazos, 2016), 17.

15. Roland Allen, *Missionary Methods: God's Plan for Missions According to Paul* (Abbotsford, WI: Aneko, 2017), viii.

trained into—modern church planters. Unfortunately, we will never have "how to plant a church in five easy steps" laid out for us from the pages of Scripture. Ott and Wilson observed that although we can't repeat the events and methods exactly, due to our situation being different, "we do seek to continue in the same trajectory, in continuity with the dynamic of mission as depicted in Acts."[16]

THE SCIENCE OF REDISCOVERY

Inventors take credit for what they've created. Scientists make discoveries. The pioneers of the scientific method didn't see themselves as inventing anything. Johannes Kepler is credited with saying, "Science is the process of thinking God's thoughts after him." Isaac Newton echoed Kepler, saying, "This most beautiful system of the sun, planets, and comets, could only proceed from the counsel and dominion of an intelligent and powerful Being."[17] Rather than their science positioning them to invent new theories, their belief that everything had an intelligent design positioned them to "rediscover" what God had hidden. Thus, properly understood, a discovery is uncovering something that was already there. In church planting, so-called discoveries are actually just a process of rediscovering God's original design.

To me, church planting has always felt this way, like we are rediscovering what somebody else designed. Despite having been a part of intentional church planting in Hungary, New Zealand, and Huntington Beach, I accidentally started a church in a Starbucks in South Wales in 2005.

There were three principles at work on my church-planting journey that I retroactively discovered were also in Acts:

1. Paul infiltrated the marketplace. (I was bivocationally working as a barista at the Starbucks.)
2. Paul's ministry was often infiltrating a public venue where people were already gathered: "He went to the synagogue, as was his custom."
3. Paul had learned to master gospel discussion as he "reasoned with the Jews concerning Jesus."

At first, planting out of a Starbucks sounds sexy and new; the more I ventured out in seemingly innovative practices, though, the more the Scriptures humbled me by showing me that there was nothing new under the sun. The apostles

---

16. Craig Ott and Gene Wilson, *Global Church Planting: Biblical Principles and Best Practices for Multiplications* (Grand Rapids: Baker Academic, 2011), 49–50.

17. Isaac Newton, *Delphi Collected Works of Sir Isaac Newton* (Hastings, East Sussex, UK: Delphi, 2016).

had mastered church in public spaces millennia before I did. Stripped of my illusions of originality, I discovered my faith in Scripture had been weak. Studying the missional practices in Acts led me to study the missional practices in the Epistles, and this finally led me to understand the practices of Jesus in the Gospels. From the Gospels, I gleaned the principles that Paul modeled to those he trained. We should not leave planters to discover New Testament mission retroactively on their own. We should train them to approach mission with a New Testament mindset before they begin. Plantology is the study of mission as modeled by Jesus and the apostles that results in church planting. As I progressed in my understanding of church in public space, I came to discover that the Anabaptists, Moravians, Methodists, and many throughout the world today continue to embrace ministry in public spaces.

Plantology involves the overlap of biblical principles, best missionary experience and practice, and church history. Where these three overlap, it is reasonable to conclude the discovery of timeless principles. Plantology avoids the pragmatism of the church growth movement that based its approach only on results but robbed the church of other valuable assets. If it is practical but not biblical, it does not qualify as a timeless plantology principle.

If the principles of plantology are timeless principles, then we should be able to trace the re-emergence of them throughout church history when the kingdom catapulted forward in catalytic expansion, before they were suppressed by Constantine. Therefore, throughout this book, we'll attempt to trace the overlapping of these three lenses like a microscope to bring the first-century plantology principles into focus. The rediscovery of these principles is intended to serve as a sort of Church Planting 101 for this generation to build upon as they discover more.

Church Plantology

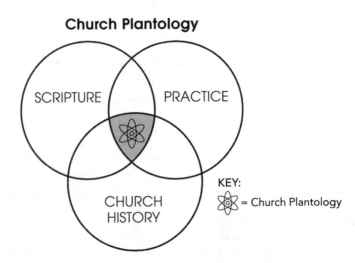

SCRIPTURE

PRACTICE

CHURCH HISTORY

KEY:
⚛ = Church Plantology

Church planting has suffered from philosophies of ministry that insist that one circle should be adhered to at the expense of the others.

- Biblicism—a legalistic adherence to one biblical truth at the expense of others.
- Antiquarianism—an adherence to the practices of historical periods for the sake of their antiquity.
- Pragmatism—an adherence to practices that produce results regardless of other factors.

Movement historian Steve Addison chronicles multiple movements throughout history across the globe. At the beginning of his book *Movements that Change the World*, Addison summarizes the principles that Roland Allen attributed to spontaneous kingdom expansion:

- When new converts immediately tell their story to those who know them.
- When, from the beginning, evangelism is the work of those within the culture.
- When true doctrine results from the true experience of the power of Christ rather than mere intellectual instruction.
- When the church is self-supporting and provides for its own leaders and facilities.
- When new churches are given the freedom to learn by experience and are supported but not controlled.[18]

Addison demonstrates these principles present in all movements that began in Acts, re-emerged throughout history, and are still applied by movement makers today. Plantology is the application of first-century apostolic church planting principles in Acts, church history, and contemporary missionary practice.

EXPERIMENTATION WITH REPRODUCIBLE RESULTS

Aubrey Malphurs defines church planting as "An exhausting but exciting venture of faith, the planned process of starting and growing local churches

---

18. Steve Addison, *Movements That Change the World: Five Keys to Spreading the Gospel* (Downers Grove, IL: InterVarsity Press, 2011), 93.

based on Jesus's promise to build his church and in obedience to his Great Commission."[19]

While this is an excellent description of what church planting feels like to the planter, and what planters think they are doing, it doesn't truly define church planting in its essence. In order to define what church planting is, we will also have to define what church planting is not, and for that, we will have to return to Mr. Keating's lesson of "Rip, Shred, Tear" before we get to an adequate definition.

J. D. Payne's definition of biblical church planting in *The Challenge of the Great Commission* is a useful way to begin this book. He wrote, "Biblical church planting follows the way modeled by Jesus and imitated by the Apostolic Church for global disciple-making. It is a methodology and strategy for bringing in the harvest, raising up leaders from the harvest, and sending leaders to work in the harvest fields."[20]

Science only establishes the veracity of a theory after experimentation demonstrates it to be reproducible and predictable. What if what was done in the New Testament is the basic pattern that many later experiments in ministry have helped practitioners rediscover in times of the church's greatest advancement? What if there was a study of the science of church planting? Where would you go for your data? Wouldn't you look at the first planters, the subsequent planters throughout history, and then examine that data against the modern practice of planting?

The first lesson of church plantology is that planting a church should never be our focus. Christ never commanded his disciples to plant churches, because it's not what He wanted them to focus on. Focusing on the church to be planted leads to church starting, whereas focusing on the Great Commission itself leads to church planting. One of the biggest criticisms leveled at the resurgence of church planting books and conferences is that God never commanded us to plant churches. What did he command? Let's carefully examine what the Twelve were commanded by Christ to do:

- Then Jesus came to them and said, "All authority in heaven and on earth has been given to me. Therefore go and make disciples of all nations, baptizing them in the name of the Father and of the Son and of the Holy Spirit, and teaching them to obey everything I have commanded you. And surely I am with you always, to the very end of the age" (Matt. 28:18–20).

---

19. Aubrey Malphurs, *The Nuts and Bolts of Church Planting: A Guide for Starting Any Kind of Church* (Grand Rapids: Baker, 2011), 22.

20. Thom S. Rainer and Chuck Lawless, eds., *The Challenge of the Great Commission* (Bemidji: Pinnacle Publishing, 2005), 107–108.

- He said to them, "Go into all the world and preach the gospel to all creation" (Mark 16:15).
- He told them, "This is what is written: The Messiah will suffer and rise from the dead on the third day, and repentance for the forgiveness of sins will be preached in his name to all nations, beginning at Jerusalem" (Luke 24:46–47).
- Again Jesus said, "Peace be with you! As the Father has sent me, I am sending you" (John 20:21).

If you boil down all four of those recordings of the same conversation, you come up with five things he wanted them to focus on.

- Make disciples.
- Baptize them in the name of the triune God.
- Teach them to obey Christ's commands.
- Go to all nations.
- Preach.

Yet every time these things are done, church plants are left in our wake. Church planting is what inevitably happens when you focus on these things, yet you can start a church *without accomplishing any of them*. Therefore, any focus on the church itself is misplaced and a hallmark of church starting. We are not called to plant churches, but to make disciples. Ralph Moore once remarked to me in conversation, "If you plant churches, discipleship may or may not happen. Yet if you devote yourself to making disciples, churches will inevitably be planted."

Much of what the church growth movement teaches leaders to do isn't found in the book of Acts, and conversely, most leaders at the helms of America's largest churches still can't do much of what we read about in Acts either. How many leaders of large churches can you think of who are making disciples and evangelizing their community outside of the pulpit?

The issue is clear: What modern planters usually mean by church planting is very different from what it meant to the first-century missionaries. Eckhart Schnabel quoted Ferdinand Hahn, saying, "The early church was a missionary church. The proclamation, the teaching, all activities of the early Christians had a missionary dimension. The fact that it is not possible to find a defined concept of 'missions' in the New Testament does not alter the fact that early Christianity was controlled by the missionary task in their entire existence and in all their activities."[21]

---

21. Eckhard J. Schnabel, *Early Christian Mission: Jesus and the Twelve* (Downers Grove, IL: InterVarsity Press, 2004), 5.

George Whitefield, who was used to stoke the fires of the same movement spent weeks in agony attempting to discern his calling. Before him was the choice to go to Gloucester or continue studying Divinity at the University. After finding no help from asking ministers' advice, he wrote: "The remainder of the fortnight I spent in reading the several missions of the prophets and apostles, and wrestled with God to give me grace to follow their good examples."[22] Those two weeks proved a turning point that brought in the great evangelical awakening, as Whitefield determined to live, minister, and die if need be, like the first century apostles.

John Wesley, at the forefront of the great evangelical awakening, advanced the kingdom by a return to the methods of what he termed "primitive Christianity," a return to the practices of the apostles. The results of his experimentation were remarkable. Within forty years, 10 percent of England's populace claimed to be Methodists. Wesley's mission statement to the American Methodists included "to reform the continent and spread scriptural holiness over these lands."[23]

He tirelessly traversed fields and roads, travelling over 250,000 miles on horseback; he preached 40,000 sermons and wrote over 400 publications.[24] In 1768, Wesley established circuits for his circuit riders—apostolic preachers bent on discipleship—to travel in pursuit of his mission. By his death, there were 115 circuits and 300 preachers carrying out his work. By 1840, the circuits numbered 399, and the number of preachers was 492 in the UK, and 2,000 in America.[25] Today, over 20 million Methodists trace their spiritual heritage back to Wesley's ministry. He was the closest thing the church has ever had to the apostle Paul. First-century methods produced first-century results.

CAUSE AND EFFECT

In the study of physics, there is the law of cause and effect. Every action has an opposite and equal reaction. In Church plantology, the law of cause and effect can also explain the connection between what we focus on and what happens. Church planting is not the *cause* of anything in the New Testament, but rather the *effect* of carrying out the Great Commission. It's the difference

---

22. Luke Tyerman, *The Life of the Reverend George Whitefield* (Azle, TX: Need of the Times, 1995), 43.

23. John Hucks, *John Wesley and Eighteenth Century Methodist Movement: A Model for Effective Leadership* (San Diego: Point Loma Nazarene University, 2003), 27.

24. Hucks, *John Wesley*, 10.

25. Hucks, *John Wesley*, 27.

between starting a church *for* evangelism, versus starting a church *from* evangelism.[26] The focus on church starting is a component of our twenty-first century church-centric approach based on Western Christendom that has gotten us into the current problems the church faces. The church still sees itself as the center, the hub of all activity, and as we've seen, the frontier was the focus of the apostles.

The proclamation of Jesus as Lord is central to the book of Acts. Church planting is not. As Schnabel observes in his two-volume tome on early Christian mission, "The oral proclamation of the gospel is the central action of missionary work."[27]

David Peterson, in his scholarship on Acts, observes, "The growth of the word is clearly coextensive with the growth of the church. Luke uses the verb to 'grow' in connection with the 'word' . . . recalling Jesus's parable about the seed of the word of God being sown in good soil and yielding an amazing crop."[28] He cites the following passages as evidence.

- 6:7—"So the word of God spread. The number of disciples in Jerusalem increased rapidly, and a large number of priests became obedient to the faith."
- 12:24—"But the word of God continued to spread and flourish."
- 19:20—"In this way the word of the Lord spread widely and grew in power."

Therefore, when Acts chronicles the progress of kingdom expansion, it's not measured in terms of churches planted. Acts never summarizes Paul's activity in any town by saying something to the effect of, "And a church was planted in Corinth." Instead, the summary passages[29] closing each section of the book focus on the number of disciples made:

- "And the Lord added to their number daily those who were being saved" (2:47).
- "Nevertheless, more and more men and women believed in the Lord and were added to their number" (5:14).

---

26. Jeff Christopherson and Mac Lake, *Kingdom First: Starting Churches that Shape Movements* (Nashville: Broadman & Holman, 2015).
27. Schnabel, *Early Christian Mission*, 977.
28. David Peterson, *The Acts of the Apostles* (Grand Rapids: Eerdmans, 2009), 33.
29. Including those listed above by Peterson that were omitted from this list to avoid needless repetition.

- "So the word of God spread. The number of disciples in Jerusalem increased rapidly, and a large number of priests became obedient to the faith" (6:7).
- "The Lord's hand was with them, and a great number of people believed and turned to the Lord" (11:21).
- "He was a good man, full of the Holy Spirit and faith, and a great number of people were brought to the Lord" (11:24).
- "So the churches were strengthened in the faith and grew daily in numbers" (16:5).

To truly define church planting, start by answering one of the first questions I ask planters as part of their training assignments: "If you were not allowed to start a Sunday service, describe what your church looks like." Once you can answer that question, you're beginning to crack the code to defining what church planting is. This book works from a central premise: If at any time you're focused on the church you're going to plant, you're focused on the wrong thing.

Our call is to preach the gospel. Jesus said that building the church was actually his job, declaring, "On this rock, *I* will build my church" (Matt. 16:18 ESV, emphasis mine). Many church planting books quote this passage but fail to point out that planting churches is what *God* does, while we engage in the Great Commission. Paul reinforces this concept by stating that he and Apollos engaged in gospel work, leaving the results to God: "I planted the seed, Apollos watered it, but God has been making it grow" (1 Cor. 3:6 ESV). Further, when Jesus sent out the seventy-two, he was teaching them to focus on the cause; he focused them on mission. Jesus didn't ask them to plant congregations during either mission trip; he gave instructions that focused them on mission itself. When church starting becomes the mission, the real mission has been lost.

Here is the pattern that Paul repeatedly followed:

- sowing the gospel
- watering it with a sustained presence and a gospel lifestyle
- reaping converts
- discipling them for greater multiplication

PAUL'S PRACTICES

Consider Paul's practice of church planting on his first missionary journey on Cyprus after leaving Antioch in Acts chapter 13.

1. INTENSE DEPENDENCE—13:1–3—Paul, Barnabas, and John Mark engage in fasting and prayer to entreat God to go ahead of them and be the first one there.
2. SUPERNATURAL WITNESS—13:4–12—The preaching of the gospel is followed with signs and wonders that affirm the message.
3. RHYTHMIC PRESENCE—13:15—They entered into the rhythms of the community, joining the gathering in the synagogue. Later, they adapted to cultural hubs such as Mars Hill and everyday marketplace ministry.
4. OBLIGATORY PREACHING—13:16–48—"We had to speak the word of God to you first." This is emphasized by verse 46 and is supported by Paul's affirmation elsewhere that "I am innocent of the blood of all" (Acts 20:26) and "woe to me if I do not preach the gospel." (1 Cor. 9:16)
5. STRATEGIC CONTROVERSY—13:49–50—Paul and Barnabas upset the local authorities who, in turn, expelled them from the city. Nevertheless, the word of God spread.
6. APOSTOLIC AGILITY—13:51–52—Paul, Barnabas, and John Mark possess the ability to reposition themselves, move on, and, as they engage in their mission, the disciples left behind continue to be filled with the Holy Spirit and continue the work.

Chapter 13 transitions to 14, when Paul and Barnabas arrive in Iconium and proclaim Christ, and the exact same six elements are present but in a different order:

1. INTENSE DEPENDENCE—13:52
2. RHYTHMIC PRESENCE—14:1
3. OBLIGATORY PREACHING—14:1
4. SUPERNATURAL PRESENCE—14:3
5. STRATEGIC CONTROVERSY—14:2, 5
6. APOSTOLIC AGILITY—14:6

As a word of caution, this is not *the* definitive sequence to implement in church planting. When we observe Paul's tactics, they are ever-changing, making it difficult to observe a definitive "Pauline sequence." Just when we've mastered the elements of Paul's first missionary journey, he begins his second mission, and his tactics on that journey are very different. Michael Pocock observes, "Whenever we treat a Pauline practice as a pattern, we immediately find examples where he did not follow that plan."[30]

We must remember that Luke, the author of Acts, was himself a missionary practitioner, and he chronicled what Paul did at that time. Typical of all New Testament narratives, Acts is transparent in demonstrating Paul's mistakes as much as his successes. Much of what occurred on Paul's first missionary journey was chalked up as mistakes Paul chose not to replicate in his later ministry, nor should we.

However, Luke's intention was to transfer to the readers of his narrative the same principles he'd witnessed Paul passing to the elders established in each church plant. Contrast Paul's practices with how planters are trained today, and the chasm between our practices and first-century principles widens. The principles we can draw from the Acts of the Apostles are timeless and, therefore, can be applied to any and every situation that a planter may face. Perhaps, as Luke penned his masterpiece, he wasn't even aware of what we now know to be true: that a post-Christian world is not so different from a pre-Christian world, and therefore the principles applied to reach each one are not dissimilar.

Consider how the two are similar:

Let's briefly examine the intersection of the first and twenty-first centuries to find common ground. Like society today, the first century in the Roman Empire was a blend of religions in a unified political system that had loosely thrown them together. Faiths, values, and cultural customs blended due to the trade routes connecting the world, similar to the way the Internet brings us new goods and information. Among the educated was a deep skepticism of religion—in spite of the social norms of public Roman worship and competing world religions—complete with the ensuing confusion, cynicism, and distrust of religion in general. Philosophy was elevated above religious dogma among the educated, but masked deep primitive superstitions below the surface among the general populace. Despite intellectual ascension over religious beliefs in Western society, the underlying pervasive belief in aliens, fear of ghosts, and acceptance of karma live in contradiction to the claims of science. Thus the inconsistency of our core beliefs betrays that we still fear what we don't understand even while we unconvincingly claim to understand everything. Superstition remains the underside of our intellectual achievements because our souls intrinsically know something

---

30. Michael Pocock, "Paul's Strategy: Determinative for Today?" in *Paul's Missionary Methods: In His Time and Ours*, ed. Robert L. Plummer and John Mark Terry (Downers Grove, IL: InterVarsity Press, 2012), 147.

that rationalism cannot prove and won't be dismissed: the knowledge that we are not alone in the universe.[31]

Pre-Christian*	Post-Christian
Competing religions due to open trade routes	Competing religions due to globalism
Philosophy elevated above religious dogma	Science elevated above religious dogma
Superstitious belief in ghosts, devils, and curses	Superstitious belief in ghosts, demons, and aliens
Belief in moral retribution	Belief in cosmic justice or karma
The belief that we are not alone in the universe	The belief that we are not alone in the universe
Absence of exclusivism in religion	Relativism: Pick what works for you
The emperor was a God.	The state is put in the place of God and the church.

*N. T. Wright and Michael F. Bird, *The New Testament in its World: An Introduction to the History, Literature, and Theology of the First Christians* (Grand Rapids: Zondervan Academic, 2015), 150–51.

Therefore, as we face the current challenges a post-Christian society presents, we must increasingly look back to a pre-Christian society for answers. Reggie McNeal observes, "In the last decades of the twentieth century, a new leadership genus began appearing on the North American church scene. This leadership type is what I and others have dubbed 'apostolic leadership.' This connotation seems appropriate primarily because the challenges to church leaders in the emerging twenty-first century parallel those that faced leaders in the first Christian century (commonly called the apostolic era). These include religious pluralism, globalism, and the collapse of institutional religion, accompanied by an increased interest in personal spiritual development."[32]

FUTURING

Therefore, in order to reach a post-Christian world with the gospel, we must study how the pre-Christian churched reached theirs. In his ground-breaking work *Futuring: the Exploration of the Future World Future Society*, Edward

---

31. Peyton Jones, *Reaching the Unreached: Becoming Raiders of the Lost Art* (Grand Rapids: Zondervan, 2017), 33.

32. Reggie McNeal, *The Present Future: Six Tough Questions for the Church* (San Francisco: Jossey-Bass, 2003), 125.

Cornish states, "Futuring can be thought of as the art of converting knowledge of the past into knowledge of the future."[33] It is the science behind predicting world trends and patterns in order to make a better future. In sociology, the practice is useful for equipping society for what is coming next, despite the challenge that we are, in fact, 99.999 percent ignorant of what comes next. Nevertheless, what comes next is inevitable. The church was unprepared for post-modernism when it impacted society, as it most likely remains unprepared for what's coming after it. Yet God did not leave us without a map, so to speak.

Likening the practice of navigating an uncharted future to the famous explorers of the past, Corning describes the poor maps and tools that some of the most famous exploration expeditions had to work from. Describing the crude, vague, and untrustworthy maps that Captain Lewis of the famed Lewis and Clark expedition studied, he writes,

> At the time, maps had almost no information about most of the territory that the expedition would be exploring; but, whatever there was, Lewis got hold of it. By the time the expedition set out, he knew all there was to know about the Missouri River and what lay West of it. This error-prone knowledge enabled Lewis to make excellent preparations for the journey, with the great result that the Lewis and Clark expedition become one of the great triumphs of American history.[34]

He concludes, "Use poor information when necessary."[35]

Acts may at times look like a crude map. Church history and the periods of kingdom advancement, such as the evangelical awakening under Wesley or the Jesus movement, may at times seem crude, naïve, and primitive. Every generation suffers from what Dr. D. Martyn Lloyd-Jones called "chronological snobbery," the view that subsequent generations are superior to their predecessors. But it is important to remember with humility that, although they had their collective blind spots, other generations have gotten right what we have gotten wrong.

For example, Lewis and Clark did not possess the cloud-based satellite maps that we possess on our mobile phones. Even if we could have delivered such

---

33. Edward Cornish, *Futuring: The Exploration of the Future* (Bethesda: World Future Society, 2004), 134.
34. Hucks, *Futuring*, 2–3.
35. Hucks, *Futuring*, 3.

technology to them prior to their journey, without roads or airplanes, they still would have had to navigate the journey personally, climbing ice sheets in the Rocky Mountains, braving native hostility, and evading grizzly bears. We have superior technology, yet we still couldn't traverse the wild country as skillfully because we weren't the explorers they were. A phone in the hand is no substitute for grit on the ground. Having the information on a satellite map would not be enough to open the transcontinental passage. We may have better maps, but not better pioneers.

BETTER PIONEERS

If we are to follow these trailblazers to learn how to pioneer into our post-Christian culture, what principles did they utilize to pioneer on a pre-Christian mission? What principles did they pass on to the churches they left behind? What were the principles of church plantology that revolutionized their world and are necessary to reform ours?

1. They planted churches instead of starting churches.
2. They modeled their ministry after Jesus's apostolic model.
3. They rejected top-down leadership and embodied Christ on mission together.
4. They resisted stationary entrenchment and formed apostolic strike teams.
5. They forsook pragmatism but listened to hear God's heart for the community.
6. They refused to enable solo performers, but rather chose to equip team mobilizers.
7. They shunned bravado in favor of the Spirit's empowerment.
8. They didn't compartmentalize evangelism but lived as sent.
9. They sacrificed full funding for apostolically agile mobility.
10. They didn't build upward but spread outward.

The result of all this was kingdom expansion, or God's original intent to cover the earth with his glory, through his people. Incidentally, these ten church plantology principles make up the breakdown of this entire book. If you peruse the table of contents, you will notice that each section unpacks one of these principles. This list was not picked arbitrarily but emerged from Scripture, church history, and missionary practices that can be applied universally today.

REDISCOVERING FIRST-CENTURY PRACTICE

On the first day of class, without warning them, Mr. Keating strolls straight out of the classroom. His head appears back in the doorway for a moment, and before disappearing again, Keating says, "Well, come on!"

Keating parades them before a glass case full of trophies and class photos dating back to the 1800s. He presses them to lean in, telling them:

> They're not that different from you, are they? Same haircuts, full of hormones just like you. Invincible just like you feel. The world is their oyster. They believe they're destined for great things, just like many of you. Their eyes are full of hope, just like you. Did they wait until it was too late to make from their lives even one iota of what they were capable? Because, you see, gentlemen, those boys are now fertilizing daffodils. But if you listen real close, you can hear them whisper their legacy to you. Go on, lean in. Listen. Do you hear it? *Carpe.* Hear it? *Carpe. Carpe diem.* Seize the day, boys. Make your lives extraordinary.[36]

This book will ask you to peer at the pictures taken of the first-century apostles and ask you to listen to them. If you're open to it, the apostles felt the same things you do. They were unsure, wondering how they got picked for Jesus's team. They felt full of doubts and faith in equal measure. But they have much to say to us. If you'll lean in a little bit further, and strain yourselves to hear, you'll hear them whisper:

Carpe Diem. Seize the day, planters. Make your lives extraordinary.

REFLECT

- Are you more interested in church planting or church starting?
- Imagine that you are from another culture: European, Asian, African, or South American. You visit a new North American church plant. What do you see? What are some similarities and differences between a new North American church plant and a first-century church plant?
- Imagine that you have a time machine and travel back to the first century to visit a church that Paul planted, such as the church at Ephesus.

---

36. *Dead Poets Society*, produced by Steven Haft, directed by Peter Weir (Touchstone, 1989).

What do you see? What are some similarities and differences between that church and a twenty-first century North American church plant?

DISCUSS

- Why is the distinction between church planting and church starting important for church planters to understand? What are the implications?
- What are your plans for church planting? What is your role in church planting?
- The author argues that there are three Pauline principles of church planting:
    1. infiltrating the marketplace
    2. infiltrating public gathering places
    3. effective discussions about the gospel

How do you see these being implemented in your plans for church planting?

CHALLENGE

- The author argues that effective church planting will look very different from the common conception of starting new churches. How prepared are you to violate cultural norms? What will it take to pursue church planting from a biblical perspective as opposed to the way it's been portrayed in your denomination, seminary, or fellowship?

REDISCOVERING FIRST-CENTURY-STYLE MINISTRY

From Church Starting to
Church Planting

THE PLANTER'S ROOKIE MISTAKES

2

Man's practices are the best indexes of his principles.

—STEPHEN CHARNOCK

Ferdinand Hahn said, "We cannot, with integrity, reflect on what mission might mean today unless we turn to the Jesus of the New Testament, since our mission is 'moored to Jesus's person and ministry.'"[1] Many church planters imbibe church planting materials that highlight the latest fads and trends without questioning whether the foundation of those methods is secure. Building a church on the assumptions planters bring to the table is tantamount to building on sand. Sand, like our fads and whims, shifts over time as the tides change, taking bits and pieces of our first impressions back out to sea, and depositing new assumptions in their place. That's not the sort of thing you can build anything on. Therefore, we need to lay the correct foundations with plantology principles. Paul famously told the Corinthians, "By the grace God has given me, I laid a foundation as a wise builder, and someone else is building on it. But each one should build with care. For no one can lay any foundation other than the one already laid, which is Jesus Christ. If anyone builds on this foundation using gold, silver, costly stones, wood, hay or straw, their work will be shown for what it is" (1 Cor. 3:10–13).

If we break that verse into bite-sized chunks, Paul is identifying three things as important when building:

1. You must understand what a good foundation is.
2. You must lay the foundation wisely and skillfully.
3. You must know how to build upon that foundation.

---

1. Ferdinand Hahn, *Mission in the New Testament Hymns, Ancient and Modern Ltd.* (Norfolk, England UK, 1984), 269.

Paul juxtaposes the foundation of Christ and his gospel laid on his founding visit to Corinth with the later constructions of wood, hay, and stubble that others were using to gain a following for themselves.[2] To ensure we're not building something God never designed, this chapter will examine the New Testament and use it as a plumb line to ensure that the church planting foundation is level and true to square. It may surprise you to learn that Paul did not start off as a wise and master builder. He made a ton of rookie mistakes. Oscar Wilde said, "Experience is the name everyone gives to their mistakes."[3] All teachers were once students, and Paul, the master builder (1 Cor. 3:10) and expert church planter, was once a novice, and novices make mistakes. At face value, the difference between a novice and a master craftsman is simply the number of mistakes made. The following undocumented quote is often attributed to Winston Churchill, the man who inspired the British nation after London had been blitzed repeatedly and seen its buildings flattened by Nazi airpower: "Success is not final, failure is not fatal: it is the courage to continue that counts."

ACTS AND EXPANSION

To set the stage for analyzing Paul's mistakes, we must first understand the missionary context of Acts itself. The early church had never known any church experience outside of church planting organically produced by gospel proclamation. Planting became synonymous with church, and therefore it was an unconscious practice—as invisible to them as water is to fish. Yet church planting provides the context and infrastructure of the New Testament from Acts to Revelation, the latter featuring seven churches planted within the Ephesus network during Paul's third missionary journey. If church planting were stripped out of the New Testament, there would be nothing to hang the epistles on, nor recipients to write them to. Planting functions are like the hidden iOS of the New Testament that runs silently behind all the apps on an iPhone screen. Without planting, the book of Acts would simply be the travel log of itinerant preachers, a train making stops without stations. Though Paul's gospel work was his focus, because it was done properly, it left faith communities in his wake. After the denizens of a province responded to the gospel, Paul sailed away from each port with a heavier burden than he had arrived with: "Besides everything else, I face daily the pressure of my concern for all the churches" (2 Cor. 11:28).

---

2. Gordon Fee, *The First Epistle to the Corinthians: The New International Commentary on the New Testament* (Grand Rapids: Eerdmans, 1987), 135–136.

3. Oscar Wilde, *Vera; Or, the Nihilists* (Project Gutenberg: 2008 edition), Act II p30.

Acts wasn't written to demonstrate how to plant a church. Rather, the book of Acts was written to trace the expansion of the kingdom: "But you will receive power when the Holy Spirit comes on you; and you will be my witnesses in Jerusalem, and in all Judea and Samaria, and to the ends of the earth" (Acts 1:8). The structural breakdown of the book chronicles the expansion of the gospel in that same order of geographical expansion: outward to the ends of the earth with Jerusalem as the epicenter to:

- Judah
- Samaria
- And the ends of the earth

Luke quotes Jesus's mission mandate as a call for his followers to be "witnesses" in concentric circles through Judah and Samaria before breaking into the Gentile world (or the ends of the earth).

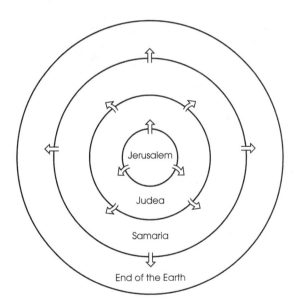

If you opened up a map of the Mediterranean at the back of your Bible, the geographical spread of the gospel in Acts can literally be traced on it following the outline Jesus gives in Acts 1:8.

- THE FIRST FRONTIER—JERUSALEM (Acts 1–7)—Starting with Jerusalem, the focal point of cosmic redemption at the crucifixion and resurrection of Jesus, it also became the *ground zero* epicenter of a global mission. In Acts 1, the apostles obediently wait in Jerusalem for the promised power to accomplish their mission of kingdom expansion. "You will receive power . . . and you will be my witnesses in Jerusalem" (Acts 1:8). The feast of Pentecost, or the "Feast of the First Fruits" was Israel's early harvest festival designed to give God thanks for the first fruits of the crops. In faith, worshipers offered to Yahweh for what was to come later when the full harvest was brought in. Thus, the thousands who came to faith as a result of Peter's preaching became a picture of "the first fruits" of a much greater harvest. Luke trusts that the worshipers originating from every part of the Roman Empire provide a glimpse of a greater global harvest from every nation. After Pentecost, the apostles boldly preach the gospel, create community, make disciples, and challenge the powers. Stephen is introduced and is martyred with the approval Saul of Tarsus, setting us up for the transition of chapter 8.

- THE SECOND FRONTIER—JUDEA (Acts 8)—Thanks to the persecution of Saul, the kingdom expands throughout Judea as the persecuted church exits the city. They live as refugees, resettling in the surrounding regions until "all except the apostles were scattered throughout Judea and Samaria" (Acts 8:1). Further, we are told that after baptizing the Ethiopian, "Philip, however, appeared at Azotus and traveled about, preaching the gospel in all the towns until he reached Caesarea" (Acts 8:40). This bridge serves as a transition to show that the gospel cannot be contained, but will spread despite the efforts to contain it.

- THE THIRD FRONTIER—SAMARIA (Acts 8)—Prior to going to Judea, Philip travels north from Jerusalem to Samaria. After ministering there, encountering Simon the Sorcerer, and baptizing the Ethiopian Eunuch, he travels south towards Jerusalem, taking the Desert Road southwest to the coast of the Mediterranean Sea. From there, he hits every coastal town on his journey north to Caesarea, spreading the gospel to the coastlands.

- THE FOURTH OR FINAL FRONTIER—THE ENDS OF THE EARTH (Acts 9–28)—The kingdom breaks beyond the Jewish barrier into "the ends of the earth." Between chapter 8 and 9, the gospel travels to Judea, Samaria, and Ethiopia. Technically, Acts 6 and 7, which focus on Stephen, are a transition between Jerusalem's Israel-centric focus and setting the stage for Paul's entrance as the "apostle to the Gentiles," the MVP of spreading the gospel to the fourth frontier (Rom. 1:5, 11:13; Gal. 2:8). Chapter 8 chronicles the spread of the gospel by others as a result of his persecution of the church, and chapter 9 is about his conversion.

Chapters 9 and 10 are the fulcrum of the book of Acts, where it turns on a hinge to face towards "the ends of the earth." Chapter 10 focuses on Peter's independent mission to Cornelius, demonstrating solidarity with Jesus's mission to reach the Gentiles through these two men. These chapters serve as the pivot point of outward expansion to the greater Gentile world. In chapter 11, Barnabas is sent to Antioch, after which he recruits Paul from Tarsus. In chapter 11, the camera angle of Luke's narrative swings away from Peter, who had occupied twelve years in the spotlight, to center in on Paul from chapter 11 onward. For the next twenty-five years of Peter's life and ministry, we hear virtually nothing about him.[4] From chapter 11 to the end of the book, Luke chronicles the expansion of the kingdom, eventually to Rome, the epicenter of the known world.

From Rome, the world was their oyster. Just as all roads led to Rome, so all roads in the ancient world led out from it like Grand Central Station. Within 300 years, the gospel spread so rapidly that Christians made up 10 percent of the population of the Roman Empire.[5] The gospel had moved from its point of origin to the epicenter of the known world. Acts isn't a comprehensive account of the mission of the New Testament, nor is it a theology of planting or a philosophy of ministry. To read Acts in that way would be to misrepresent the author's intention. F. F. Bruce likens Acts to a slideshow with brief explanations, while N. T. Wright suggests that "Luke wants his book to fit onto a single scroll."[6] Therefore, in order to understand Acts correctly and not twist it to our own liking, we need to understand that the book of Acts was *not* written to give us a step-by-step methodology for how to plant a church. The book of Acts is our primary source for church planting principles, since it is our primary record of the gospel of Jesus Christ being preached throughout the known world.

Proclaiming the gospel produced the effect of faith communities springing up across the Middle East, North Africa, and parts of Europe within a forty-year timespan.

After the initial scattering of the church under Saul's persecution, the immediate focus had to be re-establishing Jerusalem as a hub of mission to Israel. The irony at the close of the Jerusalem narrative is that every believer

---

4. Eckhard J. Schnabel, *Early Christian Mission: Jesus and the Twelve* (Downers Grove, IL: InterVarsity Press, 2004), 522.

5. Steve Addison, *What Jesus Started: Joining the Movement Changing the World* (Downers Grove, IL: InterVarsity Press, 2012), 15.

6. N. T. Wright, *Paul: A Biography* (New York: HarperCollins, 2011), 64.

except for the apostles had been sent out, a fact that those who romanticize a return to Acts 2:42 would do well to consider. Nevertheless, God's intention was to continue to empower and equip every believer on mission from day one in Jerusalem. This intention is evidenced by:

- The *empowering* of every believer: The gifts were promised to all at Pentecost and poured out on them through the Spirit. When Peter explains what the Spirit is doing through empowering the apostles with power and the gift of tongues, he quotes Joel's prophesy, "'In the last days, God says, I will pour out my Spirit on all people' . . . and you will receive the gift of the Holy Spirit. The promise is for you and your children . . ." (Acts 2:17, 38–39).
- The *activation* of every believer in their gifts: The result of the Spirit filling the people is the enabling of their gifts, allowing them to minister to each other, facilitating the body ministry demonstrated in Acts 2:42–47.
- The *deployment* of every believer: The scattering of the believers to Antioch led to the founding of the church there. Note that this founding wasn't accomplished by the apostles, but by the empowered, activated believers who had been scattered out from Jerusalem. "Those who had been scattered preached the word wherever they went" (Acts 8:4). Luke gives further commentary on this evangelistic activity and the way it led to a plant in Antioch: "Now those who had been scattered by the persecution that broke out when Stephen was killed traveled as far as Phoenicia, Cyprus and Antioch, spreading the word only among Jews. Some of them, however, men from Cyprus and Cyrene, went to Antioch and began to speak to Greeks also, telling them the good news about the Lord Jesus. The Lord's hand was with them, and a great number of people believed and turned to the Lord" (Acts 11:19–21).

This progression of empowering, activating, and deploying every believer was the key to first-century ministry, mobilizing all believers on mission. Therefore, facilitating this progression is one of the planter's primary goals in every successive age. Some argue that this was accidental on the part of the apostles because the scattering happened by persecution, but this speaks only to the deployment aspect. On Pentecost, Peter keenly understood God's intention in mobilizing the laity, and the body ministry in Jerusalem was very intentional. The apostles allowed the people to minister, just as Jesus had encouraged the Twelve to minister during his ministry. Schnabel argues that the apostles understood their role as radical catalysts of a unique movement: "There were no real parallels in the ancient world for the project of a group of people or organization operating in an international scope, neither in the religious nor in the philosophical realms. The impression that Luke's account in the book of Acts conveys is, at first glance, misleading: the apostles were not conservative men who were neither willing nor able to take missionary initiatives. Rather they were well aware of their responsibility to carry out Jesus' missionary commission, including the directive to take the gospel to the nations."[7]

What they lacked was Paul.

PAUL

When Luke introduces his readers to Paul in the first verse of chapter 8, the future apostle is introduced in passing and portrayed as hostile, "And Saul approved of their killing him" (Stephen). By the time of his conversion in Acts chapter 9, the gospel had already gone to Ethiopia, Samaria, and Antioch, not despite him, but *because of him*. "...[A]ll except the apostles were scattered throughout Judea and Samaria . . ." so that "those who had been scattered preached the word wherever they went" (Acts 8:1, 4). It is incredible that Paul inadvertently spread the gospel without trying, prompting him to say later that God had "set me apart from my mother's womb" (Gal. 1:15) to apostolic mission. In Romans 9:17, Paul quotes Exodus, commenting on the way Pharaoh was unwittingly caught in the web of God's sovereignty: "I raised you up for this very purpose, that I might display *my power* in you and that *my name might be proclaimed in all the earth*" (emphasis mine). Ironically, he understood personally what it was to fulfill the purposes of God despite his own rage against God, proving that "surely the wrath of man shall praise you" (Ps. 76:10 ESV). In retrospect, Paul functioned apostolically prior to his own conversion. Paul is nearly as wonderful a specimen as Jesus, proving the validity of the gospel message itself. Like his Lord, Paul is so real, so human, so committed. He was obviously a man transformed, who subsequently transformed the world around him.

Think what you will of the apostle Paul, but there is no doubt that he was a first-century multiplication machine. Charles Jefferson summarizes Paul's importance in the Acts narrative, and his impact in history:

He was great in his aims and plans. There was nothing small in his ambitions. He had in him the spirit of a world conqueror. He was far greater

---

7. Schnabel, *Early Christian Mission*, 554.

than Alexander the Great. He was always dreaming of other worlds to conquer. Nothing less than the whole world for Christ would satisfy his heart. He carried in his eye Rome, the center of the world, and Spain, the end of it. In his imagination, he could see every knee bending and every tongue confessing that Jesus is the Master, indeed.

He is the Christian Hercules, and his labors are so varied and wonderful that we sometimes lose the man in the blaze and glory of all that he accomplished. It was he who lifted the Christian religion out of its Palestinian cradle, tore away its swaddling clothes and trained it to walk along the highways of the Roman Empire. It was he who chipped the shell and set the imprisoned eagle free. It was he who lit the first Christian lamp in the palace of the Caesars. It was he who converted a Jewish sect into a world religion. It was he who saw Jesus not simply as the Jewish Messiah, but as divine Savior of all mankind. It was he who placed the cross of Jesus at the center of human history and also at the center of the Universe.[8]

Paul achieves more than merely preaching the gospel and leaving churches in his wake. Each missionary journey also established a network of churches that became crucial to his system of multiplication. If Paul had merely planted solitary churches, his speed alone would be enough to impress us at an average of one plant every three to four months. But Paul's true stroke of genius on his serial missionary journeys was his creation of multiple church planting networks that geographically spanned a continent in just over a decade.

Paul was a genius of kingdom expansion on a trans-local level. His networking abilities are equaled by few in church history. Paul stated in Romans 15:19, 23 (ESV), "From Jerusalem to Illyricum I have fulfilled the ministry of the gospel" and "I no longer have any room for work in these regions." Craig Ott and Gene Wilson maintain that this only makes sense if his goal was to "establish *strategic regional bases* that could later lead to the evangelization of entire provinces."[9] Paul's goal was not to hit every village, but to create multiple church planting networks in Roman Provinces. This fact is demonstrated by his statement to the Corinthians after he left: "Neither do we go beyond our limits by boasting of work done by others. Our hope is that, as your faith continues to grow, our sphere of activity among you will greatly expand, so that we can preach the gospel in the regions beyond you. For we do not want to boast about work already done in someone else's territory" (2 Cor. 10:15–16). Paul set a high

---

8. Charles Jefferson, *The Character of Paul* (New York: MacMillan, 1923), 376.
9. Craig Ott and Gene Wilson, *Global Church Planting: Biblical Principles and Best Practices for Multiplications* (Grand Rapids: Baker Academic, 2011), 53.

bar for planters to be engaged in front-line gospel work rather than babysitting Christians.[10] Paul was seeking to plant more than individual churches. He was creating movements—*multiple* movements in various provinces across the Mediterranean. Each missionary journey was a movement unto itself, the start of another network that would grow beyond him. Most planters establish churches that depend on the charisma and leadership of the planter as a central figure to function. The difference between this and what Paul did is that he sustained a movement that would outlast him. Therefore, the first lesson Paul taught us is that it's not about your church plant; it is about raising others up, equipping them, and allowing them to deploy outward from whatever church you plant. It's about multiplying yourself, creating disciples who learn from you—both your mistakes and successes—and surpass what you've done. If you plant a church, it stops there. If you reproduce yourself, you will reproduce others who reproduce themselves, which will create a movement. Paul's catalytic networks that multiplied long after he left were the reason he could boast of fulfilling the ministry of the gospel from Jerusalem to Illyricum (Rom. 15:19). Paul was so much more than the "one-stop" variety of church planters who dream of building the epic church of their dreams, instead leaving a string of churches behind. Paul was a serial, or sequential, church planter—a pioneering, groundbreaking, foundation-laying, community-founding, team-building, mobile-discipling, self-replacing, multi-generational, church multiplication missionary.

How can we recapture that momentum and make sure that there isn't just one movement of multiplication in the West, but rather an army of movement makers? Unless we reproduce what he *was*, we can never reproduce what he *did*.

PAUL'S LEARNING CURVE

That is not to say that Paul didn't make his share of church planting mistakes. Paul's three missionary journeys allow us to trace his tactical development as he fails, adjusts, and corrects his mistakes. Brian Sanders from Tampa Underground observes, "In each of his first three journeys, Paul started from and returned to Antioch. One can only assume it was his place to reflect on all he had learned. And so it was that in Antioch they reflected on their experiences, so they could go out again better prepared, but also so they could share what would become the core content of the New Testament."[11] Paul's first

---

10. Paul Barnett, *The Second Epistle to the Corinthians: The New International Commentary on the New Testament* (Grand Rapids: Eerdmans, 1997).

11. Brian Sanders, "Appendix: The First Microchurches" in *Microchurches: A Smaller Way* (Tampa, FL: UG Media, 2019), loc. 2236 of 2309, Kindle.

missionary journey was a near disaster, rife with mistakes he didn't want to repeat. In response, Paul corrected the oversights of the journey and remedied them on his second mission. Each journey Paul took provided an opportunity for course correction in his quest for greater kingdom impact on successive trips.

The difference between a master and a rookie is that the master has failed more times than the beginner has ever tried. Like Paul, you will make your share of planting mistakes, but Jesus will prune you to make you even more fruitful. In ministry, we often experience just as much learning and sanctifica-tion as those to whom we minister, for, "The hardworking farmer should be the first to receive a share of the crops" (2 Tim. 2:6). Like physicians who sample their own medicine, we live off the crops we've sown and often eat our mistakes for breakfast. Thus, we are sanctified in the process of mission as much as the targets of our mission are.

LESSONS FROM PAUL'S FIRST MISSIONARY JOURNEY—ACTS 13–14

Summary of the First Journey

In Acts 13–14, Luke chronicles the first missionary journey in which Paul, a native of Turkey, and Barnabas, from the isle of Cyprus, tag-team their respec-tive homelands. Originating in Antioch, they sail to Cyprus, cross the island by foot, hop a ship to Perga on the Southern Coast of Turkey, and make their way into the southern coastland known as Galatia.

Before they reach the Galatians, John Mark turns back to Jerusalem, setting sail from Perga (Acts 13:13).[12] Depending upon the part of Galatia in which Paul and the team ministered, they most likely spent some time in the coastal lowlands to get their bearings before setting out. Even today, disease-bearing mosquitos dominate the coastal plains in the warmer months, contributing to some scholars' conclusion that John Mark probably turned back after the team was struck down with malaria.

Paul references an illness that caused him to be laid up in Galatia, "and even though my illness was a trial to you, you did not treat me with contempt or scorn. Instead, you welcomed me as if I were an angel of God, as if I were Christ Jesus himself. Where, then, is your blessing of me now? I can testify that, if you could have done so, you would have torn out your eyes and given them to me"

---

12. Scholars argue whether Paul's mission into Turkey, or the Galatian region, was south or north. If it was south, it was on the coastal plains, but if north, it would have been accessible only through the treacherous dagger-peaked Taurus mountains notorious for murderous bandits who mugged unwary travelers braving its paths to the uplands. Southern Galatia is favored by Wright and F. F. Bruce, *Paul: Apostle of the Heart Set Free* (Grand Rapids: Eerdmans, 1996), 163.

(Gal. 4:14–15). Malaria can cause anemia and jaundice in the eyes as a result of the loss of red blood cells. Severe cases can affect the retina and lead to partial loss of vision. Paul may have stayed in Southern Turkey longer than he'd planned because he was recuperating until he was fit to travel. Luke records the Galatian ministry as taking place in Perga, Antioch Pisidia, Iconium, Lystra, and Derbe.

Received well by the Galatians, Paul formed lifelong friendships in Lystra, meeting Eunice, Lois, and her grandson Timothy, a man of mixed Jewish and Gentile blood, who was most likely converted on this journey.[13] Less happily, it was also here that the Gentiles tried offering sacrifices to them as incarnate pagan deities (Acts 14:11–13). This was the *last* thing that Paul needed in his efforts to reach the Gentiles with the gospel, because this further incited the Jews in these areas by seemingly associating Christianity with idolatry and paganism.

Paul reminded the Corinthians that once he was stoned, referring to being stoned by the inhabitants of Lystra and Derbe (2 Cor. 11:25). He reminded the Galatians, "I bear on my body the marks of Jesus" (Gal. 6:17), knowing that the Galatians would remember the scars he earned when this happened in their own neighborhood. This incident is recorded in Acts 14:19, where we learn that they dragged Paul out of the city, stoned him, and left him for dead. Each stone would have shaved off skin on his head and face, leaving huge gashes, scars, and possibly even broken facial bones. Paul was somewhere around forty-five years old when he embarked on the first missionary journey to the Gentiles; the fact that he endured external beatings, the internal deterioration common to a man of that age, and this kind of hard traveling speaks volumes about both Paul's constitution and mental fiber. At the close of their mission, they arrived back in Antioch by boat, reporting "all that God had done through them and how he had opened a door of faith to the Gentiles" (Acts 14:27). In summary, the trip seemed like an apparent success. But appearances can be deceptive, for the true test of any church plant is how it fares once the planter departs.

Lessons Learned on the First Missionary Journey: Building an Adequate Team

Tireless, seemingly fearless, and undeterred by hardship, Paul and Barnabas had sailed from Antioch to Cyprus, been whipped, beaten, and stricken with malaria, and possibly even passed over the Taurus mountain range to get into Galatia. They traveled across the map, traversing the uplands of Asia Minor and planting multiple churches across Galatia before traveling eastward again towards their adopted home and missionary hub in Antioch. The journey took

---

13. F. F. Bruce, *Paul: Apostle of the Heart Set Free* (Grand Rapids: Eerdmans, 1996), 169.

approximately a year, and when they arrived back in Antioch, they simply continued ministering there—business as usual. However, sorting through his mail one fine morning, Paul read about the condition of the churches he had planted less than one year earlier. It would seem that the churches in the region of Galatia had adopted a "Jesus and . . ." theology. It was reported that they now looked for salvation in both Christ and their own obedience to the ceremonial law.

Putting reed to papyrus, Paul shot off an emotional, pain-filled letter that is bitter with disappointment, tinged with grief, and filled with regrets and fears that he'd wasted his time with them: "I fear for you, that somehow I have wasted my efforts on you" (Gal. 4:11). Paul wrote his harshest letter on record to the Galatians, and through Paul's large handwriting, hastily scrawled, we detect the shock of a missionary who is still finding it hard to believe that the church he so painstakingly founded seems to be faced with imminent collapse. He'd suffered for them, been beaten before their eyes, suffered permanent physiological damage and detriment to his health; now, it all seemed to have been for naught. He would have to go back, but this time it would be different. This time he'd leave people behind when he planted a church. In order to do that, he'd need to learn to build stronger teams.

One of the most common rookie mistakes planters make is being overconfident in their own abilities and simultaneously underestimating the challenges they will face. For this reason, they don't invest the time in building a suitable planting team. Paul's first missionary journey could be summed up as unintentional. Most planters don't see the big picture or the consequences of not raising up others. A strong team will help mitigate nearly every disaster that can befall a planter, yet few planters are intentional about it on their first try.

SECOND MISSIONARY JOURNEY: ACTS 15:36–18:22

Paul's second missionary journey is not as easily deconstructed as the first. That's because the second missionary journey is complicated by a split before they even start. As is the case in most splits, there is a backstory. There are also multiple target cities and many moving parts. Therefore, we will analyze a few lessons along the way between Acts 15:36–18:22.

The Lesson Learned Before the Missionary Journey: Team Splits

People often quip when someone finishes a job well that it was "not their first rodeo," but the first rodeo can't be skipped or undersold because it is where one learns. If I could go back and apply what I know now to churches I planted early on, I might sleep better at night. But if I had skipped those hurts, I'd never have learned what I know now. Paul carried his burden for the churches daily, so when he and his team received a bad report about the Galatians a year after their return to Antioch, they were bucked hard, and landed harder. The pain they felt was about to become a powerful teacher.

The news that the Galatian churches had embraced heresy is what actually prompted his second missionary journey. Paul turned to Barnabas saying, "Let's go back and visit each city where we previously preached the word of the Lord, to see how the new believers are doing" (Acts 15:36 NLT).

With a small team of three, Paul, Barnabas, and John Mark had attempted to change the world by themselves, and their work was in peril. The team first began to disintegrate in Perga when John Mark sailed home, dealing Paul a bitter blow. Since John Mark was Barnabas's nephew, Barnabas was inclined to give him a second chance. Paul, who viewed John Mark as a liability, "did not think it wise to take him, because he had deserted them in Pamphylia and had not continued with them in the work. They had such a sharp disagreement that they parted company. Barnabas took Mark and sailed for Cyprus" to strengthen the churches planted there on the first missionary journey (Acts 15:38–39). Wright notes, "Barnabas and Mark sail away, not only to Cyprus, but right out of the narrative of Acts."[14]

There is more in the dispute between Barnabas and Paul than meets the eye. Most likely, the Jerusalem council that took place prior to this passage caused a wedge in their friendship, contributing to their split. The Jerusalem council was a crucial event that established ground rules for the Gentile converts, but it also provided accepted boundaries for the selective ministries of Peter and Paul, carving up the mission field, apportioning the Jews of the Diaspora to Peter, and placing the mission to the Gentiles in the capable hands of Paul. It was at this meeting that the twelve officially recognized the validity of Paul's ministry: "[T]hey recognized that I had been entrusted with the task of preaching the gospel to the uncircumcised, just as Peter had been to the circumcised" (Gal. 2:7).

Once the Jerusalem council had settled those boundaries, everything would have been fine if everyone had simply stayed in their lanes. Paul, however, encountered the Judaizers—men not unlike himself, "zealous for the traditions of my fathers" (Gal. 1:14) who wreaked havoc on the new converts. Paul states that the "men came from James" (Gal. 2:12), that is, from Jerusalem. When they came to Antioch, Paul noted that a change came over Peter, who was visiting

---

14. Wright, *Paul*, 172.

Paul and Barnabas. Recounting the event, Paul wrote "When Cephas came to Antioch, I opposed him to his face, because he stood condemned. For before certain men came from James, he used to eat with the Gentiles. But when they arrived, he began to draw back and separate himself from the Gentiles because he was afraid of those who belonged to the circumcision group. The other Jews joined him in his hypocrisy, so that by their hypocrisy *even Barnabas* was led astray" (Gal. 2:11–13, emphasis mine). This phrase "even Barnabas" indicates Paul's shock. You can almost hear the Shakespearian tone of *"et tu Brute?"* as Paul receives it as a personal dagger in his back. This would have strained their relationship and undermined Paul's trust in Barnabas to a degree, contributing to their split over John Mark. Paul was already convinced that John Mark was unreliable, but now he likely had doubts concerning Barnabas as well.

Once a planter recruits a team, it takes constant communication to maintain the bond of working together. In the same way that a modern soldier must clean his gun, so the planter must regularly look after the team. Many planters have not been taught basic leadership principles and know little about managing teams. Therefore, wise planters learn everything they can about interpersonal communication, team leadership, conflict resolution, and Christlike leadership.

The Lesson Learned in the Second Rodeo in Galatia: Recruiting Others

Paul had failed to recruit others to his team on the first missionary journey, but he would remedy that oversight on his second swipe through Galatia. The Jerusalem letter was another reason for the second missionary journey. On their way to check up on the churches, they were also commissioned to deliver the letter from the Jerusalem council with the guidelines for the Jerusalem churches (Acts 15:27). Not only would this greatly help his cause, but Paul would also start making collections for Jerusalem, to help strengthen the strained relationships between Jews and Gentiles in the church. The twelve had sent an additional missionary from the Jerusalem church to accompany Paul: Silas who, like Paul, was a Roman citizen.

With Barnabas heading to Cyprus, Paul's second missionary journey focuses on traveling back through Syria and Cilicia, strengthening the existing churches and planting new ones in Philippi, Thessalonica, Berea, and even preaching in the pagan stronghold of Athens. Stopping first in Lystra and Derbe, Paul recruited Timothy, starting a mentoring relationship with this young man who was like the son he had always wanted, but who John Mark could never be. Years later, Paul boasted, "For I have no one like him, who will genuinely care for your needs" (Phil. 2:20 ESV).

Raising people up from within to govern the church had been part of Paul's methodology from the start: "Paul and Barnabas appointed elders for them in each church and, with prayer and fasting, committed them to the Lord, in whom they had put their trust" (Acts 14:23). This practice continued on into the end of his ministry. On his first missionary journey, he'd left nobody behind; however, on this journey, Paul also learned to "appoint elders in every town, as I directed you" (Titus 1:5). Addison points out that "most of his team members came from the churches he started."[15] The recruitment of others is part of the apostolic planter's gifting. Like Paul, the planter can comb through relationships built in previous years of ministry, seeking to partner with them for the ministry years ahead. Less work will have to be done to re-establish relationships that you've previously built with people you've already poured into. On his second missionary journey, Paul planted churches in Philippi, Thessalonica, and Berea, recruiting new team members as he went.

Lessons Learned in Thessalonica and Berea: Allowing Your Team to Spread Their Wings

At first, Paul's second missionary journey was strangely difficult, "having been kept by the Holy Spirit from preaching the word in the province of Asia" (Acts 16:6). As they tried to enter into the next region over, "the Spirit of Jesus would not allow them to" (16:7). During this frustrating period of stops and starts, they took a rest in Troas, where they met Luke, and he joined the team. Paul probably thought he could use a good doctor, after all. From Acts 16:10 onward, Luke inserted himself into the narrative, the pronouns changing from "they" to "we." It was in Troas that Paul received his vision of the man from Macedonia, and then the "forbidding" of the Holy Spirit began to make sense. Had they attempted to go to Asia, they'd never have met Dr. Luke, and we would not have the book of Acts or possibly even Luke's Gospel. But even more significant is the fact that their first venture into Macedonia was met with success when they met Lydia, a wealthy cloth merchant who offered them a place to stay and a house from which to minister. Perhaps Paul's team needed that vision of the Man from Macedonia to remind them that it was God's will to minister in Macedonia, because they would also soon receive severe beatings there.

Paul and Silas were imprisoned and beaten in jail until they cashed in on their Roman citizen card to walk free. Not willing to repeat the Galatian tragedy, Paul left Luke behind in Philippi to lay the foundation of Christ firmly.

---

15. Steve Addison, *What Jesus Started: Joining the Movement, Changing the World* (Downers Grove, IL: InterVarsity Press, 2012), 152.

The narrative reverts back from the personal pronoun "we" to "they" until Luke rejoins the team once again in Troas (Acts 20:5).

Now, with Silas, Timothy, and Luke, Paul was beginning to pick up quite the team! Paul recruited young men and women in one city, then deposited them in the one or two cities down the line.[16] Schnabel gives a snapshot of some of the game of apostolic leapfrog that Paul played with the missionaries he trained: "Paul waited in Athens for Silas and Timothy (Acts 17:15), who had stayed in Berea (Acts 17:14), with Timothy having been active in Thessalonica as well. They probably met Paul in Athens, who sent them back to Macedonia with new assignments: Timothy evidently went to Thessalonica (1 Thess 3:1–5), and Silas to Philippi (2 Cor 11:9). They both rejoined Paul in Corinth."[17]

Figuring they'd taken one too many beatings in Philippi, the team moved on, leaving Luke behind. Bound for Thessalonica, the most populated city in Achaia,[18] Paul was about to go to the next level in his experiment of leaving others behind. Luke's account of the mission to Thessalonica is brief (Acts 17:1–9). In Thessalonica, Paul accidentally developed field training for his team like Jesus did when sending out the seventy-two. Jesus's field training was intentional, while Paul's was accidental and born out of necessity.

Paul ministered in the synagogue and Jason's house for less than three weeks before the Jews drove him out of the city. Leaving secretly under the cover of night, Paul and Silas traveled to the next town over, leaving the rest of the team behind in Thessalonica to continue ministering the gospel. Paul's team learned to stand on their own, and Paul learned what his team was capable of. As Paul moved on, the seeds of sequential team planting were sown, giving Paul an idea: If he could train and mobilize others, he could take the gospel farther, faster. Jason was recruited and discipled in Thessalonica and was later active in Rome (Romans 16:21).[19]

When I planted Refuge Long Beach, I was living in San Diego County. For three years, I drove multiple times a week to Long Beach, staying the night with my wife and little girl. We had agreed to help train up a team who could take over the church within a year. The problem was that all the leaders I trained kept leaving to plant out.

Right as I was phasing out on a six-month trajectory, leadership firmly in place, intense medical issues hit my family members; we felt like Job listening

---

16. Women are there too. See Schnabel, *Early Christian Mission*, 285. This is also one of the things that Paul inherited from Jesus. Jesus traveled with women as well, and Paul built his team with respect for both genders, as evidenced by the significant percentage of women in Romans 16, naming them as his "fellow workers."

17. Schnabel, *Early Christian Mission*, 1169.

18. Schnabel, *Early Christian Mission*, 1160.

19. F. B. Meyer, *Paul: A Servant of Jesus Christ* (London: Morgan and Scott, 2011), 118.

to his messengers as they reported one catastrophe hot on the heels of the last. In addition, we had just adopted a baby with special needs who had the habit of ceasing to breathe in the middle of the night. I had to make a choice then and there: Did I trust my team enough to take over the church? Had I trained them well enough to stand on their own? To top it all off, the church service was just heading into the open air again in Bixby Park.

If you've never done open-air church in urban Long Beach, saying it's the extreme sport of ministry is not an overstatement. We experienced everything from knife fights, muggings, prostitutes attending in drag, the mentally ill, overdoses, exorcisms, pit bulls biting people in church, and our newly baptized members being shot and killed by police for being at the wrong place at the wrong time. Our team members *were* ready, and they grew far more by not having me there than if I'd attempted to be their training wheels indefinitely. It wasn't until I read the account of Thessalonica that I realized what God had done. He'd taken the lifeguard off duty and thrown my team in the deep end of the pool because it was time to sink or swim.

Recruiting, training, and deploying others with confidence was a luxury Paul didn't have on his first missionary journey. This major development would make all the difference if Paul was to be martyred or locked up anytime soon. Both were reasonable possibilities for Paul to expect and were, in fact, in the hand of cards he would be dealt in the near future. Nevertheless, developing his own brand of apostolic sequential team planters would be the ace up his sleeve.

The key to training your team for your absence is to take them with you wherever you go, having them shadow you like a disciple would a rabbi. Too often, we've been told that leadership training needs to be time carved out of your schedule, away from ministry. Paul took them on mission *with him*, then sent them out to learn what they could. This book will explore a recalibration of mentoring individuals, training teams, and training planters in the way of Jesus and Paul.

Lessons Learned in Corinth: You Can't Fake It Till You Make It

For most of Acts 17, Paul, and Silas ministered in separation from the rest of the team. With Luke in Philippi and Timothy in Thessalonica, Paul began preaching in Berea until the Jews heard he was preaching Christ there and followed him. Shortly after, Timothy arrived in Berea and committed to stay behind to tackle Berea with Silas after evacuating Saul. Paul's experiment of leaving teams behind graduated to strategically dividing and reuniting interchangeable teams. This would become extremely important to Paul's church planting strategy, as it should be to ours.

After Paul was evacuated from Berea, an escort accompanied him to Athens. Most likely, Paul walked into Athens a little worse for wear. After he preached at Mars Hill, Paul sent a message back with his escort "for Silas and Timothy to join him as soon as possible" (Acts 17:15). Exhausted, Paul made his way to Corinth, which was known as "the seat of Achaia." Paul spent eighteen months there, mainly because of the life-long ministry partnership he forged during that time with Aquila and Priscilla.[20] Jews from Rome, they were a breath of fresh air to him, gave him work for his hands, a bed to sleep in, and a place to hide out for a time. Paul couldn't have known then how strategic this partnership would become for the spread of the gospel throughout the entire Mediterranean. Years later, Paul looked back on this time, and told the Corinthians that "I came to you in weakness with great fear and trembling" (1 Cor. 2:3). The apostle was harried and hunted, not quite feeling himself after having been beaten, persecuted, separated from his team, and fatigued from travel. Schnabel calculates that Paul's second missionary journey totaled nearly six months of travel: 155 days on foot and roughly twenty days at sea (roughly 2,800 miles total).[21]

Paul knew, however, that when he was weak, he was strong. Therefore, when Silas and Timothy arrived in Corinth, the Spirit had been moving powerfully through Paul, despite his fatigue. In himself, Paul had nothing left to give, but the power of Christ rested upon him, and Paul confounded the Jews in the synagogue with supernatural authority, resulting in many of them coming to faith.

Timothy brought good news with him from Thessalonica that led Paul to breathe a huge sigh of relief. "Like cold water to a weary soul is good news from a distant land" (Prov. 25:25). He shot off a letter in response saying, "But now that Timothy has come to us from you, and has brought us the good news of your faith and love and reported that you always remember us kindly and long to see us, as we long to see you" (1 Thess. 3:6 ESV). Although he had left Timothy behind to do the work, he was worried about the experiment, a strategy born out of necessity. But it had worked. This was a shot in the arm to Paul, whose strategic mind was beginning to see immense possibilities for the future.

That the reappearance of his companions re-energized Paul is evident by what Luke wrote next: "When Silas and Timothy came from Macedonia, Paul devoted himself exclusively to preaching, testifying to the Jews that Jesus was the Messiah" (Acts 18:5). Yet Paul is still wary of having to leave suddenly due to persecution just as things are beginning to build momentum. One night he

---

20. Schnabel, *Early Christian Mission*, 1169.
21. Schnabel, *Early Christian Mission*, 1150.

has a vision of Jesus speaking to him and saying, "'Do not be afraid; keep on speaking, do not be silent. For I am with you, and no one is going to attack and harm you, because I have many people in this city.' So Paul stayed in Corinth for a year and a half, teaching them the word of God" (Acts 18:9–11).

Perhaps the greatest blessing of this second missionary journey was the recruitment of Priscilla and Aquila to the cause. As wealthy, kingdom-minded owner-entrepreneurs of a thriving tent-making business, they provided work for Paul; more than that, they owned a home that could serve as a base of operations in Corinth (1 Cor. 16:19). Years later, they would establish a house church with Paul in Ephesus, and eventually another in Rome (Rom. 16:4). In Romans, Paul added that when he was in prison "they risked their lives for me." Priscilla and Aquila would be at the center of every church planting hub that Paul established. Meeting this couple provided reproducible economic sustainability, as they were able to franchise, branch out, train others, and fund mission. Even better, after he left for Ephesus, he deposited them there, and they were able to recruit others for him, as is seen in the case of their recruitment of Apollos.

The entire second missionary journey ended with Paul briefly visiting Ephesus before heading on to Antioch. Priscilla and Aquila begged him to stay, but Paul needed to go visit the Galatian churches (Acts 18:23). "But as he left, he promised, 'I will come back if it is God's will'" (Acts 18:21). Apparently it was, for Paul would return to that region for nearly the entirety of his third missionary journey, largely because Priscilla and Aquila were there and, with their help, he could do something truly amazing.

Many leaders have learned the unfortunate habit of fronting a "fake it till you make it" routine. After being frazzled and unable to catch his breath, Paul learned that the Spirit worked through his brokenness. The best thing you can do in church planting is to be authentic and real. When you need a break, take it. Having team leadership in your plant will ensure that the church plant doesn't fall apart when the leader needs a break. In the military, it's called a strategic retreat.

Paul realized that it wasn't about him, and when he was resting, imprisoned, or absent, God was still working through his team, maturing them in ways that he never could if Paul had been there. This led to greater experimentation with making mobile teams that could travel together, branch off, and reunite when needed. Paul would later greet many of his "fellow workers" in Rome, when he, himself, had never been there. He'd trained them so well that he didn't have to go there to have an impact. As a planter, one of the major tasks you will undertake is to multiply yourself so that others can grow beyond you and take the gospel where you can't.

PAUL'S THIRD MISSIONARY
JOURNEY—18:23-21:17

The Lessons Learned in Ephesus: Bivocational Training Hubs

The city of Ephesus had about two hundred thousand inhabitants and was connected to the outside world by two major highways, one of which ran to Laodicea, and the other to Hierapolis and the bustling trade port it rested on.[22] It was the greatest trade city west of the Taurus mountains.[23] The medical school also had an excellent reputation and provided a place for Luke to practice.[24] Steve Addison notes, "Ephesus was Paul's last major campaign as a free man. It was not just another stop along the way; it was the climax of his ministry, and it touched the whole Roman province of Asia. For centuries to come, the churches formed throughout Asia were among the most influential in the world."[25] It is also where Paul spent three years, the longest period he'd ever spent anywhere to this point. Obviously, though, staying put had its advantages, since "all the residents of Asia heard the word of the Lord, both Jews and Greeks" (Acts 19:10 ESV).

Paradoxically, Ephesus was Paul's most fruitful time, and simultaneously his most painful. Wright says that Ephesus is where Paul's darkest times and deepest depression afflicted him, arguing that Paul's letter of 2 Corinthians records his suffering in Ephesus. "We do not want you to be uninformed, brothers and sisters, about the troubles we experienced in the province of Asia. We were under great pressure, far beyond our ability to endure, so that we despaired of life itself. Indeed, we felt we had received the sentence of death" (2 Cor. 1:8–9). Wright suggests that this comment referred to the riot that occurred in Ephesus after which Paul was put in prison for an extended amount of time. This trial was why he wrote to Philemon (the letter was written in Ephesus) to have a guest room ready for him in Colossae.[26] Incidentally, fifty years after Paul's time in Ephesus, history records that the bishop of Ephesus was a man named Philemon, possibly the very same man.[27] Paul believed that when he was released, he would need to leave to avoid starting another riot.

Wright believes Paul to have had a type of PTSD that broke his spirit and left a scar. "His emotions, his imagination, his innermost heart had been unbearably crushed."[28] Upon release, he went to Colossae where a room was waiting for him. He had promised the Corinthians that he'd visit them when

---

22. Schnabel, *Early Christian Mission*, 1210.
23. Bruce, *Paul*, 288.
24. Schnabel, *Early Christian Mission*, 1210.
25. Addison, *What Jesus Started*, 155.
26. Wright, *Paul*, 304.
27. Wright, *Paul*, 284.
28. Wright, *Paul*, 304.

free, but instead he went to Troas. Paul just couldn't bear dealing with them in the mental shape he was in, explaining to them that he wanted to spare them an uncomfortable visit. But it was most likely himself he was sparing. He went to Troas hoping to see Titus there, putting a distance of 200 miles between himself and the Corinthians, then taking heat for it later.

From there he pressed on to Macedonia, Philippi, and Thessalonica. Paul wrote them about when Titus found him: "For when we came into Macedonia, we had no rest, but we were harassed at every turn on the outside, fears within. But God, who comforts the downcast, comforted us by the coming of Titus, and not only by his coming but also by the comfort you had given him. He told us about your longing for me, your deep sorrow, your ardent concern for me, so that my joy was greater than ever" (2 Cor. 7:5–7).

As Paul's crowds of new disciples grew, he switched from preaching in the synagogues to the hall of Tyrannus to accommodate the numbers. Priscilla and Aquila moved to Ephesus to help with the work and opened up a tent-making business there. Most likely, they helped fund the rental of the hall with the help of Erastus, another patron of Paul's.

What Paul actually accomplished in Ephesus, however, is often missed. Paul started a bivocational mission hub from Ephesus that funded and facilitated an entire network of churches. Lecturing disciples in the hall of Tyrannus resulted in the gospel spreading throughout the entire region: "He took the disciples with him and had discussions daily in the lecture hall of Tyrannus. This went on for two years, *so that all the Jews and Greeks who lived in the province of Asia heard the word of the Lord*" (Acts 19:9–10, emphasis mine).

Why did such a significant impact come from something so seemingly insignificant? Paul trained planters intentionally in the hall of Tyrannus and provided field training by sending them out to plant. In the book of Revelation, the seven churches of Asia are grouped together because they were sister churches, all planted during this time; Epaphras planted churches in the surrounding cities of Colossae, Laodicea, and Hierapolis (Col. 1:3–8; 4:13).[29] According to Addison, the churches in the cities of Smyrna, Pergamon, Thyatira, Sardis, and Philadelphia could have also been started around this time.[30]

Priscilla and Aquila relocated to Ephesus, setting up their tent-making business and provide bivocational training for Paul's students to empower them to go anywhere, anytime, to anyone with the message of the gospel. As a powerhouse ministry couple, they trained both genders to be missionaries alongside

---

29. Colossae would have been destroyed in the earthquake in AD 60 and thus was not mentioned in the letter to the seven churches.

30. Addison, *What Jesus Started*, 157.

Paul. Paul mentioned Andronicus and Junia as his "fellow prisoners." Bruce asks, "When and where had they shared an imprisonment with Paul, if not at Ephesus?" demonstrating that multiple gospel workers were raised up there.[31] When Paul wrote to them in Rome, they were opening their home, training the next generation of leaders there to spread the gospel among the Gentiles.

Ephesus was the true stroke of genius for the apostle, his master stroke of foundation laying. If not for the training center Paul established during his three years at Ephesus, there would have been no churches in Rome. In Romans 16, Paul greeted five households and twenty-six individuals by name. Because of Paul and his establishment of an intentional bivocational training hub, "Christianity came to Rome before any apostle was seen in the city."[32]

REFLECT

- The author argues that Paul learned from mistakes he made early in his church planting efforts. What mistakes have you made? What did you learn?

DISCUSS

- Successful church planting requires the empowering, activation, and deployment of every believer. How does this look in your denomination, fellowship, or organization? What are some areas for improvement? What are some areas of strength?
- The author argues that Paul learned from each of his missionary journeys. What did he learn on each journey, and how did each lesson build upon what he had learned before?
- What are some advantages and disadvantages of bivocational church planting?
- What are some advantages and disadvantages of church planting as a vocational ministry?

CHALLENGE

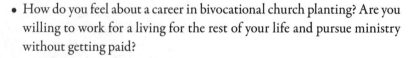

- How do you feel about a career in bivocational church planting? Are you willing to work for a living for the rest of your life and pursue ministry without getting paid?

31. Bruce, *Paul*, 298.
32. Bruce, *Paul*, 379.

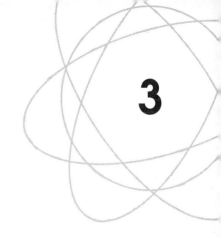

3

THE BIBLICAL PATTERNS OF PLANTING

For too long we've read scripture with 19th-century eyes and 16th-century questions. It's time we get back to reading with 1st-century eyes and 21st-century questions.

—N. T. WRIGHT

Paul's statement, "I laid a foundation as a wise builder, and someone else is building on it" (1 Cor. 3:10), outlines the normal sequence of events for those who apostolically lay foundations when planting churches. Paul successfully accomplished this goal multiple times. Therefore, accepting Paul's wisdom and skill means that we glean what we can from him, studying how he put the teachings of Jesus into practice on mission.

A failure to learn from the expertise of a builder like Paul will most likely result in building an unhealthy church to the detriment of all, including the planter. Arrogant planters (and there are many) start out with a refusal to *learn* from anyone, convinced that they have much to *teach*. They learn in the end, but they learn the hard way. In contrast, most successful planters who embark on their first voyage with wisdom are afraid, unsure, and doubt they are up to the task. And for good reason. Of the churches planted, 68 percent don't survive past year four.[1] Fearful learners make for a teachable audience, and Paul has much to offer such students.

Rather than building from his imagination, like all wise and master contractors, Paul worked from a set of plans. Therefore, the objective for this

---

1. Clint Clifton, *Church Planting Thresholds: A Gospel-Centered Guide* (Chattanooga, TN: New City Network, 2016), xx.

chapter is to further unpack the church plantology principle of "Rediscovering First-Century-Style Ministry: From Church Starting to Church Planting," and thereby provide a biblical blueprint so that you can start the groundwork of planting with wisdom and skill. When I built my own home as a homeowner-builder, the first two people I contacted were an architect and a foundation layer. The former drafted up the plans, and the latter applied them to the physical soil, measuring up, preparing the ground, digging the footings, and pouring the foundation. In this sense, Paul knew his place—he was not the architect, but rather the builder, carrying out the plans of the Chief Architect and manifesting his thoughts into a physical reality.

Paul did not start as a master builder, he started as a journeyman. Nevertheless, Paul possessed a rich tradition of training he brought with him prior to setting out on his first missionary journey. As a pharisaical student (a rabbi in training), Paul had practically memorized the Scriptures. He also possessed firsthand knowledge of shadowing a rabbi and imitating his every move; he knew how to study Jesus's life and ministry and pull it into his own context. Lastly, as a rabbi in training, Paul would frequently be given tasks to carry out that would be considered "hands-on" ministry training, similar to the way Jesus trained the twelve. This was Paul's rich background that trained him to lay foundations wisely, and for the purpose of this chapter, we will call these Paul's blueprints for foundation laying. If you've ever perused a set of plans, you know that each trade has their own page that informs the work they'll be carrying out. These plans can overlay one another—the foundation, the electrical layout, the plumbing layout, etc. The three blueprints that informed his wisdom in building were:

1. **Old Testament Blueprints:** Paul was well acquainted with the Hebrew scriptures and could extract Old Testament principles and apply them to mission in a New Testament era.

2. **Gospel Blueprints:** Having been trained under Gamaliel (Acts 22:3), one of the most respected and quoted rabbis in history, Paul had developed the practice of studying and imitating the life of his teacher. Thus, his ability to study and mimic Jesus's life and teaching were paramount to his idea of ministry. He would not have considered serving Jesus without imitating his example of life and practices.

3. **Practical Experience:** Paul's own experiences provided ample opportunity to make mistakes and learn from them. That last point may comfort you on your journey ahead, because you'll make tons of mistakes and, by journey's end of your first plant, you'll be as much of an expert on what *not* to do as the wisest and most skillful builders.

1. OLD TESTAMENT BLUEPRINTS

Paul drew abstract application out of Old Testament principles for the New Testament era, applying them to multiple facets of mission. For example, Paul quoted Deuteronomy 25:4 about the humane treatment of animals, applying it to treating ministers well: "Do I say this from a human perspective? Doesn't the law say the same thing? For it is written in the Law of Moses: "'You shall not muzzle an ox when it treads out the grain.' Is it for oxen that God is concerned? Does he not certainly speak for our sake?" (1 Cor. 9:8–10 ESV). For Paul, passages about livestock applied to how one should treat human beings, particularly those who are laboring for the gospel. The fact that we need to tell people how to treat animals and humans at all belies an even deeper problem within the church and proves theologically revealing in terms of the nature of human beings. The deeper lesson here, however, is how Paul interacted with the Old Testament scriptures, applying them to a New Testament age in a way that suggests how we should utilize the New Testament to apply first-century principles to the modern context.

Even the aforementioned passage describing the foundation he laid among them when founding the church—"For no one can lay a foundation other than that which is laid, which is Jesus Christ" (1 Corinthians 3:11 ESV)—is a clear reference to Isaiah's prophecy of Christ in Isaiah 28:16: "See, I lay a stone in Zion, a tested stone, a precious cornerstone for a sure foundation; the one who relies on it will never be stricken with panic." The Old Testament was never far from Paul's understanding of God's plan, any more than it was for Jesus.

Among the Old Testament foundations for planting that Paul applied to church planting were:

- a reliance on the Holy Spirit
- an understanding of the missional mandate
- a global mission
- a rich community model

The Holy Spirit

For Paul, becoming the wise and master builder began with a foundational understanding of the Old Testament, where God is portrayed as the wise master builder, the architect of creation. His creative insight is poetically personified in the feminine voice of wisdom from Proverbs 8:27–28:

> "I was there when he set the heavens in place,
>   when he marked out the horizon on the face of the deep,

when he established the clouds above
and fixed securely the fountains of the deep ..."

God was also the architect of the temple who dictated precise plans to Moses. As a contractor building God's house, Paul knew that God had painstakingly dictated precise blueprints to Moses for the instructions for the tabernacle in Exodus, Numbers, and Deuteronomy. In Acts 7:44 (ESV), Stephen recounts God's exhortation to Moses to craft the tabernacle "according to the pattern that he had seen" in heaven, linking Christ to the fulfillment of its meaning and informing the as-yet-unconverted-but-listening Saul of Tarsus that Christ was the true foundation and that the church of the New Covenant fulfilled the Old one in all things.

Paul developed a biblical theology of church, mission, and gospel work knowing that the temple artisans who built God's house in the Old Testament were said to receive that skill from God's Spirit:

- "... and I have filled him with the Spirit of God, with ability, and intelligence, and knowledge and all craftsmanship" (Ex. 31:3 ESV).
- "You shall speak to all the skillful, whom I have filled with a spirit of skill, that they make Aaron's garments ..." (Ex. 28:3 ESV).
- "And he has filled him with the Spirit of God, with skill, with intelligence, with knowledge, and with all craftsmanship" (Ex. 35:31 ESV).

Paul would need the same anointing of wisdom by the same Spirit to craft the New Testament–era churches among the Gentiles.

The Mission Mandate of the Old Testament

Aside from the obvious fulfillment of Christ as the long-awaited Messiah, Paul also recognized that the mission of the Old Testament had not changed, despite the fact that the *method* had. The first mission mandate laid down at creation called for humans to "be fruitful and multiply" (Gen. 1:22). This call was renewed and applied in Jesus's Great Commission, where the church was called to spread out, be fruitful, and multiply. Since Adam and Eve were made in God's image, in their unfallen state, sexual reproduction was all that was required to fill the earth with his glory. More image bearers filling the earth equaled more glory covering it.

But the fall interrupted this simple plan; the temple, or temporary dwelling place of God would be where God's glory would shine out to the world, serving as a place holder for Jesus. A key theme in the New Testament is Christ fulfilling the role of the temple, housing the glory of God. Under the New Covenant, Christ blesses and resends his people, as God did Adam and Eve, placing his Spirit within them and restoring them as image bearers and making them the new temple of God. In a new creation mandate, Jesus commissioned the people of God to go and make disciples, bearing fruit as his image bearers, redeemed from the ranks of humanity. The mission that "the earth will be filled with the knowledge of the glory of the LORD as the waters cover the sea" (Hab. 2:14) never changed, but was merely delayed until new missionaries could carry it out.[2] The fulfillment of the mission would result in the people of God functioning as the new temple, bearing the image of God.

The Global Mission of the Old Testament

Despite God limiting himself to working exclusively with Israel in the Old Testament, a global mission motif is present. If the prophets are to be believed, Yahweh was a missionary God who desired the worship of all nations. Pagan gods might be content with the worship of a regional people, but the calling God gave Abraham was pregnant with the promise that "all peoples on earth will be blessed through you" (Gen. 12:3).

God speaks prophetically to foreigners like Balaam, a pagan prophet who sees Christ's glory. Balaam says, "I see him, but not now; I behold him, but not near. A star will come out of Jacob; a scepter shall rise out of Israel" (Num. 24:17). God speaks to the Babylonian wise men through Daniel about a star from heaven that destroys all world kingdoms; this is the prophecy that inspired the Eastern Magi who claimed, "We saw his star when it rose and have come to worship him" (Matt. 2:2). The first prophetic book to be written in the

---

2. Gerald Hiestand and Todd Wilson, eds., *Creation and Doxology: The Beginning and the End of God's Good World*, Center for Pastor Theologians Series (Downers Grove, IL: IVP Academic, 2018), 138–139. Walton views the metanarrative of the Old Testament in the sense of restoring order to the universe after humanity reintroduces chaos (symbolized by the absence of God's activity in Genesis 1:1–2). In this view, Genesis 3 is not understood primarily as the entrance of sin into the world. Furthermore, the Old Testament never looks back to revisit that moment to explore its significance or probe its implications. The prophets never invoke Genesis 3 in any way as they frequently discuss the problem of sin in Israel. When Adam and Eve ate from the tree of wisdom, they were rejecting partnership with God, desiring instead to position themselves as the source and center of order. In that sense they would 'become like God,' because order is the result of wisdom. The garden was a place of God's order, and since they had desired to find order on their own, they were driven from the presence of God, where his order reigned, to seek out their own order. In this way God granted them what they had desired, but it was to their detriment and, in the process, relationship was thus broken. Genesis 4–11 traces how people worked at establishing order for themselves, with results. Eventual, overwhelming disorder resulted in Genesis 6–9. Tracking order and disorder is inherent in and recapitulated in the rhetorical strategy of Genesis 1–11, as that theme brings coherence to the variety of narratives and genealogies found there. What is not inherent in the rhetorical strategy of Genesis 1–11 is the idea that God has a plan for future redemption and restoration. That element is traditionally located in Genesis 3:15, which is generally considered the launching pad for the salvation metanarrative.

Old Testament canon, Jonah, is about a cross-cultural mission to the Assyrian capital of Nineveh in modern Iraq. God asks, "Should I not pity Nineveh, that great city?" (Jon. 4:11 ESV).

Israel was not intended to go the nations until it had a gospel, but God's concern for the world at large is clearly demonstrated.[3] Mission surrounded Israel's perimeter but, until Christ ascended, the plan remained unrealized. As Paul studied in Arabia, he pieced these things together as he tried to understand the mission that had been personally given to him by the risen Lord, "I will rescue you from your own people and from the Gentiles. I am sending you to them to open their eyes . . ." (Acts 26:17–18).[4] God's interactions with the world at large in the opening eleven chapters of Genesis, combined with the future promise to bless the world through Abraham's descendants, forecast a global mission tied to the creation of all humanity. As John H. Walton observed, "the theme of God's presence and his desire to be in relationship with his people demonstrates that the doctrine of creation itself, rightly understood, launches the mission of God."[5]

A Model of Community

The covenant community of God began with Abraham. He was separated from the rest of humanity by the sign of circumcision. Despite being surrounded by pagans, the community of God would always live in a sort of Eden, walled off from the rest of the earth, yet present in its midst. When creating a nation, God chose Moses, whose very name means "drawn out," and uses him to draw a people out from Egypt. Unlike the gods of Egypt, however, this God would present himself as a relational being who desired to live in community with his people. David Niringiye notes that when the earth is created, God acts singularly, but, on day six, he acts communally in the creation of man, discussing it in the context of relationship within the Trinity.[6] When God says, "Let us make man in our image," it proves that, for man to be in God's image, he must be communal by nature (Gen. 1:26 KJV). The Christian community would embody this aspect of the image of God together.

---

3. Andreas J. Köstenberger and Peter T. O'Brien, *Salvation to the Ends of the Earth: A Biblical Theology of Mission* (Nottingham, England: Apollos, 2001), 45.

4. This passage was itself a quote from Isaiah 42:6–7 (Berean Study Biblemark): "I, the LORD, have called you for a righteous purpose, and I will take hold of your hand. I will keep you and appoint you to be a covenant for the people and a light to the nations, to open the eyes of the blind, to bring prisoners out of the dungeon, and those sitting in darkness out from the prison house."

5. Hiestand and Wilson, eds., *Creation and Doxology*, 144.

6. David Zac Niringiye, *The Church: God's Pilgrim People* (Downers Grove, IL: IVP Academic, 2015), 41–42.

2. THE GOSPEL BLUEPRINTS

Christ's missional practice supplied the second page of plans that Paul used as he laid foundations. As Ott and Wilson point out, "The one who said 'I will build my church' also prepared his followers to participate in its establishment and provided seminal concepts that can serve as foundations of a church-planting ministry today."[7] Jesus meant us to hang on his every word, and to employ the kingdom principles as a solid foundation: "Therefore everyone who hears these words of mine and puts them into practice is like a wise man who built his house on the rock" (Matt. 7:24).

Paul used ample examples from Jesus that contributed to his wisdom and skill in establishing churches through the modeled ministry of Jesus. Paul quotes from the sending of the Twelve, "In the same way, the Lord has commanded that those who preach the gospel should receive their living from the gospel" (1 Cor. 9:14), referring to Jesus's statement in Luke 10:7, "Stay there, eating and drinking whatever they give you, for the worker deserves his wages. Do not move around from house to house."

There are primarily three sources that Paul could have drawn his knowledge from regarding Jesus's ministry practices: eye witnesses, Barnabas, and gospel fragments.

Eye-witness Accounts: Paul's eleven-to-twelve years between his conversion and his ministry with Barnabas are considered preparation years for his mission to the Gentiles. Paul would have undoubtedly come across Diaspora believers who had returned from Jerusalem after the events of the Pentecost. These Jewish sojourners would have been witness to how the apostles practiced their ministry, and Paul absorbed all he could. It is possible that Paul had also previously gleaned patterns and practices of the apostles from prisoners he interrogated during the persecution when, "Going from house to house, he dragged off both men and women and put them in prison" (Acts 8:3). As Paul traveled to Syria, Arabia, Jerusalem, and eventually Tarsus, he listened intently to the stories of anyone who would fill in the gaps.

Barnabas: Barnabas was a resident of Jerusalem who was directly discipled by the twelve apostles for twelve years. Therefore, he was a direct link to the ministry practices instilled into the Twelve by Jesus himself. Joseph, the Levite, received the nickname *Barnabas*, "the son of encouragement," and lived up to his moniker. He was the only believer in Jerusalem who trusted

---

7. Craig Ott and Gene Wilson, *Global Church Planting: Biblical Principles and Best Practices for Multiplications* (Grand Rapids: Baker Academic, 2011), 40.

that Paul's conversion was genuine. "When he came to Jerusalem, he tried to join the disciples, but they were all afraid of him, not believing that he really was a disciple. But Barnabas took him and brought him to the apostles" (Acts 9:26–27). The two formed a friendship then and there. Barnabas was a wealthy landowner from Cyprus who had sold his property and laid it at the feet of the apostles. Barnabas's devotion to the mission of Jesus made him a reasonable choice for the mission of investigating the sincerity of Gentiles coming to faith in Antioch.

After his initial visit to Antioch, "Barnabas went to Tarsus to look for Saul" (Acts 11:25), ostensibly remembering that Paul had been babbling about needing to reach the Gentiles. Because Peter had not yet received his vision of unclean animals, Paul's passion for Gentile conversion was easily dismissed. Things had changed since then, and Barnabas needed help. During their year serving together in Antioch, Barnabas would have been an invaluable source of information to Paul, training him in the way of the apostles.

It is significant that Luke mentions Barnabas first in describing the duo saying, "Barnabas and Saul" (Acts 11:26, 11:30, 12:25, 13:1, 13:2, 13:7) until Acts 13:42, where we read, "As Paul and Barnabas were leaving the synagogue, the people invited them to speak further about these things on the next Sabbath." Somewhere along the way, Paul had begun to take the lead in their relationship. At some point, Paul emerged as the chief speaker (Acts 14:4). Only when they returned to Jerusalem to attend the Jerusalem council does Luke reverse the order back to the original order that the Twelve would have recognized (Acts 15:12, 22, 25). Immediately after the Jerusalem council, however, the order switches back, with Paul listed as the prominent partner. In this way, Barnabas served as Paul's training wheels as Paul learned the missional practices of the apostles.

Gospel Fragments: When Paul planted, he would not have had access to the canonical Gospels as they exist today, but scholars point to a possible "Q" fragment, or possible Gospel fragments that were circulated.[8]

---

8. Although there is no proof of the existence of the Q fragment, there may be an earlier Gospel that both Matthew and Luke used as source material. The reasoning behind this is that Mark is the shortest Gospel with the fewest stories, most of them occurring in Matthew and Luke, but both Matthew and Luke seem to have used Mark and another document to compile their stories. Luke sets out to write a more comprehensive Gospel than the others, telling us, "Many have undertaken to draw up an account of the things that have been fulfilled among us, just as they were handed down to us by those who from the first were eyewitnesses and servants of the word. With this in mind, since I myself have carefully investigated everything from the beginning, I too decided to write an orderly account for you" (Luke 1:1–3). Perhaps there were other fragments Paul had access to that were written and circulated prior to the compiling and editing of the definitive four canonical Gospels as we know them.

What Paul Learned from Jesus

The three sources listed above tell us *how* Paul might have learned from Jesus, but they don't tell us *what* he learned. The missional practices that Jesus modeled for Paul as a wise and master builder are as follows:

1. Christ's Missionary Stance

The first thing that Paul learned from Jesus is the modeling of a missionary stance. During his earthly ministry, Jesus viewed and conducted himself as a missionary. He spoke as a missionary, telling people he had come from heaven, and from the Father. He identified his mission when preaching in his hometown: "The Spirit of the Lord is upon me, because he has anointed me to proclaim good news to the poor. He has *sent me* to proclaim liberty to the captives and recovering of sight to the blind, to set at liberty those who are, to proclaim the year of the Lord's favor" (Luke 4:18–19 ESV, emphasis mine). Not only does Jesus himself *model* apostleship (being a sent one), he is *called* one: "Jesus, whom we acknowledge as our *apostle* and high priest" (Heb. 3:1, emphasis mine). Jesus's disciples likewise were called *apostles*, or "sent ones." As a missionary, Paul was willing to suffer in the same way as the one who had sent him and who said, "the Son of Man must suffer many things . . ." (Luke 9:22) and "I must work the works of him that *sent me*" (John 9:4 KJV, emphasis mine).[9]

2. Christ's Gospel Proclamation

The same compulsion that Paul expressed when he said, "For when I preach the gospel, I cannot boast, since I am compelled to preach. Woe to me if I do not preach the gospel" (1 Cor. 9:16) was also upon his Master, who said, "I must preach the kingdom of God" (Luke 4:43 KJV). John the Baptist and Paul both preached Jesus, but Jesus preached himself. John the Baptist preached: The King is coming! Jesus preached: The King is here! Paul preached: The King came, went, and is coming back! Furthermore, Paul labored to know nothing among the churches save Christ, and him crucified, and he observed that some preached themselves rather than Christ. We live in a day where preaching has been undervalued, but solid preaching was central to Jesus's ministry, and therefore to Paul's. Schnabel emphasizes that "Peter would not have preached a 'missionary' sermon at Pentecost if he had not been a student of Jesus for three years."[10] Jesus planted

---

9. Schnabel maintains that Paul may have seen himself as the suffering servant, like Jesus.
10. Eckhard J. Schnabel, *Early Christian Mission: Jesus and the Twelve* (Downers Grove, IL: InterVarsity Press, 2004), 3.

no churches, but he said that he'd build his church through Peter's proclamation of who he was. Incidentally, this was literally fulfilled on Pentecost when Peter boldly proclaimed Christ to the very crowds he had feared only weeks before.

3. Christ's Targeted Mission

Jesus focuses his ministry primarily in Galilee (a region whose contemporary population was approximately 200,000 people),[11] and Matthew reports that he went through "all the cities and villages" (Matt. 9:35). Luke reports that he walked "from village to village" (Luke 9:6). Jesus's itinerant ministry has been well documented by the Gospel writers:

- Matthew 9:35 (NRSV)—"Then Jesus went about all the cities and villages, teaching in their synagogues, and proclaiming the good news of the kingdom, and curing every disease and every sickness."
- Matthew 11:1 (NRSV)—"Now when Jesus had finished instructing his twelve disciples, he went on from there to teach and proclaim his message in their cities."
- Matthew 14:13 (NRSV)—"Now when Jesus heard this, he withdrew from there in a boat to a deserted place by himself. But when the crowds heard it, they followed him on foot from the towns."
- Matt 4:23 (NRSV)—"Jesus went throughout Galilee, teaching in their synagogues and proclaiming the good news of the kingdom and curing every sickness among the people."
- Luke 4:14–15—"Jesus returned to Galilee in the power of the Spirit, and news about him spread through the whole countryside. He was teaching in their synagogues, and everyone praised him."
- Mark 6:56 (NRSV)—"And wherever he went, into villages or cities or farms, they laid the sick in marketplaces, and begged him that they might touch even the fringe of his cloak; and all who touched it were healed."
- Luke 9:6 (NRSV)—"They departed and went through the villages, bringing the good news and curing diseases everywhere."

According to these passages, Jesus was committed to a small geographic area during most of his ministry, which resulted in a gospel saturation strategy.[12]

---

11. Schnabel, *Early Christian Mission*, 383.
12. This is the genius of Mac Lake, one of my mentors. Find him at https://www.maclakeonline.com.

Jesus' Gospel Saturation Strategy					

Sending of the 12 (6 teams of 2)

240 Villages	40 vill	40	40
	40	40	40

= 40 villages per team

Sending of the 72 (36 teams of 2)

240 Villages						
1	6	6	6	6	6	6
2	6	6	6	6	6	6
3	6	6	6	6	6	6
4	6	6	6	6	6	6
5	6	6	6	6	6	6
6	6	6	6	6	6	6

= 6 villages per team

In Matthew 10:5, Jesus tells the Twelve not to go to the Gentiles or to any towns of the Samaritans. Matthew tells us that, "Then Jesus began to denounce the towns in which most of his miracles had been performed, because they did not repent. 'Woe to you, Chorazin! Woe to you, Bethsaida! For if the miracles that were performed in you had been performed in Tyre and Sidon, they would have repented long ago in sackcloth and ashes'" (Matthew 11:20–21). Jesus told the Syrophoenician woman that he had been called to the Jews, and not the Gentiles. Like Jesus, who intentionally focused on the regional environs of the lost sheep of Israel, Paul knew that Jesus had called him to target his mission strategically in key provinces where Gentiles lived.

Paul's choice of cities was mainly to "concentrate on major population centers, relying on the movement of people and trade in and out of the great cities to help spread the word"[13] where "the message might flow outward."[14] Paul may have also strategically chosen those cities to challenge Caesar's rule and, therefore, chose capital cities that were known as Caesar's strategic centers. For example, Corinth was the capital of Achaia, and Thessalonica was the capital of Macedonia.[15] He made sure that they had commercial, religious, or regional importance, and were in key Roman provinces. Tarsus was the capital city of

---

13. N. T. Wright, *Paul: A Biography* (New York: HarperCollins, 2011), 104.
14. Wright, *Paul*, 112.
15. Ott and Wilson, *Global Church Planting*, 52–53. Schnabel, *Early Christian Mission*, 1161.

Cilicia, a Roman province not far from Jerusalem (Acts 9:30), and Paul also established a base in Syrian Antioch, the fourth city of Roman importance.[16] Likewise, Philippi also fits all the requirements listed above. Wright asserts that, "Paul's geographical strategy had a quiet but definite political undertone."[17] Caesar claimed to be divine, God incarnate, but Paul had encountered the only King to whom he would ever bend a knee, and to fail to swear allegiance to Christ was to incur a far greater wrath than anything Caesar could mete out. In this way, Paul would have called to mind Jesus's injunction not to fear what man could do to the body, but what God could do to body and soul. Paul's confessional "Christ is Lord" is a direct rip-off of Rome's "Caesar is Lord," yet in his defense, he could answer, "I may be declaring Jesus to be God, but Caesar started it!" In preaching "*Christos kurios*," he was challenging it.

4. Christ's Base of Operations

Jesus modeled a base of operations from which he extended outward. Capernaum was the base of his missionary activity in the New Testament, according to Matthew 9:1: "Jesus stepped into a boat, crossed over and came to his own town." Although Jesus was from Nazareth, and even identified as "Jesus of Nazareth," Capernaum became known as his home base as well as his home. Later, the apostles would establish this same model in Jerusalem, using it as a base of operations to reach all of Israel. Antioch became the base of operations from which Paul operated, returning to it in between mission trips. "From Attalia they sailed back to Antioch, where they had been committed to the grace of God for the work they had now completed. On arriving there, they gathered the church together and reported all that God had done through them and how he had opened a door of faith to the Gentiles. And they stayed there a long time with the disciples" (Acts 14:26–28).

Although it may not initially have been intentional, Paul established his base of operations in Antioch in the same way that Jesus established his base in Capernaum. Moving from Antioch, Paul would begin to establish other bases of operations, such as Ephesus, eventually training his fellow workers to establish a hub in Rome before he had even been there.

5. Christ's Strike-Team Model

Jesus's primary business after his baptism and temptation was to choose a team. Far from being like today's "professional" leader who feels the need

---

16. Ott and Wilson, *Global Church Planting*, 49.
17. Wright, *Paul*, 113.

to drum up business and get people *in* the door, Paul and Jesus focused on getting people *out* the door. Like Jesus did, Paul started a network of apostles (thirty-two in all whom he trained and sent out), who could go where he couldn't. From Paul's first missionary journey, he learned to minister in a team that continued to grow, fragment, reassemble, recruit, and disperse over the years. Strike teams became Paul's secret weapon of kingdom expansion, just as they were for the One who sent him. Jesus deployed his strike team of twelve into Judah on mission (Matt. 10), and a follow-up strike team of seventy-two (Luke 10). We catch a glimpse of one when Paul awaited trial, "Aristarchus my fellow prisoner greets you, and Mark the cousin of Barnabas (concerning whom you have received instructions—if he comes to you, welcome him), and Jesus who is called Justus. These are the only men of the circumcision among my fellow workers . . ." (Col. 4:10–11 ESV). As a plantology principle, the overlap between New Testament practice and church history occurs in the ministry of Saint Patrick, who led apostolic bands of twelve to catalyze mission in Ireland.[18] In Africa, C. T. Studd sent teams of apostolic missionaries into the bush to plant, and in contemporary missionary practice, church planting movements in Tanzania mimic Paul's strike-team approach.

6. A Network Approach

Jesus had a network approach in mind long before one was ever established. The network hubs that formed the basis of the New Testament world were Jerusalem in Israel, Ephesus in Asia, and Rome in Italy. Not by coincidence, Jesus poured himself into the three who would end up taking the leadership roles in those three cities: James, Peter, and John. James stayed in Jerusalem until his death, Peter traveled to Rome ministering among the Jewish Diaspora, and John took up residence in Ephesus with Mary, the mother of Jesus. The reason Jesus singled those three out was because he was training apostles who would eventually function within networks, but focused special time, care, attention, and training into his three key network leaders.

7. Finding the Man of Peace

Jesus found the "man of peace," and sometimes it was a woman, like the unnamed woman at the well. Zacchaeus was the person of peace who threw a party, inviting all his friends to meet Jesus. Paul also found numerous persons of peace in the Philippian jailer, Erastus in Ephesus, and the "chief man of the

---

18. George G. Hunter III, *The Celtic Way of Evangelism: How Christianity Can Reach the West Again* (Nashville: Abingdon Press, 2010), 9.

island" among the Manoans (Acts 28:7 ESV).[19] This is one of many ways that Paul embraced the missional practices Jesus instructed the Twelve and the seventy-two to observe before sending them out.

8. A Discipleship Method

Mentoring the next generation. Jesus modeled missionary discipleship. As a rabbi, Jesus didn't simply teach theory. Rabbis modeled their entire life to their disciples. Jesus's message, lifestyle, and ministry could be imitated, imbibed, and implemented. His message became their message; his lifestyle became theirs. But, unlike traditional rabbis, Jesus didn't want his disciples to become rabbis themselves, for Jesus was first and foremost a missionary. This was the great task he was preparing them for over the course of three years. As we will see later in this book, Paul's method of discipling his "fellow workers" was identical to the one Jesus modeled.

9. A Field-Training Mission

Although the Twelve constantly accompanied Jesus on missions for three years, Jesus sent the Twelve on missionary excursions on multiple occasions in groupings of two. Schnabel says that "Jesus instructs the Twelve in terms of a short-term missionary tour through Galilean villages. At the same time he describes their imminent mission as a paradigm of a permanent mission in the future. The short-term mission is training for their later missionary activity."[20] Schnabel observes that if Jesus spent two days in each of the 138 settlements of Galilee that Mordichai Aviam mentions, it would have taken him 276 days, or forty-six weeks, to cover.[21] However, if he was sending out six teams of two missionaries, this same area could be covered in forty-six days (or a month and a half). If he sent out the seventy-two, we presume that we simply divide that number into teams of two, giving us thirty-six teams, and Galilee could have been covered in eight days—just over one week! The first trip sent twelve to provide a broader sweep, but the second trip of seventy-two missionaries allowed for a greater gospel saturation.

The instructions of Matthew 10 indicate that the key objective of this trip was to foster the missionaries' dependence upon the Holy Spirit. As Steve Addison says in *What Jesus Started*, "This was not a classroom approach to learning."[22] The only way they could practice dependence upon the Holy Spirit

---

19. Schnabel, *Early Christian Mission*, 1370.

20. Schnabel, *Early Christian Mission*, 293.

21. Schnabel, *Early Christian Mission*, 305.

22. Steve Addison, *What Jesus Started: Joining the Movement, Changing the World* (Downers Grove, IL: InterVarsity Press, 2012), 47.

was to place themselves in situations where they'd need him. When they were with Jesus, they had been operating under the umbrella of his dependence upon the Father and the Spirit, but Jesus's unique instructions to them were designed to take them outside their comfort zone where they, too, would need to personally depend on the Holy Spirit for:

Power: "Heal the sick, raise the dead, cleanse those who have leprosy, drive out demons. Freely you have received; freely give" (10:8).

Provision: "Do not get any gold or silver or copper to take with you in your belts—no bag for the journey or extra shirt or sandals or a staff, for the worker is worth his keep. Whatever town or village you enter, search there for some worthy person and stay at their house until you leave" (10:9–12).

Place: "As you enter the home, give it your greeting. If the home is deserving, let your peace rest on it; if it is not, let your peace return to you. If anyone will not welcome you or listen to your words, leave that home or town and shake the dust off your feet. Truly I tell you, it will be more bearable for Sodom and Gomorrah on the day of judgment than for that town" (10:12–15).

Protection: "I am sending you out like sheep among wolves. Therefore be as shrewd as snakes and as innocent as doves. Be on your guard; you will be handed over to the local councils and be flogged in the synagogues. On my account you will be brought before governors and kings as witnesses to them and to the Gentiles. But when they arrest you, do not worry about what to say or how to say it. At that time you will be given what to say, for it will not be you speaking, but the Spirit of your Father speaking through you" (10:16–20).

When Paul wrote " In the same way, the Lord has commanded that those who preach the gospel should receive their living from the gospel" in 1 Corinthians 9:14, he was referring to the command from Luke 10:7: "Stay there, eating and drinking whatever they give you, for the worker deserves his wages." This demonstrates that Paul was familiar with the sending of the Twelve and how they were trained to go on mission. Paul also shakes his feet in Acts 13:51 in fulfillment of Jesus's command in the sending out the Twelve and the seventy-two (Matt 10:14; Mark 6:11; Luke 9:5; 10:10–11). Paul knew Jesus's practices as taught to the Twelve, and he did his best to follow them.

10. Ministry in Public Space

Paul's methodology was to proclaim Christ in the synagogue, home, workshop, city square, hall, and even when publicly on trial.[23] Jesus had primarily preached, too, but about himself. Jesus modeled taking the gospel to the people, rather than expecting them to come to him. Schnabel points out that Jesus says that gospel proclamation must take place in palaces (Luke 7:25), marketplaces (Luke 7:32; 11:43), roads and streets (Luke 10:10; 13:26; 14:21), law courts and prisons (Luke 12:57–59; 18:2), and city gates (Luke 13:24).[24] Jesus modeled preaching in every single one of these environments and called for his disciples to do the same.

Paul followed suit and preached in all these venues without exception.[25] Paul's practice was exactly like that of Jesus, using public spaces and houses. The apostles followed suit, too, meeting house to house and in temple courts (Acts 5:42), demonstrating that homes for smaller gatherings and public spaces for larger evangelistic events were used. Paul, in turn, made it a part of his apostolic rhythm, saying, "I have not hesitated to preach anything that would be helpful to you but have taught you publicly and from house to house" (Acts 20:20).[26] When Paul wrote to the Corinthians about when "the whole church comes together" (1 Cor. 14:23), he was implying that they sometimes alternatively met in smaller gatherings in a rhythm. Therefore, public space was the norm, not the exception, for the regular gatherings of the early church.

11. A Love for People

Paul wrote that the love of Christ compelled him. When Paul writes that he himself would be willing to be cut off from God in exchange for the conversion of all Jewish people, he is coming as close as one can to the love of Christ, who laid down his life for us. Paul says, "For if we are beside ourselves, it is for God; if we are in our right mind, it is for you" (2 Cor. 5:13 NRSV). Paul saw himself as filling up in his flesh what was lacking in the sufferings of Christ, and said, "I bear on my body the marks of Christ Jesus" (Gal. 6:17), referring to his many scars, injuries, and ailments that accumulated during a lifetime of frontline mission. Paul's back was scarred like a walnut, and Josephus attests to his bow-leggedness from having received "the forty lashes minus one" (2 Cor. 11:24).[27]

---

23. Addison, *What Jesus Started*, 127–31.
24. Schnabel, *Early Christian Mission*, 238.
25. Schnabel, *Early Christian Mission*, 247.
26. Tom Wolfe, "Oikos Evangelism—The Biblical Pattern," Apostolic Information Service, February 8, 2008, https://www.apostolic.edu/oikos-evangelism-the-biblical-pattern.
27. Pollock makes a good case that Paul received this Jewish punishment prior to Antioch during his twelve years in obscurity as he attempted to reach his own people. As this was not a Gentile punishment,

Standing as the greatest missionary who ever lived, Paul replicated much of what he knew from Jesus's ministry. Why wouldn't he? Some sobering questions to ask this generation are, "Upon which model do we base our missionary activities? Have we been careful to follow the patterns Jesus set down for us? Have you ever asked why your activities as a minister look nothing like what Jesus or Paul did?" The reason for unpacking all of this is because it took me nearly two decades of ministry before I began to pay attention to Jesus's ministry and how he conducted it.

3. HIS OWN EXPERIENCE

Paul's own experience is the third set of plans he used when learning to minister like a wise and master builder. But Paul's experiences of trial and error made for the laying of better foundations. He disappears from the story for nearly two chapters of Luke's narrative, and Luke casts Peter to take the center stage, revealing that God is speaking the same things to Peter. It is during this time that Paul went to Cilicia and Syria, re-emerging in Tarsus. But what was he doing during the "lost years"? Schnabel pieces together those early days of Paul, or the lost years, cross-referencing Galatians 1:15–17; 2 Corinthians 11:32–33; and Acts 9:20–25:[28]

> The following seven stages emerge. (1) Paul began to speak about Jesus the Messiah in the synagogues of Damascus right after his conversion. (Acts 9:19, 20, 22) (2) Paul initiated missionary work in Arabia-Nabatea, based in Damascus. (Gal 1:17) (3) Paul returned to Damascus, where he continued to preach the gospel. (Gal 1:17) (4) Paul evidently was so successful in his missionary activity in Damascus and Arabia that the local Jews sought to eliminate him. (Acts 9:23–24) (5) The Jews of Damascus succeeded in winning the support of the ethnarch of the Nabatean king for plans to arrest Paul. (2 Cor 11:32) (6) Paul managed to evade capture by escaping over the city walls. (Acts 9:25; 2 Cor 11:33) (7) Paul went to Jerusalem—his first visit since his conversion three years earlier. (Gal 1:18)[29]

---

it is likely that he received it from the Jewish community as he ministered until Barnabas comes to call for him. The thirty-nine lashes were broken into three sets of thirteen; the first thirteen blows went across the left shoulders and back, the second across the right, and the third set of blows came between the legs and grabbed at the tendons of the inner thighs, causing bow-legged crippling from the torn tendons and sadly, the shredded genitalia, which would have led to no ability to have children. In this respect Paul could have been considered a eunuch for the sake of heaven (Matt. 19:12).

28. Schnabel, *Early Christian Mission*, 1032.
29. Schnabel, *Early Christian Mission*, 1032.

Some suppose that Paul was idle immediately after his conversion, isolating himself in Arabia. To the contrary, we see him immediately engaging in mission to the Jews in Damascus, and there is significant evidence to make a case that Paul was nothing but active for the twelve years leading up to Barnabas turning up on his doorstep to invite him to Antioch. Paul couldn't stay still for long, and Jesus merely channeled his zeal, rather than tempering it.[30]

Until Antioch, Paul concentrated his efforts among the Jews in these regions, visiting the synagogues (as was his custom) not yet understanding how to reach the Gentiles.[31] N. T. Wright argues that rather than evangelizing, Paul went to Mount Sinai in Arabia as part of questioning his "whole life and mission to date," but this seems to ignore the fact that Paul had already started evangelizing in Damascus quite successfully before being lowered in a basket. A stronger argument that Wright gives is that Paul may have been overwhelmed following his expulsion from Sinai and may have had a fainting fit similar to Elijah's as he wondered how he would be able to carry out the mission alone.

Whatever the case, Paul didn't stay inactive for long, and if he did attempt to evangelize the Gentiles in Arabia during his stint there, we may infer that he was most likely unsuccessful. This can be deduced from the fact that, when he returned from Arabia and until he went to Antioch, he focused on reaching Jews. Paul's transition to focusing on the Gentiles happened in Acts 13:46: "We now turn to the Gentiles."

During his twelve years in "exile," he went to Cilicia, Syria, and Tarsus. It was there, Bruce argues, that he got his forty lashes minus one (2 Cor. 11:22–27), a Jewish punishment.[32] This is supported by the fact that in 2 Corinthians 12:2–10, Paul refers to this time "fourteen years ago."

Many also believe that it was during these early formative years that Paul had his heavenly vision, followed by the thorn in his flesh, humbling him early on.[33] Saul's trip from Damascus, including the trip to Arabia and back, probably took three years, after which he returned to Tarsus via Jerusalem.[34] It was most here that the amazing vision and humbling weakness played out.

---

30. Schnabel makes a case that when Paul states in Galatians 1:17 that he went to Arabia after his conversion that it was immediate. As we will see, there is sufficient evidence to suggest that Paul engaged in missionary activity in Arabia, which refers to the Nabatean kingdom east of the Jordan River, ruled at the time by King Aretas IV. Paul had lived as a student of Rabbi Gamaliel for several years and would have been able to see Arabia from the Psephinus Tower (Josephus, B.J. 5.159–160). Damascus was situated at the northern edge of Nabatea. Ibid., 952.

31. Addison, *What Jesus Started*, 126.

32. F. F. Bruce, *Paul: Apostle of the Heart Set Free* (Grand Rapids: Eerdmans, 1996), 127.

33. Bruce, *Paul*, 134.

34. Wright, *Paul*, 66.

This experience greatly mirrors Peter's own rise and fall, as he boldly proclaimed Jesus as the Christ and was subsequently called Satan. During all this time, Paul was receiving the equivalent of the mission training that Jesus had given the Twelve and that Barnabas had received in Jerusalem while spending eleven years with them. During those years, he applied his hands to rudimentary mission among the Jewish Diaspora in Turkey, working as a tentmaker in his family trade.

During those twelve years, Paul began to forge a robust philosophy of ministry and mission strategy. E. Stange summarizes the factors influencing Paul's strategy.[35] Each of these factors is something Paul could have developed during his twelve years between Damascus and Antioch:

- Paul began in the Jewish synagogue (Rom. 1:16) and included the "God fearers."
- Paul focused on Roman provinces and centers (1 Cor. 16:19; Rom. 15:19).
- Paul used reception of—or opposition to—the gospel as the determining factor in deciding whether to stay or move on (1 Thess. 2:18).
- Paul worked in previously unevangelized areas (2 Cor. 10:16; Rom. 15:20–23).
- Paul operated under the leading of the Holy Spirit (Gal. 2:2; 2 Cor. 2:12).

The one missing tactic on this list is the development and delegation of care for viable churches (1 Thess. 3:10; 2 Cor. 1:15; 2:10–13). This would, of course, develop later after churches were planted; however, this was something Paul wasn't proficient at until a few missionary journeys in. Antioch served as his apprenticeship in ministry. Named after Antiochus Epiphanes, its founder, Metropolitan Antioch was home to approximately 250,000 people, a classic melting pot with every culture represented.[36] There Paul learned the rhythms of ministry and church life and developed a sense of how God worked among Gentile believers in a frontier context.

Paul's skill developed with time and experience, and the wisdom gleaned came as much from his many failures as from his successes, as all planters do before they set out. True to the Old Testament depiction of patriarchs, prophets, and kings, Luke does not gloss over Paul's weaknesses, but allows us to witness his learning curve. Abraham's, David's, and Peter's learning curves are

---

35. Quoted in Craig Ott and Gene Wilson, *Global Church Planting*, 53.
36. Wright, *Paul*, 88.

not glossed over in Scripture. Luke allows us to glimpse such weaknesses as Paul's outburst against being struck at the command of the high priest, leading to an apologetic confession of his disrespect as coming from a temper not yet fully under submission. Nevertheless, all planters greatly relate to Paul in all his humanness.

To see Paul's humanity only endears us to him and reminds us that he, too, was learning. Only the fool thinks he knows everything, whereas those with a teachable spirit realize that despite the fact that we each bring a unique set of experiences to contribute in our church planting, there is still so much more to learn. To admit a lack of wisdom is the first step on the journey to acquiring it. Nobody could have been so prepped for the journey ahead as Saul of Tarsus, the missionary who would eventually open the eyes of the world yet started out his faith having been made completely blind.

REFLECT

- How do you feel God has prepared you to plant churches? What experiences have shaped your practical theology of church planting? What vocational and educational training shaped your ideas and values regarding church planting?
- Who are the key people who shaped your understanding of church planting?

DISCUSS

- At the time when Paul and other first-century Christians planted churches, the vast majority of their scriptures were the Old Testament. Read Romans 15, noting verse 4, and 1 Corinthians 10, noting verse 11. How does Paul use his knowledge of the Old Testament to apply principles to the churches? What are some other examples of how our knowledge of the Old Testament can inform our church planting efforts?
- What is a "missionary stance"? How do we imitate Christ in adopting this posture toward ministry?
- When is it necessary or advisable to have a "base of operations" from which to launch church planting missions? What are the alternatives, and when are they called for?
- Jesus's disciples learned from Jesus and from their experiences doing ministry, which the author calls "a field-training mission." You're

reading a textbook on church planting. What can be learned in the field that cannot be learned from a book?

- Paul learned to build churches from his own experience. However, experience is more valuable for knowing *how* (i.e., skill) than for knowing *what* (i.e., facts). When lessons learned from experience conflict with more reliable sources of truth, such as Scripture, how can we gain wisdom from experience without straying from the truth?

CHALLENGE

The author identifies eleven missional practices Paul learned from Jesus:

1. Missionary stance
2. Gospel proclamation
3. Targeted mission
4. Base of operations
5. Strike-team model
6. Network approach
7. Finding the man of peace
8. A discipleship method
9. A field-training mission
10. Ministry in a public space
11. Love for people

Evaluate your readiness for church planting against these missional practices. Where are you lacking? Where are you prepared?

REDISCOVERING APOSTOLIC MINISTRY

From Moses's Model to
Missionary Multiplication

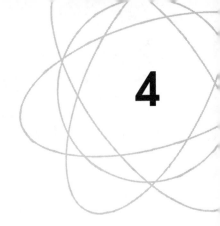

4

THE PLANTER'S GIFTING

"As the Father has sent me into
this world, so I am sending you."

—JESUS

Jack London's novel *The Call of the Wild*, set in the Yukon during the Klondike Gold Rush, tells the story through the eyes of a dog named Buck.[1] Through one tragedy after another, Buck goes from sled dog to loyal companion of John Thornton, a gold miner who becomes Buck's final master. Buck and Thornton seek a rumored "lost cabin" but instead find a gold-filled river and stake a prosperous claim. As a former sled dog having no work to do, Buck begins to explore the wilderness and encounters a phantom wolf called "The Wild Brother" who is the personification of his forgotten wolf instincts. With each encounter, Buck's canine instincts re-awaken his inner wolf, an ancestor that's been all but domesticated out of him. As Buck gets a taste of his own inner wildness, Thornton notes that he spends more and more time in the woods, until finally answering the call of the wild and running away for good. Like Buck, apostolic planters have a sense of wildness in them that doesn't function in the domesticated church system. They are wired to be wild like wolves but can safely live among the sheep. My hope is that, as you read this chapter about the wild brothers and their gifting, something may re-awaken in you; perhaps you will sense a need to unleash your latent gifting that mere ministerial sled dogging can't provide.

The wild brother who calls to us from Scripture is the apostle Paul. There was surely no one wilder. Analyzing the scriptural terms used to describe the apostolic function will give the most accurate picture of the gifting and

---

1. Jack London, *Call of the Wild* (New York: Greenwich Unabridged Library Classics, 1980).

function of the apostolic planter. Alan Hirsch outlines five subcategories of apostolic function that Paul listed in his letters to the Corinthians. Note the composite picture drawn by the following images when Paul laid the foundations in Corinth: Planter (1 Cor. 3:6–8), Foundation Layer (1 Cor. 3:10–15), Architect (translation of *architektōn*, "wise builder" in the passage above),[2] Father (1 Cor. 4:14–15), and Ambassador (2 Cor. 5:20).

Regarding the architect role, Neil Cole points to this role as putting systems in place that can be replicated and reproduced. As examples, Cole cites Zinzendorf's Mustard Seed Society that consisted of three simple pledges but produced missionary disciples and exponential multiplication; Wesley's comprehensive group system (including bands, societies, and classes); and Watchman Nee and his Little Flock of churches in China that spawned one of the largest and most prolific revival and renewal movements in history.[3] Each of these movements placed an emphasis on experience (or as Wesley termed it, "heart religion"), the Holy Spirit, and holiness.

Paul describes the apostolic role here in disconnected terms, but to summarize the function of each metaphor:

- A planter spreads new life where there was none by planting seeds.
- A foundation-layer makes it possible for all the other bits of work to go on.
- An architect understands the overall plan of what something is supposed to become and how all the other trades intersect.
- A father loves the family deeply because, indirectly, it came from his actions.
- An ambassador mediates the gospel between God and the people to make peace.

Church planting involves all this, simultaneously and, unlike the real-life construction trades he's describing, it does not involve switching hats. This is because the apostolic role is the perfect blend of all five metaphors. This chapter will unpack the role of apostle further, branching out from the descriptions in Corinthians and identifying additional functions that we can see Paul modeling in his apostolic role throughout Scripture.

---

2. Spiros Zodhiates, *The Complete Word Study Dictionary: New Testament* (Chattanooga, TN: AMG, 1992), 753.

3. Neil Cole, *Primal Fire: Reigniting the Church with the Five Gifts of Jesus* (Carol Stream, IL: Tyndale, 2014), 144–45.

CHURCH PLANTERS ARE SENT ONES

The word *Apostolos*, from which we get our word *apostle* (literally "sent one"), is the typical way Paul identifies his own ministry. Traditionally in the West, we have given preference to the word "calling," from the Greek *kletos* (literally "appointed"). Although we give preference to it, Paul used it sparingly; it came up twice: once when his authority was being questioned in 1 Corinthians 1:1, and again when he was writing to many who had never met him personally in his letter to the Romans.[4]

Paul's preference, therefore, was to describe himself as someone who was sent specifically by God: "Paul, an apostle—sent not from men nor by a man, but by Jesus Christ" (Gal. 1:1). In this sense, Paul is likening himself to the other apostles, yet, in another sense, to the prophets of the Old Testament. Someone who claims to be sent, therefore, must have a sender to be legitimate. In the literal sense, Paul had been called directly by the risen Lord Jesus, who physically appeared to him and commissioned him.

When Jesus called his apostles in the Gospels by special invitation, they permanently exited tax booths and discarded their nets in a crumpled heap on the shores of the Sea of Galilee. Matthew 4:21 recounts, "And going on from there he saw two other brothers, James the son of Zebedee and John his brother, in the boat with Zebedee their father, mending their nets; and *He called them*" (NASB, emphasis added). Paul's physical commissioning by Jesus placed him in the same category as the Twelve—but what does this say to the rest of us? Is a sending necessary? Is there a sense in which the planter today can be a *sent one*?

WHAT ABOUT US?

Apostolos is used eighty times in the New Testament, but not exclusively for Paul and the twelve apostles. Consider the use of *apostolos* when Paul described the list of his nine partners (*apostolos*, plural: *apostoloi*), none whom were part of the Twelve:

- Titus (2 Cor. 8:23)
- James, the Lord's brother, not John's brother (Gal. 1:18–19)
- Barnabas (Acts 14:14)
- Apollos (1 Cor. 4:6–9)

---

4. Gordon Fee, *The First Epistle to the Corinthians: The New International Commentary on the New Testament* (Grand Rapids: Eerdmans, 1987), 28.

- Andronicus (Rom. 16:7)
- Junia (Rom. 16:7)
- Epaphroditus (Phil. 2:25)
- Timothy (1 Tim. 1:1–2:6)
- Silas/Silvanus (1 Thess. 1:1–2:6)

Unfortunately, those translating the Bible into English rendered the word *apostolos* in our Bibles as *messenger* or *representative* because, since the Reformation, it was inconsistent with the theology of the translators. The word "missionary" does not exist in the New Testament, only the word apostle. Ask yourself whether it makes more sense to simply translate the word *apostolos* into English as "apostle" in order to describe the missionary function. *Apostle* is the New Testament word for a pioneering, groundbreaking, foundation-laying, community-founding, team-building, mobile-discipling, self-replacing, church-planting missionary.

To be clear, anyone who embarks on apostolic ministry does not share the authority or characteristics of the Twelve, who were designated by a specific number to demonstrate that there were *only twelve of them*. Only the apostle Paul would add himself to their number, "as of one born out of due time" (1 Cor. 15:8 KJV), describing what had happened when the resurrected Lord appeared to him, thus making him the thirteenth warrior. Therefore, this special cadre of apostles was only available in the first century due to the set criteria for apostles of their caliber. The nine "fellow workers" of Paul listed above were not listed among their ranks, nor will an apostolic worker be listed today; this is because they fail to meet the qualifications of *apostles with a capital* A:

Criterion #1: You had to have seen the risen Lord.

Peter said, "One of these men must become with us a witness to his resurrection" (Acts 1:22 ESV), and as a result, the church appointed Matthias. Paul met this qualification, and therefore stated, "Am I not an apostle? Have I not seen Jesus our Lord?" (1 Cor. 9:1 NRSV). That one encounter, however, was not enough to validate his apostleship to the Gentiles; he had to meet another.

Criterion #2: You had to be there from the beginning.

Luke quoted Peter as saying that Judas's replacement had to be somebody who "accompanied us during all the time that the Lord Jesus went in and out among us, beginning from the baptism of John until the day when he was taken up from us" (Acts 1:21–22 NRSV). Paul was aware that he was born later than the others (1 Cor. 15:8 NKJV), but he also knew that he received a special pass from Jesus. Because of his meeting with the resurrected Jesus, Paul said he was equal to the Twelve.[5]

Criterion #3: You had to do miracles.

Paul reminded the Corinthians that "I persevered in demonstrating among you the marks of a true apostle, including signs, wonders and miracles" as a sign among them (2 Cor. 12:12).

Those who met those criteria we may term Apostles with a capital *A*. If we are to refer to apostles today, it must be with a lowercase *a*. They are different from the Twelve in significant ways, and yet similar in others.

In Paul's postresurrection appearance chronology, he mentioned that Jesus appeared to "the twelve" (1 Cor. 15:5), and then "to all the apostles" (1 Cor. 15:7). We conclude that there were "lesser apostles" in Jerusalem who neither met the criteria of the Twelve, nor possessed their authority, yet possessed their *missionary functionality*. Who were the "rest of the apostles" Paul referred to in Jerusalem outside of the Twelve?

It is fair to speculate that Barnabas and John Mark were among them. Luke referred to them as *apostolos* in Acts 14:4, "The people of the city were divided; some sided with the Jews, *others with the apostles*" (emphasis added, note that apostles is plural). As only Barnabas, Paul, and John Mark were described in the passage, and since they were functioning apostolically as missionaries, expanding the kingdom to new frontiers, the moniker fits. The "other apostles" in Jerusalem may also refer to the seventy-two who were "sent out," and were thus *apostolos* in the truest sense. Paul understood that there were twelve

---

5. One of the major objections to this theory is the assertion that there were only twelve apostles, and that Matthias was mistakenly chosen to take Judas's place instead of Paul. Some have asserted that when the apostles replaced Judas, they made a mistake. They assert that Paul had been chosen to replace Judas the traitor, but because the apostles rolled the dice too soon, Matthias was mistakenly appointed. This view is refuted by Acts 6:2, "the twelve summoned the full number of the disciples." Luke wrote those words knowing that Matthias was one of those twelve when Paul wasn't even saved yet. If Luke in Acts 6:2 didn't have a problem identifying Matthias as one of the Twelve, then why would we? If Luke called him one of the Twelve, not contesting or even intimating it should have been Paul, why would we? A counterargument to this is to respond that Matthias is never heard of again in the book of Acts. If that's the case, then we'd better dismiss Andrew, Thomas, Bartholomew, James son of Alpheus, and Simon the Zealot from the Twelve as well, because after Acts 1:13 they're never mentioned again either. Furthermore, Paul never considered himself a member of the exclusive group known as "The Twelve." True, he believed himself to be equal to the Twelve in authority, abilities, and qualifications, yet not one of their number. In other words, he didn't rename the apostolic posse as "The Thirteen." There were twelve tribes of Israel, and the Twelve were sent to Jerusalem first to establish a hub there that would spread out into the entire region of Israel. Paul was the apostle to the Gentiles, therefore, he was rightly separated from them.

apostles who were called to the twelve tribes, and that he was "the apostle to the Gentiles," distinguishing Peter's ministry among the dispersion of the Jews throughout the Gentile world from his ministry to the Gentiles themselves: "For God, who was at work in Peter as an apostle to the circumcised, was also at work in me as an apostle to the Gentiles" (Galatians 2:8).

David Devenish observed three different categories of apostleship:

1. Jesus "the apostle and high priest whom we confess" (Hebrews 3:1 NET). Nobody is an apostle of his caliber.
2. The Twelve—including Judas's replacement, Matthias, and adding in the late-born apostle Paul on a similar level, only thirteen of them will ever exist and remain. Interestingly, though, in Revelation there are only twelve pillars with Apostles' names on them; presumably this includes Matthias but not Paul, maintaining a distinction from the Twelve.
3. The apostles of the ascended Christ given to equip the church (Eph. 4:11). These are different from the Twelve, in that they were not witnesses of the resurrection but gifts of his ascension (Eph. 4:8). This category is without number and continues into the present day, functioning as missionary planters.[6]

Over centuries, a mythology has developed regarding "calling." If we revert back to the scriptural terminology of a *sent one* or of *sent-ness* to describe our ministry as Paul did, instead of perpetuating the language of *calling*, things become clearer. Many who claim to be called refer to their choice to go into full-time vocational ministry without any conception of undertaking missionary work or anything that involves being *sent*. The elders and deacons *stay*, whereas church planters *go*. There is no required calling for local church elders and deacons *to stay*.

The modern-day pastor's role is essentially the role of a first-century elder: somebody who teaches and governs the church and, most important, stays behind when the apostolic planter moves on. Nowhere in Scripture do church elders receive a special call. The biblical pattern was for the apostolic leaders who planted a church to appoint elders before they exited it. The issue is not whether you're called, but whether you're *sent*. Aubrey Malphurs notes that using Old Testament examples as parallels to our calling employs "questionable hermeneutics," and it is more helpful to discern your internal wiring or design

6. David Devenish, *Fathering Leaders, Motivating Mission: Restoring the Role of the Apostle in Today's Church* (Milton Keynes, UK: Authentic Media, 2011), 502.

to plant as a church planter.[7] Despite the accurate claim that we are all sent in the context of the great commission, we do not all possess the wiring for apostolic ministry as "sent ones." Thus, Paul asks rhetorically, "Are all apostles?" (1 Cor. 12:29).

There are those of the missional movement who would argue that we are all missionaries, but the words of J. Herbert Kane regarding the "sentness" aspect of the apostle (The New Testament word for missionary) are helpful here:

> The use of the term missionary. There are those who advocate that we drop the word altogether. Others insist that it should be applied to all committed Christians. Stephen Neill has warned that if everybody is a missionary, nobody is a missionary. The Chinese have a proverb: "If two men feed a horse, it will lose weight; if two men keep a boat, it will soon leak." What is everybody's job is nobody's job. If every Christian is a missionary, missionary work is bound to suffer. It is correct to say that every Christian is, or should be, a witness. It is not correct to say that every Christian is a missionary.[8]

In Jerusalem, the apostles served as elders for a significant time, allowing Peter to later greet the leaders as being their "fellow elder" (1 Pet. 5:1). But in Acts 14:23 (ESV), when Paul and Barnabas appoint elders before taking leave of the region of Galatia, "with prayer and fasting they committed them to the Lord in whom they had believed." The apostolic team moved onward to take the gospel deeper into the region while local elders were appointed to serve the church that was left in their wake. Observe the pattern of Paul instructing Timothy and Titus regarding the appointing of elders and the language used:

> "This is why I left you in Crete, so that you might put what remained into order, and appoint elders in every town as I directed you."—Titus 1:5 (ESV)

> "And let them also be tested first; then let them serve as deacons if they prove themselves blameless."—1 Timothy 3:10 (ESV)

> "He must not be a recent convert, or he may become puffed up with conceit and fall into the condemnation of the devil."—1 Timothy 3:6 (ESV)

---

7. Aubrey Malphurs, *The Nuts and Bolts of Church Planting: A Guide for Starting Any Kind of Church* (Grand Rapids: Baker Books, 2011), 37.

8. J. Herbert Kane, *Understanding Christian Missions* (Grand Rapids: Baker, 1974), 41.

Upon what basis then should Timothy and Titus appoint elders and deacons? Prior to exiting the city, the apostle appoints elders and deacons based primarily on character with a slight nod to gifting. There are qualifications of ministry—hence, Paul refers to himself not being disqualified: "But I discipline my body and keep it under control, lest after preaching to others I myself should be disqualified" (1 Cor. 9:27 ESV). And not everyone is qualified. Not all are "full of faith and the Holy Spirit" (Acts 6:5 ESV) as the original seven appointed deacons were. J. Oswald Sanders said of elders, "The only method is that of qualifying to be a leader."[9]

Further, when we trace Paul's calling and activity as an apostle, we observe a transition in his ministry when he shifts from functioning as a local elder in Antioch who *stays*, to being set apart as an apostle who *goes*. On the Damascus road Jesus gave Paul the vision of what he'd do, but it's not until Acts 13:1–3 (ESV) that he received the commissioning: "Now there were in the church at Antioch prophets and teachers, Barnabas, Simeon who was called Niger, Lucius of Cyrene, Manaen a lifelong friend of Herod the tetrarch, and Saul. While they were worshiping the Lord and fasting, the Holy Spirit said, 'Set apart for me Barnabas and Saul for the work to which I have called them.' Then after fasting and praying they laid their hands on them and sent them off."

Overnight, their ministry changed to what David Ollerton called "mobile ministry" or "ministry on the move." They transitioned from stationary ministers in Antioch to "sent ones" who ministered in a much broader context. This special setting apart included *both* Barnabas and Paul, indicating that this sending is experienced by both greater and lesser apostles. Similarly, Timothy receives a special empowering of his apostolic gifting that was confirmed by prophecies: "Do not neglect your gift, which was given you through prophecy when the body of elders laid their hands on you" (1 Tim. 4:14). F. F. Bruce comments that "there are hints in the Pastoral Epistles of prophetic utterances which clearly marked out this course as the divine will for Timothy and which were confirmed by a special spiritual endowment received by him at the same time."[10]

Therefore, it is crucially important to confirm a calling in the role of apostleship to avoid the presumption of taking it upon ourselves. Paul assured his readers of his call to apostleship regularly in his epistles so he would not be left open to the criticism so often gossiped about in the church-planting world: Some are sent; others just went.

---

9. J. Oswald Sanders, *Spiritual Leadership* (Chicago: Moody, 1967), 17.
10. F. F. Bruce, *Paul: Apostle of the Heart Set Free* (Grand Rapids: Eerdmans, 1996), 214.

THE SENT-NESS OF PATRICK

St. Patrick, as he is commonly known, lived in the fifth century as a missionary to Ireland. Because he is a mystical figure, shrouded in the mists of myth and legend, it is difficult to compose an accurate picture of Patrick. Scholars believe his real name was Maewyn, indicating that he likely grew up in Wales, where raiders captured him while he was herding pigs and forced him into slavery. Upon being freed, Patrick returned to Ireland as a missionary, and legend speaks of three churches planted and over one hundred thousand baptized due to his influence. Only two of his writings survive, the Confession and the Letter to the Soldiers of Coroticus. Patrick wrote of this inward compulsion in his letter: "I, Patrick, a sinner, unlearned, resident in Ireland, declare myself to be a bishop. Most assuredly I believe that what I am I have received from God. And so I live among the barbarians, a stranger and exile for the love of God. He is witness that this is so."[11] Patrick's words highlight the following characteristics of the apostolic sent-ness:

- He felt unqualified to be one, since he is a *"sinner, unlearned."*
- He demonstrated a subjective and internal confidence in his call: *"I declare myself to be a bishop."*
- He recognized that it is not something he did, but something he was: *"what I am."*
- He acknowledged that God had given him this calling: *"I have received from God."*
- He was among the lost who needed him: *"And so I live among the barbarians."*
- He was alienated from his comforts and contacts as a missionary: *"a stranger and exile."*
- He felt the love of Christ compelling him: *"for the love of God."*
- He saw an external confirmation of the call: *"He is witness that this is so."*

Every year, 3,700 churches are planted in America. Nobody knows how many of them are successful, and the oft-quoted failure rate of 70–80 percent, although undocumented, may not be far from inaccurate, especially if the numerous failures we've personally encountered are any indication.[12]

---

11. Patrick's letter to Coroticus in Philip Freeman, *St. Patrick of Ireland: A Biography* (New York: Simon & Schuster, 2004), loc 2333 of 3508, Kindle.

12. Stetzer and Bird report, "Until recently, there was little research that addressed the health and survivability of new churches. Several oft-quoted statistics, such as those indicating an 80% failure rate

Undoubtedly, some who plant are self-appointed, rather than sent, yet others, like David Watson, who moved to Northern India, begged for two months that God would allow him to go home after six of his coworkers were martyred within eighteen months. Sensing God would not release him from being sent, Watson complained, "God, I can't plant churches anymore. I didn't sign on to love people, train people, send people, and get them killed."[13] This tension is maintained by the overwhelming love an apostle feels for the people to whom they are sent, as legendary planting mentor Don Overstreet observed: "the apostolic call originates in the heart of God."[14] Paul would have stopped if it weren't for the greater inward motor of love driving him on, for, as he said, "the love of Christ compels us" (2 Cor. 5:14 NKJV).

Planters who are sent by God are nearly impossible to stop. The only way to slow the apostle Paul was to lock him up, and the only way to stop him was to separate his head from his shoulders. Eventually, as an apostolic planter, you will wrestle with every kind of argument and excuse throughout the process of your calling; but, in the end, that call to sent-ness will defy logic, haunt you in bed at night, and keep you awake when the rest of the house is sleeping. You'll want to come out of your chest when you hear bad preaching or missed opportunities. Your appetite for Scripture will grow ravenous, your awareness of your need for prayer will deepen, and your compassion for the lost will be enflamed to the point of pain. When God enlists us on apostolic mission, it will take every bit of strength we have, and so he begins to change everything that we are. Like Patrick understood, this is about what you are, rather than what you do.

As Patrick demonstrates, an apostolic planter can be distinguished by the following characteristics of *sent-ness*:

for new church plants, seem to have no basis in actual research. Other pertinent church planting studies address issues of church plant survivability, health, and the factors which contribute to both. Multiple church planting studies, 54 doctoral dissertations, 41 journal articles, over 100 church planting books and manuals, and a few relevant studies are included in the research and literature review for this article." Found in Stetzer and Bird, *The State of Church Planting in the United States: Research Overview and Qualitative Study of Primary Church Planting Entities* (Lifeway Research: 2015), 21, https://www.wesleyan.org/wp-content/uploads/Lifeway-2015-ChurchPlanting-Survey.pdf. The original qualitative study for this report was conducted by a team of researchers who surveyed over 200 church planting churches, over 100 leaders from 40 denominations, 45 church planting networks, 84 organic church leaders, 12 nationally known experts, and 81 colleges and seminaries. Still, it seems strange that no serious research has been done concerning the failure rate of churches planted. Perhaps no one really wants the answer. There certainly doesn't seem to be any motivation for it by those who pay for such studies.

13. Quoted in Steve Addison, *Pioneering Movements: Leadership That Multiplies Disciples and Churches* (Downers Grove, IL: InterVarsity Press, 2015), 156.

14. Don Overstreet, *Sent Out: The Calling, the Character, and the Challenge of the Apostle Missionary* (Bloomington, IN: Cross Books, 2009), 62.

a. The apostolic planter is wired to cross over to new frontiers and cultures.
b. The apostolic planter is called to proclaim Christ where his name is not known or revered. As Piper said, "Mission is not the goal of the church. Worship is. Mission exists, because worship doesn't."[15]
c. The apostolic ministry is designed to be mobile, rather than stationary.

The combination of these three characteristics of apostolic ministry can contribute greatly to successful church planting. This does not mean that all church planting is done exclusively by those with an apostolic function; those who have this bent are just more uniquely outfitted for it.

Robert Johnson, King of the Mississippi Delta River Blues, was said to possess extra-long fingers that made it sound like two people were playing the guitar at the same time, and that skill defined an entire genre of music. In the same way, Paul the apostle defined an entire genre of ministry. A minister may plant a church, but that does not make that minister apostolic. Devenish quotes Daniel Sinclair: "While the various teams in the New Testament were no doubt engaged in 'apostolic ministry,' the actual title 'apostle' seems to have been applied somewhat sparingly, perhaps only to those whose calling, gifting and fruitfulness in pioneer work had become confirmed over time. As 1 Corinthians 9:2 shows, not even Paul's apostleship was universally recognized. Having said that, I do believe that over time other leaders may come to recognize that a particular person has a clear gift of apostleship, and may legitimately refer to him as an apostle."[16]

Mike Breen, author and founder of 3DM, recounts the shift he felt in moving from an evangelistic leader to an apostolic leader when he was in prayer, and God "seemed to say, 'You know, you can have the whole megachurch thing. Or you can have something else.' That something else was that the Lord gave me this vision for a continually reproducible network of lightweight and low-maintenance communities. . . . We wouldn't simply grow by adding people to worship services; we'd grow by multiplying disciples who could then multiply missional communities, who could multiply worshiping campuses who could multiply churches and into other networks and cities."[17] St. Patrick himself claims he received a vision of a man named Victoricus, who handed him a letter with the heading *The Voice of the Irish* entreating, "We appeal to you,

---

15. John Piper, *Let the Nations Be Glad: The Supremacy of God in Missions* (Grand Rapids: Baker, 2010), 15.
16. Devenish, *Fathering Leaders, Motivating Mission*, 16.
17. Quoted by Alan Hirsch and Tim Catchim in *The Permanent Revolution Playbook: APEST for the People of God: A Six Week Exploration* (Denver: Missio Publishing, 2014), 64.

holy servant boy, to come and walk among us."[18] Such a clear sense of personal calling and sent-ness from the Lord and his people is essential fuel for the apostolic heart.

YOU ARE SENT TO SOMEONE, SOMEWHERE, OR SOMETHING

Many people are unaware of the different types of sending. They wrongfully assume that when God sends apostles, it's one-size-fits-all. There are actually three different types of sending in Scripture:

1. Sent to perform an activity—Paul noted that he was sent to preach the gospel. Jesus also identified preaching as his chief activity, "that is why I was sent" (Luke 4:34). Of course, there isn't always one activity associated with our sent-ness, but sometimes we are sent for a particular purpose.

2. Sent to a people—Jesus was sent to the lost sheep of Israel. Paul was sent to the Gentiles. Each of them had a separate group of people to whom they were sent, and they focused their ministry on that people group. You can't reach every people group with your little church plant, but you could partner with other church planters and ministers who will; then work together and share resources. Rick Warren felt sent to the upwardly mobile yuppie in Orange County, California. He could have gone after anyone, but he felt that if he went strategically after the businessman in Orange County, he'd eventually have the resources to go after everyone, and that their families would eventually follow. Targeting a specific cross-section of humanity is not wrong according to Scripture. True, Paul said we become all things to all men in order to reach some, but those were different seasons of his ministry career that he was describing. You can't be everything to everybody, every time. Paul flipped the switch when he declared, "From now on I will go to the Gentiles" (Acts 18:6). He was sent to a specific people; even though Jesus had expressly outlined his ministry to the Gentiles, Paul was slower to catch on.

18. Liam De Paor, *Saint Patrick's World: The Christian Culture of Ireland's Apostolic Age* (Dublin: Four Courts Press, 1993), 100.

3. <u>Sent to a place</u>—Paul was also called at various times to specific places. Jesus met the Samaritan woman because, as John 4:4 says, "Now he had to go through Samaria" on his way from Galilee to Judah. Most Jews skirted around Samaria, refusing to go through it, but Jesus was sent to that well in that village at that time of day. Jesus also told his disciples "that he must go to Jerusalem" (Matt. 16:21). Paul was also *sent to a place* when he received the Macedonian call. The Twelve only stayed in Jerusalem for a time. Acts tells us that Peter traveled, as did John (else he would not have been exiled in Patmos). Others traveled according to church history, and eventually received martyrdom as a result of their missionary work. Apostles may serve locally for a time, as Paul did in Ephesus, but it will be short-lived. Paul served in Ephesus for three years; James served in Jerusalem until he died.

In summary, the apostolic planter delivers a specific message to a specific people, in a specific place, at a specific time.

QUALITIES OF APOSTOLIC PLANTERS

Unfortunately, there are those who have hijacked the role of apostleship and fail to embrace the missionary aspect of it by modeling themselves on Paul, who modeled himself on Jesus as the suffering servant in Isaiah. Instead, they model themselves on false teachers, claiming special revelation and superpowers. For this reason, many choose to opt for different terminology. Some recognize the activity of the apostolic planter but choose to call them "missionary-pastors," reasoning that "missionary + pastor = missionary pastor."[19] Similarly, Grudem recognizes the functioning of a "church encourager" but refuses to call them prophets or prophetic leaders.[20] In Shakespeare's *Romeo and Juliet*, Juliet asserts that "a rose by any other name would smell as sweet."[21] In the same way, regardless of the term one uses to label it, the fragrant offering of apostolic sent-ness is still sweet in the throne room of God and essential in the mission field.

---

19. Clint Clifton, *Church Planting Thresholds: A Gospel-Centered Guide* (Chattanooga, TN: New City Network, 2016), xviii.

20. Wayne Grudem, *The Gift of Prophecy in the New Testament and Today* (Wheaton, IL: Crossway Books, 1988), 93, 94.

21. William Shakespeare, *Romeo and Juliet*, Act 2, Scene 2.

ACTIVITIES OF APOSTOLIC PLANTERS

Reggie McNeal outlines the parallels between the apostolic leader of the first and twenty-first centuries: "The focus of apostolic leadership is not on office or gifts (these are how people in the church culture deal with the term apostle), but on the content of leadership that responds to the new spiritual landscape by shaping a church movement that more resembles the world of Acts than America in the last half of the twentieth century."[22] Paul's activities in the New Testament mirror the tasks of the planter today:

1. heralds the gospel
2. recruits and trains others
3. models bold, pioneering faith
4. plants churches
5. strategically sends
6. pioneers cross-cultural bridges
7. catalyzes mission
8. seeds contagious vision

1. Apostolic Planters Herald the Gospel

Paul's overwhelming description of his own ministry as an apostle is that of a proclaimer of the message of Jesus. Paul saw himself as a herald of the gospel above and beyond all that he was commissioned and sent to do. In each account of his commissioning by the risen Christ, the public preaching of the gospel is central.

Each of the accounts in Acts 9, 22, and 26 demonstrate the preaching of the gospel to be central to his apostolic calling:

- "But the Lord said to him, 'Go, for he is a chosen instrument of mine to carry my name before the Gentiles and kings and the children of Israel'" (Acts 9:15 ESV).
- "And he said, 'The God of our fathers appointed you to know his will, to see the Righteous One and to hear a voice from his mouth; for you will be a witness for him to everyone of what you have seen and heard'" (Acts 22:14–15 ESV).

---

22. Reggie McNeal, *The Present Future*, Jossey-Bass Leadership Network Series (San Francisco: Jossey Bass, 2009), 125–26.

- "'...I have appeared to you for this purpose, to appoint you as a servant and witness to the things in which you have seen me and to those in which I will appear to you, delivering you from your people and from the Gentiles—to whom I am sending you to open their eyes, so that they may turn from darkness to light and from the power of Satan to God, that they may receive forgiveness of sins and a place among those who are sanctified by faith in me'" (Acts 26:16–18 ESV).

Regarding laying foundations as a planter, Paul states, "thus I make it my ambition to preach the gospel, not where Christ has already been named, lest I build on someone else's foundation, but as it is written, 'Those who have never been told of him will see, and those who have never heard will understand'" (Rom. 15:20–21 ESV). Schnabel notes that "The oral proclamation of the gospel is the central action of missionary work."[23] This holds significant application to planters embarking on apostolic planting in light of common assertions that appear to reduce the importance of evangelization and preaching, particularly within the very circles where APEST roles are championed. (The acronym APEST was articulated by Alan Hirsch and refers to the five functions of Christ's ministry gifted to the church and enumerated in Ephesians 4:11— Apostolic function, Prophetic function, Evangelistic function, Shepherding function, and Teaching function).

To be true to the apostolic function, those who plant apostolically will not be able to resist the urge to preach the gospel, but will echo the apostle, "For necessity is laid upon me. Woe to me if I do not preach the gospel!" (1 Cor. 9:16 RSV). You may plant a church without being evangelistic, but you can't function apostolically without being evangelistic. To claim this would be contrary to the makeup and gifting of the apostolic function, not to mention Paul's description of his role. For this reason, many advocates of APEST have been mistaken for being apostolic, yet they are merely teachers who have discovered how to talk the talk of APEST. They are not apostolic if proclaiming and heralding Christ is not at the center of what they do. How could they be? How would it serve a missionary function if Christ's proclamation were not central to being apostolic like it was for every apostle in Scripture? Claiming the apostolic gift for yourself as an entrepreneurial teacher who popularizes APEST cannot replace actually being an apostolic practitioner.

---

23. Eckhard J. Schnabel, *Early Christian Mission: Paul and the Early Church.* (Downers Grove, IL: InterVarsity Press, 2004), 977.

2. The Apostolic Planter as Recruiter and Trainer

When Todd Hunter interviewed twenty-two failed planters within the Vineyard denominational tradition, he found that "95% of them possessed the inability to recruit, train, and deploy workers and leaders."[24] Yet everywhere Paul went, he recruited and mentored apprentices. "Paul and Barnabas appointed elders for them in each church" (Acts 14:23). It was also one of the first things that Jesus did in his own ministry. True planters have an unconscious competence in recruiting that often eludes mere church starters. They often aren't even aware of what they're doing. They have an inspiring quality that makes people want to follow them into doing the impossible.

Walt Disney convinced shareholders to invest in a submarine ride based on *20,000 Leagues Under the Sea*. Unprecedented in theme park engineering, it involved digging a massive hole to hold 34,000 m³ of water. That was the easy part. Whereas others would have designed a walk-through aquarium, or a glass-bottom boat, Disney wanted to move people under the water in submarines operated on tracks in the 1950s.[25] Disney reproduced himself by inspiring a team he called "the Imagineers." They have since come to be known as "Disney's Nine Old Men," Disney legends who were his apostolic recruits and who animated most of his films, designed his theme parks, and went on to direct and produce. Had Disney merely hired artists to do jobs, instead of pouring himself into them and discipling them to be world builders, the Walt Disney Company would have a very different legacy today.

Perhaps Paul's exhaustive greeting to thirty individuals in Romans 16 evidences the most striking example of his apostolic training recruitment. Paul had never been to Rome, but after multiple missionary journeys, he had left a string of pearls across an entire continent. Perhaps more significantly, Stetzer asserts that "he risked delegation to young Christians" to expand the movement.[26]

Consider the fellow workers Paul recruited from the following regions. Despite this not being an exhaustive list, it represents what can be pieced together from his letters and Acts:

24. Fred Herron, *Expanding God's Kingdom through Church Planting* (Bloomington, IN: iUniverse, 2003), 85.

25. Bob Thomas, *Walt Disney: An American Original* (New York: Simon and Schuster, 1976), 291.

26. Ed Stetzer and Daniel Im, *Planting Missional Churches: Your Guide to Starting Churches that Multiply* (Nashville: B&H Academic, 2016), 37. Ralph Moore argues the same in *How to Multiply Your Church* (Grand Rapids: Baker Books, 2009), 163.

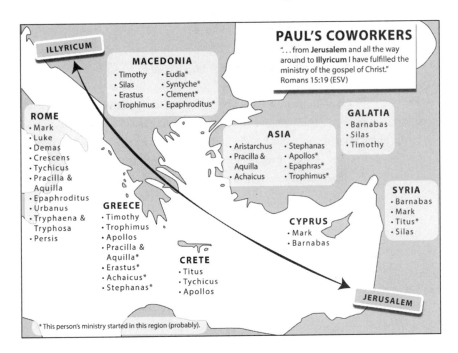

PAUL'S COWORKERS

"...from **Jerusalem** and all the way around to **Illyricum** I have fulfilled the ministry of the gospel of Christ."
Romans 15:19 (ESV)

ILLYRICUM

MACEDONIA
- Timothy
- Silas
- Erastus
- Trophimus
- Eudia*
- Syntyche*
- Clement*
- Epaphroditus*

ROME
- Mark
- Luke
- Demas
- Crescens
- Tychicus
- Pracilla & Aquilla
- Epaphroditus
- Urbanus
- Tryphaena & Tryphosa
- Persis

GREECE
- Timothy
- Trophimus
- Apollos
- Pracilla & Aquilla*
- Erastus*
- Achaicus*
- Stephanas*

CRETE
- Titus
- Tychicus
- Apollos

ASIA
- Aristarchus
- Pracilla & Aquilla
- Achaicus
- Stephanas
- Apollos*
- Epaphras*
- Trophimus*

GALATIA
- Barnabas
- Silas
- Timothy

CYPRUS
- Mark
- Barnabas

SYRIA
- Barnabas
- Mark
- Titus*
- Silas

JERUSALEM

* This person's ministry started in this region (probably).

3. Apostolic Planters Are Role Models

The apostle Paul was able to inspire people to follow him and want to be mentored by him simply because he lived a life of faith that few did. Paul ran circles around his contemporaries, wore young men out, and ate hirelings for breakfast. I've included examples of these traits here to emphasize the importance of this role. What we do speaks louder than what we say:

> You, however, have followed *my teaching, my conduct, my aim in life, my faith, my patience, my love, my steadfastness, my persecutions and sufferings* that happened to me at Antioch, at Iconium, and at Lystra . . . (2 Tim. 3:10–11 ESV, emphasis mine).

In nearly every epistle, Paul gives an invitation to imitate the pattern of his own life, leaving us a powerful message about the importance of leadership. The apostle's character, boldness, sacrifice, faith, attendance to God's will, compulsion under Christ's love, and willingness to risk should inspire everyone around the apostle. In all things, Paul modeled what a follower of Christ should be:

> What you have learned and received and heard and seen in me—practice these things. (Phil. 4:9 ESV)

Therefore I urge you to imitate me. (1 Cor. 4:16)

Be imitators of me, as I am of Christ. (1 Cor. 11:1 ESV)

For you yourselves know how *you ought to imitate us*, because we were not idle when we were with you, nor did we eat anyone's bread without paying for it, but with toil and labor we worked night and day, that we might not be a burden to any of you. It was not because we do not have that right, but *to give you in ourselves an example to imitate.* (2 Thess. 3:7–9 ESV, emphasis mine)

Brothers, join in imitating me, and keep your eyes on those who walk according to the example you have in us. (Phil. 3:17 ESV)

What you have learned and received and heard and seen *in me*—practice these things, and the God of peace will be with you. (Phil. 4:9 ESV, emphasis mine)

For this reason, apostles will often have little patience for those who talk about things they don't do. No wonder Paul called his opponents "empty talkers" (Tit. 1:10 ESV) the ancient equivalent of big-mouthed-do-nothings. One of Wesley's Methodist contemporaries, John Fletcher, remarked that John Wesley "has generally blown the gospel trumpet, and rode twenty miles, before most of the professors, who despise his labors, have left their downy pillows."[27] He inspired a generation of circuit-riders to do the same.

4. The Apostle as Planter

Paul specifically said that he planted. Further, Paul contrasted his role as an apostle, planting churches, with Apollos's function of watering as an evangelist. Schnabel observes that "Paul sees himself as a pioneer missionary called by God to 'plant' (1 Corinthians 3:6) and to 'lay the foundation' (1 Corinthians 3:10)—that is, to establish new churches, Apollos and the other preachers and teachers 'water' (1 Corinthians 3:6). [Thus, we have] Paul's statement that the Lord assigned different tasks to 'each.' (1 Corinthians 3:5)"[28] The apostolic function comes first chronologically in the case of the Corinthians; Paul visited them

---

27. Iain H. Murray, *Wesley and Men Who Followed* (Edinburgh, UK: Banner of Truth, 2003), 152.
28. Schnabel, *Early Christian Mission*, 949.

apostolically, then afterward Priscilla and Aquilla served as teachers along with others who served as elders. This also implies that there is a risk factor. Planting something is always risky; one must be willing to risk death and loss of what's invested in the soil before new life can emerge.[29]

5. Apostolic Planters Are Senders

Once Paul recruited and trained missionaries and served as a role model to develop their character, he sent them on mission, thus extending his own reach. Consider those whom Paul sent out:

Paul sent Timothy to Corinth (1 Cor. 4:17).
Paul sent Timothy to Ephesus (1 Tim. 1:3).
Paul sent Timothy to Thessalonica (1 Thess. 3:2).
Paul sent Timothy to Philippi (Phil. 2:19).
Paul sent Epaphroditus to Philippi (Phil. 2:25).
Paul sent Titus to Corinth (2 Cor. 7:14; 8:16–17).
Paul sent Titus to Dalmatia (2 Tim. 4:10).
Paul left Titus on Crete (Tit. 1:5).
Paul sent Tychicus to Ephesus (Eph. 6:21; 2 Tim. 4:12).
Paul sent Tychicus to Colossae (Col. 4:7).
Paul sent Tychicus to Crete (Tit. 3:12).

In this sense, the apostolic planters live vicariously through fellow workers and reproduce themselves through discipleship and deployment.

6. Apostolic Planters Are Pioneers

Like explorers, apostles want to go where Christ is not named. Kenneth Scott Latourette quotes the *Didache Ton Dodeka Apostolon*, an early Christian document that describes the way churches operated in the first century. The church operated with the leadership of both "traveling apostles and prophets and of resident prophets and teachers. It instructs the Christians to appoint for themselves bishops and deacons and to hold them in honor, along with the prophets and teachers."[30] Apostolic planters are more excited to reach a cross-section of people who aren't being reached than church starters are to

---

29. Jim Peterson, *Church without Walls: Moving Beyond Traditional Boundaries* (Colorado Springs: NavPress, 1992), 55.

30. Kenneth Scott Latourette, *Beginnings to 1500, A History of Christianity*, vol. 1 (New York: Harper and Row, 1975), 117.

have a crowd. As pioneers, apostolic planters aren't wired for high numbers, but for high challenge. Branson calls the pioneering activity of apostolic planters "boundary crossing," noting that the frontiers breached by apostles are sometimes more cultural than physical.[31] This is demonstrated in Paul's ministry to the Gentiles, Peter's ministry in the house of Cornelius, and Christ's ministry to Samaritans, lepers, tax collectors, and prostitutes.

Hirsch identifies the anatomy of a pioneer:

1. An ability to invent the future while dealing with the past
2. A willingness to break with traditional ideas and methods
3. An ability to play multiple roles at the same time
4. A high tolerance for risk
5. A need to be different despite supporters wanting the pioneer to stay the same
6. An understanding that many want the pioneer to fail.[32]

7. The Apostle as Catalyst

People think they need an evangelist when actually they need an apostle. An evangelist will come and do it for you, but when they're gone, the church simply waits until the next time an evangelist blows back into town. An apostle, however, is a mobilizer, and will not merely do the work of an evangelist but also demonstrate to others that they, too, can do the work of an evangelist! This catalytic element is so pronounced in apostolic planters that Fred Herron labels serial planters as apostolic catalysts.[33]

Dwight Moody volunteered to teach Sunday school at the mission on Chicago Avenue and Wells Street in Chicago. The superintendent informed him that they already had enough teachers, but if he could "work up a class of his own," he could teach. The next Sunday he brought eighteen poor street urchins from the poorest part of the neighborhood known as *Little Hell*. Not only did he catalyze that Sunday school, he recruited two helpers immediately, and started a Sunday school in Little Hell in an abandoned freight car. From there, he started a class for the older boys in a derelict saloon. As the Sunday

---

31. Mark Lau Branson, "Perspectives from the Missional Conversation," in *Starting Missional Churches: Life With God in the Neighborhood*, ed. Mark Lau Branson and Nicholas Warnes (Downers Grove, IL: InterVarsity Press, 2014), 40.

32. Alan Hirsch and Tim Catchim, *The Permanent Revolution: Apostolic Imagination and Practice for the 21st Century Church* (San Francisco: Jossey-Bass, 2012), 161–165.

33. Herron, *Expanding God's Kingdom*, 69.

schools grew into the hundreds, Moody began to catalyze others to assist the expanding mission that grew out of thin air.[34]

8. Apostolic Planters Are Vision Casters

Tied to the mobilization of others is the ability to seed contagious vision in those who stay behind and in those who are sent out from the church plant. In other words, the apostolic planter seeds the contagious vision in others rather than usurping all of the vision-casting role. The prominent pastor-only model seeks to make the lead pastor the sole visionary, despite the fact there is no mandate in Scripture demanding that a senior leader must cast the vision. Karl Vaters says, "This may be one of the primary reasons for the growth of New Age, Find-Your-Inner-Vision books being gobbled up by otherwise Christian people. People want to know how to dream their own dreams, like Acts 2:17 says they will, but that's seldom what they get at church. What they usually hear is 'You're here to help me fulfill my vision for this group.' So they go elsewhere and receive unbiblical advice, instead."[35] Vaters is kicking at something that goads us, the dream that we should all play a part in developing the collective vision of our churches.

Leaders often quote (and twist) Proverbs 29:18: "Where there is no revelation, people cast off restraint; but blessed is the one who heeds wisdom's instruction," and also Hosea 4:6, "my people are destroyed from lack of knowledge," using the authorized version that translates knowledge or revelation as "vision" to suit their agenda and pirate vision away from God's people. Besides, those passages focus on the people rightfully resisting the leadership of pastors to make it all about themselves.

Hirsch notes that Paul's use of *master builder* "is loaded with notions of design, innovation and strategic craftsmanship."[36] God's house is neither a Craftsman prefabricated home ordered from of the Sears catalogue, nor a flat-packed vision to build an Ikea church. Paul learned from experience that each church plant would incarnate Christ differently depending on the gift matrix of the community in which he planted it. What many call vision is actually the strategic organization of the gifts of God's people.[37]

---

34. Kevin Belmonte, *D. L. Moody: A Life* (Chicago: Moody, 2014), 53–54.

35. Karl Vaters, "5 Problems with Top-Down Vision-Casting—And a New Testament Alternative," *Christianity Today*, Pivot blog, December 19, 2016, https://www.christianitytoday.com/karl-vaters/2016/december/5-problems-top-down-vision-casting-new-testament-alternativ.html?paging=off.

36. Hirsch and Catchim, *The Permanent Revolution*, 103.

37. This will be explored more thoroughly in the section on participation, mission, and values.

REFLECT

The author argues that an apostle, properly understood, is a person sent on mission. However, some apostles were the twelve Jesus chose, who were distinguished by their having seen the risen Lord, having been there from the beginning, and having performed miracles. Review the material on the distinction between the twelve apostles and all the other Christians who were also sent on mission. Is this consistent with what you have been taught? Have you ever considered yourself to have the spiritual gifting of being an apostle?

DISCUSS

- Paul uses five metaphors to describe the apostolic role:
    1. Planter
    2. Foundation layer
    3. Architect
    4. Father
    5. Ambassador
- Review the passages in 1 Corinthians that use these metaphors. How do they combine to provide a more complete picture than any one metaphor alone? Why were five metaphors necessary to capture the role that Paul is describing?
- The author argues that apostles are sent, as opposed to being called. How does this look in your denomination, fellowship, or organization? What is the process by which the leadership chooses people to send? Is there a role for a church planter's sense of calling in this process?
- The author lists eight activities of apostolic planters:
    1. Heralds the gospel
    2. Recruits and trains others
    3. Models bold pioneering faith
    4. Plants churches
    5. Strategically sends
    6. Pioneers cross-cultural bridges
    7. Catalyzes mission
    8. Seeds contagious vision
- Are these core competencies for every church planter? Which are mandatory for every church planter, and which could be accomplished by a specific member(s) of the team?

CHALLENGE

- Review the sidebar on being sent to someone, somewhere, or something. Do any of these types of sending apply to you? How might viewing being sent from this perspective help you understand your mission as a church planter?
- The author lists ten statements that might reveal if you are an apostle (i.e., "you are an apostle if . . ."). Read each statement and rate yourself from 0 (not at all like me) to 10 (completely like me). What are your lowest and highest scores? Why? Ask someone who knows you (e.g., someone you disciple, someone who disciples you) to rate you on these statements. Do their ratings match yours?

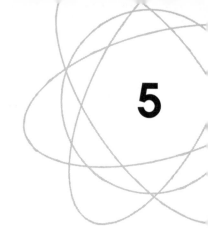

THE PLANTER'S CHARACTER AND HEALTH

5

I have more trouble with D. L. Moody than with any other man I've ever met.

—D. L. MOODY

In *Lectures to My Students,* Charles Spurgeon titled the first chapter *The Minister's Self Watch,* quoting the proverb, "If the axe be dull, the workman must exert much force."[1] Just as a wholly yielded person is a powerful weapon in the hands of God, the converse is equally true. Any damage dealer for the kingdom possesses potential for doing damage for the other side. A painful question we must all ask as sent ones is *Am I someone I would send?*" There are many church planting assessments throughout the country that will attempt to help you answer that question and clarify your qualifications for a call to plant. However, there is no system devised that can replace the self-assessment to which planters must first subject themselves internally. Any external church planting assessment should only complement and confirm the internal assessment the planter undertakes. Asking a series of probing questions will help prospective planters assess their church planting call. This chapter digs deeper into these questions in order to help the aspiring planter perform the necessary self-assessment. Any planter must start with the why question. "Why am I doing this?"

Attempting to express our goals can often expose our motives when we're not honest or aware enough to bring them out into the light in other ways. John Eldredge was speaking with a pastor in his thirties who had wound up working in the publishing industry. As a young man fresh out of seminary, he'd wanted

---

1. Charles Spurgeon, *The Minister's Self-Watch* (Pensacola: Chapel Library, 1999), 9.

to become a famous pastor with a church bigger than Swindoll's. "He wondered aloud why God hadn't let that happen. 'Perhaps' I offered, 'because you wanted a church bigger than Swindoll's.' He didn't like my answer. And that was the end of the conversation."[2] Contrast this with a statement by Count Zinzendorf, the founder of the Moravian movement who catalyzed John Wesley's mission: "Preach the gospel, die, and be forgotten."[3] Without question, church planting is sexy in some segments of contemporary Christian culture, but what is an acceptable motive for planting a church? How would your motives change if you were called to lift up the name of Jesus in Tanzania? Some of the best church planters in the world are there and have planted 350 churches in the last ten years through viral church planting. Teams travel through the bush and disperse in smaller teams to plant. Their final exam is to plant a church that has planted churches. When those students return within three years, the usual result is that each student's church has planted around ten churches that have also planted churches, themselves!

To clarify if you are planting more for ego or impact, ask yourself:

- Would you plant exclusively in developing nations?
- Would you take the gospel to a nation where you'd be persecuted?
- Would you plant if nobody ever learned your name?
- Would you invest your life leading a movement for which you would never get any credit?
- Would you plant churches if you still had to work another job and nobody paid you?

If your answer to any of these is no, then you probably shouldn't be a planter. Bernard of Clairvaux's maxim may be true of you: "He thinks only of what he wants and he does not ask himself whether he ought to want it."[4]

God doesn't delight in using planters who crave fortune and glory, who strive and clamor for the best seats at banquets and conferences, like the Pharisees. They will find themselves at cross-purposes with the mission of the

---

2. John Elderedge, *The Way of the Wild Heart: A Map for the Masculine Journey* (Nashville: Nelson Books, 2006).

3. Attributed to Count Zinzendorf, yet undocumented. Zinzendorf was the founder and bishop of the Moravian church 700–1760, and had a profound impact on John Wesley. In this chapter we discuss legacy, so my hope is that although this may inspire our motives to make it about him, we don't miss the importance of leaving something behind that helps others follow Christ more nearly, see him more clearly, or serve him more dearly.

4. Quoted without reference in Zack Eswine, *The Imperfect Pastor: Discovering Joy in our Limitations through a Daily Apprenticeship with Jesus* (Wheaton, IL: Crossway, 2015), 17.

Holy Spirit, of whom Jesus said, "When [he] comes . . . he will glorify me" (John 16:13–14). That leaves little room for the vainglory of men. George Whitefield confessed that popularity nearly destroyed him as a young man before he learned to crucify it. "The tide of popularity began to run very high. In a short time I could no longer walk on foot as usual, but was constrained to go in a coach from place to place, to avoid the hosannas of the multitude. They grew quite extravagant in their applauses, and had it not been for my compassionate high priest, popularity would have destroyed me. I used to plead with Him to take me by the hand and lead me unhurt through this fiery furnace. He heard my request and gave me to see the vanity of all commendations but his own."[5] Having a large church does not indicate success. Many large, "successful" churches are simply in the way of kingdom expansion.

Sadly, many leaders in this social media–driven platform ministry have failed to make the distinction between being popular and being successful. Success is truly to be great in the eyes of heaven, where Jesus proclaims us before the Father, but all too many leaders choke when asked difficult questions on CNN. Paul stood before governors, kings, and emperors and didn't flinch. He knew his call was to proclaim Christ as Lord, and because his calling was clear, the mandate was decided. Paul boldly proclaimed the gospel despite the aspersions cast on his own reputation. If the choice was to be popular or to be useful, which would you choose? If the current *modus operandi* of tracking church growth and followers on social media are the hermeneutic by which we interpret ministry success, few would sacrifice such a precious platform. They will never know how God could have filled them with bread that satisfied, or the food from the Father with which Jesus was satisfied as he met one person at the side of the well in Samaria, making his journey worth the trek.

FALSE MOTIVES

Ministry can become a hotbed of doing the right things for the wrong reasons. In Philippians 1:15 Paul says, "It is true that some preach Christ out of envy and rivalry, but others out of goodwill." Paul rejoices that Christ is being preached at all but lists off the wrong motives. Paul's list of "false motives" include:

- Envy (Phil. 1:15)
- Rivalry (Phil. 1:15)
- Selfish ambition (Phil. 1:17)

---

5. Luke Tyerman, *The Life of the Reverend George Whitefield* (Azle, TX: Need of the Times, 1995), 85.

Envy, rivalry, and selfish ambition all go together, and are among the pitfalls of our sickening Christian celebrity culture. *Radiohead*, punk music prophets of the 1990s, penned the lyrics to *High and Dry* about the perils of fame and the desire to have it by using famed stuntman, Evel Kneivel, as a metaphor. In the song, singer Thom York chides himself for allowing the envy of other artists to drive him to self-comparisons with others until it becomes a self-destructive force. What if I told you that God just called and told me that he didn't want to be your agent? What if I said he didn't want to promote your brand or make you famous? The way the apostles made it look, they were making him famous, promoting him. As a church planter, you're God's promoter.

CHARACTER TRUMPS GIFTING

Paul claimed that the greatest gift was love, positioning it at a higher level than raising the dead or working miracles. Heart motives and personal character always trump gifting. The stronger the influence created by your gifting, the greater the swathe of devastation that will be created by any failing of your moral character.[6] Church planting eats the most gifted preachers for breakfast and wipes the floor with what's left of them. A few months in reality hits as hard as Mike Tyson. When they realize it's going to be a long, slow grind, many planters peter out because they thought that all they needed was to be gifted. The most valuable character virtue for any church planter is endurance.[7] Endurance is not character in and of itself, but it certainly demonstrates the strength of your character.

Paul tells Timothy three times in 1 and 2 Timothy to endure:

- "But you, man of God, flee from all this, and pursue righteousness, godliness, faith, love, **endurance** and gentleness" (1 Tim. 6:11).
- "You therefore must **endure** hardship as a good soldier of Jesus Christ" (2 Tim. 2:3 NKJV).
- "But you, keep your head in all situations, **endure** hardship, do the work of an evangelist, discharge all the duties of your ministry" (2 Tim. 4:5).

Paul needed endurance himself:

6. Jeff Christopherson and Mac Lake, *Kingdom First: Starting Churches that Shape Movements* (Nashville: B&H Publishing, 2015), 33.

7. In expanding God's kingdom through church planting, Fred Herron remarks that when he was asked at a conference what the most important quality in a planter was, he answered without hesitation, "endurance." Most seasoned veterans of planting would answer the same. Fred Herron, *Expanding God's Kingdom Through Church Planting* (Lincoln: iUniverse, 2003), 86.

- "Rather, as servants of God we commend ourselves in every way: in great **endurance**; in troubles, hardships and distresses" (2 Cor. 6:4).
- "Therefore I **endure** everything for the sake of the elect, that they too may obtain the salvation that is in Christ Jesus, with eternal glory" (2 Tim. 2:10).
- "You, however, know all about my teaching, my way of life, my purpose, faith, patience, love, **endurance**" (2 Tim. 3:10).

He tells Titus to instruct the older men to model endurance for the younger men.

- "Teach the older men to be temperate, worthy of respect, self-controlled, and sound in faith, in love and in **endurance**" (Titus 2:2).

The strength of character manifests through emotional resilience, the ability to bounce back. Proverbs 24:10 says, "If you falter in a time of trouble, how small is your strength!" Perhaps this is why Paul had such high expectations of his fellow workers, as exhibited by his refusal to take John Mark back into the field after he proved not to possess the quality of endurance.[8] There was something in Paul that respected someone who could suffer like his Lord. Paul saw himself as an endurance athlete to be imitated by those around him:

For though you have countless guides in Christ, you do not have many fathers. For I became your father in Christ Jesus through the gospel. *I urge you, then, be imitators of me.* That is why I sent you Timothy, my beloved and faithful child in the Lord, *to remind you of my ways in Christ*, as I teach them everywhere in every church. (1 Cor. 4:15–17 ESV, emphasis mine)

Character was such a primal factor in Paul's ministry that if he was unable to visit a church, he needed someone who had similar character traits, like Timothy, whose example would be just as powerful. He exhorts Timothy to be the example to others that Paul was to him:

Let no one despise you for your youth, but *set the believers an example in speech, in conduct, in love, in faith, in purity.* (1 Tim. 4:12 ESV, emphasis mine)

---

8. In Ryan Lokkesmoe, *Paul and His Team: What the Early Church Can Teach Us about Leadership and Influence* (Chicago: Moody, 2017), Lokkesmoe observes that Mark was with Paul in Rome and was a comfort to him (Col 4:10–11). He mentions Mark again in Philemon 24.

Show yourself in all respects to be a model of good works. (Titus 2:7 ESV, emphasis mine)

This should inspire all of us to live the type of life that others can emulate. After all, when you lead a church planting team, others will be looking to you, sizing you up, carefully watching how you handle hardship and challenges to assess whether your leadership is worth following. Luckily for us, Paul left a trail for those who entered leadership in the churches planted by him—or anyone on his team—that we can still follow today.

RUNNING THE GAUNTLET

If anyone is above reproach, the husband of one wife, and his children are believers and not open to the charge of debauchery or insubordination. For an overseer, as God's steward, must be above reproach. He must not be arrogant or quick-tempered or a drunkard or violent or greedy for gain, but hospitable, a lover of good, self-controlled, upright, holy, and disciplined. (Titus 1:6–8, ESV)

If these are the requirements for the elders appointed to replace the church planter, we can safely assume that they are also part of the requirements for church planters themselves. If we can't honestly say that our lives are examples to be followed, then it's safe to say that we shouldn't be leading. Thankfully, Paul practiced what he preached and modeled a lifestyle of fearless proclamation, a life that adorned the gospel that he called others to imitate in every one of his epistles.

"Above reproach" is not part of the list; it's the summary of it. What follows is the unpacking of what "above reproach" looks like. Being above reproach is so vital to Paul that he emphasizes it by stating it twice; once in verse 6, then again in verse 7, leaving us to conclude that there should be no gaping holes in the character of anyone who desires to lead others.

Despite the fact that this list is intended to make us slightly uncomfortable, let me comfort you with this: every truly humble, qualified leader wrestles with this passage, wondering if the list washes them out. No leader truly feels above reproach apart from divine intervention and, if they do, they are far from being the type of apostles Jesus chose. This long list of leaders includes Peter, who told the Lord to depart from him because he was too sinful. It also includes Paul, who counted himself the chief of sinners. Thankfully, however, Paul elaborates by providing a list of character traits that define what "above reproach" means.

These qualities of character, when assembled together and analyzed, construct a composite model of Jesus; this is a fitting pattern for those who aspire to disciple others into his likeness.

The first target on our list is arrogance. Arrogance causes casualty by self-sabotage, making you your own worst enemy. When leaders have slain almost every other beast lurking in their character, arrogance is the hydra with seven regenerative heads that grow back, constantly needing to be lopped off with the gospel that brings humility.

In Melville's masterpiece *Moby-Dick*, Captain Ahab and first mate Starbuck face off in a confrontation on deck. Seizing a loaded musket, Ahab points it at Starbuck exclaiming that there is only room for one captain on the ship. Starbuck composes himself and pauses before he exits the room: "Thou hast outraged, not insulted me, sir; but for that I ask thee not to beware of Starbuck; thou wouldst but laugh; but let Ahab beware of Ahab; beware of thyself, old man."[9] That is because leaders themselves are often the monster at the door.

Perhaps this is why Peter asked leaders to be "examples to the flock" (1 Pet. 5:3). In verse 5, he tells them to cloak themselves with humility, like wrapping a garment over all their abilities, so that humility becomes the most obvious thing about them, outshining their gifts. Peter would forever have his own pride on display. At the Last Supper, he boasted he'd never deny Jesus even if the other eleven did; later, he proceeded to deny him three times before the rooster crowed. To make things worse, humility had been the centerpiece in Jesus's instructions at the meal as he modeled servant leadership; he had washed their feet in the same upper room where Peter's pride had erupted. As Peter went over that night repeatedly in his mind after that painful failure, the fact that a humble leader like the Jesus of Philippians 2 shouldn't be preached about by an arrogant braggart must have hit home. Church planters often clean toilets, load trailers, sweep floors, and sub in Sunday school classes.

Paul adds to the list and, in a sort of reverse-negative, we see ourselves all too clearly dabbling in things we should not be, like "quick-tempered." "The anger of man does not produce the righteousness of God" (Jas. 1:20 ESV). James said that, and he should know. Growing up as Jesus's imperfect half-brother teaches you a lot about your own flaws. Paul suffered a bad temper, as evidenced by the quick tongue-lashing he delivered before the high priest after being struck. When he realized his temper had gotten the better of him, he apologized. He adds drunkenness, greed, and others to the list. The significance? These are the deadly traps that take planters out of the game for good. This is what Paul

---

9. Herman Melville, *Moby-Dick* (1851), 1102.

meant by watching your life and doctrine closely in order to "save yourself." The word "save" in the Greek here means "to preserve." If Timothy lived a life worth modeling, like Paul, it would preserve him, as well as those modeling themselves after him. It would keep him safe as a good defensive maneuver, but it would also make him formidable on the offense.

Kevin DeYoung, in his book *The Hole in Our Holiness*, identifies the following scriptures in a section called "Effort is Not a Four-Letter Word":

- "Put off your old self, which belongs to your former manner of life and is corrupt through deceitful desires, and to be renewed in the Spirit of your minds, and to put on the new self, created after the likeness of Good in true righteousness and holiness" (Eph. 4:22–24 ESV).
- "Put to death what is earthly in you: sexual immorality, impurity, passion, evil desire, and covetousness, which is idolatry" (Col. 3:5 ESV).
- Fight the good fight of the faith. Take hold of the eternal life, to which you were called and about which you made the good confession in the presence of many witnesses" (1 Tim. 6:12 ESV).
- "Do you not know that in a race all the runners run, but only one receives the prize? So run that you may obtain it. Every athlete exercises self-control in all things. They do it to receive a perishable wreath, but we an imperishable. So I do not run aimlessly; I do not box as one beating the air. But I discipline my body and keep it under control, lest after preaching to others I myself should be disqualified" (1 Cor. 9:24–27 ESV).
- "Not that I have already obtained this or am already perfect, but I press on to make it my own because Jesus has made me his own. Brothers, I do not consider that I have made it my own. But one thing I do: forgetting what lies behind and straining forward to what lies ahead, I press on toward the goal for the prize of the upward call of God in Christ Jesus" (Phil. 3:12–14 ESV).
- "For this I toil, struggling with all his energy that he powerfully works within me" (Col. 1:29 ESV).
- Lastly, Revelation 2–3 speaks repeatedly of those "who overcome."[10]

If these verses give you pause, then you've understood them correctly. If, however, you're brushing them off, please find something else to do. Those verses

---

10. Kevin DeYoung, *The Hole in Our Holiness: Filling the Gap between Gospel Passion and the Pursuit of Godliness* (Wheaton, IL: Crossway, 2012), 88–89. See G. K. Beale, *The New International Greek Testament Commentary: The Book of Revelation* (Grand Rapids: Eerdmans, 1999), 235. To overcome in these passages means *to conquer* in 2 Clement.

are there for good reason. Church planting is no more for the faint of heart than Christianity itself is. Paul laid out requirements for ministry that serve as barbed wire obstacles that every church planter has to either climb over, crawl under, or walk away from. Even when you think you have what it takes to press forward in the call to lead, you will still get hung up on them and need to spend some time unhooking yourself with the Lord's help. Besides Paul's list of qualifications for those in leadership, a church planter will also need to exhibit certain qualities requisite to church planting.

Hypocrisy is the art of play-acting in a religious context or holding a discrepancy between how you speak and act publicly versus privately. You project a hero in public, but you know who you are in private. Those who are faithful in the small things can be entrusted with the big things. Years ago, the band *Van Halen* sent out a rider in advance of playing gigs with a request for a bowl of M&Ms with no brown M&Ms in it. The *No-Brown-M&Ms* clause was found in article 126f, but it served as an indicator of the venue's overall compliance with the contract: "Van Halen was the first band to take huge productions into tertiary, third-level markets. We'd pull up with nine 18-wheeler trucks, full of gear, where the standard was three trucks, max. And there were many, many technical errors—whether it was the girders that couldn't support the weight, or the flooring would sink in, or the doors weren't big enough to move the gear through. The contract rider read like a Yellow Pages because there was so much equipment and so many human beings to make it function. . . . When I would walk backstage, if I saw a brown M&M in that bowl, we'd line-check the entire production. Guaranteed you'd run into a problem."[11]

This is why the military insists that you make your bed taut enough to bounce a quarter off it. One of my planters who was formerly in the British special forces said that the first week of Commando School was spent teaching them how to iron and do other domestic chores. At first, he thought the instructors were joking and expected an officer to burst through the doors like it was an April Fool's joke; later, though, he understood that they were training him to give attention to detail in the small things so that when life-and-death situations presented themselves, he would be attentive to every little thing. Warren W. Wiersbe, Author of the famous *Be* series of commentaries, kept a plaque on his desk throughout his ministry that read, "Remember whenever occupying a smaller space, someone is measuring you for a larger one."

11. Chris McDaniel, *Ignite Your Generosity: A 21-Day Experience in Stewardship* (Downers Grove, IL: InterVarsity Press, 2015), 23.

MORAL FIBER—THE PLANTER'S WORK ETHIC

Some planters who have met the moral character requirements of elders and deacons nevertheless lack the necessary moral fiber to plant a church. Often, sloth, or a failure to complete tasks, is an indication that a planter lacks the requisite maturity for the responsibility of church planting. Other indicators of personal issues that need to be worked out are a high degree of debt, an inability to deliver on promises made, or a failure to keep appointments. Such issues point to a gap in one's ability to undertake the level of responsibility needed to care for a church.

Paul made a few statements about his own work ethic:

I have worked much harder, been in prison more frequently, been flogged more severely, and been exposed to death again and again. (2 Cor. 11:23)

But by the grace of God I am what I am, and his grace to me was not without effect. No, I worked harder than all of them—yet not I, but the grace of God that was with me. (1 Cor. 15:10)

Today, we call this a work ethic and, by God's grace, Paul had the moral character to work circles around most of us. We may speak of someone in terms of being sacrificial, industrious, and diligent. Nobody could outwork Paul. Listen to Paul describe what he was modeling for those left behind in the churches he planted: "For you yourselves know how *you ought to imitate us*, because we were not idle when we were with you, nor did we eat anyone's bread without paying for it, but with toil and labor we worked night and day, that we might not be a burden to any of you. It was not because we do not have that right, but *to give you in ourselves an example to imitate*" (2 Thess. 3:7–9 ESV, emphasis mine).

Church planting is going to be hard work, and few planters are ready for the amount of multi-tasking that they will encounter in the process. Planting takes organizational skills, communication skills, and interpersonal skills. You don't have to be a master of all of them, because that's where your team comes in. But if you're not working hard, nothing hardly works. Hudson Taylor said, "A man may be consecrated, dedicated and devoted but of little use if undisciplined."[12]

And there's still a plethora of tasks that planters have to do behind the scenes

---

12. Quoted in Patrick Lai, *Tentmaking: The Life and Work of Business as Missions* (Downers Grove, IL: InterVarsity Press, 2005), 155.

that are required for taking care of others but that the planter simply dislikes doing. On the one hand, preaching, adventure, open road, radical conversions, and intimate groups all beckon. Yet, on the other hand, more ungratifying tasks line the path to planting. Because money is an issue, you don't have people you can hire, and so you will find yourself rolling up your sleeves, taking a deep breath, sucking it up, and jumping feet first into stuff you hate. When people are critical of how you spend your time, simply smile. They have no idea, and you don't need to tell them; but, like Paul, you know that you're working harder than most. For Paul, being stoned, shipwrecked, hungry, sleepless, and naked were some of the entry fees to the process of church planting in the first century. What's a little pencil pushing, after all? You can delegate and a team can share the burden, but like Tom Bennardo says, "no one else will ... care half as deeply as you."[13]

WAIT NOT, WASTE NOT

There is a reason that every soldier must pass a physical before deployment. Just because planters are being sent does not mean they are ready. When a planter deploys without the proper health certificate, it amounts to a waste of the planter as a human resource. The amount of financial resources deployed also go to waste. J. Oswald Sanders wrote in his classic *Spiritual Leadership*, "God wants to show such people how strong He really is (2 Chronicles 16:9). But not all who aspire to leadership are willing to pay such a high personal price. Yet there is no compromise here: in the secret reaches of the heart, this price is paid, before any public office or honor. Our Lord made clear to James and John that high position in the kingdom of God is reserved for those whose hearts—even the secret places where no one else probes—are qualified."[14]

As a church planter, it is important to stop and reflect regularly. This will be difficult, as you will constantly feel the pull from many directions to constantly stay on the go, running forever on an imaginary treadmill, but you must remember what Charles Spurgeon said about caring for yourself as a minister. He begins his *Lectures to My Students* by telling the students at the Pastor's College in London that, whereas other professions have tools, they, as ministers, are their own tools.

---

13. Tom Bennardo, *The Honest Guide to Church Planting: What No One Ever Tells You About Planting and Leading a New Church* (Grand Rapids: Zondervan, 2019), 73.

14. J. Oswald Sanders, *Spiritual Leadership/Spiritual Discipleship/Spiritual Maturity* Set (Chicago: Moody, 1994), 37.

RELATIONAL, PHYSICAL, MENTAL, AND SPIRITUAL HEALTH

For years, I took part in an RPMS group of planters who met regularly to ensure its members were healthy in our relationships, physically responsible, mentally whole, and spiritually abiding in Christ. Every Monday morning, four or five of us met for an hour. Monday mornings can be a killer; the mental and emotional depletion of preaching made me neurotic after my adrenal glands went into overdrive. As someone who suffers chronic hypoadrenia, I found that when my body didn't have enough change to pay the full toll, it borrowed from my psyche. I would awake in the morning with dark thoughts swarming, many of them fruits of an endocrine hangover, some of them burning barbs from the pit of hell. We brewed coffee, sat in a circle, laughed, cried, and shared our deepest fears, struggles, and pain, and peeled one another off the asphalt. Together, we walked through processing the death of a child, infertility, coming to grips with what dealing with a special-needs child means, the loss of vision, marital stress, and anything else life could throw at us.

How RPMS works is that you take turns sharing about four aspects of your life and well-being, based on the acronym RPMS:

R—Relational: How are your relationships with your spouse, kids, friends, and others?
P—Physical: How are you stewarding your body physically (rest, exercise, nutrition)?
M—Mental: How are you feeding, nurturing, and caring for your mind?
S—Spiritual: How are you personally walking with and being led by God?

Normally leaders feel unable discuss their personal lives, so talking about ministry is used to fabricate fig leaves of borrowed worth. Therefore, the ground rules of our Monday Fight Club was that we didn't talk about ministry, nor were we allowed to lecture or counsel one another; only listen with and pray for one another. Keeping a check on the four RPMS with other planters will assist you to minister from a place of integrated wholeness rather than a deficit in integrity.

MINISTERING FROM A PLACE OF WHOLENESS

In 1976 Sister Callista Roy developed the adaptive model of nursing that stated humans are complex bio-psycho-social beings who interact and adapt to their environment. In the years that followed, a spiritual component would be added to the description. As a nun, Roy had developed a model that incorporated a very Hebraic way of understanding human beings made in the image of God. When all these components work together, we experience "wholeness" or balance.[15]

The word "shalom" means wholeness, or "all things functioning in harmony" as a result of the reign of the king.[16] When the Jews greeted one another with "shalom," they were wishing the blessing of God upon one another. When Jesus spoke of abiding in him, he was communicating the idea of shalom, or wholeness. This was the blessedness that the psalmist spoke of in Psalm 1, "He is like a tree planted by streams of water that yields its fruit in season, and its leaf does not wither" (Ps. 1:3 ESV). Jesus pointedly used the imagery here of a tree when he spoke of abiding in him so that we could bear more fruit. The opposite of shalom (usually translated from Hebrew into English as "peace") is anxiety, and church planting is filled with anxiety. The root word for anxiety means to be pulled apart or stretched in different directions. Consider the results of a survey listing the top struggles among planters' spouses, ranked in order:

1. Personal finances
2. Feeling overwhelmed with needs/responsibilities
3. Time management/priorities
4. Boundaries between home life and church life[17]
5. Effect of church plant on the family
6. Lack of time with spouse
7. Loneliness/isolation
8. Lack of emotional/spiritual support from local churches
9. Criticism/rejection from individuals
10. Understanding your role as the spouse of a planter[18]

We are all too familiar with anxious feelings of being drawn and quartered as human beings in modern society, but wholeness can only be experienced when all facets of the RPMS are balanced and working as God intended.

---

15. Frances Monahan et al., *Phipps Medical Surgical Nursing: Concepts and Clinical Process, fourth edition* (St. Louis: Mosby Year Book, 1991), 172.

16. Mark L. Russell, *The Missional Entrepreneur: Principles and Practices for Business and Mission* (Birmingham, AL: New Hope, 2010), 47.

17. Brian and Amy Bloye, *It's Not Personal, Surviving and Thriving on the Journey of Church Planting* (Grand Rapids: Zondervan, 2012). The Bloyes outline healthy boundaries, such as not answering the phone during dinner, screening calls at home, etc.

18. This study is quoted by J. D. Payne and was taken among Southern Baptists, making the spouses women only, but there is surely crossover for male spouses of planters as well. J. D. Payne, *Discovering*

Relational Health

Paul wrote to Timothy, "For if someone does not know how to manage his own household, how will he care for God's church?" (1 Tim. 3:5 ESV). Despite the fact that Paul told Timothy to endure hardship like a good soldier, planters' families can be the first casualties of war if we don't fight for their territory. Gary Thomas quotes a friend, "People who marry well aren't lucky in love. They're intentional in their path." He continues, "Too many Christians are lazy in love."[19]

In the way that God is a relational being who exists in the relationship of the Trinity, so humans are created male and female, and called to represent God in their marriages. "So God created man in his own image, in the image of God he created him; male and female he created them" (Gen. 1:27 ESV). Our ability to reproduce children mirrors creating something in our own image, making the family the closest earthly expression to God. A hallmark of the Jewish faith was that the family was the primary vehicle of ministry (Deut. 6:7; 11:19). Therefore, Paul concludes that a minister will be unable to minister outside the home if not first ministering within it. Therefore, the family is not to be seen as a "lesser pursuit" that takes second place to the "really important work" of ministry. Rather, family takes a prominent place in advancing God's kingdom purposes in both the Old and New Testaments. Caesar Kalinowski speaks about how the idea of family is at the heart of all that the church does.

> We were created to live in grace-based relationships, which is why true gospel communities are an irresistible call to return home. That family represents the open arms of God and a place at his dinner table.[20]

During the church growth movement, America witnessed large ecclesiastical empires being built like the pagan temples of old with the foundations being laid upon the sacrificial deaths of their firstborns. Your church plant can always obtain another minister, but your kids only have one mother or father; those are not so easily replaced. As scores of ministers have resigned over the past few decades, it's become clear that the family bedrock eroded over time as the structure of the church was being built. In the end, it was a growing public façade, while the personal life was secretly crumbling away.

Church Planting: An Introduction to the Whats, Whys, and Hows of Global Church Planting (Colorado Springs: Authentic Publishing, 2009), 300.

19. Gary Thomas, *The Sacred Search: What If It's Not About Who You Marry, But Why?* (Colorado Springs: David C. Cook, 2013), 80.

20. Caesar Kalinowski, *Transformed: A New Way of Being Christian* (Grand Rapids: Zondervan, 2014), 51.

My wife and I have been bivocational church planting missionaries for two decades. Ecclesiastes says, "A cord of three strands is not quickly broken" (4:12). Many interpret this to be speaking about the unity between husband, wife, and the Lord, but it also reminds us of three threads that we have committed to nurture in keeping those parties all connected:

- Physical: Anything to do with physical intimacy (kissing, sex, holding hands)
- Emotional: Anything involving quality time that fosters emotional connection (walking together, talking, reading a book together)
- Spiritual: Anything that helps us connect with God (devotional prayer, reading the Bible to each other and discussing it)

All three don't have to be connecting us for our marriage to be healthy. Two out of three keeps us connected. All three make our marriage epic. If we only maintain one, our marriage feels like it hangs by a thread. We have also been in counseling for a quarter of a century. When I married my wife, I was the next pastor in line to take the helm of a megachurch. The pastor I trained under resigned due to moral failure. Therefore, the elders required my wife and me to attend counseling as a preventative measure. We have continued the tradition, even after the assignment ended. We go regularly whether our marriage is in trouble or not. It is maintenance rather than repair.

These measures may seem like overkill, but consider the results of a recent study from Lifeway. It reports that 90% of church leaders work more than fifty hours a week, 90% say they can't cope with the demands, and 70% say that they have no close friends because they're unable to maintain those relationships. Clearly, preventative measures are called for!

PHYSICAL

D. Martyn Lloyd-Jones, a renowned Welsh minister, used to say that when he approached a problem, he always asked first if it was physical. Depression may appear in men like Charles Darwin, whom Freudian psychologists diagnosed as suffering from a psychosomatic illness originating as a neurosis rooted in hating his father. It was later discovered that he had contracted Chaga's disease in Argentina, which led to the symptoms of depression. Similarly, Charles Spurgeon often faced depressive bouts due to suffering from gout. Therefore, it was not Scripture he needed, or more time in prayer, but rather months spent in the warm climate and fresh air of Montagne, France, to convalesce and improve his circulation and diet. One condition may have an effect in another area. Lloyd-Jones, himself a medical doctor, asserted that spiritual problems have spiritual prescriptions, while physical problems must be treated physically.[21] Wesley believed that health of the body was crucial to serving the Lord to the extent that he slept on the ground, took cold baths, and wrote a medical textbook in his spare time![22]

Our society is constantly urging physical fitness in relation to diet and exercise but often neglects rest in the relentless desire for self-improvement and productivity. Rest has been hardwired by God into the rhythm of the universe. Therefore, it is no surprise that God commanded regular rest as a part of our worship to him, calling it holy in the Ten Commandments. As the earth rests from the growth activities of the sun as it rotates into darkness each night, God's people rest every week in a cycle that a loving God designed for our wellbeing.

Sleep coincides with our body's circadian rhythm, the daily light/dark cycle caused by the rotation of the earth. During the hours of daylight, our bodies release stimulating hormones, and when the sun goes down, our body has been releasing chemicals for hours to sedate us so it can repair our tissues and process our collected mental data. In this way, our very bodies respond to the environment around us, perfectly designed to adapt and survive in the world we inhabit.

Our circadian rhythm can repair damaged DNA, meaning that rest is hardwired into the very genetic code, the core of your being. In addition, sleep regulates most of your hormone production.[23] When you rob your body of God's design for rest, your chance of getting cancer quadruples. Chronic lack of sleep produces more cortisol, the stress hormone, which causes you to eat more and store more fat, and unbalances your emotional reactions. Further, your ability to concentrate and work efficiently decreases. Proper sleep releases growth hormones to repair muscle, burn fat, consolidate your memory, and wash cerebral spinal fluid through your central nervous system to flush out damaging molecules that cause neuro-degeneration.[24] Rest is no joke. Only a loving God would design us this way, then include a regular rhythm of rest as part of our worship of him.

The Guinness Book of World Records abandoned attempts to break the sleep deprivation record due to the overwhelming scientific evidence of damage to the human body. Sleep neurologist Matt Walker contrasts this with what *is* allowed, "Recall that Guinness deems it acceptable for a man (Felix Baumgartner) to ascend 128,000 feet into the outer reaches of our atmosphere in a hot-air balloon wearing a spacesuit, open the door of his capsule, stand

---

21. D. Martyn Lloyd-Jones, *Healing and the Scriptures* (Nashville: Thomas Nelson, 1988), 149–50.

22. Edgar W. Wesley Thompson, *Apostolic Man* (Eugene, OR: Wipf & Stock, 2015).

23. Shawn Stevenson, *Sleep Smarter: 21 Essential Ways to Sleep Yourself to a Better Body, Better Health, and Bigger Success* (New York: Rodale Books, 2016), vii.

24. Stevenson, *Sleep Smarter*, ix.

atop a ladder suspended about the planet, then free-fall back down to Earth at a top speed of 843 mph (1,358 kmh), passing through the sound barrier while creating a sonic boom with just his body. But the risks associated with sleep deprivation are considered to be far, far higher."[25]

Conversely, those who live the longest in the world take naps, such as the Greek isles and parts of South America. When Harvard University conducted a study of 23,000 Greek adults from age twenty to eighty-three, they found that the mortality risk of not napping in men was as high as 60%.[26] Every planter must monitor their sleep to ensure that they are able to take voluntary rests before being forced to by a mental breakdown or burnout. Carey Nieuwhof calls burnout something that "no one expects, and everyone experiences" likening it to suddenly falling off a cliff without noticing the warning signs. Some possible signs that a cliff might be approaching can include:

1. Your passion fades.
2. You can't feel highs or lows.
3. Little things make you disproportionately emotional.
4. Everybody drains you.
5. You've become cynical.
6. Nothing satisfies you.
7. You can't think straight.
8. Your productivity is dropping.
9. You're self-medicating.
10. You don't laugh anymore.
11. Sleep and time off no longer refuel you.[27]

Even the Son of God rested, falling asleep in a boat. Perhaps Paul's prison stretches were forced rests. The ministry can wait. Sometimes the minister can't.

MENTAL

The absence of mental illness in a person does not equate mental health. Periodically, the world awakens to the tragic news that another pastor has taken his life. In some cases, there is chronic depression brought on by chemical

25. Matthew Walker, *Why We Sleep: Unlocking the Power of Sleep and Dreams* (New York: Scribner, 2017), 135.

26. Walker, *Why We Sleep*, 71.

27. Carey Nieuwhof, *Didn't See It Coming: Overcoming the 7 Greatest Challenges That No One and Everyone Experiences* (New York: WaterBrook, 2018), 151–54.

imbalances, and in others there is situational depression brought on by extreme duress and tragic circumstances.

Charles Spurgeon's depression, as previously stated, was made worse in later years by his battle with multiple chronic illnesses; it started, though, during his twenties in the aftermath of a horrific church tragedy. Someone had yelled "fire" while Spurgeon was preaching and a panic ensued, resulting in a balcony collapsing under the weight of too many jostling people. In his book *Lectures to My Students*, Spurgeon wrote a unique chapter on ministerial depression, revolutionary for its day, called "The Minister's Fainting Fits." Spurgeon observed, "This evil will also come upon us, we know not why, and then it is all the more difficult to drive it away. Causeless depression is not to be reasoned with, nor can David's harp charm it away by sweet discoursings. As well fight with the mist as with this shapeless, undefinable, yet all-beclouding hopelessness."[28]

Spurgeon learned to take a break every summer as much for his mental health as his physical constitution. Sabbaths are periods of rest that cycle every seven days, while taking a sabbatical means taking all or part of the seventh year off. Seven years is a long time to wait, so mini-sabbaticals are weeks or seasons off in the interim. For example, taking five or six weeks off a year is a mental survival skill. Recreational hobbies or sports can also provide mental rest in short bursts.

I have long felt the Spirit in times of leisure, whether hiking in the woods or just doing something amusing for the pure enjoyment of it. Not having to be anything, do anything, accomplish anything, or save anything creates margin for us to simply enjoy God. I have been playing video games for decades, watching films, reading books and comics, and learning that some things are holy because they bring joy in and of themselves. This is what recreation was designed for, and it is why children, who are close to the heart of God, play.

Unfortunately, there is a belief that play should be left behind during adulthood, and many buy into this lie. Mark Buchanan, in his wonderful book with the playful title *The Rest of God*, wrote "adulthood is mostly about getting things done. Past a certain age, our existence is consumed by obligation. Deadlines loom. Assignments are due. Responsibilities are mountainous. Chores are piling up. . . . So one of the first things to die in adults is playfulness."[29]

Play has been hardwired into the universe, in the same way that rest has. Perhaps the most beautiful and redemptive picture of play is found in *The Lion, the Witch and the Wardrobe*. The first thing that Aslan (the Christ character

---

28. Charles Haddon Spurgeon, *Lectures to My Students* (Pantianos Classics ebook edition, first published in 1875), 288.
29. Mark Buchanan, *The Rest of God* (Nashville: Thomas Nelson, 2008), 143.

in the book) does after he rises from the dead is play. He shouts, "Oh, children, catch me if you can!" and the narrator tells us that "a mad chase began. . . . And whether it was more like playing with a thunderstorm or playing with a kitten Lucy could never make up her mind."[30] The children later realize that they didn't feel any sense of hunger, thirst, or tiredness while they were playing with Aslan. This shouldn't surprise us coming from the man who said, "Our leisure, even our play, is a matter of serious concern."[31] Ever the prophetic poet, Lewis is telling us something—namely that heaven is a place where we feel like children at play. Perhaps we don't have to wait until heaven.

In modern society, we've come to accept that our lives are compartmentalized. We speak of first, second, and third spaces; these are "the place I live" (first place), "the place I work" (second place), and "the place I take recreation/play/rest" (third space). For this reason, people talk about their work/life balance. When some hear that phrase, they immediately ask, "Balance? What balance?" In 2018, only 51 percent of Americans were satisfied with their jobs, making work/life balance nearly impossible.[32] If there is no satisfaction in work, then part of the day becomes drudgery, draining the mental reserves, and depleting other areas.

This is why Mark R. Shaw's assessment of the "work hard–play hard" model is important. Shaw points out that in this philosophy, relationships tend to suffer, and only single people can sustain it. This may be one of the reasons that people are prolonging their season of singlehood, realizing internally that one of these dynamics will suffer if relationships that need to be nurtured are added to the mix. Shaw identifies the "wisdom worker" model taken from the Bible's wisdom literature, forming the Hebrew philosophy of life, in which everything is sacred: work, rest, and relationships. Satisfaction, or wholeness, is found in the balance of the three.

Solomon summarized this work/life balance in Ecclesiastes when he wrote, "So *here is what you should do:* go and enjoy your meals, drink your wine and love *every minute of* it because God is already pleased with what you do. Dress your best, and don't forget a splash of scented fragrance. Enjoy life with the woman you love. Cherish every moment of the fleeting life which God has given you under the sun. For this is your lot in life, *your great reward* for all your hard work under the sun. Whatever you find to do, do it well because where you are going—the grave—there will be no working or thinking or knowing or wisdom" (Ecc. 9:7–10, emphasis mine).[33] Shaw quotes Tremper Longman's translation of Hebrews

30. C. S. Lewis, *The Essential C.S. Lewis* (New York: Scribner, 1996), 128–29.

31. Leland Ryken, *Culture in Christian Perspective* (Portland, OR: Multnomah, 1986), 93.

32. Hailey Lynn McKeefry, "Employees Mostly Happy: Labor Day Survey Finds." EBN World news .com, August 31, 2018, https://world.einnews.com/article/460506084?lcf=4wwzRcP70mUgCwd nXAWeCPF7D3EI7OcEiFdyVlLOnHQ%3D.

33. Holy Bible, "The Voice" edition (Nashville: Thomas Nelson, 2014). For this quote I used "The

8:30–31, which brings out the Hebrew word for play, *mishak*: "I was beside him as a craftsman. I was *playing* daily, *laughing* before him all the time. *Laughing* with all the inhabitants of the earth and *playing* with all the human race."[34]

Eric Liddell, the famed Scottish runner whose life is portrayed in the movie *Chariots of Fire*, felt God's pleasure when he ran; I feel it when I play, and it's been this connection with God in recreation that has kept me in the ministry for decades, despite being wrongfully told that recreation was secular, not sacred. Fortunately, I continued to walk with God in the way he'd revealed himself to me. I started taking days off during the week because Sundays seemed less a sabbath since it is "lawful to do good on the Sabbath" (Matthew 12:12 ESV). Because Sundays were exhausting, Mondays left me neurotically drained and were therefore relegated to mindless admin days where I dove into tasks in the morning and discipleship in the evening, taking a break with my wife during the day to recharge. Martyn Lloyd-Jones regularly listened to jazz in the afternoons in the kitchen with his wife as a way to connect with her and relax his mind.

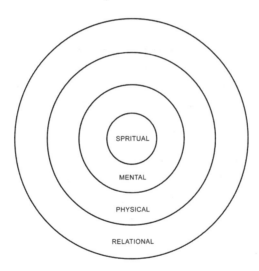

In ministry, as in life, we can only go so far clocking miles on the odometer before we have to pop the hood and check the fluid levels. We can ignore the rattling of the muffler or steam coming out of the radiator for only so long before the engine fails. Having others riding along who can say, "What's that

---

Voice" translation by Thomas Nelson because it translates the Jewish word *heved* (lit. vapor) as fleeting, instead of vanity. Translating "heved" to vanity ruins the sense of the book, and leads to misunderstanding of the message of the book of Ecclesiastes which is to enjoy life. It is the *carpe diem* book of the Bible, not the confessions of a king who got it wrong.

34. Ryan Shaw, *Spiritual Equipping for Missions: Thriving as God's Message Bearers* (Downers Grove, IL: InterVarsity Press, 2014), 33.

burning smell?" or "Is that brake fluid I see leaking behind you?" ensures we don't blow a piston. If you're intent on holding up a mask, please get another profession before you hurt yourself irreparably or harm others. Too many people pretend to be one thing though they're an entirely different thing altogether.

But if you want to be transparent and honest and find healing in Jesus, then learn from Peter. Standing on the beach with Jesus, he surrendered to him. "Lord, you know all things" (John 21:17). That surrender came from being broken. He had blown a piston once already and did not want to repeat the process. Taking your car off the road to pop the hood is never convenient, but it keeps the car roadworthy enough to carry others safely to their destination. In ministry, you're carrying others, therefore your life is more than a demolition derby vehicle designed to entertain others until it just can't move anymore. Taking care of yourself ensures handing down a vintage beauty that becomes more impressive as it ages.

REFLECT

- What are your motives for church planting?
- "Character trumps gifting," but we seek to use our spiritual gifts. What areas of your character prevent you from fully using your spiritual gifts?

DISCUSS

- How do you reconcile the need for holistic health in church planters— relational, physical, mental, and spiritual—with the need for sufficient church planters and the need to mobilize every Christian? What is the role of a Christian who is not particularly healthy? How much of this chapter is aspirational?
- "Character trumps gifting," but we prefer gifted individuals for certain roles in the church. How can your leadership guard against overlooking character flaws in gifted people?

CHALLENGE

- What are your motives for church planting? Interview a few people who really know you. Ask them to describe your motives for planting churches. Did they identify any false motives? Do their descriptions match yours?

REDISCOVERING TEAM LEADERSHIP

From Top-Down Leadership to Embodying Christ on Mission

TEAM LEADERSHIP

6

> There has never been a Jesus movement with long-term societal impact that did not have the fivefold fully operative in its organization and among its members.
> —ALAN HIRSCH

My apostolic training network is dubbed the New Breed Network. A member of the New Breed tribe, who had successfully served as a missionary in Central America and Asia, went through a church planting assessment with one of the largest denominations in America. After two days of intense assessment and analysis, they failed him. Although they marked his assessment report with a "fail" rating, it was actually the majority of church planting assessments that were exposed as failures that day. The planter being assessed was not only a humble leader but also a veteran missionary who had served in Columbia and Southeast Asia, made cross-cultural disciples, experienced and performed miracles, and led many people to faith. Because he was a prophetic leader, the Western system of assessing planters was baffled about what to do with him and lacked a box to put him in. Instead of saying, "Here are some things to work on, come back in a year," they said, "We don't think you're called to this." It nearly deflated every bit of confidence he had, and he took a bench in the dugout for a few years. If he'd been coupled with an apostolic planter after that assessment, the team would have been nearly unstoppable with him on it. Further, had there been a system of assessment that took the APEST gifts into account, he would have aced his assessment.

There are a few conclusions we can draw from situations like this:

1. Nobody should ever fail a church planting assessment. A fail grade simply should not exist. The alternative is to link the "not ready" candidates with someone who *is ready* and to assign them to a planting team to develop in their gifts.

2. There is not an APEST assessment at this time that can adequately assess planting teams, due to the "pastor-only" model that approaches the assessment process as a quest to find a one-size-fits-all kind of leader. To learn more about how I assess apostolic planting teams, visit www.newbreednetwork.org to access my comprehensive CityWide Training.
3. Apostolic leaders have been designed to serve alongside a team of variably gifted individuals who accent and complement their own selective gift type.

Unfortunately, because we fail to assess planters alongside their church planting teams, we also fail to equip and deploy them in teams. A church plant is only as strong as the weakest link in the planting team. Therefore, we never know how strong the chain truly is unless we assess the team itself. We also don't often know, therefore, where leaders are most likely to break.

PAUL MODELED TEAM PLANTING

Paul was eleven years into his missionary work when he penned these words, "From Jerusalem to Illyricum, I have *fulfilled* the ministry of the gospel" (Rom. 15:19 ESV). What was *the ministry of the gospel* to which Paul was referring? God sent Paul to proclaim Christ and establish multiplying churches in every major city on the Mediterranean islands, Macedonia, and Asia Minor. Just over a decade into his mission, Paul had to push on to Spain because he had run out of new frontiers to cross, but before he did, he'd left a string of six networks throughout the Mediterranean.[1] For all who have ever wondered how Paul accomplished so much in so little time, the answer is simple: he did not do it alone. As an apostolic planter, Paul specialized in team church planting. Paul is not taking credit for the labors of others, because he not only put the systems and strategy in place to disseminate the gospel into all these regions but had also trained the gospel workers who populated those systems and enacted those strategies.

In Acts 20:4 (ESV), we catch a glimpse of Paul forming apostolic strike teams after he had created a network of regional planters out of Ephesus. When he left Ephesus, "Sopater the Berean, son of Pyrrhus, accompanied him; and of the Thessalonians, Aristarchus and Secundus; and Gaius of Derbe, and Timothy; and the Asians, Tychicus and Trophimus." Paul had leveraged this

---

1. Chapter 8 breaks down strike teams in detail, and chapter 20 is dedicated to exploring Paul's strategic use of networks.

strategic church planting team of eight gifted, qualified, experienced church planters who banded together, yet were ready to be deployed across the local network of Asia in teams of two.[2] In case you're not convinced that a solo leader isn't enough, remember that Jesus sent his disciples in teams of two, propelling them out into the towns of Judea in dynamic duos like double-barreled shotgun blasts. Jesus himself modeled team leadership by traveling with twelve disciples and prioritizing their recruitment to himself as his first order of business. Similarly, when sent by the Twelve to investigate Antioch, Barnabas's first *modus operandi* in Acts 11:25 was to recruit a once-legendary figure named Saul who had faded into obscurity after eleven years. Recruiting a team will, therefore, be one of your first orders of business.

Paul's first-century church planting teams of interchangeable players enabled multiple groups to strategically hit numerous targets throughout a broader area. Paul's first network was Asia Minor, and he moved his "fellow workers," like carpenters, plumbers, and electricians all around this little piece of Turkish real estate whenever and however needed. These strike teams were a blend of apostolic planters like Titus, prophets like Agabus, teachers like Priscilla and Aquila, and evangelists like Apollos. Despite the West's failure to employ the first-century team leadership depicted in Acts, the Holy Spirit still continues to gift individuals for flourishing in teams, like the aforementioned global missionary planter who "failed" assessment.

WHY PLANTERS QUIT

Almost all the reasons planters quit can be traced back to the fact that the planter had an inadequate team to help share the load. As a solo operative, almost any planter would be doomed to failure with these pressures:

- Overworked
- Bivocational
- Stressed
- Family implodes
- Insufficient finances
- Shrinking church

---

2. We know that they traveled in teams of two because of the way that they've been grouped into teams of two by their ethnicity. Luke purposefully groups them together this way so that we can catch a glimpse of how Paul organized such teams. With the word count easily double this size, the author was forced to cut half of the manuscript, including much about multicultural teams. Perhaps if there is a Church Plantology 201, that material will still see the light of day.

Most of these things could have been prevented if they'd tapped into Paul's pattern of team planting. At the outset, it's important to remember that no matter how strong or seasoned the leader:

- Nobody can be expected to know everything.
- Nobody can be expected to do everything.
- Nobody can be expected to wisely handle everything.

Jesus knew this, and so he gave us team ministry so we could get our lives back, stop shouldering the weight of the world, and prevent burnout out in isolation. The sum of a team is greater than its parts, and it will accomplish more collectively than any individual member could. Moses led with seventy elders. David had his thirty-seven mighty men. Jesus traveled with his twelve. Paul created a network of thirty-two missionary partners. Yet we still ignore the emphasis in Scripture on team leadership.

Jesus's giftedness equipped him to be an army of one; yours does not. Only Jesus was capable of doing it all, *yet even he chose not to do it alone!*

APOSTOLIC PLANTERS ARE ONE OF FIVE TYPES OF LEADERS

And he gave the apostles, the prophets, the evangelists, the shepherds, and the teachers to equip the saints for the work of the ministry, for building up the body of Christ (Eph. 4:11–12 ESV)

Some refer to the team leadership of the New Testament as APEST because it is a convenient acronym for the five roles listed: Apostle, Prophet, Evangelist, Shepherd, and Teacher.[3] I call it fist leadership. Make a fist. Now look at it. You've just created a weapon; it is a powerful one if the arm behind it knows how to throw a punch. Fist leadership brings the five individual fingers together in a unity to pack a powerful punch for kingdom impact.

Now, unfolding your fingers so they're extended, examine them individually. By itself, each finger isn't particularly intimidating. You wouldn't expect to see anybody fighting with just a finger unless you were watching a Kung Fu B-movie. Examining the fingers in reverse order, the pinky finger is our built-in toothpick. Nothing picks spinach from between the bicuspids like an extended pinky. The ring finger tells my spouse I'm committed to her for life.

---

3. I will forever be indebted to Alan Hirsch's work on this concept.

The middle finger tells people I'm angry with them. The index finger points. Lastly, the thumb gathers and touches the other four fingers, bringing them together into a fist. In this chapter, we'll look at each of them individually and unpack what their role and function is. For now, it's enough to know that each of them acts on their own in a unique way, yet when they come together, they pack a hard-hitting punch.

What if our churches were trying to fight the good fight with only one finger extended against the onslaught of the kingdom of darkness? Would it explain why we keep getting our tail kicked and our butt handed to us in a doggy bag? It might explain all the broken fingers—solo planters who were brave enough to stand out from the crowd but were never designed to fight alone.

The New Testament presents five different types of leaders that work together to form a fist. The Holy Spirit uses it to deliver a knockout punch to the enemy time and again, throughout every age, and in every culture.

Apostolic-type leaders are church-planting, front-line missionaries committed to taking the people of God back out to the front lines to aggressively expand the kingdom of God. They are your spiritual entrepreneurs and team leaders. The apostle identifies the gifts of others, mobilizes the church towards the fringes of the frontier, and lays a foundation of grace through Christ crucified. The apostles *sent-ness* ensures that the lost and marginalized are considered. The apostolic team, or "A-team" can do the impossible on the cheap, and apostolic planters function as the team's thumb that gathers and touches the other four fingers, bringing them together into a fist.

Prophetic-type leaders are concerned with hearing from God, collectively or individually. They are concerned that people aren't just "playing church," but actually meeting with God. They tend to walk in the supernatural a bit more than average, bringing God into the body as a reality rather than an idea. Like the Old Testament prophets, they are the index finger, always pointing people back to Jesus. The prophet stirs up the gifts of others, keeps the church focused on God, and keeps the atmosphere tinged with the supernatural. Just when the church wants to get established and comfortable, prophets rattle the cages.

Evangelistic-type leaders do the opposite of the apostle. Rather than constantly motivating the church to go out, the evangelist compels the lost to come in. They are the middle finger because they bring the scandal of the cross and the offense of the gospel before people's eyes. The evangelist presents the gospel, is no stranger to confrontation, is task driven, and is high energy. When things start to become too insular, he tips the scales to ensure the church exists for those outside its walls.

Shepherd leaders are consumed with discipleship, development, counseling, and relationships. They are inwardly focused and concerned with nurturing healthy sheep. For this reason, they tend to appear more conservative, but they are the ring finger, committed to the sheep, willing to lay down their lives for them "till death do them part." When a church is tempted to make decisions that could leave families in the dust, the shepherd makes sure that everyone is being considered and can make the journey.

Teaching-type leaders are the pinky. They can pick the poppy seeds of bad theology out of the hard-to-reach places. They don't want you ingesting that stuff, and they also don't want the world to see the embarrassing broccoli of false teaching, moral error, and weak logic messing up the church's welcoming smile. They are exact and delicate. They spend time on the finer points of theology to convey revelation from Scripture that will reshape the thinking of disciples.

One finger is cool. One finger is quirky. One finger breaks easily. Put them together, though, and you can do some damage. A return to the team leadership of the New Testament is essential in these dark times. The church is the outworking of the ministry of Jesus after his ascension. When Jesus ascended with his work unfinished, he knew that no one person was going to be able to follow in his wake. Therefore, he broke his ministry into five different pieces, and "when he ascended on high, he took many captives and gave gifts to his people" (Eph. 4:8). These gifts were specializations like you would see on a special-forces team—individual experts working together strategically. "A church planter is never a splinter cell who acts alone, but the leader of a platoon of daredevil pathfinders. Church planting resembles a covert commando operation that travels covertly in small teams, creates an opening for other special teams, and gets the heck out of Dodge when the mission is accomplished."[4]

JESUS AS THE EMBODIMENT OF APEST

The only One who could do the jobs of five leaders was Jesus, the lone master of all five roles:

He was the **Apostle**: "Consider Jesus, the apostle" (Heb. 3:1 ESV). Let's face it, he is the ultimate pioneer, missionary, messenger, and sent one.

He was a **Prophet**: "The LORD your God will raise up for you a prophet like me from among you, from your brothers—it is to him you shall listen" (Deut.

---

4. Peyton Jones, *Church Zero* (Colorado Springs: Cook, 2013), 74.

18:15 ESV). The people who ate the bread he multiplied in the wilderness attributed this passage to Jesus, identifying him as the prophet Moses spoke about, "When the people saw the sign that he had done, they said, 'This is indeed the Prophet who is to come into the world!'" (John 6:14 ESV).

He was an **Evangelist**: Taking the scroll in Nazareth, Jesus read Isaiah 61:1 in the synagogue, which says that he was anointed to "bring good news [gospel] to the poor" as well as liberty and the Lord's favor. "I must preach the good news of the kingdom of God to the other towns as well; for I was sent for this purpose" (Luke 4:43 ESV).

He was the **Shepherd**: "I am the good shepherd" (John 10:11). Peter, the one told to tend Christ's lambs for him, calls Jesus our "chief Shepherd" (1 Pet. 5:4).

He was the **Teacher**: "He opened his mouth and taught them" (Matt. 5:2 NKJV). When the crowds heard him on the Mount, they were stunned, and in John they reported to the Pharisees, "Never man spake like this man" (John 7:46 KJV).

Hirsch calls the APEST in Jesus the J-APEST.[5] Jesus is the perfect embodiment of the five roles, and the church, as his body, was designed to be as well.[6] Want to know what Jesus looks like? Put all five of these leaders in a blender. When Jesus ascended, he left a "Jesus-shaped hole" in the world that the church was meant to fill, and each of these various gifts helps to fill it in with something that the world can recognize as Jesus's body still active on earth. That's why Paul said these leaders are given "to equip the saints for the work of ministry, for building up the body of Christ, until we all attain to . . . the measure of the stature of the fullness of Christ" (Eph. 4:12–13 ESV). When

---

5. Alan Hirsch, *5Q: Reactivating the Original Intelligence and Capacity of the Body of Christ* (100 Movements, 2017), xxxiv.

6. Hirsch, *5Q*, xxxiv. The genius of 5Q is that Hirsch traces backward from the vocational callings of the functions of leaders, to the embodiment of the APEST ministry of the entire church, which is the body of Jesus on earth, ministering as he did. That alone is profound enough, but Hirsch digs deeper, claiming that if the APEST is the image of Christ's ministry, and Christ was the Son of his Father, then the creator of the universe has hardwired these roles into creation itself. And why wouldn't he if humans are made in God's image? Therefore, Hirsch traces the APEST back to heroic expressions in culture and history, and further back again to primitive archetypes. For apostles, Hirsch identifies designers, innovators, entrepreneurs, paradigm shifters, and *imagineers* as APEST expressions in culture. The archetypes would be pioneer, general, adventurer, visionary. For the prophetic in culture and history, we see artists, poets, iconoclasts, and futurists. The archetypes of APEST are the seer, sage, and reformer.

children are growing, some parents measure their growth annually by marking the doorjamb with a pencil. Paul is marking the shape of Jesus on the door for us, saying we have a big place to fill, and progress can only be made through the outworking of these five gifts.

Giving these gifts to the church is part of Jesus's strategy to "fill all things" by building up the body through the functioning of these gifts (Eph. 4:10 ESV). The more these five functions operate, the more Jesus's ministry operates at full capacity. If your church only has a teacher functioning, then it is showing the world only a part of who Jesus was. Jesus was a teacher, but also a prophet. Two out of five isn't bad, but it neglects Jesus's evangelistic, apostolic, and shepherding ministries. Each of the APEST functions is essential for effectively discipling believers to become Christlike because these are the functions Christ gifted to the church to help it become mature and "grow up in every way into him who is the head, into Christ" (Eph. 4:15 ESV).

RELATIONAL OVER HIERARCHICAL PARTNERSHIPS

Some confuse the apostles' initial leadership in a church plant with hierarchical misunderstanding of the function. Paul's relationship to his fellow workers was not based on a hierarchical pecking order. Paul does strategically run the mission game in the Mediterranean, yet he doesn't insist on the movements of the missionaries. Paul allowed autonomy among his fellow workers, showing respect and deferring to their own leading from the Spirit. Titus and the other fellow workers of Paul demonstrated their own initiative. Paul reported, "For Titus not only welcomed our appeal, but he is coming to you with much enthusiasm and on his own initiative" (2 Cor. 8:17). Of Apollos, Paul said, "Now about our brother Apollos: I strongly urged him to go to you with the brothers. He was quite unwilling to go now, but he will go when he has the opportunity" (1 Cor. 16:12). Apollos didn't obey Paul's every whim or wish because he wasn't expected to.

To the churches, Paul was gentle "like a mother" to the Thessalonians (1 Thess. 2:7) and like a father to the Corinthians, "For though you have countless guides in Christ, you do not have many fathers" (1 Cor. 4:15 ESV). To those he discipled and trained, he was like a father, affectionately addressing Timothy as "my son" (1 Timothy

1:2, 18). Paul embodied the paternal task of training his fellow workers in the way they should go, such as writing letters of fatherly advice to Timothy while stationed in Ephesus. This is important for planters to remember. You will best serve people and get the most out of them if you invest in them like Jesus did in the Twelve and like Paul did with his fellow workers. His fellow workers followed him, not because they were compelled by his authority, but because they were inspired by his character, life, and sacrifice in following Christ on mission. Therefore, when they deferred to him out of respect and admiration for the man himself.

STRIKE TEAMS AND FIST TEAMS

Although we've briefly discussed the APEST gifting, there are also two types of teams that can be formed: teams that stay, and teams that are sent.

- Fist teams are the APEST teams that stay behind.
- Strike teams are the APEST teams that venture out to plant more churches.

A strike team is a band of APEST leaders (usually apostles, prophets, and evangelists) who combine to form a temporary bond with the goal of splitting off at a future date to multiply out. This approach is what made Paul able to go farther faster.

A fist team is a multidisciplinary team of all the five functions who stay behind indefinitely to ensure that the church is stable until proper leadership is in place. Sometimes they stay permanently. Elders and deacons who make up the fist team are appointed to stay behind, while apostles and other APEST functions may be sent out with a strike team. Murray and Metcalf argue that these are modalities and sodalities operating through the ministry of the local church.[7] Terry and Payne chronicle the weaknesses of church planting movements. While these movements may move fast, they are susceptible to false teaching, like the Galatians after Paul left them to themselves. God designed the ministry of Christ to provide width through the APE roles, while providing

---

7. Stuart Murray, *Church Planting: Laying Foundations* (Scottdale, PA: Herald Press, 2001), 107; Sam Metcalf, *Beyond the Local Church: How Apostolic Movements Can Change the World* (Downers Grove, IL: InterVarsity Press, 2016).

necessary depth through the ST roles more apt to stay behind.[8] This accounts for much of the tension between "theorists" and "practitioners."

Church planting without solid team leadership is like trying to ride a tandem bike alone; it is possible but ridiculous. Contrast Paul's team planting methodology with the modern approach to church planting. For too long, we've been sending planters out alone, as if we're flinging them at the wall like spaghetti and waiting to see what sticks. This is tantamount to the trench warfare strategy of WWI, in which armies sent soldiers out of the trenches and over the top to rush into No Man's Land in a battle of attrition. No wonder the casualties and failure rates are high![9]

George Miley helps to contrast the church at Antioch and Paul's strike team, which was to be "set apart." The team that stayed behind in Antioch had the following qualities:

- Designed to be stationary
- Focused on local issues
- Valued stability
- Wanted to grow where it was
- Financed by its members
- Led by God through its leaders
- Linked with the team spiritually

Paul's strike team, by contrast:

- Was designed to be mobile
- Was focused on cross-cultural ministry
- Valued advance, even if risky
- Wanted to go to new locations
- Was responsible for its own finances
- Was linked with the church spiritually[10]

---

8. John Mark Terry and J. D. Payne, *Developing a Strategy for Missions: A Biblical, Historical, and Cultural Introduction* (Grand Rapids, MI: Baker, 2013), 134–35.

9. Ed Stetzer, "That Stat that Says Pastors are All Miserable and Want to Quit (Part 1)," *Christianity Today*, October 2015, https://www.christianitytoday.com/edstetzer/2015/october/that-stat-that-says-pastors-are-all-miserable-and-want-to-q.html. Author refers to Setzer contesting the 70 percent failure rate (of pastors), but not with statistical evidence to the contrary.

10. George Miley, *Loving the Church . . . Blessing the Nations: Pursuing the Role of Local Churches in Global Missions* (Downers Grove, IL: InterVarsity Press, 2003), 88–89.

Nevertheless, here is a list of Paul's thirty-two interchangeable strike team members[11]:

Agabus	Epaphras	Luke	Sosipater
Apollos	Epaphroditus	Onesimus	Sosthenes
Aristarchus	Erastus	Onesiphorus	Stephanas
Artemas	Gaius	Priscilla and	Timothy
Barnabas	Jesus (Justus)	Aquila	Titus
Clement	John Mark	Secundus	Trophimus
Crecens	Lucas	Silas	Tychicus
Demas	Lucias	Sopater	Zenas

At any one time they could be left behind to serve on a fist team, or they could set out as part of one of the strategic strike teams into the next city.

The goal of utilizing the strike-team approach is to produce sustainable church plants at an ever-increasing rate. Imagine if, instead of five churches launching this year in one city, those five planters launched together in one place, forming a super team. Imagine also that after the church is stable in six to twelve months, the team would perform cellular mitosis and split in half. As they start to multiply by amicably splitting, the strike team brings some newly discipled believers along with them. Then, imagine the process repeats itself six to twelve months later and both of those teams break in half, repeating the process by striking out into newer areas. Now we would have three solid church plants in three years![12]

And what if each of those churches continues to designate strike-team members to the local network in order to keep the ecclesiastical cellular mitosis reproducing the model indefinitely? This was Paul's methodology. Paul usually moved on after appointing a fist team of elders, depositing one of his strike-team members as he did with Timothy in Ephesus, or Titus on Crete. As Timothy and Titus stayed behind, they focused on discipling strike-team members to exit with them and fist-team members to leave behind. Scholars estimate that Paul planted anywhere from twelve to twenty-four churches in the eleven-year period of his active ministry. Many fail to miss that when Paul sends Onesimus, the runaway slave, back to Philemon, he is sending him from Ephesus to Colossae, where Epaphras planted, as either part of that strike team, or to strengthen the fist team there. Eusebius wrote that when Ignatius came to Ephesus, years later,

---

11. Metcalf, *Beyond the Local Church*. Author's Note: Metcalf distinguishes between those who stay and those who go with the terms modality and sodality.

12. Chapter 20 will explore this concept at greater length.

the pastor there was named Onesimus.[13] Imagine being strategic enough to build a super team of planters who could rapidly deploy in any given city and take on various roles, increasing and decreasing according to their gifting and the need of the plant. In chapter 20, we will discuss this in greater depth to assist planters in perceiving the multiplicative potential of team planting.

THE FRUITS

Besides how successful such ventures would be, the benefits of a team-planting strategy would be:

- Stronger launches
- Greater discipleship capacity
- Leaders able to take a break when needed
- Shared responsibilities of mission and management
- Multiple types of leaders who would be able to use their gifts
- More congregations that have shared in kingdom work together
- Kingdom advancement that replaces competition and empire building
- Local networks formed between multiple churches
- Special teams formed for evangelism
- Rapid multiplication
- Greater support for planters

Daniel Sinclair justifies the need to plant in teams with the following apologetic:

- It's the only New Testament model
- One person can't make it alone
- You need to stay vibrant in community relationships
- You need to stay on task and spiritually thriving[14]

George Miley notes many of the same benefits of team planting, adding a few more:

- Teams allow a diversity of gifts to be applied to a common purpose.
- Teams carry an enhanced capacity to engage in spiritual warfare.

---

13. Eusebius, Eusebius' Ecclesiastical History (Grand Rapids: Baker, 1989), 121.
14. Daniel Sinclair, Vision of the Possible (Downers Grove, IL: InterVarsity Press, 2012), 34.

- Teams can provide nurture and pastoral care for their members.
- Healthy teams are small communities, and Christian community is one of the most powerful agents for evangelism.[15]

In addition, such an approach would shift churches from addition to multiplication. Alan Hirsch asserts: "Apostles almost always catalyze movement primarily through mission and church planting, whereas evangelists create church growth by adding people to the movement through conversions." For instance, when Bill Hybels went on record stating that Willow Creek did not do church planting, he was indicating that his primary vision and motivation was evangelistic, not apostolic. Hirsch goes on to point out that many megachurches are largely focused on church growth, which accomplishes numerical addition through evangelism, whereas apostolic leaders focus on multiplication. A team-leadership model harnesses the power of both!

RADICALS AND CONSERVATIVES

In the APEST functions of the church, there is a 3:2 ratio of radicals to conservatives. Three of the roles are primarily focused outward, while two are primarily focused inward. This means that God has hardwired the balance of team leadership to favor a more radical, outward stance. This helps maintain a forward-leaning position of the church toward mission. The church may not be anti-establishment, but it was also never meant to be the establishment. The church in its purest form has always been an underground, radical community of multiplying believers who shook the local authorities. The powers that be don't fear a conservative church that knows to keep its place in sidelined obscurity. But let Martin Luther King Jr. mobilize the church into the mainstream, and the CIA and FBI take notice.[16] Therefore, any strike or fist team should have one more radical member than the total of its conservative members. And, because the APEST functions are pieces of Jesus, ask yourself whether Jesus was more radical than conservative. Whatever the answer, it should determine how the church should be.

---

15. Miley, *Loving the Church*, 75–79.

16. In 2010, classified documents from the CIA were released to the public showing the amount of surveillance that the CIA was conducting on King. There was also a letter sent to King anonymously that is believed to have been authored by William C. Sullivan, Deputy FBI Director. The letter was used in 1975 during the Church Committee hearings, and was part of a secret FBI operation called COINTELPRO, aimed at eliminating MLK as a national threat.

Radicals	Conservatives
• apostle • prophet • evangelist	• shepherd • teacher

The tensions between the APE (radical-leaning) members of the team and the ST (conservative-leaning) ones are noted by Miley. He emphasizes that ST leaders who stay are:[17]

- Motivated to nurture the saints
- Focused on stability
- Invested in building consensus
- Tend to avoid risks
- Work for gradual change

Contrast that with APE leaders who are:

- Motivated to initiate new works
- Focused on change
- Invested in blazing trails for others to follow
- Embracing risk
- Asking God for dynamic breakthroughs and are eager to follow up

YOUR TEAM'S APEST FOCUS

When it comes to working together, the individuals operating in these five roles have to ensure that they are able to function as a cohesive whole. This can be difficult when team members don't see things the same way. If you've stood in the ophthalmologist's office and covered one eye to read an eye chart, you've noticed that the letters are various sizes. In the same way, we could map out our individual makeup of the five functions of Christ's ministry to determine how developed each of us is in each of them. Some of the letters are bigger, meaning you see through that lens better, and others are small, meaning you struggle to see through those lenses.[18]

---

17. Miley, *Loving the Church*, 88–89.
18. Alan Hirsch drew something similar in *The Permanent Revolution* (New York: Jossey-Bass, 2012).

Apest

In this eye chart you can see that, in my personal gift mix, apostleship is the most developed of my functions, and shepherding is my smallest. My prophetic and evangelistic functions actually operate in tandem, and almost never apart from one another. If I'm sharing the gospel with people, I will often understand things about them that I couldn't understand by natural means. This is explained by J. R. Woodward and Dan White Jr., "So if God gives you a word of knowledge (a manifestation gift), and your vocational intelligence is a pastor, you would likely use that word of knowledge to help people work through past hurts and move toward healing and wholeness. But if you've been given a word of knowledge and happen to have the vocational intelligence of an evangelist, you are likely to use that word of knowledge to help bring people to Christ."[19] Teaching is my second biggest function, which probably explains why I don't only train others while sequentially planting churches, but also write books and record podcasts. The teacher function is too large to mind its own business and, combined with the high apostolic gifting, seeks to mobilize others.

What this means for your plant is that there will be a wide array of varying dynamics determined by the makeup of your strike team. You can make a chart for your team's collective gifting, as well as for an individual. This chart could help determine how your strike team develops and disciples everyone in your church plant. Perhaps another leader presents this way on the eye chart:

aPESt

We'll call this hypothetical leader Beau. Beau has a strong shepherding gift, an apostolic blind spot, and a fairly developed evangelistic second functioning. In this combination, Beau is almost my polar opposite. We'd make a fantastic team and cover each other's blind spots. Any church the two of us led together would develop fairly evenly.

Discovering the makeup of your team will not only help you discern how you will work together, but also which kind of disciples you will make. Hirsch

---

19. J. R. Woodward and Dan White Jr., *Church as a Movement: Starting and Sustaining Missional Incarnational Communities* (Downers Grove, IL: InterVarsity Press, 2016), 43.

observes that "if a church lacks a missional vision or capacities, it's probably because the apostolic (A) function has been degraded or entirely delegitimized . . . a lack of concern for prayer, holiness, and justice is very likely due to a dysfunctional prophetic (P) function."[20] If this concept is new to you, there may seem to be an overemphasis on the APEST gifting in this book. However, when boots are on the ground, it will help you to make sense of how you're ministering Christ to your community; it will show you where you're misrepresenting him by not representing *all of him*, and thus making incomplete disciples.

Picture the body of Christ as consisting of five sections, including four limbs and a torso. People might mistake a single leg for the entire Body if all we've done is show them the pastor-only model of leadership. If a full team model is used, the work of your team discipling the individual believers in the church will stretch them in five separate directions, pulling them like a piece of taffy until they resemble Jesus, the only one to embody all five functions.

If all I've been exposed to is a teacher, I'll develop more as a student and no stretching takes place. If only a prophet is pulling on me, I'll focus on the Spirit and justice issues, but will function more like a balled lump of putty than like Jesus. Paul describes the Body growing through the leadership of the five functions in Ephesians 4, each role pulling on it until it fills the Jesus-shaped hole left by the ascension. What's really happening is that they are pulling on your gifts and helping them to emerge, "to equip the saints for the work of ministry" (Eph. 4:12).

But a strength can also become a weakness. Paul Shreiner says, "The five ministry functions also share two common areas of risk. Each of the five runs the risk of using their function in a way that does not equip believers for ministry. If one's ministry does not produce active ministers one's ministry is not an equipping ministry."[21] Instead, the church becomes the showcase for that one person's gift. The balance of the APEST keeps the church in perfect harmony:

- Disciples need to be missionaries, so they will need the apostolic.
- Disciples need to walk in the power of the Holy Spirit and be unleashed in their gifts, so they need the prophetic.
- Disciples need to be romanced by the gospel and know how to share their faith, so they need the evangelistic.
- Disciples need to be cared for and, as a result, need shepherding.
- Disciples need to be taught. That's where teachers come in.

---

20. Hirsch, *5Q*, xxxiv.
21. Paul Shreiner, *Paul, Apostle of God's Glory in Christ: A Pauline Theology* (Downers Grove, IL: InterVarsity Press, 2001), 356.

The balance of these five roles will keep the church plant itself balanced, developing well-balanced disciples. If the APEST gifting becomes imbalanced to favor the gift of an individual, then the church will become unbalanced:

- If all you have pulling on a congregation is the apostolic, then your church becomes a mission station.
- If all you have pulling on a congregation is the prophetic leader, the church becomes a circus.
- If all you have pulling on a congregation is the evangelist, the church becomes a stadium crusade.
- If all you have pulling on a congregation is the shepherd, the church becomes a counseling session.
- If all you have pulling on a congregation is the teacher, the church becomes a classroom, and when we multiply them, we call them campuses.

SYNERGY AND BALANCE

The Synergy and Blind Spots of the APEST Functions

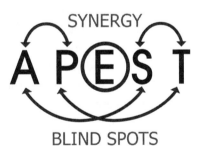

Some of the team members work together forming a synergy, as in the case of the apostle and prophet, or the bond between the teacher and shepherd. In these combinations certain APEST functions enhance the effect of the other. When forming a team, it is important to be aware of the team dynamics and how the APEST functions complement and counter one another. Naïve leaders are tempted to favor synergistic combinations when forming a team, but despite the conservatives working well in tandem and the radicals likewise working well with their own kind, synergistic functions fail to balance each other. The apostle and prophet are both radicals, whereas the shepherd and teacher are both conservatives. Both, however, are needed. God overbalanced Christianity with a ratio of 3:2 by inserting the radical evangelist into the mix, but there is still a counterbalance within the APEST makeup as God designed it. Sometimes it is more helpful on the team to work with those who balance our APEST gifting rather than those who enhance it. Synergy may feel nice, but balance is necessary. David Fitch wrote, "Recognizing our weaknesses makes us more readily dependent on everyone else."[22]

The following is a summary of synergy and balance among the APEST functions:

- Apostles and prophets work in synergy.
- Shepherds and teachers work in synergy.
- Apostles and shepherds balance each other's blind spots.
- Prophets and teachers balance each other other's bind spots.
- Evangelists unsettle everybody.

The evangelist is the radical in the bunch who requires the other combined concentration of the other four APEST functions to pull on them to keep them in check. This is because the evangelist's weakness is the tendency to function independently from the other four ministry functions. Tomlinson observes, "It is distressing to note that a large number of very talented evangelists end up 'going it alone.' Probably because of the pioneer instinct in them, but the evangelist needs a relationship with men of different ministry who can consolidate his work."[23] For this reason, in the diagram below, the evangelist is isolated by a circle to show their loner tendencies and seeming independence in their ministry. Despite the illusion of independence, the evangelist needs the others to provide equilibrium. The desire to proclaim to the lost can outweigh the need to develop strong relationships with ministers who are fulfilling the other functions necessary to the church. That said, an evangelist is a valuable asset to any church plant and will make your church plant grow, but the price tag of this role—if it operates without balance—is ample conflict and weary people trailing behind being told to keep up. Many megachurches during the church growth movement were built and led by evangelists desperately in need of APEST team members to balance them out.

Here is a glimpse of how the teams work together:

---

22. David E. Fitch, *Faithful Presence: Seven Disciplines that Shape the Church for Mission* (Downers Grove, IL: InterVarsity Press, 2016), 156.

23. David Tomlinson, "Apostolic Teams: A Strategy for Corporate Maturity," in *Apostles Today*, ed. David Matthew (West Yorkshire, UK: Harvestime, 1988), 125, quoting David Sills, *Changing World, Unchanging Mission: Responding to Global Challenges* (Downers Grove, IL: InterVarsity Press, 2015), 203.

Role	Synergy	Balance	Notes
Apostle	Prophet	Shepherd	Works well with all to a certain degree as a mobilizer
Prophet	Apostle	Teacher	Fades to the background without other APEs
Evangelist	Minimally all to a degree	All	The Apostle becomes a champion to the rest of the team
Shepherd	Teacher	Apostle	Shepherd is the most sensitive on the team
Teacher	Shepherd	Prophet	Teacher is the stabilizing factor for all

If team leadership were united, the church would be unconquerable. Our distinctions should not become divisions. When a leader learns that using teams rather than indulging the whim of one leader only can more readily reflect God's heart, their quest to discover the heart of God begins. Surprisingly, God's heart sounds like the collective wisdom of the five functions speaking in unison.

Each of the APEST functions involves helping us experience an aspect of Jesus, to help us experience who God really is.

- The apostle wants you to experience God through mission.
- The prophet wants you to experience God through the gifts.
- The evangelist wants you to experience God through the gospel.
- The shepherd wants you to experience God through community.
- The teacher wants you to experience God through Scripture.

All believers need the five APEST functions developed within them by one of these types of leaders. Therefore, an unbalanced team will hinder or distort the development of a congregation. Few apostolic teams contain all five at the beginning, however, and it is difficult to maintain all five functions on a team indefinitely due to apostles, prophets, and evangelists (APEs) being mobile in nature. Regardless of their APEST function, there are behaviors that all your team members should exhibit—what J. D. Payne calls the *Barnabas Factors*: walks with the Lord, maintains outstanding character, serves the church, remains faithful to the call, shares the gospel regularly, raises up leaders, encourages with speech and actions, and responds appropriately to conflict.[24]

24. J. D. Payne, *The Barnabas Factors: Eight Essential Practices of Church Planting Team Members* (Charleston, SC: CreateSpace, 2012), 214–16.

All APEST functions are valid, and Jesus performed them all during earthly ministry just as he continues to express himself through them in the church today. His prayer that we would be one, as he and the Father are one, was a prayer for unity. Instead of fulfilling that prayer, the church has fragmented; the prophets have been scattered to the Pentecostal camp, and teachers have become entrenched in the Word-based camps like the Baptists and the Reformed movement. Jesus's prayer was for unity amidst diversity.

It is helpful to remember the functionality of the Trinity within God himself as each member embodies different functions to redeem humanity. The Godhead maintains distinct persons with unique roles, yet is still one God—the profound root of teamwork hardwired into the universe, reflecting the creator.

Will your church plant model this same teamwork modeled by the Trinity and bring this aspect of the kingdom to earth?

Apostle
- Strategy
- Structure of organization
- Protect DNA
- New ways of doing thinking
- Multiplication
- Empowering others
- Outward oriented
- Growing mission, not maintaining it
- Vision casting
- Movement-style approaches
- Questions status quo

Prophet
- Questions status quo
- Justice
- Mouthpiece of God
- Critiques institutionalism
- Calls people back to the purity of worship
- Stirs up the gifts
- Calls people to the supernatural

Evangelist
- Outward oriented
- Gospel focused
- Equips others for evangelism
- Equips others for apologetics

Shepherd
- Enables discipleship
- Calls people to community
- Moves people into the community
- Fosters relationships
- Comes alongside people
- Plans meals together
- Builds community

Teacher
- Immerses themselves in the text
- Develops a biblical worldview
- Brings clarity to Scripture
- Applies Word of God to their personal lives

REFLECT

- Church planting is a team sport. Imagine your favorite professional (or collegiate) basketball team. Now visualize the opposing coach sending only one player to take on your team.

DISCUSS

- How does your denomination, fellowship, or organization understand church planting teams? What are some similarities and differences with the APEST approach?
- Write down APEST like an eye chart, with bigger letters for the roles you identify with more closely and smaller letters for the others. Compare your eye charts with those of your your teammates and discuss.

- Another word that describes synergy is potentiation. For example, caffeine potentiates the effects of acetaminophen, so they are often given together for certain types of headaches. How might a team member gifted in prophecy potentiate the effectiveness of the apostle on the team? Why does a teacher potentiate the effectiveness of a shepherd?
- Another way of describing the way team roles balance each other is to say they complement one another. For example, in Genesis, Adam needed a person who corresponded to him, and God provided Eve, who would complement his gifts, abilities, and temperament. How does a shepherd complement an apostle on a church planting team? How does a prophet complement a teacher? Why do team members primarily gifted in evangelism need the complementary gifting of the other four giftings on the team?

CHALLENGE

- Interview a few people who really know you. Explain the APEST model of church planting teams if they are unfamiliar with it. Then, show them your APEST eye chart and ask them to comment. Do they concur with your self-assessment?

FUNCTIONS OF THE PLANTER'S TEAM

There was an idea to bring together a group of remarkable people, to see if we could become something more.

—NICK FURY

Jon R. Katznebach defines the church planting team as "a small number of people with complementary skills who are committed to a common purpose, performance, goals, and approach for which they hold themselves mutually accountable."[1] The divine Trinity entered into a division of labor and worked as a team to accomplish the mission of redemption, giving the church, as the body, a model for how the "head" operates in a plurality of leadership. Payne states, "Working as a team is a divine characteristic and must be a component of missionary endeavor."[2]

My first book, *Church Zero*, was an apologetic on team planting, but the most common request I had from readers was, *show us what it looks like*. Therefore, this chapter seeks to explore the various APEST functions of Christ's ministry in detail on a team, unpacking the daily responsibilities that each member shoulders. In short, we will explore the division of labor among the APEST roles to assist you to:

- Make sense of your own APEST function and the functions of others on your team
- Keep your team members operating effectively in their lane
- Embrace the economy of the five roles to achieve team synergy on mission

---

1. Jon R. Katznebach and Douglas K. Smith, *The Wisdom of Teams: Creating the High Performance Organization* (Cambridge, MA: Harvard Business Review Press, 1993), 45.

2. J. D. Payne, *Discovering Church Planting: An Introduction to the Whats, Whys and Hows of Global Church Planting* (Downers Grove, IL: InterVarsity Press, 2012), 236.

- Envision what the day-to-day responsibilities of the APEST functions are on a team so your team members can keep operating out of their strengths
- Speak confidently about superheroes

A number of books have been written that explore the functions of APEST and, so far, none have exhausted the topic. Alan Hirsch's monumental book *5Q* traces the fingerprints of the APEST functions that God hardwired throughout creation and humanity. Specifically, humans made in the image of God still bear a natural imprint of APEST in the natural order. Traces of the apostolic may be witnessed in entrepreneurs, pioneers, and scientists bent on discovery. If Jesus was perfect humanity personified, and he embodied all five roles perfectly, then humankind's original mission to fill the earth with God's glory, involved embodying the functionality of APEST to accomplish that mission prior to the fall. Now that Christ has redeemed humanity through his life, death, resurrection, and ascension, he has restored this original missiological mandate to the church. As the APEST functions, Christ's glory fills the earth. This theological breakthrough explains how the five-functioning ministry of the church fills the Jesus-shaped hole in the world.

To trace the APEST functions in the church, we will focus on the following in respect to each of the APEST functions—Apostles, Prophets, Evangelists, Shepherds, and Teachers—and examine their burdens, functions, responsibilities, voice, and tension.

1. Burden: Each of the APEST functioning leaders possesses a unique burden that drives them.
2. Function: Each APEST function has an *internal* (inward facing) ministry within the church and an *external* (outward facing) ministry to the world.
3. Responsibilities: How should the various APEST functioning leaders best spend their time on a team? What piece of the ministry pie should they take?[3]

---

3. Ed Stetzer, *Planting New Churches in a Postmodern Age* (Nashville: Broadman & Holman, 2003). Stetzer outlines the daily responsibilities and schedule of planters. They suggest mapping out a productive work schedule based on the following breakdown: Evangelistic outreach: 15 hours per week (full-time); three hours per week (bivocational). They include sermon study and preparation (10 hrs FT/ 3 hrs bivo), administration (10 hrs FT/ 3 hrs bivo), and ministry care (15 hrs FT/ 3 hrs bivo). This is not necessary when a planter has a team. Plus, there's no real way of knowing how to accurately divide your time if it's not leaning into the APEST function. In this model, the shepherd and teacher functions are getting the majority of the time, totaling 35 hours if you include administration. In a 50-hour week, this allows for 15 hours of evangelism. One-third of the leader's time is given to the actual work of planting. Further,

4. Voice: Each of these functions contains a speaking gift, yet each manifests differently, and sounds unique in the context of preaching. The teacher tends to be methodical, organized, and expositional, whereas the prophet preaches from burden. For this reason, some teams prepare a message together to ensure all APEST perspectives are covered, while others rotate in the pulpit to accomplish the goal of representing all five aspects of Christ's ministry.

5. Tension: Each functioning team member has strengths and weaknesses that need to be acknowledged and accounted for to avoid unnecessary tension, but which also provide the right amount of tension for growth.

When all gifts are working together in a church, it's like a synchronized martial arts movie that's been painstakingly choreographed. The various functions serving the body in unison help the church to fire on all five cylinders and prevent it from operating at a fifth of its capacity, as it would under just one type of leader. Ott and Wilson cite additional advantages, among them: complementary gifts, deeper development of gifts, accountability, intensification of vision, being able to focus on areas of strength, and being able to tackle bigger challenges.[4]

APOSTLES

The apostle is the pioneer with an injection of faith for the whole team, having confidence in things not seen yet. For this reason, people call them the strategic visionary of the team, but that's misleading. Vision can only truly be determined by the shared collective dreams and discernment of the team. Faith, not vision, causes the apostle to lead the charge (1 Cor. 12:28) and excel at taking ground so that others on the team can hold ground. Apostles are always up for a challenge and get even more fired up when others are discouraged. When the church shrinks after multiplying outward, the apostle gains a second wind. Apostolic pioneer William Carey failed to see a convert in twelve years but penned the following words in his journal upon witnessing his first convert, Krishna Pal, coming to faith:

---

for the bivo planter, there is no division of labor implied, meaning that the individual is attempting to take the plant by themselves as a bivocational planter. Frankly, that's ministerial suicide without a team. After working a full-time job, having 11 hours left over to run the whole church is the stuff burn-out is made of.

4. Gene Wilson and Craig Ott, *Global Church Planting: Biblical Principals and Best Practices for Multiplication* (Grand Rapids: Baker Academic, 2011), 333.

He was only one, but a continent was coming behind him. The divine grace which changed one Indian's heart, could obviously change a hundred thousand.[5]

Like *Titanic* survivor Molly Brown urged the crew in lifeboat number 6 to ceaselessly search the water for survivors, the apostle champions the rescue efforts of the church. This brings us to their burden.

1. An Apostle's Burden

One might think that the apostle is burdened for the lost, but that's only a part of it. Apostles are dominated by a burden for the expansion of the kingdom of God and are passionate to see the glory of God cover the earth like the seas. The first order of business, therefore, is kingdom expansion. Apostles yearn to see the kingdom broadening into new territory—not just geographically, but crossing societal frontiers into marginalized groups where Christ is not named.

2. Apostolic Function

Each of the APEST functions faces both inward and outward in their gifting.

Outward Focus

As our apostle and forerunner, Jesus crossed frontiers as the ultimate pioneer missionary, bridging two cultures that could not be more different: heaven and earth. As long as there is a frontier or another mountain to climb, apostles keep their packs on when others want to take them off and air out their hiking boots. Therefore, the apostle does not stay long. As Len Tang points out, "Planter's gifts and wiring are, broadly speaking, apostolic and entrepreneurial."[6]

Inward Focus

Apostolic leaders' inward function is to mobilize the church for ministry outward to the edges of its own borders by developing others. Because apostles' time is limited, they facilitate leadership development by raising up and discipling others to take their place when they are gone.

---

5. Iain H. Murray, *The Puritan Hope* (Edinburgh: Banner, 1971), 141.
6. Len Tang and Charles E. Cotherman, *Sent to Flourish: A Guide to Planting and Multiplying Churches* (Downers Grove, IL: InterVarsity Press, 2019), 105.

3. Apostolic Responsibility

Because of their function, the bulk of the apostles' contribution to the team and areas of responsibility will be:

- Discipling their replacements
- Mobilizing every believer on mission
- Strategizing the gifts of others and planning how to match those gifts to needs
- Analyzing culture
- Penetrating culture
- Developing stratagies to engage the church in risky maneuvers
- Working with prophetic leaders to hear God's collective voice on the team
- Prioritizing prayer in advance of mission
- Calling attention to the marginalized

Gifts commonly associated with apostolic functioning are faith, administration, wisdom, and knowledge.

4. Speaking Voice

When apostles preach, they mobilize the congregation outward, empowering and releasing people in their gifts. Their preaching creates a kingdom atmosphere by preaching kingdom ethics and seeding kingdom priorities into the church's DNA. They lay the foundation of Christ so that the church inhales an atmosphere of grace, and exhales mission in response to the gospel. Further, they instill courage, faith, and a sense of adventure. Before departing from my multiplying urban plant in Long Beach, I preached a final message that I hoped would mobilize the team for years to come called, "The World I Love, the Trains I Hop." The effect of apostolic preaching is motivational, leaving listeners excited, empowered, and activated in their gifts for unfinished mission.

5. Apostolic Tension

Apostolic leaders are pioneers, and, according to Hirsch, if they are left to function too long without settlers coming after them, they "will seek to delegitimize the others."[7] J. R. Woodward confesses that another tension apostles bring is that sometimes for the apostolic leader, "mission comes before people

---

7. Alan Hirsch and Tim Catchim, *The Permanent Revolution: Apostolic Imagination and Practice for the 21st Century Church* (San Francisco: Jossey-Bass, 2012), 71.

instead of mission being for people."[8] When apostolic leaders admit they need shepherds to cover their blind spots, they experience a freeing sense of unburdening from a weight they were never meant to carry.

I realized late in ministry that I'm a horrible shepherd. I have hurt many people due to the unconcerned ways I've interacted with them in the past. Daniel Sinclair, in his book *Vision of the Possible*, identifies some of the weaknesses of the apostolic leader, listing self-confidence, over-assertiveness, and independence. The core traits of apostles can either be harnessed by the Spirit for a positive impact, or by the flesh for a negative one. For example, taking the apostolic core traits of faith, persuasion, and pioneering, they will exhibit the following when acted on by the flesh or Spirit:

Apostolic Traits in the Spirit and the Flesh

Trait	Spirit	Flesh
Faith	Confidence	Arrogance
Persuasion	Conviction	Over-assertiveness
Pioneer spirit	Independence	Rebellion

PROPHETS

The word *prophet* is used over 150 times in the New Testament. In Acts 15:32 (ESV), we see Silas and Barnabas "encouraged and strengthened the brothers with many words." Paul often conjoins prophets and apostles, due to their frontline aspect (see Eph. 3:5; 2:20, 1 Cor. 12:28). A. W. Tozer said we need biblically balanced prophets who can strengthen and encourage new works:

> For a generation certain evangelical teachers have told us that the gifts of the Spirit ceased at the death of the apostles or at the completion of the New Testament. This, of course, is a doctrine without a syllable of biblical authority back of it. Its advocates must accept full responsibility for thus manipulating the Word of God.
>
> The result of this erroneous teaching is that spiritually gifted persons are ominously few among us. When we so desperately need leaders with the gift of discernment, for instance, we do not have them and are compelled

8. J. R. Woodward and Dan White Jr., *Church as a Movement: Starting and Sustaining Missional Incarnational Communities* (Downers Grove, IL: InterVarsity Press, 2016), 49.

to fall back upon the techniques of the world. This frightening hour calls aloud for men with the gift of prophetic insight."[9]

Paul wrote of the foundational role of a prophet, saying the church is "built on the foundation of the apostles and prophets" (Eph. 2:20 ESV). Some interpret the passage to refer to New Testament apostles and Old Testament prophets. However, Paul's context is New Testament, because the church is built on the foundation of apostles and prophets who are presented as contemporaries. Six verses later, Paul said that the mystery of Christ (God's plan to save the Gentiles) was "not made known to the sons of men in other generations as it has *now been revealed* to his holy apostles and prophets by the Spirit" (Eph. 3:5 ESV, emphasis mine). Failing to recognize the New Testament prophetic office is an example of an ecclesiastical paradigm interfering with proper exegesis. Luke mentions nameless prophets (Acts 11:27), Agabus (Acts 11:28), Barnabas, Simeon (Acts 13:1), and Judas and Silas (Acts 15:32), and Paul wrote, "God has appointed in the church first apostles, second prophets, third teachers" (1 Cor. 12:28 ESV).

In *Church Zero*, I addressed some of the other concerns that people have with the notion of New Testament–era prophetic leaders. "Many people struggle with the idea of a New Testament prophet because the canon of Scripture is closed. Their concern is that a license to create biblical literature is being handed out with the title. We fail to remember that the Old Testament is packed with prophets who made cameos in Israel's history and never wrote a line of Scripture. They spoke into the moment. This string of pearls kicks off with Enoch (Jude 1:14–15) and is followed by Deborah (Judg. 4–5), Gad (1 Sam. 22:5; 2 Sam. 24:11–19; 1 Chron. 29:29; 2 Chron. 29:25), Nathan (2 Sam. 7:2–4; 12; 2 Chron. 9:29; 29:25), and others. There were unknown prophets in the days of Eli (1 Sam. 2:27–36) and Gideon (Judges 6:7–10). Under Samuel there were schools of prophets (1 Sam. 10:10–12; 19:20–24); and Scripture also shows us the "man of God" from Judah (1 Kings 13), Ahijah (1 Kings 11:26–40; 14:1–18), Shemaiah (1 Kings 12:21–24; 2 Chron. 12:1–8), Iddo the seer (2 Chron. 12:15; 13:22), Azariah (2 Chron. 15), Hanani (2 Chron. 16:7–10), Jehu son of Hanani (2 Chron. 19:1–3), Micaiah (1 Kings 22), Oded (2 Chron. 28:8–15), Huldah the prophetess (2 Kings 22:12–20), Uriah (Jer. 26:20–23), Jahaziel (2 Chron. 20:14–17), Eliezer (2 Chron. 20:37), the prophetic school of Elisha (2 Kings 9:1–13), Zechariah son of Jehoiada

---

9. A. W. Tozer, *Keys to the Deeper Christian Life* (Pioneer Library, 2014; first ed. 1959), location 267 of 392, Kindle.

(2 Chron. 24:20–22), the "Man of God" who forbade Amaziah's league with Israel (2 Chron. 25:7–10), the unknown prophet who rebuked Amaziah (2 Chron. 25:15–16), and another unknown prophet who encouraged and rebuked Ahab (1 Kings 20:13–15, 35–43). Similarly, prophets that are walking around today may speak into the moment, but don't write scripture. That said, their messages better not violate scripture, but be tested."[10]

1. A Prophet's Burden

The prophet operates from a place of burden. Whereas the apostle is burdened for the kingdom and the evangelist is burdened for the lost, the prophet is burdened for God himself. To the other roles, the church is the beautiful bride, but to the prophet, the bride is not always faithful. In some cases, the prophet speaks more about the faithful covenant love of God to the church, and this brings great comfort; but in other cases, the prophet also speaks of the unfaithfulness of the church, which brings sorrow leading to repentance. The message of a prophet must always be laced with hope if it is authentic. Whereas the apostle sees wasted mission potential when the church is sick, the prophet sees a stubborn bride refusing to listen. The prophet is burdened for the gifts of the spirit to be active because they usher the supernatural presence and voice of God into a congregation. The prophet doesn't want the church to hear the prophet, but to hear God *through the prophet* as prophecy, tongues, and other gifts of the Spirit operate.

Gifts commonly useful for prophets are *miracles, signs, healing, prophesy, word of knowledge, tongues, and encouragement.*

2. Prophetic Function

The prophet's chief function is encouragement, and this gift is applied internally and externally to the church.

Inward Focus

The prophet's inward focus is to share God's burden for his people. This functions to encourage believers in their faith and spur them to use their gifts. Like Elijah's "school of the prophets," modern prophets seek to train up others in their gifts. Believers understand their value when experiencing the ministry of prophets. "And Judas and Silas, who were themselves **prophets**, encouraged and strengthened the brothers with many words" (Acts 15:32 ESV). Paul and

---

10. Peyton Jones, *Church Zero* (Colorado Springs: Cook, 2013), 107.

Barnabas functioned apostolically in Antioch to establish faith communities and support early gospel work demonstrating that the role of a prophet was also mobile in nature:

- "Now in these days **prophet**s came down from Jerusalem to Antioch" (Acts 11:27 ESV).
- "Now there were in the church at Antioch **prophet**s and teachers, Barnabas, Simeon who was called Niger, Lucius of Cyrene, Manaen a lifelong friend of Herod the tetrarch, and Saul" (Acts 13:1 ESV).
- "While we were staying for many days, a **prophet** named Agabus came down from Judea" (Acts 21:10 ESV).

Not only are prophets helpful with new works and churches in trouble, they are also extremely useful for works that need re-establishing, such as Judas and Silas after the Jerusalem council: "And Judas and Silas, who were themselves prophets, encouraged and strengthened the brothers with many words" (Acts 15:32 ESV).

Outward Focus

The outward focus of the prophet is to share what things in our society grieve God, such as sin, social injustice, and inequality. This helps to mobilize the church to embody solutions for whatever burdens God's heart. Bryn Jones describes the unction of the church encourager with these words, "when he speaks, he *inspires people to action*. The word he carries from God demands decision, action, change or adjustment. . . . Not only does he bring men and women to the point of decision; he also *communicates faith for action*."[11]

3. Responsibilities
- Prayer
- Visiting small groups to stir up the gifts
- Visiting new workers to encourage them
- Training other prophetic leaders
- Visiting the sick and those in need of supernatural empowering
- Counseling
- Calling the church to fasting and prayer

---

11. Bryn Jones, "Apostles and Prophets: What's the Difference?" *Apostles Today*, ed. David Matthew (West Yorkshire, UK: Harvestime, 1988), 109.

- Accompanying the apostolic leader in performing exorcisms
- Focusing on God's global activities together within the global body of Christ

4. Speaking

When the prophet speaks, it comes across less as expositional, and more as *sharing from burden*. The prophet's preaching often uses mental pictures, symbols, and illustrations to communicate scriptural principles.

5. Tension

If the other leaders on the team are not secure in themselves, having a prophet in their midst can be unsettling. Learning to laugh at oneself on a leadership team serves as the necessary confession that you do not have all the answers. When corrected by prophets, a healthy leader is keenly aware that, for every bullet of rebuke that hits, the leader has also dodged 100 more bullets that could have struck true. A prophet's rebuke and instruction, however, are always an indirect encouragement because they are the expression of God's heart. In Revelation 2 and 3 where Jesus says some difficult things to his church, he encourages every one of them, giving them hope and opportunity because that is his heart toward us. "To him who overcomes . . ." is the upward note on the end of any true prophetic message. The love of the Holy Spirit is behind everything, and when the prophet isn't getting in the way of the message, God's love is tangible.

Bashfulness is the weakness of prophets. Despite a necessary degree of courage requisite to share their burdens and step out in faith regarding the gifts of the Spirit, prophets don't always want to go and can be reluctant to share. Particularly when prophetic leaders are in non-charismatic circles and not encouraged by apostolic leaders to step out, they will sometimes withdraw and hold back. When this happens, it's the responsibility of the apostolic leader to encourage prophets to speak. On opposite ends of the spectrum, prophets can be shy and withdrawn when they are the only prophet, or they can be overzealous and get carried away if they find themselves in a group of other prophets.

Prophetic Traits in the Spirit and the Flesh

Trait	Spirit	Flesh
Watchful	Burdened	Judgmental
Messenger	Encouraging	People-pleasing
Intervener	Disrupter	Interrupter

EVANGELIST

Famous evangelists in church history have included Dwight L. Moody, Billy Graham, and George Whitefield. Evangelists have no churches to speak of generally but leave a mass of converts in their wake.

1. An Evangelist's Burden

The evangelist is the gospel-centered leader who is burdened for the lost. They serve both inward and outward functions.

2. Evangelistic Function

Evangelists preach the gospel.

Inward Focus

Although the outward function is more evident, it is the inward function that people may have experienced more without realizing it. Many leaders who lead level-3 churches (churches that grow by addition only, merely increasing their size, rather than multiplying) tend to be evangelists. The church grows quickly by addition, and Christians are brought into a romance with the gospel itself once more.

Outward Focus

The evangelist doesn't wait for people to come and hear the gospel; the evangelist takes the gospel to the people. The evangelist seeks to invite Christians to share their faith outside the walls of the church, in imitation of the evangelist. If you see evangelists coming down the hallway, you might want to hide, duck, or run, because they will recruit you to share your faith unless you've got a note from the doctor.

3. Evangelistic Responsibilities:

Evangelists spend their days primarily focusing on being out in public places and sharing via conversations.

- Engaging the marketplace
- Training others how to share their faith and testimonies
- Evangelizing of strangers
- Leading evangelistic discussion groups and forums
- Apologetics training
- Engaging people with the gospel online
- Inviting others to come

- Organizing outreach events
- Focusing on nations

4. Evangelistic Speaking

An evangelist is a blessing to any congregation. Less the mobilizer and more the romancer, the evangelist brings everyone back to seeing the need for grace and gospel in their lives. Having an evangelist preach to the congregation ensures that Christians don't wander too far from the cross. The evangelist is gifted with strong persuasion and compels them to come in.

5. Tension

Whenever I see a large congregation that has quickly sprouted up numerically, I tend to think it is either an evangelist at the helm or someone of another role who has the strong evangelistic gift. Their zeal can overtake them as their activities overtake their knowledge and wisdom. Teachers Aquila and Priscilla had to explain the way of God more accurately to Apollos despite his flurry of evangelistic activity (Acts 18:24–26). Because souls are at stake, no price is too high to pay, and evangelists can be slave drivers, wearing people out by incessantly promoting gospel work.

All three radical functions of the APEST matrix of leadership are unsettling to the conservative functions of shepherds and teachers. Some teachers masquerade as apostles, teaching on APEST with zeal but, because they are conservatives who are unaware they aren't radicals, they minimalize evangelism and give a distorted picture of it, even becoming hostile toward it at times. Teaching on APEST doesn't necessarily make you radical; it is possible that it only makes you a conservative teacher with a pet subject.

Conservatives would rather talk about "abiding," discipleship, and community —all low-risk activities—and would rather describe the work of evangelists as simply being excellent neighbors who throw good barbeques. This is the domesticated version of what shepherds and teachers think evangelists *should be*. In truth, evangelists cause offense with frontline preaching of the gospel in public. If your evangelists don't cause your leadership team occasional embarrassment, they are not evangelists. Remember that the Corinthians were embarrassed by Paul's evangelism as an apostle, which led to his remark, "For if we are beside ourselves, it is for God; if we are in our right mind, it is for you" (2 Cor. 5:13 ESV).

You can be assured that those who disparage evangelism are actually in the conservative camp. Despite teaching at universities, cycling speaker's circuits, and teaching frequently about APEST and other apostolic things, they are still just teachers, theorizing about what others practice. Similarly, when some misinformed APEST teachers speak of prophets, they strip them of the supernatural and portray them merely as politically correct social justice warriors. Many of these champions of APEST unwittingly distort the radical roles of apostle, prophet, and evangelist into conservative roles. When they do this, they are actually describing the outward functions of the shepherds and teachers without realizing it. Apostolic, prophetic, and evangelistic leaders understand their own radical and embarrassing nature among conservatives and therefore do not disparage one another's functions or practices. Evangelists can be the most difficult team members, but they should be appreciated.

Evangelistic Traits in the Spirit and the Flesh

Trait	Spirit	Flesh
Passion	Passionate	Fanatical
Boldness	Fearless	Foolish
Single-minded	Focused	Stubborn

SHEPHERD

The job of a first-century shepherd was a smelly, dirty, and inherently socially distancing profession. Shepherds are down and dirty with the sheep, close with them, and very compassionate to their needs and protection. If you intend to mess with sheep, you have to go through the shepherd first. Don't underestimate shepherds just because they are conservatives—I've seen shepherds ready to throw down on a leadership team over the needs of the sheep, and I'd sooner tangle with a grizzly guarding her cubs.

1. A Shepherd's Burden

The burden of the shepherd is entirely ecclesiastical. They live for the church and define the church as people. Others might see the church as gospel bearers, a missionary force, or God's voice on earth. The shepherds fight for everyone to know that the church is still made up of people.

2. Shepherding Function
Inward Focus

The shepherd provides safety and stability to the family of God. They sustain community and seek to enrich relationships wherever God's people gather. George Miley says of the shepherd,

People with a strong pastoral gifting may not be the first to respond with a radical challenge to mission, to a call to be missionaries. But watch them come forward when they see God's servants wounded and needy! There are casualties in this battle, and God has placed among us those gifted by the Holy Spirit to minister healing to the wounded. Jesus has graciously distributed among us gifts of healing, caring, discernment, and mercy to keep us going in health for the long haul. The diversity in the church is designed to bring a godly balance between radically forsaking all and the appropriate care of individuals.[12]

Outward Focus

To a degree, all the roles share synergy with the evangelist's function, including the shepherd. Jesus noted that the Good Shepherd leaves the ninety-nine to go after the one. This is because evangelism is still about people. I've watched shepherds go after the marginalized, hunting them out from dumpsters, purposefully shopping at 7–11 to encounter addicts and to share the gospel. The difference between an evangelist and a shepherd is that the evangelist is quick to move on to others. The most powerful evangelist I'd ever met blew into my town, stayed with me overnight, and said, "I need to hit as many people as I can within two and a half hours." I was skeptical until I watched him leading multiple people to Christ. Shepherds, by contrast, will slow down, taking time to invest in the totality of people's lives, discipling them into the faith over the long haul.

3. Shepherding Responsibilities

- Counseling
- Coaching
- Visiting
- Extending hospitality
- Organizing home studies
- Training in discipleship

4. Shepherds as Speakers

When shepherds speak to a congregation, they apply the gospel to people's real-life situations and celebrate stories and testimonies. They are not known for being excellent expositors, yet God's heart shines through. What they lack in

---

12. George Miley, *Loving the Church . . . Blessing the Nations: Pursuing the Role of Local Churches in Global Missions* (Downers Grove, IL: InterVarsity Press, 2003), 61.

pulpit polish they make up for in love. Often you will hear them described like this: "Our pastor isn't the best teacher, but he is really good with the people."

5. Tension

Because people are their focus, shepherds often drive churches into the ground at worst, and see them plateau at best. Shepherds butt heads primarily with the apostle, but apostles will love them for it, because shepherds also make apostles feel loved. The weakness of a shepherd, however, is people-pleasing. They can easily be swayed by compassion to take the wrong sides of things, and sometimes they are backed into corners by wanting to please everyone.

Shepherd Traits in the Spirit and the Flesh

Trait	Spirit	Flesh
Faithful	Devoted	Over-committed
Protective	Warding	Rigid
Compassion	Attentive	People-pleasing

TEACHER

A teacher is an expositor, despite the fact that we often use the terms "pastor" or "teacher" interchangeably for the leader in the pulpit. Understanding team leadership helps rectify this.

1. A Teacher's Burden

Teachers are burdened for the truth, believing God's Word to be the link between God's people and himself. The prophet, providing balance, sees the Spirit as the link. The problem is, they are both right. Like the old saying goes,

> Only scripture, we dry up.
> Only Spirit, we blow up.
> Take them together, we grow up.

Words are the overflow of somebody's heart. Therefore, the Spirit may be God's heart dwelling within his people, but God's Word is his heart on the printed page. The teacher reveres the Bible, milking every jot and tittle for all it's worth. The words are the overflow of the heart, and out of the heart, the mouth speaks. Therefore, the teacher is burdened that everyone would know the Word of God.

2. Teacher Function
Inward Focus

As you would expect, the teacher does the lion's share of the teaching. They spend a great deal of time studying, and therefore their activities are limited to a small number of things:

- Teaching
- Studying
- Training others to teach
- Helping set series
- Touching base with small-group leaders on teaching

Outward Focus

- The outward function of the teacher is most clearly represented by apologetics, such as Tim Keller writing the *New York Times* bestseller *Reasons for God*, or writing a regular column in a newspaper to provide a Christian worldview. C. S. Lewis functioned in this way when he broadcast Mere Christianity over the airwaves.

3. Teachers Teaching

Paul said if a person's gift is teaching, let them teach (Rom. 12:6–7). Any teachers worth their salt, however, will train others to teach, and rotate them in. They will be the main teachers, yet seek to duplicate themselves, particularly under the encouragement of the apostle who needs to take some teachers with them to assemble a fist team in the next church plant. Teachers tend to be expository in nature, listening to other teachers and learning from them.

4. Teacher Tensions

The tension among teachers happens when the Word becomes all-consuming and the quest for truth matters at the expense of everything else. Knowledge quickly puffs up rather than love building up. Therefore, teachers can seem cold, mercurial, and even ruthless at times. Those within the Reformed movement have often been accused of being the greatest proponents of the doctrines of grace, yet also among those most deficient in modeling it. The lack of sensitivity when it comes to matters of truth can make the teacher appear to be less than gracious and devoid of love, like a banging gong or a clanging symbol. Over the years, John MacArthur has come under scrutiny for making unbalanced and even damaging statements. Teachers sometimes express strongly held opinions or viewpoints under the guise of "biblical truth."

Teacher Traits in the Spirit and the Flesh

Trait	Spirit	Flesh
Studious	Receptive	Rigid
Knowledgeable	Wise	Know-it-all
Apologetic	Defending	Contentious

In conclusion, your team will need to establish a division of labor and an accountability for fulfilling the five functions of Christ's ministry. Here is an example of one team's breakdown of their leadership roles:

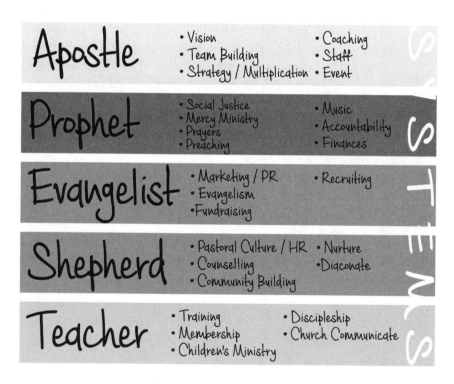

Apostle
- Vision
- Team Building
- Strategy / Multiplication
- Coaching
- Staff
- Event

Prophet
- Social Justice
- Mercy Ministry
- Prayers
- Preaching
- Music
- Accountability
- Finances

Evangelist
- Marketing / PR
- Evangelism
- Fundraising
- Recruiting

Shepherd
- Pastoral Culture / HR
- Counselling
- Community Building
- Nurture
- Diaconate

Teacher
- Training
- Membership
- Children's Ministry
- Discipleship
- Church Communicate

SYSTEMS

REFLECT

- This chapter organizes the function of each of the APEST giftings by their burden, function, responsibility, voice, and tension. Review these for your leadership gifting. What functions are you performing well? What functions need improvement? Were there any you were not aware of?

DISCUSS

- What's the difference between faith and vision?
- Read Ephesians 4:11–16. In Western Christianity, most churches have a single lead pastor. How can this be reconciled with the APEST gifts given by Christ to the church?
- Are the lists of responsibilities for each of the APEST gifts complete? What would you add?

CHALLENGE

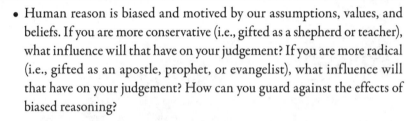

- Human reason is biased and motived by our assumptions, values, and beliefs. If you are more conservative (i.e., gifted as a shepherd or teacher), what influence will that have on your judgement? If you are more radical (i.e., gifted as an apostle, prophet, or evangelist), what influence will that have on your judgement? How can you guard against the effects of biased reasoning?

REDISCOVERING APOSTOLIC STRIKE TEAMS (FIST LEADERSHIP)

From Solo Performer to Catalyzing Teams

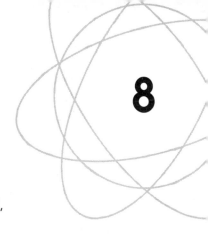

8

STRIKE TEAMS

It is no good trying to escape you. But I'm glad,
Sam. I cannot tell you how glad. Come along!
It is plain that we were meant to go together.

—FRODO, *THE LORD OF THE RINGS*

The stage lights were hot. Sweat poured down his cheeks, and he could feel a solitary bead of sweat sliding slowly down the bridge of his nose, tickling as it went. He knew that he'd never be invited back after the monologue with which he'd just challenged the crowd. Crowned with a jet-black Ronald McDonald white-man's afro, Keith Green arched his neck, sidled his mouth sideways up to the microphone that lurched out from his piano atop the stage in front of a crowd of thousands, and sang "Jesus Commands Us to Go." He sang that "we're moving so slow" and that the "church refuses to obey."

When the song was over, the reaction was as mixed as the one from the crowd on Mars Hill at Athens after Paul had spoken. Many were angry. Many were moved. Some wondered if he was theologically correct. Coming to faith at twenty years old, Keith Green was saved for a brief eight years before a fatal plane crash would rob the church of his clarion call; nevertheless, his life and death both stimulated an entire generation to join the mission field. Missionary organizations reported record numbers of people signing up for foreign missions during the final year of Keith Green's ministry, as well as in the year afterward, when they traveled the country echoing his final call to the church to get up and go. In our consumer church age today, you'd be lucky if you ever heard something as challenging from a Christian microphone, but when you recruit people to come with you on a mission-focused strike team, you're asking them to do something radical, whether or not they realize it.

You have to give it to the cults—young Mormon males press their black suits, don white dress shirts, tie black ties, and saddle their bicycles for approximately two years of their young lives. They do it in dedication to their mission to expand the borders of Joseph Smith's kingdom of make-believe. Counter-cult apologist Walter Martin used to ask, "Are you willing to do for the truth what the cults do for a lie?"

My strong conviction is that every Christian should answer that question by committing to participate in a church plant for at least two years during their lifetime. It will not only permanently and dramatically transform how they view church, but it will also wreck them for anything else besides the front lines of mission. Once you've been on mission, there's no going back to the status quo. The first casualty of those who adopt this New Testament mode of ministry is that they become fixated with *expanding outward* instead of *building upward*, putting them at odds with many existing churches in the West. The bait of a bigger widescreen, a better website, a larger parking lot, a more comfortable sanctuary seat, and multiple services no longer appeals and excites.

Paul's strike teams[1] were chosen very carefully based on his strategy. On Paul's first missionary journey, Paul and Barnabas went to Cyprus and Turkey; each of them was a native of one of the places they were trying to reach. On his second missionary journey, he strategically chose a Hellenistic Jew, Timothy, from the region of Galatia to accompany him through that region. Leaving Ephesus on his third missionary journey, he set out in Acts 20:4 with eight strike team members, each carefully selected from one of four ethnic groups, who could be divided and split off into teams of two:

- Sopater, son of Pyrrhus, from *Berea* (assuming Paul goes with Sopater to finish the work started there)
- Aristarchus and Secondus from *Thessalonica*
- Gaius and Timothy from *Derbe*
- Tychicus and Trophimus from the *province of Asia*

---

1. I will use the term "strike team" during this chapter rather than "core team" or "launch team." In recent years, some have opted to swap out core team due to hurt feelings that may arise when the church has launched. Ed Stetzer argues that "launch team" has less of a chance to demoralize a church. The issue that I take with this is threefold:

    i. Some people are only meant to be at a church plant for short periods of time. The whole concept of apostolic ministry implies this.

    ii. Planters should not encourage people to come and build crowds. Instead, a focus on quality over quantity will help form the team in a way that fosters transformation. Having a superficial group who is not invested in people feels forced and disingenuous.

    iii. Calling the same behavior by a different name will not change the way that people feel about it if they've started to develop relationships during the most important phase of a church's relational stage of development.

Paul was strategic and intentional about ethnicity in his recruitment of team members, and "deliberately manned his team in order to execute his strategy in the most effective manner."[2]

TYPES OF STRIKE TEAMS

The determining factor for recruiting strike team members is to identify which type of strike team you are forming. There are a number of different ways planters can organize their tactical entrance into a target community. Jesus picked twelve members and deployed them in teams of two, while the apostles sent Barnabas solo to Antioch. In the end, there is no right or wrong way to deploy. Here are descriptions of the three most common ways of deploying into a community that may assist you in determining what makeup your team requires.

Mitosis Teams

A cell mitosis team is sent by a sending church that hires a planter to serve for a time, and breaks off a chunk of people to accompany the planter to plant another congregation within the same city. In effect, it's a missional church split.

Benefits: Local team members from that area and local support from the sending church

Risks: The sending church's nearby location serves as a constant pull that tempts team members back to the mother ship.

Example: When I planted in Long Beach, the mother ship assembled and deployed a team. I recruited additional team members to train as multipliers, but the sending church was a major player in determining the *where, when,* and *who.*

Parachute Drop Teams

The church planter moves to a new community without a team and starts from scratch, recruiting local team members as the sending church (or denominational body) supports from a distance.

Benefits: Freedom in operations and an inescapable evangelistic pressure that keeps mission front-and-center in the planter's mind

Risks: Most expensive model, with a failure rate of 25–50 percent

---

2. Charles Chaney, *Church Planting at the End of the Twentieth Century* (Eugene, OR: Wipf & Stock, 2013), 28.

Example: This was my method in the early days. It cost nothing because I worked bivocationally in the marketplace, and the churches thrived as planting hubs. I slowly developed multiple teams for future deployment.

Migration Teams

An entire team moves with their families to a new city, living and working there to reach the community.

Benefits: Higher success rate, and higher emotional support

Risks: Difficult to find people willing to uproot and re-establish in a new community

Example: Anton Fero and a team of fifteen to thirty people from San Diego, California, migrated to Portland, Oregon. The Common Place planted simultaneously with a CrossFit gym known as Blue House CrossFit. To pull it off, the team served as employees of Blue House and even shared Fero's cramped living quarters, initially.

METHODS OF ACQUIRING A STRIKE TEAM

Once you've determined your method of deployment, you are ready to recruit. Aptitude for recruiting is part of the apostolic planter's skill set, but there are different tactical methods you can use when you go about acquiring a strike team. The biblical examples of recruiting strike teams are, themselves, diverse.

Straight Recruitment

Barnabas directly recruited Paul in Acts 11:25. Planters recruit this way by intentionally contacting friends, previous ministry colleagues, seminary classmates, or somebody suggested by their friends.

The Quickening

In the 1980s film *Highlander*, a race known as the Immortals were drawn towards each other across continents and centuries. The quickening phenomenon is when God draws your team together and you can feel that something mystical is taking place. People may suddenly turn up in your life and display a kindred passion to reach the lost in your area, just like when Apollos made his way through Corinth and Ephesus, colliding with Aquila and Priscilla and eventually joining Paul's posse. When the quickening happens, planters become aware they are not the ones in control.

Discipling Your Own

In the same way that the most serious coffee lovers graduate to roasting their own beans, apostolic planters eventually learn to intentionally disciple their own strike teams. This was Paul's chosen methodology of recruiting. Consider the amazing coworkers Paul recruited from churches he planted:[3]

Strike Team Member	Church Discipled From
Timothy	Lystra (Acts 16:1)
Gaius	Derbe (Acts 20:4)
Aristarchus, Secundus	Thessalonica (Acts 20:4, 27:2)
Sopater	Berea (Acts 20:4)
Priscilla, Aquila,	Corinth (Acts 18:2)
Stephanus	Corinth (1 Cor. 16:15–17)
Erastus	Corinth (Rom. 16:23)
Achaicus	Corinth (1 Cor. 16:15–17)
Fortunatus	Corinth (1 Cor. 16:15–17)
Apollos	Ephesus (Acts 18:24)
Trophimus	Ephesus (Acts 20:4)
Tychicus	Ephesus (Acts 20:4)
Epaphras	Colossae (Col. 4:12)
Archippus	Colossae (Col. 4:17)
Epaphroditus	Philippi (Phil. 2:25)
Phoebe	Cenchrea (Rom. 16:1)

While we're looking at Paul, it's helpful to discuss terminology. Planters have traditionally used the terms "launch team" and "core team" to attempt differentiating between people who stay indefinitely and form the leadership (core team), versus people who only prep for the launch (launch team). Launch teams focus on building a bolstered audience to create an illusion of momentum and energy that helps manipulate crowd dynamics by creating a temporary surge. In contrast, strike teams operate as splinter cells where people are invested in that community, so much so that they can only be peeled off of it

---

3. Graph built from information taken from Gene Wilson and Craig Ott, *Global Church Planting: Biblical Principals and Best Practices for Multiplication* (Grand Rapids: Baker Academic, 2011), 51.

> for the purpose of latching just as passionately onto another people for whom God has burdened them. As defined previously, your strike team that initially plants may move on and should not be confused with a fist team that stays behind fulfilling APEST equipping functions.

WHERE TO BEGIN

The initial stage of recruiting your core team involves sharing your burden with the group of believers you feel might consider joining you on the adventure of a lifetime. Whether over coffee individually or in a room of gathered strangers, there must be a rough outline of the mission, even if you don't know how you're going to accomplish it.

1. **Pray to receive God's burden for your community.** No planter has things fully figured out prior to assembling their team; an APEST team will fill in the blanks as they seek God together. Nevertheless, a wise planter will set aside significant times for prayer asking God to reveal what burdens his heart as he looks at the target community and asking him to sovereignly draw a team together. The things revealed in such prayer are essential in recruiting, as they provide resonance points where likeminded people can begin to agree together about what God is ready to do in the target community.

2. **Write up the first draft of your burden so that you can articulate it to others.** Transfer your burden to paper and clearly articulate what the gospel offers to the community. Other churches have been there before; be ready to share how your plant will uniquely embody the *gospel* and bring hope to your community.

3. **Write a letter inviting them to meet face-to-face.** An invitation letter should simply tell the recipient in a few sentences:
   ○ You would like to meet them along with a small group of people to share a burden.
   ○ They've been selected by a small group of people, and you feel they somehow might be a part of the group.

4. **When you meet with them, determine three varying levels of commitment: pray, give, and go.** We will talk about this more later, but on the handout you give them that night, there should be a tear-off portion they can return to you.

If you've already been engaged on mission and God is working so powerfully around you that you feel the need for a team, better still.

THE THREE PHASES

Proper bonding is the secret sauce to building an effective strike team, and time is the special blend of spices. Imagine traveling with Paul on one of his missionary journeys. The weeks and months of traveling by ship, horse, or on foot gave Paul and Barnabas loads of time during which to forge a tight bond.[4] Since training a team lasts only six to twelve months, my caution to all planters is to milk each and every week, counting every discussion, every teaching opportunity, and every scheduled outreach as precious. Whatever you do, don't be tempted to launch too soon. Even the military stops and trains during wartime, taking the required three months to forge a recruit into a lean, mean, killing machine. You have precious little time to accomplish the daunting task of discipling your strike team into a front-line, gospel-penetrating, multiplying, pioneering, disciple-making, self-replacing missionary band of commandos.

There will be three phases your strike team goes through before deployment, providing time for you to bond cohesively as a team over six to twelve months before your public deployment. The United States Navy uses an acronym that fits the three phases of training their recruits. They call it Recruitment Training Command. Borrowing the term, those three phases are:

Strike Team Timeline

Recruitment Phase: Gathering the team.

Months 1–3	1st–12th meeting

Training Phase: Training the team.

Months 4–9	Training for mission begins

Commitment Phase: Committing to the team.

Months 10–12	High missional engagement

Launch

---

4. Ralph Moore, *Starting a New Church* (Grand Rapids: Baker, 2002), 81. Ralph Moore spends five months developing a core team. Moore once said, "There is no special reason for five months. We did it that way during an early church plant and found that it works well."

THE RECRUITMENT PHASE

The recruitment phase begins with the initial strike team recruitment meeting. In this case, you've invited eight people to your house for a cup of coffee, a bite of cake, and some mind-blowing vision. You're about to share with them what you've put in the letter, hinted at on your phone call, or shared during your face-to-face time, but this time it's with a group—possibly *the* group.

Like the children standing in front of the portal to Narnia yawning open at the back of a wardrobe, the unsuspecting souls gathered with you have no idea that they are about to be transformed into warriors over the next year. According to studies on human dynamics, the ideal interpersonal group tracks at eight to twelve people. Over pleasantries and pouring cups of coffee, you hand them a full copy of your mission statement, explain your history to them, share your burden, and describe how they can support the burden, either by praying for it, funding it, or coming with you. After sharing your burden *briefly* (for no more than ten minutes), *be quiet*. You are listening for echoes now. You've painted the broad brushstrokes, and they will begin to fill in some of the details. At the end of the night, spend time praying and close the night within an hour. At the very end, tell them, "If this resonated with you tonight, I'll see you at the same time (next week or next month)."

Over the better part of the next year, you'll eat together, laugh, talk, get into the Word, pray, and discuss the people you're trying to reach. For this reason, homes work best to allow people to relax and just be themselves. Most of your bonding will happen naturally through prayers and conversations over a plate of food and a drink. You must learn to operate like the Mediterranean peoples who understand best that if you really want to bond with somebody, you share a meal together. During this time, you will be:

- Training them to *think*
- Training them to *be*
- Training them to *minister*

Your team will also bond during this time of transformation. This is why it's important not to jump too soon. Launching before your team is ready is one of the most common mistakes of rookie planters. Therefore, the Samurai proverb states, "You can only fight the way you practice." It is important that you and the team members all grasp the right principles that will lead to the right practices. Too often, we underestimate the value of completing our training.

In the Star Wars saga movie *Empire Strikes Back*, Yoda warned Luke, who tried to leave his training too early, "If you end your training now, if you choose the quick and easy path, as Vader did, you will become an agent of evil." From the side, an apparition of Obi-Wan urges, "Patience . . ." Even the apostles waited in Jerusalem for ten days before starting their mission.

THE TRAINING PHASE

Traditionally, a jump-school instructor teaches you to count after flinging yourself out of the hatch of an airplane before you pull a ripcord. When you show up to jump school ready to jump out of an airplane, they tell you to cool your jets. There's a red light at the front of the plane that has to turn green before you're good to go. Similarly, there's also an ideal "red light" gestation period during which a strike team needs to develop before you jump and pull the launch ripcord. You need to be able to jump in unison so you can hit the ground together and move as a unit, not be scattered around the countryside like matchsticks.

In World War Two, the ability for paratroopers to quickly form up and act like a squad after hitting the ground was impressive, but it was only possible because of the training that was done in boot camp and basic jump training. Think of your strike team development as an essential period of training that will save you time later. Training a team after the jump is both counterproductive and counterintuitive. After all, Jesus trained his team for three years before deploying them fully into mission.

When you fail to train your strike team before the launch, the yeast of unbiblical thinking and wrong expectations begins to work through the dough. The strike team boarding process is like the TSA security check. You need to go through their baggage and search them for contraband. They'll want to bring all kinds of unhelpful things from their last church, past habits, and preconceived notions with them, but you have to convince them that they won't need all that stuff where you're going.

Those months leading up to the launch serve as hands-on discipleship training. Daniel Sinclair identifies four stages during this time: forming, storming, norming, and performing. During the forming stage, people are just testing things out. By the storming phase, the honeymoon is over. People's expectations are being upended, and a new way of church—a whole new culture, really—is being adopted. There may be minor healthy conflicts at this stage as people work through ideological paradigm shifts. Norming is when the values, mission, and vision are starting to become shared among the group.

Lastly, the performing stage happens when the team can effectively engage in mission together.[5]

The military knows that it can't have a bunch of individuals running around in a squad. It needs a functioning unit, and to accomplish this, individuals need to stop thinking of themselves as individuals and reinvent themselves as members of a body with specific functions that act on behalf of the squad. The first step in this identity transformation is to buzz the head of every recruit, hand out identical standard-issue clothing, and teach him or her to march in formation as a single unit. The army requires this to instill the principle that there are no individuals in a squad. Individuality gets people killed. Therefore, they have to train them to think as a unit.

In the same way, you have to teach a church planting core team about their corporate identity. They need to know that they're no longer Christian consumers who attend church services to meet their own needs. They are no longer merely autonomous individuals. Seeds, soldiers, and missionaries all fall to the ground and die so they may bear more fruit. When Paul spoke to Timothy, he told him to reframe how he saw himself: "Join with me in suffering, like a good soldier of Christ Jesus" (2 Tim. 2:3).

They need to know that they are picking a fight with the enemy, and that the second they enlist, they are in that enemy's crosshairs. Whenever recruits join one of my core teams, I shake their hands and issue both a congratulatory welcome and my condolences in the same breath. It's usually something like, "Welcome to the team. I'm sorry. Your life is about to fall apart." In the same way, every drill sergeant is aware that he's training soldiers for death via deployment. As Bonhoeffer has so often been quoted as saying (usually without any link being made to explain the missional context of the statement), "When Jesus bids a man to follow him, he bids us come and die."[6]

This is where God's presence is most profoundly felt and experienced: on the front lines. Take it from a front-line missionary. Jesus commends the outward propulsion of a missionary leaving father, mother, brothers, and sisters because it is what he himself did in leaving his Father and his home to go on mission for us. If you desire to be Christlike, you *must* be on mission. Jesus chose to make his disciples *en route* to their deployment. John Bunyan, puritan author of *The Pilgrim's Progress*, echoes this concept in his famous hymn:

Who would true valor see,
Let him come hither;

---

5. Daniel Sinclair, *Vision of the Possible* (Downers Grove, IL: InterVarsity Press, 2012), 39.
6. Dietrich Bonhoeffer, *The Cost of Discipleship* (New York: Macmillan,1963), 89.

One here will constant be,
Come wind, come weather;
There's no discouragement
Shall make him once relent
His first avowed intent
To be a pilgrim.[7]

TRAINING AND PLANTOLOGY

Plantology is the study of the science of church planting, and that is translated as the science of mission. You're not training your team to be church planters; you're training them to be missionaries, or disciples. Whenever you train people to practice the principles of plantology on a micro level, you will see the fruit on a macro level. This is why a church was planted in Antioch; the apostles didn't train the people to plant, they trained them to be disciple makers. The timeless principles of plantology are not rocket science, but natural cause-and-effect principles we've witnessed in the early church.

Briefly review the great commission to get an overview of plantology principles. This is what you want them to be able to do:

1. Go—Take yourself and the gospel where it is not; have an outward leaning posture as a missionary.
2. Preach the gospel—Proclaim Christ with your words and life.
3. Make disciples—Reproduce yourself.

These three components have gone by other names but remain three distinct ingredients to Jesus's discipleship. Bill Donahue identifies them as the truth (teaching), the table (time), and the towel (tactics).[8] When believers learn to do these three things on a micro (individual) level, churches will be planted on a macro (community) level. This is why Paul could take the gospel to anyone, anywhere, anytime. These timeless principles will have the same cause and effect when implemented today.

In most cases, believers are not trained to do all three of these. Discipleship, the model and practice that Jesus spent the majority of his time training others to do, has been particularly neglected and even lost in many instances.

---

7. John Bunyan, *The Pilgrim's Progress: From This World to That Which Is to Come*, 32nd ed. (London: W. Johnston, 1771), Part II, 157.

8. Bill Donahue, *The Irresistible Community: An Invitation to Life Together* (Grand Rapids: Baker, 2105), 21.

The type of discipleship that *Church Plantology* focuses on is based on Jesus's model of discipling the Twelve, so we'll call it discipology. It's not rocket science, but consists of three key practices:

1. Teaching—how to think
2. Time—how to be
3. Tactics—how to act

Discipology

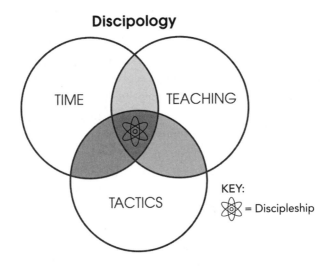

Almost any small group experiences teaching. Missional church members spend time outside the meetings, building relationship and just doing life together. You've likely been part of groups that say, "Right. Get out there. Time to put into practice what you've been learning." We become experts at talking about things we never do. We talk about reaching the world without ever venturing forth to do anything intentionally in it. If you're not careful, small groups can become a breeding ground for Christians who are experts on inactivity.

Jesus recognized this in his disciples and therefore sent them out into the villages of Judea. He actually did this twice, but have you ever wondered why? The pattern isn't one-and-done; it is repeated, like respiration. There should be a rhythm to our discipleship, as natural as breathing: We take in knowledge, fellowship, and encouragement in one giant breath, and then exhale faith, risk, and mission with the same regularity. Inhale. Exhale. Just breathe. Gather. Scatter. Breathe in. Breathe out.

Many of our small groups have been holding their collective breath for years, turning blue and hypoxic. Here's the reality: You can't fully inhale again until you've fully exhaled. In this rhythm of gathering and scattering, I've watched small groups become core teams, and pew sitters become leaders. What if our gathering were like inhaling, and our scattering were like exhaling? What if these two things became natural to every Christian in our churches? Wouldn't we find that we'd be making disciples and multiplying churches?

TEACHING—HOW TO THINK

After training teams for fifteen years, overseas and in urban contexts, I've learned to follow a consistent pattern in my training over the span of the launch year. I have broken the twelve-month training cycle down into:

1. The first three months
2. The next six months
3. The final three months

Here is the ideal twelve-month training schedule that I use to train strike teams:

Strike Team Teaching Timeline

Recruitment Phase

Months 1–3	Gospel Centered Life

Commitment Phase

Months 4–9	Jump School Training

Pre-Launch

Months 10–12	Titus

Launch

Year 2	Acts

The First Quarter: The Recruitment Phase

I typically start with something called *The Gospel Centered Life* by Bob Thune and Will Walker.[9] I recommend it to every church planting strike team, and to any leaders I train, because it is written with the assumption that Christians don't understand the gospel. The gospel won't penetrate anyone else's heart if it hasn't penetrated yours.

---

9. Bob Thune and Will Walker, *The Gospel-Centered Life: A Nine-Lesson Study* (Greensboro, NC: New Growth, 2009).

Thune and Walker maintain that most of us started our journey to Christ with a large view of the cross. Our view of our own sin and God's holiness were huge, and thus our view of the cross was massive—the symbol of grace dominated our spirituality. But over time, through behavior modification, we learned to minimize God's holiness through thinking we weren't actually that bad anymore. As time progressed, our view of the cross has grown small, and with it our appreciation of grace has been minimized. When rightly understood, the gospel allows believers to grow in both the awareness of their own sinfulness and the awareness of God's holiness. We grow in our understanding that God is holier than we could ever conceive and, as a result, our need for the cross and the grace of God to cover us grows as well.

The Next Six Months: The Training Phase

The most common question I hear is, *"How do I train my team?"* In response, I developed a six-month core team training designed to train your team between the commitment cut off and the church's launch, called *Jump School*.[10] This is the core chunk of training necessary to develop them into a planting strike team.

The Final Quarter: Training During the Commitment Phase

After training them for nine months (through *Gospel Centered Life* and *Jump School Core Team Training*), my final three months are spent training them through the book of Titus. Titus was the powerhouse apostolic trainee of Paul, as is evidenced by the challenging nature of the missions that Paul handed down to him. Contrast his mandate with that of Timothy, who had to be told to "do the work of an evangelist" (2 Tim. 4:5). Titus was frontline to the core. His Mission Impossible manila folder contained the letter of Titus with a photograph of the isle of Crete. In that briefing, he was told that his mission, should he choose to accept it, was to church plant in every major city by establishing leadership (*or fist teams*) there (Tit. 1:5). Multigenerational discipleship was the method advised—teach "reliable people who will also be qualified to teach others" (2 Tim. 2:2). If Acts is the narrative church planting book of the New Testament, then Titus is the church planting epistle. It's not by accident that Paul writes to a serial church planter with discipleship directives. Paul is directing Titus to employ plantology principles on the ground in Crete.

---

10. You can find *Jump School Core Team Training* at ministryninja.com.

TIME—HOW TO BE

The next part of discipleship involves modeling the change you'd like them to be in the world.[11] The first training regards the value of prayer. In the upper room, prayer was instilled into the early church, and the pattern of an Acts 1 type of prayer followed by an Acts 2 type of power should be an evangelistic cycle woven right into your church plant's rhythms. Teaching your team to be a people of prayer will bolster confidence in God's power. "Trust God but keep your powder dry" is a helpful maxim.

After doing everything humanly possible, prayer is the confession of dependency; the best evidence of a trusting heart is a praying mind. Desperate people pray well. Vitus Theodorus, a German theologian and friend of Martin Luther wrote of him, "I overheard him in prayer, but, good God, with what life and spirit did he pray! It was with so much reverence as if he were speaking to God, yet with so much confidence, as if he had been speaking to his friend."[12]

Charles Spurgeon learned to lean on God in desperation after being thrust into pastoral ministry at the young age of seventeen, just one year after his conversion, and then quickly becoming a popular preacher at the largest church in London. Dr. Wayland Hoyt recalled praying with Spurgeon, and afterward wrote,

> I was walking with him in the woods one day just outside London and as we strolled under the shadow of summer foliage, we came upon a log lying along the path. "Come," he said as naturally as one would say it if he were hungry and bread was put before him, "come let us pray." Kneeling beside the log he lifted his soul to God in the most loving yet reverent prayer. Then rising from his knees he went strolling on, talking about this and that. The prayer was no parenthesis interjected. It was something that belonged as much to the habit of his mind as breathing did to the habit of his body.[13]

In the mission field, prayer often happens on the go. Prayer becomes less about devotional time, and more about devotion. Wesley once wrote,

---

11. This is a modified Gandhi quote, "Be the change you want to see in the world." Mahatma Gandhi, *The Collected Works of Mahatma Gandhi*, Volume XII, April 1913 to December 1914. (Gujarati, India: Indian Opinion, gandhiheritageportal.org, 1913), 156. As Alan Hirsch remarked in a meeting I attended, "The best way to challenge the current system is to model a better one."

12. Charles Spurgeon, *Lectures to My Students* (Pantianos Classics ebook edition, first published in 1875), 24.

13. Wayland Hoyt, *Walks and Talks with Charles H. Spurgeon* (Philadelphia: American Baptist Publication Society, 1892), 10.

Frequently, it seems, it was not so much the preaching as the praying of the men that arrested attention. The two men might join a burial party, and in the midst of those kneeling and wailing in the traditional manner at a graveside, pour out fervent and sympathetic prayers. It was thus that many for the first time heard of eternal life and a loving heavenly father. The missionaries were ready to pray in every place. On one occasion a priest looked out of his church door for an overdue wedding party he was expecting. To his surprise he saw them kneeling on the road outside, with Ouseley also on his knees praying and tears flowing. Long before, Augustine had once said, the Christian teacher will succeed more by piety in prayer than by gifts of oratory.[14]

You can only disciple people by modeling desired behaviors, therefore, ensure that prayer is a regular rhythm of all that you do personally and corporately.

- Pray alone.
- Pray together with people every time you meet with them.
- Pray before your gatherings and invite people in.
- Pray during your gatherings and model it to all present.
- Ask people to pray for you, modeling yourself as someone who is dependent on the prayers of others, as Paul did in every letter.

Never let it be said of your church that Jesus stands outside the door and knocks. In modeling prayer, you will be modeling the core practice out of which everything else springs, including mission.

Prayer is not the only thing you will model to your team. As you spend time with your team, they will be observing everything you do, including how you speak with your neighbors, family, and friends. Every part of your life is on display, and spending time with others is the most unconscious yet powerful method of discipleship.

Without realizing it, my youth pastor mentored me by taking me into his house after our late-night outreaches and feeding me anything he had, which usually wasn't much. Over the years, I've realized that I ate that poor guy out of house and home; he will never know, until it is revealed in the clarity of eternity, how much he invested in me during those late-night hours. We ate tacos, reviewed that night's ministry, and laughed until we cried, poking fun at infomercials, B-movies, and low-budget cable access shows. Shadowing this man

---

14. Quoted in Iain H. Murray, *Wesley and the Men Who Followed* (Carlisle, PA: Banner of Truth Trust, 2003), 152.

of God as he unwound on the downside of intense frontline ministry, I learned what it meant to be a disciple. I'm convinced it was no different with the Twelve.

It is extremely important during this time to start sizing people up and getting a feel for them. There will be a wide range of people in your group, and time is the only way to truly tell who they really are, which is why Paul warned about being "hasty in the laying on of hands" (1 Tim. 5:22). Over time, you will observe members of your team climbing the highest heights, and you will also see them diving to unthinkable depths. All of this will unfold as you share joys and weep over sorrows with one another, carrying one another to God in prayer. I'm convinced that laughter and tears have some of the most powerful bonding properties, and I'm sure Jesus had this strategy in mind when he lived with and carried twelve poor, misguided men for three years. As a firefighter, I can attest to the raucous laughter that flows when twelve guys get together for any length of time. I'm certain that these twelve young men would have had their share of antics. Doing life together involves *all aspects of life* together.

TACTICS—HOW TO ACT

The word *tactics* refers to training. The military uses field exercises to train soldiers on the ground. These tactical maneuvers prevent all students from being theorists. The church has enough of those. Your plant will produce practitioners, but you must train them tactically. Jesus said that when a student was fully grown, he would be like his teacher. We can't fully become like Jesus until we begin to minister like he did. His goal for the disciples was that they would do "greater things than these" (John 14:12). Every leader should desire that their team grows beyond them and learns to minister more effectively than they can. Somehow, we've misunderstood ministry as "doing for" people, rather than "equipping them to do."

In order to develop the Twelve into powerful ministers, Jesus used the following methods of training:

1. Jesus *modeled ministry* for them: Jesus tirelessly healed, preached, and dealt with people's souls so that the disciples could learn by watching him.
2. Jesus *created opportunity*: Jesus provided opportunities for the Twelve to minister. When he fed the 5,000, he actually asked them to feed the people, and the miracle took place in their hands while he sat back and watched them minister. He empowered them to heal and sent them out into all the regions of Galilee. He sent not only the Twelve, but also the seventy-two to accompany them on the second missionary journey. This gave the disciples practice sharing ministry and training others.

3. *Jesus debriefed*: Jesus mentored them afterward. After the feeding of the 5,000, he debriefed with them in the boat, noting that they had not learned the lesson of the loaves (Mark 8:14–21). In every activity, there was a lesson to be learned, and Jesus followed up everything they did by reinforcing their experience with principles. After they attempted an exorcism and failed, Jesus told them that "this kind cannot be driven out by anything but prayer" (Mark 9:29 ESV).

4. Jesus *released* them: Not only did he release them periodically on short-term missions, but he then released them long-term after his ascension by sending the Spirit and his empowering at Pentecost.

Similarly, Paul's methods of discipling his team mirrored Jesus's pattern:

1. *Paul modeled*: He took Timothy, Silas, and others with him on the road.
2. *Paul created opportunity*: He allowed them to preach and baptize. This is the reason that Paul baptized only a few. He was sharing his ministry with his team.
3. *Paul debriefed*: The epistles are the best glimpse that we see into the mentoring relationship Paul had with his fellow workers, and every pastoral epistle is an example of the type of debriefing Paul did with his team as they traveled and ministered together.
4. *Paul released:* Paul deployed his fellow workers all across the map of the Mediterranean.

When you train your planters tactically, you must implement these four stages. You cannot skip stages and merely turn them loose without following these steps. Therefore, you will need to intentionally hardwire each of these four methods into your tactical training aspect of discipleship.

STARTING WITH THE LOST

Many teams busy themselves with logos, bank accounts, buildings, and websites, but Paul always began with outreach. You can't merely start with gathering Christians and expect the lost to magically turn up at your shindig. Targeting the lost prevents magical thinking. Outreach along the way is an essential part of developing the bond within your team. You can go door-to-door in the projects, like Francis Chan in the Tenderloin district, asking what prayer needs people have and providing opportunities to meet physical needs. Your team can also get involved with community events, volunteering to serve coffee at an event to facilitate conversations. You can feed the homeless or visit recovering addicts in a halfway house. Visit prisons, have a cookout in the park, offer to feed the hungry, or do anything that will deploy your people into the community you intend to reach. You may simply build relationships with your neighbors and talk to them about spiritual things over dinner. Without this, you can have the best food laid out at your launch, the coolest logo, and the best worship band, but the only people who will benefit are the Christians you invite.

The real work of church planting is gospel penetration, gospel saturation, and gospel maturation. *If your people are going to reach the ones nobody is reaching, they're going to have to go where nobody is going and do what nobody is doing.* Whitefield commented on visiting the poor, "It is remarkable that our Lord sent out his Apostles on short term missions before they were so solemnly authorized at the day of Pentecost. Would the Heads and Tutors of our Universities follow His example . . ." Whitefield urges the students to be sent to poorhouses and prisons to jumpstart their ministries.[15]

THE COMMITMENT PHASE

John and Andrew staggered behind Jesus after John the Baptist's Lamb of God declaration, not quite sure why, until Jesus turned around and asked, "What are you seeking?" The truth is, they didn't know, and supplied a bogus answer, "Where are you staying?" (John 1:38). It was a fumbled response to a more serious question. The people who follow you onto this mission venture may not know completely why they've taken those next steps, and this initial uncertainty is more than acceptable.

Preferably, you're not meeting on a Sunday morning, so your team doesn't have to ditch their own churches before they've fully committed to coming with you. They're just getting a feel for what you're about to do. Don't worry if they don't fully understand where you're going overnight. Look to Jesus and his patience with the Twelve during their three years traveling daily with him, gathering up the fragments of his vision, readjusting when they understood it, but questioning it when they didn't.

Months into the game, however, you'll need to know who is truly on the team with you. At that point you need to know because there are tasks to do, people to reach, and enemy strongholds to demolish. This is like the time Gideon crossed the stream to conquer Midian. At this time, you'll need to take note of who is drinking from their hands and who is lapping like a dog. It's cut-off time; time to put up or shut up. You've finished nailing your colors to the mast, and you need

---

15. Luke Tyerman, *The Life of the Reverend George Whitefield*, vol. I (Azle, TX: Need of the Times Publishers, 1995), 42.

to know who is ready to take to the high seas before you leave port. Six months out from launch is when the commitment cut-off needs to happen. Never be tempted to take legalistic pharisees, toxic mutants, or agenda-driven axe grinders onto your team. You may think you need them. You don't. Numbers don't validate you as a leader, and in the beginning, quality trumps quantity.

THE LAUNCH

With so much of a church starter's energies being focused on starting a Sunday service, many have wondered whether or not there is validity in setting a launch date for church planters. On the one hand, you have to train and activate the team you have before you deploy them. Jesus recruited the team in the early days of his public ministry and spent a lot of time with them in private. He had a launch date set for his ministry and argued that his mother was asking him to reveal who he was before his time at the wedding of Cana of Galilee.

Like a strike team, Jesus actively trained the Twelve on the field, equipping them for exorcisms and miracles, and ministering to people's needs, but he didn't properly activate and empower them for mission until Pentecost. As they were filled with the Spirit and empowered in their gifting, the Jerusalem church went public, resulting in conversions. Despite how much you may hear about the centrality of a public worship launch to the church starting process, there is no disputing that the church itself went public in Jerusalem on the day of Pentecost in 33 AD, despite being active in training for mission prior to that date. Launches are biblical, but the difference between the launch of a church start and a church plant is what you do to get there. The outreach we've already discussed is essential to distinguishing what type of launch you'll have.

The "If you launch it, they will come" mentality is a myth. The lost won't, anyway. Attracting a crowd is the way church starters measure a successful launch. But true harvesting only comes through consistent sowing and watering. The big launch method promotes the idea that marketing can replace the sowing and watering on which real gospel work is built. Crowds may come through marketing, but treating your church launch like the grand opening of a business will guarantee a temporary result. Just remember, planter, that by the end of your first Sunday, after all that effort, expense, and exhaustion, you can bank on one thing: You will never see most of those people again.

The second and third weeks after a "successful" big launch often leave first-time planters bewildered and confused. Whenever we divorce God's presence from our time together, the "church" becomes an idol, a thing put in the place of first importance instead of the Lord. Personally, I've never given a rip about any church I've planted as an entity or an institution. I care about the people. Although I form strong bonds with my teams, I secretly pray that they will have gone a thousand miles in a million different directions within a year's time. The launch isn't the endgame, even though many church plants treat it as such.

That all being said, though, launches are certainly exciting. Like pulling a ripcord on one's parachute from a few thousand feet up in the air, there is nothing as exhilarating as the backside of your public launch. Most want to climb back up thousands of feet and jump all over again before they've even had time to repack their parachutes.

A few words about planning your public launch: First of all, planning it is essential. Therefore, a date needs to be set in stone before you even put the other dates on the calendar. You'll be tempted to keep moving it back, but don't give in to the temptation to put off your launch. That temptation comes from nerves and fear, so draw a line in the sand from day one and refuse to move it. Unless you commit to that principle, you're going to find yourself increasingly tempted to change it the closer you get to the date. Start from the launch date and work backward, determining how long your team needs to bond before you start inviting the lost to your church. Whether you plan to launch out of a coffee shop, community center, nightclub, or even your house, commit as a team and hold each other accountable to launching on the original date upon which you agreed.

Don't make the mistake of thinking of the launch as giving birth to a baby, like the pregnancy is over. The launch is just the end of the first trimester, and it needs to be bathed in prayer before, during, and after. Praying for the work of the Holy Spirit in people's lives before your launch so that they subsequently turn up on the day of the launch is the most important lead-up to the launch itself. Remember, Pentecost happened after ten days of intense prayer! Your launch should be no different. If you're desperate enough, you'll either fling yourself onto God in dependence and powerlessness before your launch, or afterward you will wish you had.

LAUNCH PRO TIPS

- If you're in a school or community center, make sure you tip the caretaker. If you tip the caretaker every week for cleaning up, it not only builds good relations, it also shows appreciation for looking after you. And, come Monday, they will. In fact, they will come along behind you to make sure that you've not left any messes because it's in their best interest to keep you there. You are worth extra cash every month to them. If anyone objects to this practice, remind them that such custodians rarely receive any increase in pay due to a church's rental of the space, no matter what you pay the facility owners in rent. Facility managers often simply bank the rental revenue and expect the same results from their custodial teams. Your presence will mean extra work for the custodial staff with few accompanying incentives other than your care, kindness, and goodwill. It is wise to appoint a cleanup captain who can request a checklist from the custodian and ensure that the church leaves things in good order. Also, this person can be put in charge of initiating a well-timed gift basket, prayer note, box of donuts, gift card, thank you note, or moment of recognition to accompany the financial tips. This will keep lines of communication open and protect the relationship as it unfolds!

- Buy all the facility's employees a gift card from a coffee shop or anywhere else that seems appropriate. This is maintenance and part of being a blessing and giving grace. It doesn't matter if it's a school, a community center, or a library. You want to give gifts to be a blessing, with a simple note that reads, "Thank you for being a blessing to our community." You'd be surprised how far this might go if you do it at the beginning of the school year, at Christmas, Easter, and for summer break. You can also humanize the church by leaving thank you notes in the rooms you use. You can also make it a point to pray for the building's other occupants in your service and let them know you prayed for them while in their space; one day, they might trust you enough to share their prayer concerns or needs with your team.

- Walk through the parking lot and try to experience everything like somebody who has never been to a church gathering before. Keep in mind the fear and anxiety they may feel, and then do everything within your power to make sure that signs are posted and that people feel welcome. When you throw a party for kids, put balloons on the gate and a sign out front for people who've never been there. It's common sense, but when it comes to church, people get critical of it or simply forget to do it. When we've made signs for newcomers, we've included things from the gospels, such as:

  - Are you weary and tired? Find rest for your soul.
  - You are now entering a nonreligious zone.
  - No perfect people allowed.

REFLECT

- Are you the leader who will assemble a strike team? Are you an aspiring strike team member who needs a leader?

DISCUSS

- Can you identify any additional strengths and weaknesses for the three types of strike teams: Cell Mitosis, Parachute Drop, and Team Migration?
- The author describes methods for assembling a strike team. How might they look different if you are already close with many members of your local fellowship?
- Does your denomination, fellowship, or organization have a process for forming and deploying strike teams? How does it compare to the phases described in this chapter: recruitment, training, commitment?
- The three phases in this chapter take about twelve months. The second phase also takes about twelve months. Training has three subphases: commitment phase (three months), pre-launch (six months), and launch (three months). How can these timelines be reconciled?
- The author argues that strike teams must start with the lost. What is his reasoning? What is the right proportion of "convert growth" to "transfer growth" in a church plant? Why?
- Review the "pro tips" sidebar. Are there any that surprised you? What would you add?

CHALLENGE

- Compare Jesus's training methods (e.g., modeling, creating opportunity, debriefing, releasing) and Paul's with yours. How similar are they? What are you missing?

9

CHURCH PLANTING DRIVES AND BURDENS

We must learn to regard people less in the
light of what they do or omit to do, and
more in the light of what they suffer.

—DIETRICH BONHOEFFER,
LETTERS AND PAPERS FROM PRISON

All across North America, planters are being trained to fill out Will
Mancini's Kingdom Concept and Vision Frame from the book *Church
Unique* to hone their mission and vision.[1] While I greatly appreciate Will's
hard work and expertise in focusing leaders of established churches on narrowing their focus, I would argue that a church planter isn't quite ready for this
level of detail. I realize that to suggest an alternative is tantamount to church
leadership blasphemy, but after years of planting and training planters, I would
start somewhere else. *Church Unique* is extremely useful for established pastors
and leaders, but planters on the ground tend to start with a burden. To explain
this deviation from otherwise normative tools, we must explore what drives the
planter to plant.

DRIVES

Planters are driven, and most planters are driven by a specific burden. That
drive will largely determine what type of church will be planted, or what we

---

1. Will Mancini, *Church Unique: How Missional Leaders Cast Vision, Capture Culture, and Create Movement* (San Francisco: Jossey-Bass, 2008).

call "the expression of church." The nature of those burdens can vary. Some planters are burdened by mission, others by theology, and some by ecclesiological considerations. Because planters are driven by different burdens, they aren't often motivated by theorists and theologians pontificating on battling ideologies and clamoring to be heard about what church planting is and should be. Such academics rush in like bystanders at the scene of an accident, offering their opinions and cluttering the scene of an emergency. As the church bleeds out, their panicked cries offer bits of information irrelevant to the job at hand.

As a fire fighter, one of the first tasks I was expected to perform in a crisis was to get loud bystanders to back up out of the way and then create a perimeter so the actual task of lifesaving could happen. Sometimes, practitioners on the ground quietly get on with it, while the theorists' loud observations merely confuse the scene. Unfortunately, with all the noise, planters can't hear their own thoughts. Therefore, the aim of this chapter is to assist the planter in hearing what that still small voice has been saying and to give language to what their heart is telling them. Dhati Lewis calls this planting from burden.[2] This burden informs what the planter feels they *must* do. Paul testified to Agrippa that he was not disobedient to the vision he received from heaven (Acts 26:19).

The drives and expressions of church planting that are explored in this chapter have been gleaned on the other side of harvesting specific fruit from particular labor in a much wider field of mission. Many prevalent philosophies of church planting are fads, which are more microwaved than marinated,[3] while others are timeless. Yet each bears fruit in its season. A long-view analysis will not stop people from asserting that their church planting philosophy constitutes the Holy Grail that will restore eternal sustenance to all of Christendom. More often than not, their belief holds the key to "a way" rather than "the way" to plant.

John Godfrey Saxe's much quoted, but rarely read, poem *Blind Men and the Elephant* signals the danger of assuming that one's way should become everyone's way. This poem is often used by pluralists to indicate that no single world religion has a corner on understanding God. However, in this discussion, it can also be used as a metaphor for our efforts to master the mystery of church planting and our temptation to reduce it to something that can be mastered by our favorite method or brand of planting:

> It was six men of Indostan,
> > To learning much inclined,

---

2. Dhati Lewis, *Among Wolves: Disciple-Making in the City* (Nashville: Broadman & Holman, 2017), 14.

3. This is a take on the turn of phrase "Vision is marinated, not microwaved," attributed to Jason Hess in Jason Crandall, *Proliferate: A Church Planting Strategy for Everyday Churches* (Houston: Lucid, 2017), 73.

Who went to see the Elephant
   (Though all of them were blind),
That each by observation
   Might satisfy his mind.

The *First* approach'd the Elephant,
   And happening to fall
Against his broad and sturdy side,
   At once began to bawl:
"God bless me!—but the Elephant
   Is very like a wall!"

The *Second*, feeling of the tusk,
   Cried: "Ho!—what have we here
So very round and smooth and sharp?
   To me 't is mighty clear,
This wonder of an Elephant
   Is very like a spear!"

The *Third* approached the animal,
   And happening to take
The squirming trunk within his hands,
   Thus boldly up and spake:
"I see," quoth he, "the Elephant
   Is very like a snake!"

The *Fourth* reached out his eager hand,
   And felt about the knee:
"What most this wondrous beast is like
   Is mighty plain," quoth he,
"'Tis clear enough the Elephant
   Is very like a tree!"

The *Fifth*, who chanced to touch the ear,
   Said: "E'en the blindest man
Can tell what this resembles most;
   Deny the fact who can,
This marvel of an Elephant
   Is very like a fan!"

The *Sixth* no sooner had begun
    About the beast to grope,
Than, seizing on the swinging tail
    That fell within his scope,
"I see," quoth he, "the Elephant
    Is very like a rope!"

And so these men of Indostan
    Disputed loud and long,
Each in his own opinion
    Exceeding stiff and strong,
Though each was partly in the right,
    And all were in the wrong!

MORAL.
So, oft in theologic wars
    The disputants, I ween,
Rail on in utter ignorance
    Of what each other mean;
And prate about an Elephant
Not one of them has seen![4]

No matter how many books you read, philosophies you imbibe, or degrees you have in missional theology, you can still only hold so many pieces of the church planting elephant at once. With every church planted, you will discover yet another handful of pachyderm anatomy. Each part of the elephant is learned on a rotating journey around it. Successive ecclesiastical adventures are the equivalent of a seminary education, allowing the planter to experiment, majoring on one part of the elephant, while possibly minoring on another. It is possible that the adoption of a wider array of beliefs about church planting will result in greater fruit for the harvest; a seasoned planter, however, can both appreciate the beauty of a single flower and still carefully arrange each belief into a vase.

This chapter will attempt to allow for the likelihood that various parts of the methodology elephant are valid at the same time, specifically because of the role that APEST plays in diversifying the expression of style in various types of plants. This is because various ideologies of true value don't normally come

---

4. John Godfrey-Sax, *The Poems of John Godfrey Sax* (Boston: Osgood and Company, 1873), 277.

through reading books, any more than an ability to box could be gained by viewing a Rocky film. The convictions forged in church planting are a result of ample batches of trial and error. The deepest wisdom is often gleaned from experience, for a truth delivered externally is nowhere as powerful as a truth arrived at internally. Such revelatory encounters provide "the why behind the what." When we were children, our parents warned about hot stoves externally, but pain was a more effective teacher and powerfully ingrained deep convictions about them internally.

With different handfuls of elephant in tow, we approach one another, unaware that there's yet more of it to explore. We often believe that our fist clenches the "truly true" part of the elephant, the *essentia pachydermus,* but in time, we learn our foolishness. As the saying goes, "Young men think old men are fools. Old men know young men are fools," and so it is with noob and veteran planters. Hindsight reveals as much foolishness as it does wisdom. All parts of an elephant are equally valid parts of the beast and prove vitally important for differing functions. An elephant would cease to be a complete elephant with any of these parts removed. So, the church has various functions and forms, and we would do well to heed the word of caution at the beginning of the chapter to check our own attitudes and beliefs against our own experiences. Perhaps our opinions are narrow simply because our experiences are meager. When it comes to experience and enlightenment, they who sow sparingly also reap sparingly, while they who sow abundantly in experiences and faith ventures also reap abundantly.

ORTHODOXY DETERMINES ORTHOPRAXY

Before we can develop church planting praxis, we first need to look at our church planting theory. Orthopraxy (the right way of doing things) builds upon the foundation of orthodoxy (the right way of thinking). As our priorities are ordered out of our beliefs, they will inform our church planting practices more than any other factor. If planters dig deeply enough, they will discover not only how they plant, but why they plant at all. Unfortunately, many planters are never encouraged to think on that level; they are given a quick formula that encourages them to fill in the boxes in a type of ecclesiastical paint-by-numbers. Multiple church planting networks have been formed either because a set of core beliefs was lacking in another network or because the priorities and practices of the existing networks were seen to be insufficient.

The combined core beliefs about what church planting is (orthodoxy) and how it should be done (orthopraxy) form our philosophy of church planting. Any organization's philosophy of church planting becomes a driving force or key motivation for planting. Sometimes a previous negative experience with a church or a network can help the planter rethink their philosophy of planting, leading to them shifting away from a denomination or network. The planter may realign their own beliefs and practices within their own process, or cross over to another network or denomination that models their emerging church planting philosophy. Each time a planter embarks on their mission, there will be a primal drive—a calling related to their philosophy derived from hard-won convictions. Yet, there is a deeper reason that planters sometimes shift and shimmy around networks and denominations, feeling like square pegs in round holes: their APEST makeup.

Church planters are always driven by something, whether for good or ill. One church plant may be driven by theology, another may be burdened by brokenness in a community that cries out for kingdom restoration. Both convictions are important, but the elephant is large, and one can only possess two handfuls. Therefore, in exploring the various parts of the elephant, we discover that the apostle is holding one part, while the evangelist is holding another. Our drives exist in direct proportion to the specific gifting and function that God has appointed in us. Therefore, as I plant with others across the APEST spectrum, the more elephant the church is able to grasp at one time.

The key things that drive planters are theology, ecclesiology, pneumatology, eschatology, and missiology. Each of the drives can be linked to the corresponding APEST role that a planter will fulfill. Each role is driven by a different metric, causing planters to believe that church is "about" something specific. For the apostle, it's all about kingdom expansion. For the shepherd, it's all about community. For the prophet, it's about experiencing God and his presence. Each of these views is valid, with proponents grasping a specific piece of the elephant. When you speak to planters, they express that they are planting a church for the following reasons, and the reasons can give you clues about the planter's drive. Here are some examples:

"People don't know how to worship God. Churches are dead, and I want to see a place where God's majesty is felt and known when you come through the door" (prophetic drive).

"I don't think we're meant to be staring at the back of people's heads. Church should be a place where we all contribute and become family. I want to start a community" (shepherd drive).

Essentially, if you boil down the reasons planters give for planting churches, they will fall into one of these five categories:

Drive	Function
Theologically Driven	Teacher
Ecclesiastically Driven	Shepherd
Missiologically Driven	Evangelist
Pneumatologically Driven	Prophet
Eschatologically Driven	Apostle

Of course, these are all the outworking of Christ's earthly ministry that the church is meant to carry out between his ascension and return "that he might fill all things" (Eph. 4:10). Rather than functioning as five separate ministries, these drives are all aspects of what Christ's full ministry accomplishes on earth. Brad Brisco sees the ongoing ministry of Christ through the church as a continuation of his ministry between his baptism and crucifixion in the following diagram:

Robust Chistology

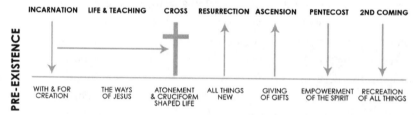

Created by North American Mission Board, copyright ©
2014 by Brad Brisco. Used by permission.

Therefore, each APEST function expresses an aspect of the ongoing ministry of Christ meant to continue on earth after his ascension. This understanding led Leslie Newbigin to conclude, "I have come to feel that the primary reality of which we have to take account in seeking for a Christian impact on public life is the Christian congregation."[5] Therefore, the drive of any planter should be to see Christ fill all things as we flesh out the five aspects of APEST incarnationally, just as he modeled them for us during his earthly ministry. For this reason, David Schwenk notes, "Even today, a congregation usually develops

---

5. Brad Brisco, *Covocational Church Planting* (Alpharetta, GA: SEND Network, 2017), 48.

a vision and commitment which is quite similar to that of the person or persons who planted the congregation . . . the team tremendously affects the form of the congregation."[6]

Let's briefly examine each of these drives and their corresponding APEST functions in order to determine the expression of church plant they likely lead to. In particular, we will examine the nature of what happens when leaders with these burdens meet up with an apostolic planter.

THEOLOGICALLY DRIVEN PLANTS

The planter driven by theology (teacher) seeks to impart a certain degree of knowledge to a community. Since the majority of teachers gravitate towards the Reformed movement, perhaps theology takes the front seat, as in the case of Mark Driscoll, Tim Keller, or the Acts 29 network. From their perspective, most issues in life can trace their roots back to good or bad theology. As Dr. David Martyn Lloyd-Jones used to say, "Bad thinking leads to bad living. Right thinking leads to right living." This view touts that a right understanding of the gospel will realign all of one's life into peace and harmony. Gospel faithfulness is seen as the antidote to works-based salvation and confinement to performance-based religious observance of Christian rules. The church is seen as the foundation and cornerstone of truth (1 Tim. 3:15), the herald of the gospel to a community. Therefore, in such churches, you will find heavy emphasis on expositional preaching and a recovery of the historic Christian faith.

To a certain degree, all denominations are theologically driven, whether Reformed or otherwise. Each brand of Christianity seeks to establish its own influence and set of beliefs. Presbyterians, Lutherans, Baptists, and Anglicans would justify planting on the same street because they differ on secondary issues. They may put those differences aside at times to work together, but their presence on opposite street corners indicates that, at some point in the history of that community, one group of Christians sought to establish a presence there to supply the "orthodoxy" they felt other churches failed to provide.

Further, there will be a focus on the Scriptures themselves. Therefore, when the teacher plants a church, the conveyance of biblical truth and teaching is seen as paramount. There will be an emphasis on preaching and a desire to educate believers in biblical theology, systematic theology, and the history of the church. Preserving orthodoxy and the evangelical tenets of the faith are

---

6. David W. Shenk and Ervin R. Stutzman, *Creating Communities of the Kingdom: New Testament Models of Church Planting* (Scottsdale, PA: Herald, 1988), 95.

primary goals. The planting of a church like this helps to establish a beacon of truth into a community and sets a lamppost on the hill that faithfully shines the light of God's Word. The spirit and authority brought by the teaching of Jesus the rabbi will be at work within the theologically driven teacher.

In the sixties and seventies there was a flood of hippies coming to Jesus through the ministry of a community known as the Jesus Movement. At the epicenter of that cultural shakedown was Chuck Smith, a Bible teacher who had learned to structure his sermons around W. H. Griffith Thomas's *Outline Studies*.[7] He pastored the sleepy little church called Calvary Chapel of Costa Mesa. But there was also another figure, an unsung hero of the Jesus Movement.

One fateful day, Chuck's daughter Cheryl brought home a young charismatic hippie named Lonnie Frisbee, who became instrumental in catalyzing Calvary Chapel into a worldwide phenomenon that would land it on the cover of *Time* magazine. At the time, Chuck recognized a gifting in the charismatic young man, not realizing then that he possessed a highly apostolic nature.[8] Over time, the legend of Calvary Chapel relegated Lonnie Frisbee to the back seat, but no amount of verse-by-verse teaching would have grown the church to the levels that it did during the pioneer stage. It was said that they came because of Lonnie and stayed because of Chuck. In a *LIFE* magazine story done at the height of the Jesus Movement, there is a photograph of Chuck and Lonnie standing in the water, both with a fist raised high in power, testifying to the power and grace of God.[9] That snapshot embodies the powerful chemical combination of an apostle-teacher team and the exponential dividends that come through ministry tag teams.

APOSTLES + TEACHERS = REFORMATION MOVEMENTS

In fact, Lonnie Frisbee's apostolic gifting would contribute to the building of three movements highlighted in this chapter: the Jesus Movement, the Signs and Wonders Movement (Vineyard), and the Discipleship-Submission Movement. Despite the shortcomings all these movements had, it is notable that Frisbee was influential in all three when they boomed.

---

7. W. H. Griffith Thomas, *Outline Studies of Matthew* (Grand Rapids: Kregel, 1985).

8. Chuck Smith and Hugh Steven, *The Reproducers* (Ventura, CA: Regal, 1972), 38. Smith is referring to Lonnie Frisbee, who would go on to develop an apostolic gifting.

9. Lonnie Frisbee with Roger Sachs, *Not by Might Nor by Power—The Jesus Revolution* (Middlebury, VT: Freedom Publications, 2012), 141, 142.

ECCLESIASTICALLY DRIVEN PLANTS

This pragmatic approach to planting is burdened for the community and communal gathering of God's people. The missional movement itself was largely a movement of shepherds, despite some apostolic influences. Churches planted during the missional movement were convinced that their way of "doing church" was the right way. From those who champion a return to APEST's five-fold/team leadership, to those focused on forming missional communities, planters holding this part of the elephant focused on orthopraxy. These desires for God's people to interact with one another in a particular way was the expression of the drive of a shepherd, who desires to enrich the experience of God's people in community. Ecclesiastically driven planters agree that, "The commands of Christ cannot be kept by one individual alone, and the kingdom of Christ cannot be demonstrated in isolation."[10]

Historically, early Methodism focused on a pragmatic approach to church by providing an interactive meeting that met in homes called "the experience meeting" where they would answer a set of questions about their "spiritual progress."[11] As the name Methodist implies, their return to what they perceived as first-century methods of ministry and preaching marked them as a sect within Anglicanism. Wesley inaugurated the circuit riders as apostolic-type ministers who covered a geographical area, working in the spirit, practice, and preaching of the apostles. Wesley was as burdened for what happened after he left a town as he was for the conviction of those who gathered to hear him preach the gospel.

Early Methodism demonstrated what happens when apostolic and shepherding leaders come together: A missional movement of house churches and microchurches is born. Both the shepherd and the apostle resist consumerism, as both want to see the quality of ministry improve, rather than just the quantity of believers. During the church growth movement, led largely by evangelists, quantity was emphasized over quality. As a result, the level of human interaction in church suffered qualitatively. Is it possible that this generation is returning to an emphasis on the quality of human relationships and interaction? Ironically, this return comes as a backlash against the social media

---

10. Gene Wilson and Craig Ott, *Global Church Planting: Biblical Principals and Best Practices for Multiplication* (Grand Rapids: Baker Academic, 2011), 23.

11. William Williams, *The Experience Meeting: An Introduction to the Welsh Societies of the Evangelical Awakening* (Vancouver, BC: Regent College Bookstore, 1995). Author note: It's fascinating to read the return to discipleship small groups during the Evangelical Awakening that parallels the contemporary focus today. They were convinced, as we are, that something was missing.

revolution and a growing disenchantment with all its inauthentic posturing. The church planter who provides consumers with an opportunity to find yet another space to "experience" religion like a ride at an amusement park will fail to connect with those burdened for community that gravitates towards house churches and missional communities.

This drive is the outworking or expression of the relational aspect of God found in the Trinity. Plass and Coffield observe,

> We are relational beings because we are created in the image of a relational God. By definition the Christian God exists in relationship as Father, Son and Spirit. While existing in three distinct persons, they share one divine essence that is described as love (1 John 4:8). God can be love only if God exists as community. The pure love the divine persons have for each other is unconditionally giving in its character. The Father gives himself for the Son, and the Son gives himself for the Father. The gift of each for the other is personified in the Spirit. And not only do they give unconditionally, they receive each other in the same manner. That is the nature of agape. It is the radical giving and receiving. . . . We were created with this relational likeness and we long for relational connection because God exists in a relationship of love.[12]

This desire to work out the relational aspect of our faith will result in the shepherd emphasizing discipleship over and above knowledge (teaching) and over and above programmatic evangelism devoid of a relational aspect. The ecclesiastically driven shepherd will plant a church that expresses the outworking of Jesus as the good shepherd who desires to see his people gathered intimately.

Again, we witness Lonnie Frisbee at the forefront of the discipleship or highly controversial "Shepherding" movement that sprung up in the 1970s. This demonstrates the following:

APOSTLE + SHEPHERDS = MISSIONAL MOVEMENTS, HOUSE
CHURCHES, AND DISCIPLE-MAKING MOVEMENTS

MISSIOLOGICALLY DRIVEN PLANTS

Evangelists tend to be missiological in nature. Whereas the teacher focuses on truth, the evangelist will be driven by the message of the gospel and the

---

12. Richard Plass and James Coffield, *The Relational Soul: Moving from False Self to Deep Connection* (Downers Grove, IL: InterVarsity Press, 2014), 13.

Great Commission. For this reason, evangelistically driven churches tend to be program heavy, and they approach mission with a shotgun blast. More is better. Evangelists aren't concerned as much with people's feelings as with faithful proclamation of the message of salvation, be it from a megaphone, online platform, or personal conversations. Evangelists tend to lack an "off switch" despite many around them desperately attempting to locate it!

Paul may have been an apostle, but his church planting Swiss Army knife had a very big evangelist blade. For this reason, Paul was active, but to an evangelist there is no conception of overactive. If you have ever been in an evangelistically driven congregation, there is a dominant focus on newcomers. Churches such as Willow Creek, Mars Hill in Seattle, and Saddleback grew consistently through faithful proclamation of the gospel message aimed at the unchurched. Through missiologically driven churches, the church growth movement and the seeker-sensitive churches grew. Yet, without the other roles of the APEST ministering to such a rapidly growing congregation, faithful discipleship, deep relationships, and a deeper understanding of the teachings of the faith will be neglected. In such a scenario, members (not to mention the evangelists themselves) burn out or find another church where they receive better teaching or can build relationships.

Evangelists must surround themselves with the other functions of the APEST team if they want to have any chance of surviving the pitfalls of rapidly growing churches and the tendency to work alone. Such unchecked risks have led to disasters in the past few decades, as evidenced by all-too-common scandals among giants of the church growth movement hitting the headlines. The fastest-growing churches in America should be cautionary tales rather than objects of envy. For, unless they subscribe to APEST and team leadership, the leaders on large stages run a higher risk of self-sabotage when their own success inevitably catches up with them.

CONCLUSION: APOSTLE + EVANGELIST = CHURCH
GROWTH AND SEEKER-SENSITIVE MOVEMENTS[2]

PNEUMATOLOGICALLY DRIVEN PLANTS

This approach is favored by the prophetic leader, who views the church primarily as a meeting place where heaven has come to earth. Most churches that are pneumatologically driven seek a return to dependence upon the Holy Spirit and a restoration of the spiritual gifts in worship and practice. Because of the tendency to work well with apostolic leaders, the prophetic movement combines with apostles to birth something that looks like the New Apostolic Reformation (NAR) founded by C. Peter Wagner. The NAR was a charismatic reformation based on Pentecostal theological interpretations of the APEST roles that was bent on reinstalling the five-fold gifting to the church. This movement of supernatural gifts spawned the return of signs and wonders and focused on the experiential nature of worship. Because the theological interpretations of the roles were unique to the charismatic circles, the NAR would have greatly benefited from the teaching functions of APEST to balance out their blind spots.

The NAR is merely one example, whereas more mainstream churches such as the Vineyard and Assemblies of God are also pneumatologically driven. John Wimber was largely a prophetic leader, who was introduced to Lonnie Frisbee after he had recently left Calvary Chapel. After Frisbee and Wimber connected, a new type of movement emerged. Vineyard became one of the fastest-growing movements in America, just as Calvary Chapel had been when Smith and Frisbee connected. At Fuller seminary, Frisbee was at the epicenter of the return to the signs and wonders as a phenomenon when he taught a class together with C. Peter Wagner on the topic.[13]

It's not surprising that many wish the pneumatological movements would cease, just as they believe the supernatural gifts have. However, Darrell Bock asserts, "the essence of the church is that she is a Spirit-indwelt community."[14] Christopher B. James summarized the position of Lukan ecclesiology as, "modeling the church as followers of Jesus empowered by the Spirit to extend God's saving mission across ethnic and cultural lines to the ends of the earth."[15] The Spirit is painstakingly portrayed in Acts as an energizing and driving force behind missionary activity. Therefore, it should not surprise us that movements such as the Vineyard—and even historic revivals—have evidenced large waves of people coming to faith in Christ as a result of Pentecostal and charismatic movements. The prophet embodies the burden of a God yearning to dwell in

---

13. C. Peter Wagner, *Your Spiritual Gifts Can Help Your Church Grow: How to Find Your Gift and Use It* (Ventura, CA: Regal, 1979). C. Peter Wagner became one of the foremost champions of the restoration of the five gifts of Ephesians 4. He was at the forefront of the New Apostolic Reformation and greatly influenced the work of church planting, missions, and charismatic renewal. Among his works are: *Latin American Theology: Radical or Evangelical* (Grand Rapids: Eerdmans, 1970); *Strategies for Church Growth* (Ventura, CA: Regal, 1987); *How to Have a Healing Ministry* (Ventura, CA: Regal, 1988); *The New Apostolic Churches* (Ventura, CA: Regal, 1998); *Churchquake!* (Ventura, CA: Regal, 1999); *Changing Church* (Ventura, CA: Regal, 2004); and *The Book of Acts: A Commentary* (Ventura, CA: Regal, 2008).

14. Christopher B. James, *Church Planting in Post-Christian Soil: Theology and Practice* (New York: Oxford University Press, 2018), 71.

15. James, *Church Planting in Post-Christian Soil*, 71.

the midst of his people. Therefore, the pneumatologically driven church will focus on God's presence in their midst.

APOSTLES + PROPHETS = SPIRITUAL REVIVAL,
RENEWAL, AND RESTORATION MOVEMENTS

ESCHATOLOGICALLY DRIVEN PLANTS

So far, we've examined what happens when apostolic leaders combine with the other members of the APEST functions, leaving us to examine what drives the apostles to plant. Apostles plant eschatologically driven churches, or churches driven by a fulfillment of kingdom expansion. When Jesus came preaching the good news of the kingdom, he was introducing his own reign and rule. The theology of the kingdom is the belief that all things that are broken will be restored, all who mourn will be made joyful, all that was lost will be found. The theology of the kingdom preaches that the kingdom of God has come, is in the process of coming, and will arrive again, establishing his kingdom fully and finally.

Therefore, as a "sent one," the apostolic-type, pioneering church planter expands the borders of the kingdom of God into the frontier, pushing further on and further out. Alexander the Great famously wept into his hands at twenty-one years old, mourning that there were no more worlds left to conquer; this incident typifies the apostle's incessant drive for outward expansion. Kingdom expansion is linked to the eschatological promise of God covering the earth with his glory. The apostle looks to Jesus's promise that "this gospel of the kingdom will be preached in the whole world as a testimony to all nations, and then the end will come" (Matt. 24:14). For the apostle, the expansion of the kingdom is less about "taking ground" than it is about magnifying the glory of the king. As Newbigin stated, "The center of the picture is not the human need of salvation (from sin, from oppression, from alienation) but God and God's immeasurable grace. So the central concern is not 'How shall the world be saved?' but 'How shall this glorious and gracious God be glorified?'"[16] As the kingdom advances, the king is glorified.

The theology of the kingdom of God stretches back to the Old Testament, when God asked Adam and Eve to spread his glory throughout the world simply by engaging in sexual reproduction. That sounds like the type of evangelistic strategy almost everybody could get behind! Since the fall, however,

---

16. Lesslie Newbigin, *A Theological Life* (Oxford, UK: Oxford University Press, 2000), 195.

things have not been so easy or simple. Just as the ground now produced thorns because of sin, missional engagement would prove more difficult and would involve much difficulty in both sowing and reaping. But, in spite of the curse, God's continuous posture was to bless. He is seen repeatedly blessing humanity as he brings forth his kingdom, the ultimate fulfillment of all blessing.

This Jewish concept of blessedness found expression in the Jewish culture through the Shalom greeting. Saying *"shalom"* to someone is a way of blessing them with the restoration, hope, and peace of God's promised kingdom. It's wishing that God's dream for his kingdom on earth will be experienced by the person receiving the blessing, as a pledge and foretaste of heaven on earth. Babel's true crime was their refusal to multiply and spread out over the face of the earth, choosing instead to build upward. The modern church bucks against God's command to *spread out*, seeking instead to "make a name for ourselves" as we *build up* to the heavens.

The past, present, and future tension of the kingdom already come, still coming, and yet to come is a promise not yet totally fulfilled, yet still powerfully in process. The church is the vehicle that most clearly embodies the kingdom on earth, and as the church plants itself in a community, it inevitably brings the cultural norms and practices of the kingdom with it.

The snow of the White Witch of Narnia's domain begins melting after the resurrection of Aslan, the changing climate hearkening the imminent arrival of summer when the sun will always shine. In Lewis's penning of Narnia, he described a land that was broken, without any kingdom influence, trapped in a reality that was always winter but never Christmas. As Father Christmas is the first sign that Aslan has returned in that story, so is the apostle showing up into the brokenness of a long-forgotten neighborhood of marginalized people. Eschatologically driven apostles share that same excitement in seeing the kingdom introduce hope, freedom, and social change. The social aspect of an apostle's mission is born out of a focus on the theology of restoration in Scripture when all things are made new, and all broken things are made whole.

This is not to pit social change against theological proclamations, for eschatological churches may be, and often are, deeply reflective, theologically. Often, eschatologically driven plants aim to plant multiethnic congregations that reflect the cultural makeup of their surrounding neighborhood. The prophetic and apostolic functions share synergy as issues like racism, social injustice, and systemic poverty are addressed. Study the social aspects of the majority of prophets, and the social sins of injustice and inequality quickly reveal their prominence in their ministries. Whereas the prophet raises awareness of God's heart on social issues, the apostle mobilizes people to take action. In order to preach the gospel, the church serves the community, becoming a force of kingdom transformation in the world. This was demonstrated by the apostles' commissioning of Paul to "remember the poor" when he consulted them in Jerusalem. Paul can't seem to help editorializing, adding that this was "the very thing I was eager to do" (Gal. 2:10). When the church operates apostolically, it will grow daily in the esteem of the people.

The church is not the kingdom of God, nor is the kingdom limited to the church. Despite the church being the clearest embodiment of the kingdom, the kingdom itself is always bigger than the church. The church functioning in the APEST ministries is a clear expression of what God is already doing in the world. The kingdom of God often advances outside of the church, as it did in the civil rights movement under Dr. Martin Luther King Jr. Despite the church's kingdom roots, the kingdom was advancing through, in spite of, and beyond the church itself. What is the growing of the awareness of racism, systemic inequality, social injustice, and other issues, if not humanity connecting with the influences of God's kingdom on earth, catching glimpses into his heart, and realizing what betrays his image in their hearts? As it was during the civil rights movement in America, so the kingdom of God is outpacing the church. The church has been playing catch up to the kingdom for decades in this country.

In addition, the apostle will always seek to plant a multiplying church that plants other churches, rather than just a single church. Instead of seeking to add to one congregation, they seek to multiply the churches themselves, further pointing to their catalytic nature and calling to birth movements.

APOSTLES + APOSTLES = SOCIAL MOVEMENTS
AND MULTIPLICATION MOVEMENTS

CONCLUSION OF PLANTER DRIVES

Thus, we see that each of the APEST roles enables the church to fulfill one aspect of Christ's ministry in his physical absence. When we imitate existing models, we may be guilty of cherry picking from Christ's ministries on earth and inadvertently missing our chance to see Christ filling all things with his glory. In the same way that the Old Testament glory is the radiance of God's attributes emanating from his character, so the APEST functions are the glory of Christ in the world today.

Who would willingly refuse to glorify Jesus in all his excellencies? Those only grasping the trunk, leg, and ears of the elephant are unaware that they are "fitly framed together" and only represent Christ as a composite whole. An APEST framework that could unite denominations, facilitate communication across lines of division, and disallow one part of the elephant pretending the other parts don't exist would hasten *kingdom come* with monumental force. God's glory will not cover the globe until this apostolic eschatological dream is realized.

Drive Summary	Planter Function	Expression
Theologically Driven	Teacher	Word-Based Church
Ecclesiastically Driven	Shepherd	House Church
Missiologically Driven	Evangelist	Megachurch
Pneumatologically Driven	Prophet	Pentecostal Church
Eschatologically Driven	Apostle	Multiplying Church

REFLECT

- In one sentence, why are you going to plant? How does your answer reveal what drives you?
- One church fellowship cannot do everything. Have you considered how many "lanes" God has given your church? Have you incorporated the drives of all the leaders into your vision?

DISCUSS

- How does our orthodoxy (the right way of thinking) inform our orthopraxy (the right way of doing things)? Share examples.
- Consider "the way we do things around here" for some of the people in your discussion group. What do assumptions about how to "do church" suggest these fellowships really believe?

CHALLENGE

- If what drives us is influenced by the people we're working with, how have the people you're working with contributed to your vision and motivation?

REDISCOVERING GOD'S HEART FOR MISSION

From Borrowed Models to Broken-Hearted Compulsion

MISSION, VALUES, AND STRATEGY

10

Before the battle is joined, plans are everything, but
once the shooting begins, plans are worthless.
—DWIGHT D. EISENHOWER

Be careful when aiming for nothing. You just might hit it.
—WILL ROGERS

VALUES

What do Tom's shoes, McDonald's, America, and the church of Satan all
share in common? They all operate by a set of values. Every church planter has
been taught that values are the principles that will guide you in accomplishing
your mission, but values are much more than how you will accomplish your
vision. You may not be able to recite what the values of an organization are,
but you will feel them as soon as you walk into their corporate spaces. Values
create the atmosphere of a church. They are the DNA that should shape
and encapsulate what people experience when looking at us or sharing space
with us.

In some cases, the written values of an organization may not match up with
its unspoken values. When this happens, an organization is in danger of believing it is about one thing on paper and feeling like another thing entirely in person. Therefore, values are useless if the leaders crafting them neglect to model
them. Core values are often forged through discipleship as someone instills
their values into us, and we operate by them as if they were second nature to us,
never realizing why we do what we do or how we are doing it.

Values are essential to how God communicates with his people. God
packaged up his values for his people by making covenants. In each covenant,

God defined the characteristics, expectations, and values of the relationship. As you prepare to launch your plant, your values embody your priorities and help ensure that these priorities are shared with all parties. Therefore, planters must ensure that their values always have scriptural roots to ensure that they are values also shared by God. Besides, if you fail to establish the core values from the start, people will smuggle their personal ideals into the place where biblical values should have been.

Values should not be confused with ideals. In *Radical Reformission*, Mark Driscoll identified values as the triggers for how people spend their time, energy, and money. "Values can be tricky because they are often little more than ideals, what people merely wish they valued and cared for, what they are committed to in theory but not in practice. Many vegetarians eat meat, environmentalists don't recycle, employees don't work, and Christians don't read their Bibles. Ideals are what you want; values are what you do. Ideals become values only if they are lived out."[1]

VALUES WON'T ALWAYS GROW WITH YOUR CHURCH

Unfortunately, many leaders have sacrificed their values on the altar of church growth. Most planters are eager for their church to grow to a certain size but are tragically unaware of the fact that increased numbers naturally change dynamics. Because many of my church plants met around coffee tables, our size quickly became an issue. We were constantly looking for new buildings. At each crossroads, our core values gave us direction.

A colleague walked through the main meeting room that we used for Pillar's services. In an effort to help us maximize what we do, he scanned the perimeter and began asking questions about the placement of our worship team, angle of the room, arrangement of the chairs, and where the preacher stood. After thinking a moment, he said, "I'd bet you could fit three times as many people in here if you eliminated these coffee table and chair setups and put in rows. You could turn the whole room to that far corner and get even more people in." After noticing my awkward silence, he smiled and said, "That is the goal, right? To get as many people in as you can?" Turning to my friend half-shocked, I said, "No. That's never been our goal."

I knew emphatically that following the values he expressed would rip

---

1. Mark Driscoll, *The Radical Reformission: Reaching Out without Selling Out* (Grand Rapids: Zondervan, 2004) 123–24.

the heart and soul out of the church. The church had been built as a place where people could be real, share real problems, get help, speak their minds, challenge others, and be used by God. Our core values had been hardwired into the way we were set up, and our setup was directly helping us reach our goal. Growing bigger would simply be a distraction away from our values. From the beginning, we'd determined that when we hit room capacity, we'd break off another church planting team. Before I left, we had broken off two church plants.

If a church plant of fifty people and an established church of 1,000 people share the same DNA, the only difference between the two should be 950 people. When you were a child, your genetic code was the same as today because your DNA does not change. Your core values also should not change with size.

Here are a couple of examples of random core values that can be shared by churches big and small:

- We value people, just as they are, over anything they can do for us.
- God gets the prime cuts, not our scraps.
- We value people over programs.

CRAFTING YOUR VALUES

One of the greatest weaknesses in how planters are trained is that they are asked to craft a vision alone, rather than with their team. A solitary planter will craft a deficient vision, if "vision" can even be used to describe it accurately. Each function of the strike team brings an ingredient to pitch into the stew. Each of the roles has a "vision," but sees only one-fifth of the big picture. If you will embark on the mission together, then it should be envisioned together. If someone only possessed the ability to see at 20 percent capacity, we would consider them legally blind. Once you've decided what the collected drives are among your APEST team, you will be in more of a position to ask God what the composite picture looks like.

When we sit down to write out our core values, it may be that we forge them from years of good experiences and think, "I want to ensure that people feel this, or know that . . ." Core values may also be formed from years of bad experiences in which leaders, churches, or circumstances left a bitter taste in our mouths and we determined to "never let somebody feel this way, if I have something to say about it." The first values I ever penned were *The Five Pillars of Pillar: Communion, Commitment, Contemporary, Compassionate, Community.*

- Communion: Knowing and experientially interacting with God personally was our priority.
- Committed: We were committed to Scripture as the authoritative, inspired, infallible way through which God primarily reveals himself to us.
- Contemporary: We used this term to speak to the desire to be innovative on mission. Functioning like any other time in history doesn't reach our current culture with the gospel.
- Community: This described our body of real people reaching out as they were released in their gifts.
- Compassion: We made Christ's compassion our passion.

These value statements were naked, flawed, raw, and could use improvement, but they worked. They accomplished what shared values are intended to do: They encoded the DNA that shaped our church's culture and created an atmosphere. Most important, they weren't borrowed from another context.

STARTING OFF RIGHT

Your values should be the embodiment of Jesus in your community and should encapsulate how your plant will flesh out the ministry and presence of Jesus in a local context. Ensure that you are laying the foundation of Christ like Paul did, pointing people away from yourself and toward Jesus. Don't make the mistake of presenting the idol of your sexy new church with the flashy name and logo as the great white hope of your target community.

When the addict is trying to get off drugs, you'd better point him to somebody who can set him free. When the couple's marriage is falling apart because a partner has been caught using pornography yet again, you'd better get them to Jesus. When a woman has been sexually abused, raped, and degraded as she's trying to escape the life of drugs and prostitution, you'd better be pointing her to the One who can heal, forgive, and restore her. The chorus of the old hymn says, "You can have all this world, just give me Jesus."

It's funny how, when you're planting a church, everybody crawls out of the woodwork to try to make the church plant about nearly everything *but* Christ. My sending pastor was fond of saying, "Where there's light, there's bugs." Church planting values rooted in Christ's ministry serve as a trusty bug zapper.

MANTRAS IN POP CULTURE

The word *mantra* originally meant a sound that a person practicing Eastern-style meditation would repeat to themselves to aid their concentration. In pop culture today, the term has morphed into meaning a phrase that someone repeats to remind themselves of something or from which to derive inspiration. Pop culture has leveraged mantras in the way that Christians use Scriptures: to remind each other of key concepts through repetition, as when believers encourage one another with a verse like, "I can do all things through Christ who strengthens me" (Phil. 4:13 NKJV).

Consider these examples of mantras in pop culture to help you get a grasp on what a mantra looks and sounds like:

Musical Mantras
- You gotta fight for your right to party.—The Beastie Boys
- All we are saying is give peace a chance.—John Lennon
- Don't stop believing.—Journey
- Jump! Go ahead and jump!—Van Halen

Movie Mantras
- I'll be back!—*Terminator*
- There's no place like home.—*The Wizard of Oz*
- May the Force be with you.—*Star Wars*
- Every man dies. Not every man really lives.—*Braveheart*

Motivational Mantras:
- Follow your dreams.
- Reach for the stars.
- Let go and let God.
- *Carpe Diem!*

VALUE MANTRAS

A mantra is a maxim learned through repetition. Mantras are catchy rewordings of our values, intended to be memorable and contagious. When you use mantras to teach your church what matters, instilling your core values, people will learn to quote them and apply them to problems. Our people self-correct and quote one of our mantras to bring comfort when everything is breaking down during our gatherings. Worthy mantras reiterate a common goal to focus everyone's eyes back on Christ. In this way, they form bite-sized chunks of vision.

Mantra #1—We Are the Church That Exists for People Who Are Outside of It

Before you launch, you have to be clear about the question that every military leader must ask: "What is an acceptable casualty rate to accomplish this mission?" In *Saving Private Ryan*, Tom Hanks tells his second-in-command that he justifies losing each and every man by saying that for every man sacrificed, ten more are saved. Unconvincingly, he mutters, "And that's how simple it is . . ."

In *Reaching the Unreached*, I tell the story of a day when I was phasing out of my role at Refuge Long Beach and a church member noticed a transgender male prostitute using the ladies' room. She asked what she should do. My response was not what she expected. With a wry grin, I responded, "Wait for them to come out?" That day, I made a calculated decision about the person I was willing to lose. Because of our values, we were willing to lose believers over nonbelievers every day of the week. When the busybody stormed up to me demanding to know what I was going to do about a transgender prostitute in the ladies' room, she made it clear that she wasn't a part of our team, because she should have already known our values and the answer they would produce.

Most of the churches planted in our New Breed Network call themselves "the last stop before hell" because of the neighborhoods surrounding them. Most people never get more than one second chance in those communities, and we performed many funerals. Witnessing many people come to Christ before entering eternity changes your perspective. Ministering to gang members, hardcore convicts, addicts, prostitutes, and just about everyone else who would probably never darken the door of a regular church required us to make plenty "Eat my flesh and drink my blood" speeches to offend and disperse unwanted crowds. Jesus didn't want crowds or numbers. Neither did we. We wanted disciples who resembled his grace, love, and compassion for broken people. With that sentiment, we threw another phrase around: "Legalism is illegal here."

Mantra #2—No Christians Allowed

In Pillar, I chose not to accept any other church's Christians because I didn't want them to stink up the newbies like an old banana in a lunchbox. Accepting

Christians into your new church plant will do a couple of things: One, it will swell your numbers and make your church plant look better, and two, it will also serve to provide your newbies with teaching from nomadic Christians who will instruct them about things they "should" be irritated about: *The worship is too loud. The sermon is too long. The church is too unloving. The overheads are too wild. The service is too jovial. The service is too serious.* These behaviors are learned, and you've provided them with teachers because you wanted a crowd.

At Pillar, we found that the new Christians were so excited to know Jesus that they never thought about these things on their own. Somebody had to plant these thoughts. Somebody they trusted. Somebody they respected. Somebody who seemed more mature than they were. For this reason, the first thing that I'd say while shaking hands with visiting Christians is "Thanks for visiting." When they said that they were actually thinking of making Pillar their home church, I'd ask where they'd come from. Unless they had newly moved into the area, I'd tell them that the church had been planted expressly for the unchurched, and I would then actively seek to identify reasons I could point out about why they'd hate Pillar.

If they said, "I left my old church because the pastor didn't seem to care. He only visited twice a year," I'd say, "Oh, you'd hate it here. I wouldn't even visit you once. I suck as a pastor." If they smiled queasily and said, "Well, it's not just that. The worship was terrible. The guy up front over there thought it was all about him." They would lean in on that last part, like they were laughing at a joke we both shared. I'd say, "Well, our worship gets pretty lame and corny. Our guy is really good, but he won't make you happy. He wears lame hats, and you know what that means . . ." I'd lean in close like I was telling a secret, and lower my voice to a half-whisper, "He's come over from a Pentecostal church. He might be a bit wacky." As their eyes widened with fear, I'd wink and touch my nose, like it was our dirty little secret.

Later, I'd smile as I told my co-pastor, Jeff, and he'd laugh, shake his head, reprimand me a bit, and say, "One of these days you've got to stop kicking people out before they've even gotten in." I had decided, however, that there were certain attitudes and motivations that would inevitably lead to angry departures in the future, and it was better to send them running early than to let them settle in and infect others.

Mantra # 3—Jesus Is Our Senior Pastor

This mantra gets to the core of the ownership issue; some planters can get very enmeshed with their plants and take excessive ownership of the ministry. Instead, healthy churches insist that the church is owned by Christ alone, and behave as if he is perfectly capable of fighting for it with or without the help of the pastor. I found this out accidentally. Honestly.

I planted a church accidentally in a Starbucks in Europe. I had quit ministry and told Jesus I wanted nothing to do with his church anymore, labeling myself a deserter. Instead of hanging me high, Jesus showed me the real battle and surrounded me with his power, in spite of my weakness. He dropped some spiritual napalm around me and did all the work as I stood there watching, protesting, and trying to run. The night before our big launch, the guy who was supposed to take the church plant confessed that he was taking off and left me holding the bag. I stood there feeling like a sucker, but I told Jesus again that I thought I'd made it clear that I didn't want to be in ministry anymore. I told my strike team over and over that I wasn't their pastor, and if any of them wanted to lead the team, they could have it. They all took one massive step backward, leaving me looking like the guy who had stepped forward for leadership.

When that plan blew up in my face, I told them that I was leaving in a year and didn't care what happened to the team as long as we saw the lost saved. I told them that I didn't care about the church plant, and I really didn't. But I also told them that if Jesus did, he'd show up and lead it, because I didn't want to. It never backfired. It got them excited, and they looked for him and to him for everything we did. Eventually, I did start to care and actually like ministry again, but I've never changed my tactic. I've never been so involved, yet so free.

Mantra #4—What Did the Early Church Do?

Have you ever been cheesed off on a Sunday morning and then had to mount the pulpit steps to preach? I have, and when you get to that state, it's very difficult to do much that could be of any spiritual benefit to anyone. In fact, after a number of years in ministry and enough time on the mission field, I became aware that there were technical problems in the minutes leading up to our gatherings. All the things that were putting everybody in a funk were twenty-first-century problems. Reminding ourselves that the early church got all the essentials done without twenty-first-century technology helps put things into perspective.

Before the invention of microphones, you had to be a barrel-chested man to be a gospel preacher, at least according to Charles Spurgeon.[2] If the sound system broke—which is highly probable in a planting situation—we learned

---

2. Charles Haddon Spurgeon, *Lectures to My Students* (Pantianos Classics ebook edition, first published in 1875), 24. Spurgeon once wrote a chapter in *Lectures to my Students* called, "To Ministers of Slender Apparatus," meaning their chests and frames. To sum it up, Spurgeon asserted, "You're not called. God calls barrel-chested men to preach the gospel," In today's terms we'd say, "Sorry, you just don't have the hardware to run this software."

to laugh. We'd tell people, "If you're here to watch a show, you're in the wrong church. We're here to reach the lost." We learned to laugh at ourselves, and so did our people. Now, the setup crew repeats this mantra to each other, despite being the most dedicated team I've ever seen.

Mantra #5—We Care More about You Than about Anything You Can Do for Us

I can't emphasize how important this is. Many of our people are coming from churches where the leadership used them to build their personal empires. Rather than exercising their spiritual gifts, they were forced to do church chores to run the machine. When they slackened their pace in building the pyramid of the pastor's glory, the whip of manipulation cracked harder, their commitment to Jesus was questioned, and the cry "More bricks, less straw!" rang louder.

You must make it plain to all the people that they are more important to God than anything they can do for him or for the church. In the same way that a woman wants to be valued for her heart instead of used for her body, so the bride of Jesus needs to know that Jesus died for their souls because he delights to reveal his own glory in them and to them, not because of any goodies he thought he'd get in return. Performance Christianity may not ring out from your pulpit, but it may still fester in the pews. Help people check their baggage by giving them breaks. Don't guilt them when they aren't there. Encourage them to take a well-deserved rest, free of ministerial guilt. God never takes from us; he is overjoyed by what we freely give.

MISSION

Once your burdens, drives, and values have coalesced with your team members, they should be distilled into your mission. Engaging people on mission first is key to engaging with a meaningful mission statement. Your values will inform your mission, as expressed by the authors of *Tradecraft*, "Mission is not something we do, it's something we are."[3] Paul said he wasn't like a boxer just beating at the air. He knew what he was swinging for.

Inexperienced church planters suffer from a myopic vision that fails to look beyond simply launching the plant off the ground. As long as their bucket of bolts gets airborne and doesn't crash and burn, they consider it a success. Filling a room with crowds of Christians is not a successful church plant. Statistically, fourteen out of fifteen churches that significantly increase in attendance do so

---

3. Caleb Crider et al., *Tradecraft: For the Church on Mission* (Portland, OR: Urban Loft, 2013), 24.

by transfer growth. The risk of modern church planting is that your plant may "grow" and appear to have been successful without reaching a single lost person.

If launching the church is your mission, don't be surprised if you wake to find you've not been on the same mission as the Holy Spirit. There is irony in having to remind planters that the mission statement is about the mission rather than the church plant. A mission statement will remind you that you're getting the band together not to play great music but, like the Blues Brothers, because you're "on a mission from God."

Many church planting training programs tell you to get the vision up front. The problem is that planters don't naturally start there, nor should they. Planters should plant from burden because burden informs mission. When I'm assessing entry-level planters, the first thing I notice is the presence—or lack—of the drives we discussed earlier. The ones who possess a drive that comes from burden are the ones I know are going to make it.

Drive, burden, and values are all you need to begin. Mission, vision, and strategy become revealed along the way, not before the journey has begun. Despite our attempts to train them before they plant, much of what they develop will be changed as they begin to truly reach their targeted community. Values are stationary, while mission, strategy, and vision are all moving targets. Therefore, much of the mission and strategy you develop at an early stage should be written in pencil rather than ink, at least until you understand your community and how God is at work within it. Only as planters engage in mission do they begin to experience what God has already been doing before they arrived. This may be the reason God has us embark on mission prior to revealing the mission and strategy to planters.

Although the Holy Spirit could simply deliver the information cerebrally to a planter, the experiential learning on mission is where the breakthroughs actually happen. On Paul's first missionary journey to the Galatians, his approach was methodical, pragmatic, and opportunistic. On his second missionary journey, however, when he tried to apply the same approach to mission, he was "forbidden by the Holy Spirit to speak the word in Asia" (Acts 16:6 ESV). He found himself frustrated in every attempt to reach the people *he thought he should be reaching*. Attempting to enter Bithynia "the Spirit of Jesus did not allow them" (Acts 16:7 ESV), leading to greater frustration. This continued until Paul's dream of the man from Macedonia, whereby Paul was given divine revelation into what he should do next. No chart, system, or diagram could have prepared Paul for that breakthrough.

For planters, this is the typical process on mission. Why wasn't Paul given the Macedonian call back in Antioch before he'd set out on the second missionary journey? Because the real journey Paul took wasn't to Macedonia, it was to greater dependence upon the Holy Spirit. Paul wasn't the same man on his second missionary journey as he was on his first. He had been broken, had learned from his mistakes, and had been made more pliable. This is the process of the long defeat and submission that takes us deeper into our dependence upon the Holy Spirit. The day we stop training planters to ignore the supernatural providence of God is the day things will start to turn around again.

Paul didn't discover his "missional sweet spot" until he was on the way. And this was not his first rodeo. He had already planted numerous churches. Planters should expect to be frustrated by the Holy Spirit blocking them at times. Experienced planters gain the wisdom to see that there is always more to the picture than has been communicated to them. When the paratroopers in the D-Day landings studied the maps prior to the invasion of Normandy, they were convinced they understood the aerial photographs.[4] From above, the pictures depicted hedgerows similar to those in Britain, but there was one problem. The roads weren't sunk between hedgerows in France; they were raised. That meant that mobilizing troops via roads that would expose them to enemy fire. As in battle, so in mission: The troops on the ground must *shift and maneuver* to adjust when their preconceived ideas do not match reality. Only those who are in the trenches can communicate the chasm between the two and shift accordingly.

This is why, despite training planters for years using Mancini's model, I believe that Mancini's model is more useful for established churches trying to define mission than it is for a church plant.[5] This is also the reason that this discussion has intentionally come later in the book.

MODIFYING THE KINGDOM CONCEPT

The Kingdom Concept is a helpful tool used in the business world for decades that Will Mancini modified and presented in *Church Unique* to help church leaders craft a missional mandate. It has become very popular for training

---

4. Stephen E. Ambrose, *D-Day, June 6, 1944: The Climactic Battle of World War II* (New York: Simon & Schuster, 1995).

5. Will Mancini, *Church Unique: How Missional Leaders Cast Vision, Capture Culture, and Create Movement* (San Francisco: Jossey-Bass, 2008). I greatly appreciate Will Mancini, and in no way should modifying his work be seen as criticism. As I've stated, the work is extremely helpful for churches who have already established themselves. This is because it is a defining tool, and on mission these things aren't defined yet, and can't be expected to be at the early stages of a planting scenario. Therefore, allow me to say that *Church Unique* is a fantastic book. That said, I also believe one of the limitations of the Kingdom Concept is that it focuses on the passions of the leaders for the apostolic *espirit*. The difficulty with this is that the missionary success of every church is based on equipping every believer through the APEST gifting. Until believers are released and activated in *their passions*, true mission stalls. I view the apostolic *espirit* (or passion) of all five APEST functions as equipping others in their respective lanes.

planters to determine direction for mission. The tool is made up of three circles that represent the following three factors:

1. Local predicament
2. Collective potential
3. Apostolic esprit

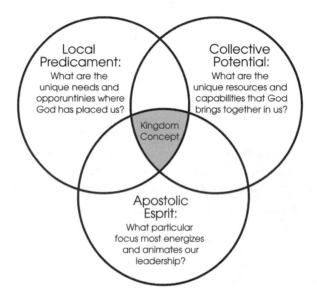

Local Predicament: This is the collection of felt needs in your community. It's the groan of your city. It's the cracks in the facade. It's where the brokenness breaks through more than anywhere else.

Collective Potential: This is the sum of the collected resources your team shares, including money, space, time, and spiritual gifts. It could also be strong families, professional abilities, or anything that might help you meet the needs in your city.

Apostolic Esprit: This term simply means the passion of your leadership or what gets them up in the morning to go on mission. This also tends to be what keeps them up at night praying and thinking about how to reach the needs of the community around them.

Listing five examples of the components in each circle, you circle the recurring themes that overlap all three in the middle triangle. When you think you see a pattern, distill it into the middle by crystalizing it into a statement where the three circles converge conceptually.

Your Kingdom Concept statement becomes distilled into a missional mandate and should begin with the phrase, "Our church exists to glorify God and make disciples by _____" (fill in the blank).

The Kingdom Concept tool is intended to prevent a team from lining up behind a mission that is wrong for their team. For example, I may have read a church planting book about reaching the urban community, but my team is ready to rock in rural Iowa. Try as we might, our mad graffiti skills (*collective potential*) and burden for the urban poor (*apostolic esprit*) fail to align with the the unsuspecting corn and dairy farmers awaiting our arrival (*local predicament*).

Now that you understand the basics of the Kingdom Concept, allow me to modify the circles slightly by merging *apostolic esprit* and *collective potential,* since I believe our burdens and passions are directly connected with our gifting. We will call the modified circle *APEST Drives.* APEST functions and their corresponding drives cannot be separated from one another, therefore a multifunctioning team manifests the various burdens of Christ's ministry represented: apostolic, prophetic, evangelistic, shepherding, and teaching.

Combining those two circles in Mancini's model of the Kingdom Concept, I would then add a third circle called "*Divine Opportunity.*" The man from Macedonia wasn't the only divine opportunity that presented itself during Paul's second missionary journey. When Paul traveled to Macedonia, he visited Ephesus and briefly stayed there, depositing Priscilla and Aquila and telling them he'd be back. He wouldn't really pursue Ephesus for all its potential until his third missionary journey, but in 1 Corinthians 16:9 he told them he was derailed from coming to Corinth because "a great door for effective work" was opened by the Lord. That door was Ephesus, and it became Paul's most powerful mission. This is why another circle representing the unpredictable, unknown variable of the Holy Spirit known as *Divine Opportunity* is necessary.

Paul's approach to each community was far from the "do or die" or "church plant or bust" mentalities displayed by planters today. Today we set our sights on a neighborhood and start a church there. Paul, however, sowed seed, constantly moving, and only slowed down to water it when it seemed to be taking hold. If he went to a town where nothing seemed to happen, he moved on and shook the dust off his feet. Paul spoke of the favorable "reception" that was given him and the team by the Thessalonians (1 Thess. 1:9) and elsewhere:

Now when I went to Troas to preach the gospel of Christ and found that *the Lord had opened a door for me.* (2 Cor. 2:12 ESV, emphasis mine)

And though my condition was a trial to you, you did not scorn or despise me, but received me as an angel of God, as Christ Jesus. (Gal. 4:14 ESV)

At the same time, pray also for us, that *God may open to us* a door for the word. (Col. 4:3 ESV, emphasis mine)

Paul interpreted these welcoming receptions as Divine Opportunities. When I played as an offensive center on the high school football team and we failed to protect the quarterback from infiltrating linebackers, our coach would throw his clipboard, and I would inevitably hear, "Jones! That hole was so big I could have driven a truck through it!" Paul entered through the doors the Holy Spirit opened for him. No matter what you're doing as a church planter, when you find that the Holy Spirit opens up a new window, you will find that he often blows your pretty papers and diagrams away. That is how church planting actually works on the ground.

Mission is incarnational in nature, and planters wade deep into their community to get a working knowledge of it. This engagement is essential before crafting a vision frame, and demographic studies are a cheap substitute for rubbing shoulders with the people and becoming incarnate among them. Incarnation takes time. Jesus gestated for nine months and matured for thirty years among people before ministering to them. Planters cannot truly know their mission until they've been immersed in the culture they're going to reach for some significant time. You can ask Mancini's questions early on, but you can only really answer them after you've started community infiltration.

We found ourselves reverse engineering our understanding of Acts from what God was doing in our churches. We learned a new appreciation and respect for the apostles, the book of Acts, and the genius of the Holy Spirit. The book you hold in your hands is, in large part, a byproduct of that experience. Therefore, be ready for God to open up opportunities for you. You may experience a restaurateur opening their space to you on Sundays. You may have a manager at Starbucks ask you to host a community meeting of your choosing because he knows you used to be a pastor. Pursue the mission that God puts in front of you by divine appointments.

When crafting your missional direction, be sure to include the following factors:

Missional Direction

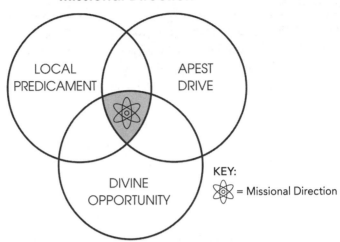

- **Local predicament:** What are the pain points in my city?
- **APEST drives:** What are the APEST drives and gifting of my team? (Formerly Collective Potential and Apostolic Esprit)
- **Divine opportunity:** What opportunities is God opening up in front of us?

ALWAYS MOVING

Like apostles themselves, the mission of your church plant never ceases to be a moving target. Every time your church sends a strike team to multiply out of your church, your collective potential changes, and the makeup of the fist team that stays behind also changes. As some of the gifting leaves with those people, your collective potential and APEST makeup shifts. The major difference between this tool and Mancini's is that the modified tool always assumes a major change is coming at any minute. That said, when you've distilled those three circles to the best of your ability with an eye toward the Holy Spirit's sovereign intervention, you've not only already been attacking the mission, you're ready to improve it.

REFLECT

- What are the core values of your church or church plant? Don't choose aspirational values—rather, try to discern the values already operating. Craft a mantra corresponding to each value.
- Examine the core values of your church. Are these the values your church plant should have?
- Read Ephesians 1:22–23. What does the "church plant shaped hole" look like in your city? That is, what does the "God-shaped hole" look like in your city, and how will your church incarnate Jesus there?

DISCUSS

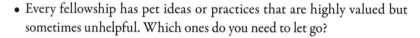

- If a new church plant adopts the mantra, "Everybody serves, everybody wins," what does that suggest about their core values?
- How are mantras helpful for persuading the fellowship to remain true to the core values of the church?

CHALLENGE

- Every fellowship has pet ideas or practices that are highly valued but sometimes unhelpful. Which ones do you need to let go?

11

CULTURE AND CONTEXTUALIZATION

I can calculate the motions of the heavenly
bodies, but not the madness of crowds.

—SIR ISAAC NEWTON

THE CULTURAL MANDATE

The process of contextualization in ministry describes the process of applying the gospel to the cultural context of the listener. Paul had the enormous task of contextualizing a gospel of Jewish origin into the cultural context of the Gentiles. The church's relationship with culture has been fraught with difficulty since the dawn of the faith.

Although the church has historically viewed culture as something to fight or contend with, if we oppose culture as an enemy to be defeated rather than a sparring partner, we will find ourselves standing outside of the ring, boxing with the air. Culture is the conversation that the world around you is having. If the church is called to one thing, missiologically speaking, it is to enter the conversation, not ignore it. The church adds a voice that is sometimes comforting, sometimes disruptive, and at other times prophetic, as in the case of Martin Luther King Jr.

Historically speaking, there has been a lingering fear within evangelical circles that engaging with culture must be a one-way street. The fear is that the church will never truly permeate the culture but, instead, the church will inevitably be permeated, and hence corrupted, by culture. But this view denies church history, both recent and ancient. As a result of this type of thinking, churches have typically treated culture with fear and suspicion. Yet neither the church global nor the church local can ever escape culture for the simple reason that the church exists within the context of culture. If the church is water, then culture is like the cup that holds it and helps give it shape, despite how little the water may desire for this to be the case.

The extent to which culture has shaped the church has been debated by missiologists for decades. Interestingly, the dissection of the relationship between culture and the church has been chiefly discussed by those returning from another culture after serving in a cross-cultural mission field. As they have exegeted a new culture from an outsider's perspective with the intention of penetrating it with the gospel, they often return home to find they are unable to switch off this missionary skill and must relearn their native culture by exegeting it in the same way. This has led to discussions on indigenous church movements led by nationals as missionaries to their own culture.

This wrestling with the intersection of culture and ecclesiology, led by notable missiologists and missionaries such as Lesslie Newbigin and others, triggered the World Council of Churches to introduce the concept of cultural contextualization, the process by which national Christians can communicate the gospel message effectively as missionaries to their own culture. Tim Keller explains that, in its early stages, the work got off to a rocky start due to the complexity of culture itself, concluding that "yet again, the Christian faith was over-adapted to culture."[1] But the church had taken the right step towards engaging culture, and that was certainly more advantageous than pretending it didn't exist or had no effect on the church's self-understanding.

Culture is the water to the fish, the air to the bird. Humans involuntarily, and often unconsciously, dwell in it. We scarcely notice it unless we are trained to do so or perhaps, as we age, we might start to sense its impact as culture keeps shifting and morphing away from the good old days of our youth. How should a church planter react to culture? Should the planter resist culture, or attempt to harness it?

The question remains, *What is the proper relationship between culture and the church?*

Mark Driscoll helpfully summarizes the role churches should play in their culture by providing a series of formulas:[2]

- Gospel + Culture – Church = Parachurch
- Culture + Church – Gospel = Liberalism
- Church + Gospel – Culture = Fundamentalism

---

1. Timothy J. Keller, *Center Church* (Grand Rapids: Zondervan, 2012), 91.
2. Mark Driscoll, *The Radical Reformission: Reaching Out without Selling Out* (Grand Rapids: Zondervan, 2004), 22–25.

The conclusion inferred from these formulas is that the way to properly engage and penetrate culture must be:

Church + Gospel + Culture

What does this formula equal? The question must be answered by each respective generation. For the first generation of the church in Jerusalem, cultural engagement was a primary question, beginning with how to contextualize the gospel into Judaism. Then the early Hellenistic converts raised cultural questions that the apostles were forced to address. Perhaps more significantly, the church had to wrestle with the process of contextualizing that same gospel into a pagan, Gentile world.

The church first has to answer three vital questions:

1. Is culture a moral force?
2. Is culture an immoral force?
3. Is culture an amoral force?

PAUL'S TREATMENT OF CULTURE AS AMORAL

The New Testament narrative chronicles the ways in which the early church saw culture as amoral as they worked to cross cultural boundaries, penetrate a vast breadth of cultures, and over time, even transform them without losing the church's essential function or doctrine. Outside of Christ, Paul stands as the central figure in the New Testament; he modeled, as Jesus did, the attitude that culture need not be the enemy of the gospel. On the contrary, culture itself may be the donkey that the Master can use as a vehicle to penetrate the crowds.

It is highly probable, according to F. F. Bruce, that Paul acquired "the rudiments of Greek learning in Gamaliel's school."[3] Gamaliel's son, Simeon, was widely known for offering instruction in both "the wisdom of the Greeks" and the Torah equally. If such prominent rabbis as Gamaliel viewed culture as an amoral tool, then it is not surprising that Paul might view it that way too. He approached culture as a two-edged sword that could cut both ways. It could be as much a danger to the wielder as it could be a tool in his or her hand. During his twelve years prior to Antioch, Paul, ever the thinker, must have hammered out the complex arguments that appear later in his writings as he worked with his hands, making tents. During those formative years, he would have mused

---

3. F. F. Bruce, *Paul: Apostle of the Heart Set Free* (Grand Rapids: Eerdmans, 1996), 126.

over Plato, Aristotle, and the other Greek philosophers and poets, imagining how the gospel could cross from being a Jewish message to a global one.[4]

PAUL'S TREATMENT OF CULTURE AS IMMORAL

To gain an understanding of Paul's double approach to culture, let's look at his view of culture as an immoral threat. Culture must bow to the gospel, not the other way around. In many of the epistles, Paul addressed behavioral concerns brought on by cultural influences that needed to be put down. Perhaps the letters to the Corinthians contain the most glaring examples of culture polluting the church. In Paul's first letter to the Corinthians, he challenged their cultural baggage and sought to change their attitudes toward a number of issues:

- Their fascination with words and wisdom (1:18–2:5)
- Ranking preachers based on popularity (3:5–17)
- Their preoccupation with the accouterments of success being a sign of commendation (4:1–21)
- Tolerating sexual deviancy (5:1–5)
- Suing one another to settle disputes (6:1–11)
- Continuing to see prostitutes (6:12–20)
- Carelessness toward divorce (7:10–16)
- Eating food sacrificed to idols (8:1–11:1)

PAUL'S TREATMENT OF CULTURE AS MORAL

Similarly, Paul changed his approach at some points and even used the culture itself as a correctional tool. When addressing an incestuous relationship, he directly appealed to the cultural norms of the day, contrasting the behavior of the perpetrator with the standard of the Gentiles: "It is actually reported that there is sexual immorality among you, and of a kind that is not tolerated even among pagans, for a man has his father's wife" (1 Cor. 5:1 ESV).

At other times, he used cultural norms to contextualize the teachings of the gospel through familiar language, appealing to popular philosophy. For example, when he spoke of virtue (literally "the good"), he was speaking of a Platonic ideal that was seen as something to strive for in life. Paul borrowed this term from culture and saved himself a great deal of explanation. Papyrus wasn't cheap!

4. N. T. Wright, *Paul: A Biography* (New York: HarperCollins, 2011), 78.

To illustrate this principle, I was once preaching the gospel at a church in the Greater London area. I was preaching on atonement and, to save time, quickly referenced the Ark of the Covenant in *Raiders of the Lost Ark*. Afterward, a kind, elderly, English gentleman approached me and said, "I enjoyed your sermon very much, but when you referenced a Hollywood film, you will have offended a great many members of the church." Knowing that friends of mine who did not yet believe were present in the audience, I quickly responded, "I wasn't speaking to those people." Time wasn't the only thing saved that morning.

Consider Paul's use of popular culture in contextualizing gospel principles:[5]

1 Corinthians 13:12

- Paul wrote, "For now we see through a glass, darkly, but then face to face" (KJV).
- Plato wrote, "I am very far from admitting that he who contemplates existences through the medium of thought, sees them only 'through a glass, darkly,' any more than he who sees them in their working effects."[6]

2 Corinthians 7:2

- Paul wrote, "We have wronged no one, we have corrupted no one, we have exploited no one."
- Plato says, "We have wronged no man; we have corrupted no man; we have defrauded no man."

1 Corinthians 12:25–26

- Paul says, "That there should be no division in the body, but that its parts should have equal concern for each other. If one part suffers, every part suffers with it; if one part is honored, every part rejoices with it."
- Socrates says, "If the finger of one of us is wounded, the entire community of bodily connections stretching to the soul for 'integration' with the dominant part is made aware, and all of it feels the pain as a whole."[7]

And why would Paul *not* quote Plato? He was well known and often quoted in the world into which Paul was planting. Eusebius wrote, "[Plato is] the only

---

5. "Paul and His Use of Greek Philosophy," Bible Things in Bible Ways, https://biblethingsinbibleways.wordpress.com/2013/07/14/paul-and-his-use-of-greek-philosophy/. See also Stuart H. Merriam, *Paul the Apostle: At the Edge of Faith* (Tucson, AZ: Wheatmark, 2003), 107.

6. Plato, *The Dialogues of Plato*, Vol. 1, ed. B. Jowett (Oxford: Clarendon, 1875), 478.

7. F. F. Powell, *Robbing Peter to Pay Paul: The Usurpation of Jesus and the Original Disciples* (iUniverse, 2008), 90.

Greek who has attained the porch of (Christian) truth." Augustine wrote, "I found that whatever truth I had read [in the Platonists] was [in the writings of Paul] combined with the exaltation of thy grace."[8]

This is not to say that Paul was directly quoting these sources. He may have been referencing popular aphorisms, but the importance is in recognizing that his use of them validates the practice of leveraging culture for the communication of the gospel. Culture is therefore amoral but may be used to serve either moral or immoral ends. It is always wise to remember that the Holy of Holies was lined with Egyptian gold that had originally been dedicated to the worship of pagan deities. Culture is like that gold, the most malleable of metals, and planters should seek to harness culture, redeem culture, and if possible, transform it.

When appealing to virtue, Paul appealed to the Platonic ideal and joined the conversation the world around him was having. Church planters today must do the same. That said, if we were only talking to people like us, this would be simple, but in the next section, I will make a case that the effective church planter cannot simply reach people like themselves because culture is no longer homogenous.

AN EVER-INCREASING COMPLEXITY

The Merriam-Webster Dictionary defines *culture* as "the characteristic features of everyday existence (such as diversions or a way of life) shared by people in a place or time."[9] In a globalized world, we may ask the questions: Which people? Does any society today really have "a people"? Today we speak of people groups within any given society. As Sproul observed, "We have a melting pot of people, and therefore, of ideas. The result has been that many different beliefs and philosophies compete for acceptance within our society."[10] The book *A New Religious America* reports, "There are more Muslim Americans than Episcopalians, more Muslims than members of the Presbyterian Church USA."[11] This means that when we speak about issues of faith, it merely comes across as "another personal preference in an ocean of cultural preferences."[12]

---

8. David Davidson, "Take It from the Church Fathers: You Should Read Plato," Logos Talk, https://blog.logos.com/2013/11/plato-christianity-church-fathers/.

9. "Culture," Merriam-Webster, https://www.merriam-webster.com/dictionary/culture, accessed June 26, 2020.

10. R. C. Sproul, *Lifeviews* (Grand Rapids: Baker, 1995), 2.

11. Quoted in Alan J. Roxburgh, *Structured for Mission: Renewing the Culture of The Church* (Downers Grove, IL: InterVarsity Press, 2015), 19.

12. Alan Noble, *Disruptive Witness* (Downers Grove, IL: InterVarsity Press, 2018), 2.

Since church planters are missionaries by definition, they must understand that the culture into which they are planting will be made up of a diverse group of people. The complexity of modern life does not allow the planter to study only one culture; the aggregation of diverse people from numerous cultural backgrounds has created subcultures within multiple cultures, and even subcultures that come from the blending of multiple cultures. It is no longer enough to discuss the Hmong tribe as a monolithic group of immigrants from Southeast Asia; time has created a subculture of second-generation Asian-Americans from the Hmong tribe whose perspectives and values may differ substantially from those of their immigrant parents.

This complexity also existed in the early church. The obvious cultures, such as the Romans, the Jews, and the prolonged presence of the Hellenistic Diaspora in the newly formed Jerusalem church posed the first clash of cultures, and the collision nearly split the church. From the beginning, the story of the Christian faith has been one of crossing cultures. The church has always brushed against a culture bigger than itself, harnessing it, at times redeeming it, and eventually transforming it.

There is an ever-increasing complexity that culture breeds with each passing generation. This chapter will not be able to address each cultural issue exhaustively, as each one warrants multiple books of this size, each with specific perspectives on the issues. Nor will this chapter be able to capture and exhaust the breadth of them. Instead, this chapter will highlight current cultural considerations with which the church is grappling in this brave new world. Indeed, it is hard to keep up with all the cultural nuances and issues that a planter faces, and yet nearly all speak to an aspect of brokenness in a fallen world.

CHRIST IN CULTURE

The answer to the question of what the church's relationship to culture should be is directly tied to where Christ stands in relationship to it. After all, the church is meant to act as his Body—an extension of him as our head. Richard Niebuhr's work *Christ in Culture* posed these five options for viewing Christ in relationship to culture: Christ against culture and Christ of culture are the two extremes. In between these two are Christ above culture, Christ and culture in paradox, and Christ transforming culture.[13]

Keller, in *Center Church*, a brilliant manifesto on Christ-centered urban

---

13. A summary of the work of Richard Niebuhr's work *Christ and Culture* (New York: Harper and Row, 1951).

ministry, outlines the four main models for the church's approach to culture: Transformationalist, Counter-culturalist, Two Kingdoms, and Relevance models. For the sake of time and space, I'd refer you to that work, as Keller spends four chapters detailing each model's strengths and weaknesses.

His conclusion is that any of the four models, in and of themselves, "are correct and essential, yet incomplete. As a result, the core-prescriptions are admirable and necessary, yet unbalanced."[14] Borrowing from the work of D. A. Carson, he attaches each model to an emphasis on one of the four essential metanarratives of redemptive history. Each emphasis may be categorized as an overemphasis at the expense of the other elements of the metanarrative. The summary looks like this:

The Two Kingdoms model (over)emphasizes the creation.
The Transformationalist model (over)emphasizes the Fall.
The Counter-culturalist model (over)emphasizes God's redemption.
The Relevance model (over)emphasizes the restoration of creation.

The planter can ignore these models, but they will influence the church nonetheless. Yet that is not the question at hand. The true question remains: "How will the church exert influence in these cultural issues?" For this reason, there are three considerations for the following issues:

- How can the gospel harness this aspect of culture?
- How can the gospel redeem this aspect of culture?
- How can the gospel transform this aspect of culture?

Harnessing Culture

Christians are able to speak into this vacuum, not because they stand outside or even above culture, but because, like Jesus, they are incarnate in the midst of it and have the ability to *harness culture* for communicating the gospel. Jesus harnessed culture when he taught about the image on a Roman coin bearing Caesar's profile. Paul harnessed culture when he hijacked the pledge of divine allegiance to the Emperor God "Caesar is Lord" and made it a picture of what a Christian confessed about Jesus.

Harnessing culture is usually the first step toward communicating the gospel with people, and Paul harnessed culture very clearly when he claims in 1 Corinthians 9:22 (ESV) that "I have become all things to all people, that by

---

14. Keller, *Center Church*, 225.

all means I might save some." Paul was not only adapting his manners to various cultures in order to reach them, he was even strategically adapting his use of circumcision to reach them. In the case of Timothy, he circumcised Timothy "for they all knew that his father was a Greek" (Acts 16:3). In so doing, he was not violating his stance about circumcision as communicated to the Galatians; he circumcised Timothy for a missional advantage, rather than for the sake of a theological principle. Titus, on the other hand was encouraged not to be circumcised so that he could be received among the Gentiles and serve as an example to them.[15] In any case, Paul accommodated culture in order to communicate something completely countercultural.

Redeeming Culture

To penetrate society, planters must learn to redeem aspects of their culture. We redeem culture by celebrating the parts that are hardwired within it that point to the Lord's heart and can begin to transform it. For example, Tim Keller argues that the modern city is a cultural trend that contains redemptive analogies and that cities in Scripture are increasingly portrayed as God's preferred setting for the thriving of human culture and potential. He sees this demonstrated in Genesis 4 and 5 where mankind achieves the invention of music and metallurgy. God's desire is not to bring us back to Eden, but to the New Jerusalem, a city whose maker and builder is God.[16] The longing to dwell together with others, forming an identity, and sharing something in common on earth is a glimpse of the heavenly city that God has been building.

Transforming Culture

Finally, the gospel will eventually work through the cultural dough like yeast to transform the whole lump. Through the church in Great Britain, William Wilberforce rose up as an abolitionist to transform the British Empire and culture forever. When the American Civil War failed to restore dignity to black Americans, the racist bus laws in America created a pressure cooker set to explode. In the center of this civil rights revolution was the church, and a black minister in Montgomery, Alabama, named Martin Luther King Jr. stepped up to make a difference. The black church served as a catalyst for cultural change in America, and the black church modeled Christianity at one of its finest hours.[17]

---

15. Bruce, *Paul*, 215.
16. Timothy Keller, *Why Did God Make Cities?* (New York: City to City, 2013), 8–9.
17. James K. A. Smith, *Desiring the Kingdom* (Grand Rapids: Baker Academic, 2009).

Social Justice Issues

America has always been a nation divided, and the roots of racism—systemic and personal—go deep. When a church plant forms a kingdom community within an existing community, the principles of the kingdom challenge and upset the earthly structures of power, inequality, and injustice.

Harness

The Gospels are laced with Jesus challenging racism, from his interactions with the Samaritan woman at the well to his conversation with the Phoenician woman. The apostles were also products of their culture, and it was rife with racist overtones. Yet the God they worshiped was incarnated as a persecuted minority; Jesus was a person of color. Despite this, the first real crunch that the apostles hit was a crisis of ethnicity between the Jews and Hellenists in Jerusalem—a clash that could only be solved by appointing non-Jewish leaders in the church.

Any church planter wanting to plant a multiethnic church would do well to pay attention to the wisdom of the apostles in the early church. For most of his ministry, the apostle Paul fought against latent, retaliatory racism aimed at the Gentiles as they attempted to join in fellowship with the Jews. As a Jew, he knew well what it felt like to be a victim of discrimination, but he was convinced that the kingdom of God meant better things for humanity.

Redeem

Glaringly absent in the discussions regarding *social justice* is the concept of *reconciliation*. Dhati Lewis, director of church planting at the North American Mission Board, remarked, "There is a place where justice exists without reconciliation. In the Bible it's called hell."[18] Restoration is hardwired into the gospel itself, and the church possesses the ability to redeem the conversation. All ethnic groups bear the responsibility to stop the spread of hate, from fighting against outright racism to stirring up compassion for the plight of another group. That said, particularly within the white church, there is a burden that must be shouldered. There is a history of not treating other races as equals or acknowledging their dignity as human beings. There has been a history of repressing minorities that has had aftershocks and consequences in modern society. The first step to overcoming the tension is for honest and open conversations to take place. Anyone planting a church must ask the question, "What does reconciliation look like in the life of our church plant?"

---

18. Dhati Lewis, *Advocates: The Narrow Path to Racial Reconciliation* (Nashville: Broadman & Holman, 2019), loc. 1582 of 1987, Kindle.

Transform

Transformation in society can take place on various fronts. It could be social, represented by fair treatment of the marginalized reflected in legislation or employment opportunities. Economic factors may improve over time. Studies have found that as people from poor and lower socioeconomic communities "adopt biblical lifestyles, they rise in social standing and standard of living."[19] For example, fathers take more responsibility for their families, with the result that money is spent on education instead of alcohol or gambling. A work ethic is adopted, and human dignity is instilled in place of fear and inferiority.[20] Transformation is a process, and the outworking of the gospel will manifest differently over time in various neighborhoods.

Conclusion

As complex as issues like this are, they cannot be solved with simple strategies. On the contrary, it's the hope of the author that planters would develop their own solutions and strategies for participation with the Spirit for harnessing, redeeming, and transforming these aspects of culture. One thing that all these cultural conversations have in common is that they are polarizing by nature.

Many run from controversy or from robust discussion. We often supply multiple reasons for avoiding these cultural conversations. We may avoid engaging culture on these topics due to feelings of being out of our depth intellectually; however, all good missionaries, negotiators, and counselors will tell you that the best skill in any conversation is listening.

The second reason a planter may avoid these cultural conversations is fear of setting off an emotional powder keg. A third reason is sociological.

In Stephen L. Carter's masterpiece *The Culture of Disbelief*, he argues that a misunderstanding of the separation of church and state has been used to trivialize the faith of millions, convincing them that their religious devotion and beliefs don't belong in the public sphere.[21] In fact, anyone making mention of a connection to a church or religion, in general, risks being labeled a fanatic. While in no way advocating religious dominance, Carter argues that religion is relevant but has been trivialized by politicians seeking power. Religion has

---

19. Donald A. McGavran and Peter C. Wagner, *Understanding Church Growth* (Grand Rapids: Eerdmans, 1980), 42–46, 295–313.

20. Gene Wilson and Craig Ott, *Global Church Planting: Biblical Principals and Best Practices for Multiplication* (Grand Rapids: Baker Academic, 2011), 335.

21. Stephen L. Carter, *The Culture of Disbelief: How American Politics Trivialize Religious Devotion* (Alpharetta, GA: North American Mission Board, 2012), 26.

now been relegated to the place of a hobby, rather than being seen as a major influencer in how the world thinks and behaves. Therefore, trivializing it is neither wise nor honest.

Early in his book, Carter compares and contrasts the biography of Maria Von Trapp with the popular Rogers and Hammerstein musical *The Sound of Music* that was inspired by her story. In it, he notes that her religious faith was the deciding factor in most of her decisions, including whether or not to marry. In the end, she submitted to the instructions of her mother superior at the convent, which by today's standards would be interpreted as belonging to a strange religious cult. Despite nearly one-third of the world's population professing to be Christian and only 2.4% describing themselves as atheist, Western society treats the theist majority (roughly 80% of humanity) as if it has nothing important to say.[22] As C. S. Lewis observed regarding the place of religion in polite conversation, "That religion should be relegated to solitude in such an age is, then, paradoxical. But it is also dangerous . . . when the modern world says to us aloud, 'You may be religious when you are alone,' and then mutters under its breath, 'I'll see to it that you never are alone.'"[23]

Nevertheless, the reluctance to enter these conversations must be overcome. While the Dunkirk evacuation was taking place in World War Two, the commander of the allies sent a message to the commanders back in Britain saying that he and his men would fight on, trusting that they would be rescued in time. However, he demonstrated his determination to endure by ending his message with three words: "AND IF NOT." This was a quote from the book of Daniel, the Jewish envoy to Babylon who faced a culture hostile to all he was. As his friends, Shadrach, Meshach, and Abednego were expecting to be delivered from the fiery furnace, they nevertheless accepted the possibility that they might yet have to stand in the fire. Such is the call to all who seek to transform a society by engaging its culture.

ENGAGING CULTURE

To be a church planter and properly exegete your city, you will require a special set of skills. The planter must *observe* the culture, or they cannot *understand* it. Once the planter *understands* the culture, they can intelligently *speak* to it. In the parable of the sower, Jesus highlights one of the reasons that

---

22. Conrad Hackett and David McClendon, "Christians Remain World's Largest Religious Group, but They Are Declining in Europe," Pew Research Center, April 5, 2017, https://www.pewresearch.org/fact-tank/2017/04/05/christians-remain-worlds-largest-religious-group-but-they-are-declining-in-europe/.

23. C. S. Lewis, *The Weight of Glory* (San Francisco: HarperOne, 2001), 161.

contextualization is crucial to communicating the gospel. In the parable, Jesus outlines three reasons that the gospel seed fails to take root. One of these is when the scattered seed falls on a hardened path and birds eat it up; Jesus explains that this scenario represents people who failed to understand. Unfortunately, this has all too often been the case. Contextualization involves being able to take the gospel and communicate it in language that is readily received by those to whom one is preaching.

Famous missionary Don Richardson, in his book *The Peace Child*, demonstrated how the gospel can be contextualized in a myriad of ways. A missionary in Indonesia among the Sawi people, Richardson and his wife came to believe that they were causing greater tensions among the three villages in the vicinity of the mission and prepared to leave as failures. They had failed to connect with the gospel among the Sawi, as their value system elevated Judas as the hero of the Gospels who successfully deceived everyone—a virtue among the Sawi. Upon news of their departure, the three chieftains of the villages met to declare peace. Each chief offered their son to be exchanged with the sons of the other chiefs. As long as the children lived, peace would be held. It was at this point that Richardson had a breakthrough in contextualizing the gospel to the Sawi. God the Father sent his son as the peace child and gave him to make peace with his enemies.

Richardson's important contribution to missiology was the creation of the Redemptive Analogy concept.[24] The Redemptive Analogy was a concept hardwired into every culture, in every age, whereby the gospel could be preached, as Paul had found at Mars Hill when he preached from the statue inscribed as dedicated to the "Unknown God" (Acts 17). Crider states, "Observe any culture in depth, and it becomes clear that the suppressed memory of the Creator is not completely forgotten. . . . The Artist has left His fingerprints on His work."[25]

When church planters contextualize the gospel, they are seeking to answer the question: "How does the gospel become good news to *this* people?" Like Richardson's near miss, many of our breakthroughs are like Bob Ross's happy accidents. Like the accidental discovery of penicillin when a petri dish was left too long in the lab, we stumble into these missional inroads like a hidden garden path. Lesslie Newbigin wrote, "My own experience as a missionary has been that significant advances of the church have not been the result of our

---

24. Ruth A. Tucker, *From Jerusalem to Irian Jaya: A Biographical History of Christian Missions* (Grand Rapids: Zondervan, 2004), 476–78.

25. Larry E. McCrary and Caleb Crider, *Tradecraft: For the Church on Mission* (Portland, OR: Urban Loft Publishers, 2013), 70.

own decisions about mobilizing and allocating of 'resources.' The significant advances in my experience have come through happenings of which the story of Peter and Cornelius is a paradigm, in ways of which we have no advance knowledge. God opens the heart of a man or woman in the gospel."[26]

MISSIONARIES KNOW THEIR COMMUNITIES

Planters can know where they are geographically without having a clue where they are culturally. Familiarity may breed contempt, but for missionaries, it breeds compassion. Before you can go on mission, you need to understand the mission field to discover how to cultivate it. Paul spent an entire day walking around Athens and studying their worship before engaging them with the gospel. Nehemiah scouted the city by night. Joshua's troops circled the city for days. Circling the city beats circling the drain. Believe it or not, many planters never pause to answer the following questions:

- What's the suicide rate in your part of the city?
- What's the ethnic make-up?
- What languages do your neighbors speak?
- What's the socioeconomic makeup?
- What percentage of the population is unemployed or on benefits?
- What's the chief type of occupation?
- What are the statistics for how many are married or divorced, with or without kids? What percentage are single parents?
- Is the crime rate high? Which crimes are the most common?
- What social concerns do the mayor or other civic leaders address the most?
- Which religions are practiced, and at what rate?

All this information is at your fingertips by simply typing your city's name into the Google search window. You just have to care.

Additionally, perusing local newspapers is also enlightening when it comes to the needs of a city or community. A newspaper is as good as a map, because the city's needs are clearly laid out in articles where hundreds of needs are documented, far more than any one church plant can reach: kids aging out of foster care, the homeless, young families, orphans, ex-cons, addicts, sex trafficking, and slavery. All of these are worthy fights to pick in your city, but you can't win a cage match with evil if you don't know where to punch.

---

26. Tony Parsons, *The Open Secret* (London: The Open Secret Publishing, 2000), 64.

Linda Berquist, catalyst for the North American Mission Board, wrote a book with Alan Karr called *The Wholehearted Church Planter* in which she speaks about "falling in love with a people."[27] When I wanted to be a missionary to Wales, I fell in love with the Welsh from afar. I read everything I could about them. I found that to know them was to love them. I read their folklore. I read their history. I read huge tomes on their politics. I attempted to learn their language. Perhaps my love for the Welsh culture could not be measured, but in hindsight, I am convinced that my love was felt.

TOOLS OF THE TRADE

So how do planters learn to think like missionaries and contextualize the gospel for their communities? Larry McCrary and Caleb Crider, in their excellent book *Tradecraft*, summarize missionary tactics for modern planters. They identify the Five Elements of a City outlined by Kevin A. Lynch in the 1960s.[28]

Paths

Paths are streets, sidewalks, or any type of thoroughfare by which people travel, be it on foot, automobile, bike, or public transport. Learning the paths of a city helps you to become familiar with the concepts of distance relative to that area and gives you a perspective to see through the eyes of the people who live there as they move about daily.

Nodes

Nodes are where people gather strategically for interaction: parks, food courts, cafés, or shopping malls. Because of the high concentration of people, these are areas where advertising is prevalent. Observing the ads and what is being communicated can help you understand the desires, hopes, and fears of the people who live there. Nodes are often defined by their borders.[29] Michael Frost advocates placecrafting, the practice of churches owning a space and seeking to shift from being *within* their neighborhood to *in-with* their neighborhood. Frost argues placecrafting isn't done in place of mission, but is essential for mission.[30]

---

27. Allan Karr and Linda Bergquist, *The Wholehearted Church Planter: Leadership from the Inside Out* (Nashville: Chalice, 2013), 82.

28. McCrary and Crider, *Tradecraft*, 52–60.

29. McCrary and Crider, *Tradecraft*, 52–60.

30. Michael Frost and Christiana Rice, *To Alter Your World: Partnering with God to Rebirth Our Communities* (Downers Grove, IL: InterVarsity Press, 2017). Frost makes this same argument in his *The Road to Missional: Journey to the Center of the Church* (Grand Rapids: Baker, 2011), 27. He also credits

Districts

These are areas where the groupings of people are commonly understood, identified, and named. We tend to think of this in terms of neighborhoods. In densely populated beach towns, they will speak of living in the village, or on the South Side. Terms like "the rainbow district" or the "art district" would be examples of a district. It is a place that has been defined by the inhabitants of the city.

Edges

Between two neighborhoods or districts, there is usually a border or boundary of sorts. Perhaps where the freeway intersects the city or a train track bisects a community you see an edge that denotes the proverbial "other side of the tracks." Rivers, walls, and streets may serve as natural edges.

Landmarks

These sites tend to define a city's identity and serve as directional guides, or anchors, in a resident's mental map. For example, in Long Beach, "The Pike" is a landmark, a shopping center that was built on top of the amusement park by the same name. The Queen Mary and the white dome that once housed Howard Hughes's infamous "Spruce Goose" also serve as landmarks marking the harbor from a great distance. In London, landmarks such as the Thames River, Big Ben, London Bridge, or the London Eye serve as landmarks to tourists and locals alike.

MAPPING

Knowing these things isn't enough. *Tradecraft* points to the practice of "mapping," the process of marking a geographic map of your community that identifies the paths, nodes, districts, edges, and landmarks. This is the first layer, or the geographical layer. Next, map out the social layer. This is done by gathering relevant information on crime, school statistics, or anything that will paint a picture of business, leisure, or relationships. The third and final layer is known as the spiritual layer.

> **Geographic**—What neighborhoods are represented, what are they called, how have they formed as distinct communities, and where do they stop and start?

Paul Sparks, Tim Soerens, and Dwight J. Friesen, *The New Parish: How Neighborhood Churches Are Transforming Mission Discipleship and Community* (Downers Grove, IL: InterVarsity Press, 2014) with the concept of placecrafting.

Social—Is there a racial identity, socioeconomic profile, or some other uniting factor?

Spiritual—What is the predominant makeup of spiritual beliefs in these communities?

Tim Keller said, "It is impossible to understand a culture without discerning its idols."[31] In the British documentary *Meet the Natives*, seven South Pacific tribesmen travel to London to understand British culture. A tribesman asks the host about the "Spirit House," pointing to a skyscraper. The host replies, "No, that is our money house." The tribesman responds, "In my village our biggest building is for our gods." The host pauses and replies sheepishly, "I think that might be what we worship more in this country after all."

When planting outward from one of our plants in Wales, we marked where all the churches were and discovered a "black spot" where there were no churches within a two-mile radius. Incidentally, it was also the poorest part of the city. Therefore, our church targeted that area as our first place to plant out. Therefore, mapping may be more strategic than we realize. N. T. Wright argued that Paul mapped his journey to the Gentiles by marking the Roman provinces on a map and selectively targeting them.

Put all these components together, and you will begin to understand the situation of the people you are trying to reach. So how do you find the needs?

When I'm working locally with a team, I take my planters out to laundromats, bars, parks, plazas, and other places to study how to reach those particular places. Whoever comes up with the best analysis gets to lead a smaller fraction of the team there. It's an exercise to teach planters to strategize how to meet people in areas where they never thought church was possible. I call it ministry in public places, because it's what Paul excelled at, and what modern America sucks at. Almost everything we've learned to do is confined within our own buildings. Take that away, and most ministers would be lost. Every bit of ministry in the New Testament, including Jesus's, however, was done outside. When performing reconnaissance outside, our teams are scouting out the land in almost any interconnecting hub in the community where people from different walks of life congregate with time on their hands.

We ask these questions:

---

31. Timothy Keller, *Counterfeit Gods: The Empty Promises of Money, Sex, and Power, and the Only Hope that Matters* (New York: Penguin Press, 2011), 119.

What are people doing here?

Why are they here?

How are they occupying their time?

What would they value?

How could church be valuable to them?

How would you reach this crowd if you did church here?

ASSIGNMENTS

Planters who are attempting to perform cultural reconnaissance must get their hands dirty. They must venture out into the culture and wade into the proverbial waters and swim in the current by doing the following.

Find Where God Is Already Working

Henry Blackaby said, "When God reveals to you where he is working, that becomes his invitation to join him in his activity."[32] Some of the ways you can discern where God has already been working is by walking around the city, as Paul did. Paul learned to read between the lines of the Athenian's existential angst in order to contextualize the gospel at Mars Hill. Without that valuable time spent walking around the city as he waited for his companions, Paul would not have been able to contextualize.

Before we speak, we must observe in order to understand. When we can trace the missional "ins" that Richardson speaks of that lie in every culture, we can fit the gospel key into the recessed lock that has held the culture entrapped and then set it free. John Wesley spoke of prevenient grace—the grace that prepares us for salvation and is at work in our lives by our sovereign God, prior to our receiving his saving grace. Planters who think like missionaries will begin to see God's prevenient grace in the conversations going on around them through films, songs, and social media posts. God is at work in the world long before we show up to the party.

Find Paths of Prayer

To avoid becoming a sociologist instead of a missionary, the planter must be careful not to divorce the spiritual from the sociological. Prayer walking is the practice of walking the city with others and praying over neighborhoods, asking God to reveal people and needs. Waiting for his companions to arrive in

---

32. Henry Blackaby, *Experiencing God: Knowing and Doing the Will of God* (Nashville: Lifeway Christian Resources, 1990), 56.

Athens, Paul had time to kill, so he walked around the city to feel its heartbeat. He breathed the air. He witnessed its wounds and felt its pain. Athens wasn't like any town he'd been to before. Paul had learned on his travels that in every place he went, there was a gospel "in." He just had to find it. The statue of the Unknown God unfolded Paul's missionary strategy. Prayer walks can be both reconnaissance and rescue at once.

Find the Story

One of the assignments you can give yourself and your team is to study the history of your city. There are even pictorial guides of the city. You can research the county and the state and see what makes the people tick. For example, the city of Los Angeles differs in many ways from San Diego. San Diego was built around a mission started by the Jesuit missionaries. As such, there is a rich religious history there, and the town developed differently from Los Angeles. Los Angeles was developed around the streetcar and, therefore, has always been a city geared towards progress and innovation. Despite being a modern city, San Diego maintains a rich old-world history as well, and to ignore that fact is to miss a vital part of the mindset of people living in San Diego. In addition to studying the history and mapping out the layout of your city, Crider and McCrary suggest mapping God's activity in your city. What has God been doing in your city over the years? Has he moved there before? What happened? What were the conditions? What were the obstacles? When did things begin to die off?

Find the Gatekeepers

If there are needs in your city, the mayor and city council know about them, and most cities now have a committee that seeks to work with local charities to meet those needs. A church planter should seek to be on it.

Find the Resting Spots

Once you identify the hangouts, nodes, and gathering places, start going there. Start meeting there. Start making that community part of the rhythm of your day. As you do, you will form relationships. You will visit the same coffee house or pub and start to recognize the regulars. As you converse with them, ask them questions like: What do you love about living here? What's the biggest challenge about living here? What do people who live here want out of life? What do people around here fear? What keeps them up at night? Talking about these things will not only give you insight, it will lead to gospel conversations. Once you know the layout of the city, you'll begin to understand how people think, move, and congregate. The next step is to travel their paths, congregate in their areas, and learn from their sacred spaces. The paths are how people move around. Where they congregate is a great way to reach them, and their values are learned from their "sacred spaces."

Find the Marketplace

Paul was bivocational—partly so he could eat, partly so he could support his team (Acts 20:4). I believe, however, that Paul could have asked for almost any amount of support from the churches, but instead he chose to go where the traffic was. In the same way, the apostles in Acts 3 were visiting the temple during the time of prayer (Acts 3:1). Church planters go where the people already are.

Alan Hirsch talks about proximity spaces rather than centralized gatherings in church buildings. If people are at a coffee shop, why start a Christian one? The name of the game is infiltration, and if you want to infiltrate people, you go where they go. You don't ask them to come to where you are. To meet them on their turf, you may need to go to an MMA gym and partner with them like Josh Boyd from Fight Church in Las Vegas. Set up church in a motel courtyard in Stanton. Have a service in a park on Sunday mornings in an inner-city neighborhood.

At a recent coaching session we did with a church planter, he mentioned that they'd moved into the old church building in the neighborhood that was used for weddings and funerals. The old church had gone bankrupt, and they were seen as the new church with money that had pushed the old one out. Damage control was needed with the community, more than anything. The message they sent to that community was crucial.

We suggested that instead of giving a modernizing overhaul and renovation to the old chapel to equip it for reaching youth, they should restore the old chapel with money from the weddings and funerals; we said they should then make sure that the people knew that the building "belonged" to the community because their most precious memories were there. They could also open up the new building to be a multi-use facility. In other words, since they had a building, they needed to use it in a strategic way. It would sit there week after week unused, except for twice a week, if it were only used for church services. Meanwhile, opening it up to karate classes, ballet classes, gardening groups, etc., would serve as a way to wave a white flag to the community. In the inner city, you could start DJ workshops, urban gardening groups, or infiltrate model car racers.

Find the Contextual Conversations

As I was speaking to my neighbor, he furrowed his brow and, with sincere incredulity, asked, "Can you help me understand the whole church thing? I just don't get it." His religious devotion was to CrossFit. I explained that, just as in his CrossFit experience, working out alone was good, but working out with others was better. "Think of church as CrossFit for your soul." He tilted his head, smiled, and said, "I get it now." Contextualization means learning the language and values of the other person so you can communicate your own. In this case, it means communicating God's.

When the apostles communicated the gospel as native Aramaic speakers of Jewish origin, they had to write their gospels in Greek. John learned the language and communicated in it. When Jesus spoke, he used examples that were familiar to his listeners, whether they were farmers in a field, wicked servants, thieves breaking in and stealing, Pharisees and tax collectors, or a man getting mugged on the road. Everything Jesus spoke about was a picture taken from something they already understood and applied to something spiritual they didn't yet grasp. Jesus contextualized the gospel. When the movie *The Matrix* came out, I capitalized on its popularity and used it to communicate the gospel by making my own Matrix-themed tracts.

Missionaries Crider and McCrary give the following advice for having conversations with people to garner trust and facilitate a meaningful conversation that may lead to the gospel:[33]

1. Listen.
2. Pay attention.
3. Read the person you're talking to.
4. Don't just talk about religion.
5. Be real.

Note that only one of them involves you talking. If I were to add a sixth point, it would be to relax. If you're nervous talking to people, it will be very difficult for them to relax enough to disclose sensitive information that will lead to a spiritual breakthrough.

---

33. McCrary and Crider, *Tradecraft*, 98–99.

REFLECT

- On a scale of 1 to 10, how would you rate yourself as a researcher of your own community? What do you think are the reasons for this? What are the "pathways" of your community? Where are the nodes? Where and how do people congregate in your community?
- What are the major cultural assumptions, themes, and values of the context in which your church or church plant operates? Consider both the larger culture (e.g., twenty-first century America, generations) and the micro-culture (e.g., the university, city, suburbs).

DISCUSS

- The author argues that you can harness, redeem, or transform culture. Which of these describes your vision for your church plant?
- Discuss the parts of culture that can be harnessed, redeemed, or transformed.
- For these examples, how would you harness culture? How would you redeem culture? How would you begin to transform culture?
- The author argues that in order to redeem culture, you need to see how the kingdom of God could infiltrate the culture somewhere. For your church or church plant, where could the kingdom of God infiltrate the culture of your city?

CHALLENGE

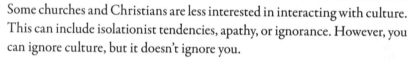

Some churches and Christians are less interested in interacting with culture. This can include isolationist tendencies, apathy, or ignorance. However, you can ignore culture, but it doesn't ignore you.

- Where do you think culture has harnessed or corrupted the church?
- How has culture conformed your church?
- Take some steps to become more of a part of the rhythms of your community. For example, hang out where people are congregating. Go to the center of the community and take part in a meeting or gathering of the members of the community. Observe the cultural norms, assumptions, and practices of your community in action. How can you harness, redeem, or transform the culture of your community?

REDISCOVERING FIRST-CENTURY PARTICIPATION

From Solo Performers to Team Mobilizers

12

DISCIPLESHIP AS A LIFESTYLE

Discipleship is the process of becoming
who Jesus would be if he were you.
—DALLAS WILLARD

WE ARE THE BOTTLENECK

In his discipleship book *Guardrails*, Alan Briggs recounts stopping daily at 10:02, morning and evening, to pray that the Lord would send more laborers into the harvest fields (Luke 10:2). In response to his prayer, Briggs felt God ask him what he'd do if he was sent ten hungry leaders the next day. He was forced to confess, "I was the bottleneck to my own prayers. My desire to disciple others, to equip everyday folks to join God's work, was clouded by unsustainability. My systems were maxed out. I either needed to change my systems or change my prayers."[1]

Just before he ascended to heaven, Jesus emphasized that discipleship was the core calling of the church and that it would continue to be so until the end of the age. The recent resurgence focusing on discipleship indicates that the church in the West may finally listen to the actual wording of the Great Commission and cease running a show on Sundays.

The concept and practice of discipleship was embedded in rabbinical training during the first century. As a rogue rabbi, Jesus was a calloused-handed carpenter, not a religious professional. As such, he made disciples out of other rough-necked, leather-faced tradesmen. Jesus modeled discipleship you could take to a jobsite. Since disciple making is our postresurrection, divine directive,

---

1. Ala Briggs, *Guardrails: Six Principles for a Multiplying Church* (Colorado Springs, CO: Navpress, 2016), 2.

one would think the church would excel at it, cornering the market on disciple-
ship. Perhaps if Jesus wrote the letters to the seven churches to the American
church, they would say, "You had one job." What the chicken sandwich is to
Chick-fil-A, discipleship is to Christ's church, but we've been serving hotdogs.
If the church were a peanut butter sandwich, discipleship would be our jam.
Why then do so few in the church understand and practice discipleship?

If the average Christian were asked how to disciple, the answers would vary
from person to person because of a basic principle regarding discipleship: *We
tend to disciple how we, ourselves, were discipled.* And sadly, if you don't disciple,
it's because of the same principle in reverse; *People tend to not disciple because
they weren't themselves discipled.*

The closest experience with discipleship most converts encounter is
being told:

- Read the Bible.
- Pray.
- Share your faith.
- Watch out for spiritual attack.

We basically tell new believers, "Welcome to Jesus. You're on your own from
here. Good luck!"

When multiplication rock star Ralph Moore was asked how nearly 2,800
churches resulted from his ministry, he popped the hood on his process and
revealed the engine of his discipleship machine. He maintained that the resulting 2,800 churches were born out of the leaders created over a fifty-year span
of he and his wife personally maintaining three active disciples at any given
time for six-month terms. The Moores discipled disciple-makers, resulting in
exponential multiplication. You may not have 2,800 churches spawn from your
loins, but Rick Warren observes that "Jesus doesn't expect us to produce *more*
than we can, but he does expect us to produce *all* that we can by his power
within us."[2] It turns out that our potential is higher than we thought.

When Jesus said, "Go and make disciples," the word *disciple* was pregnant
with meaning, unlike the neutered version in our culture that has become
devoid of its inherent richness. Today, "learning" can be passively achieved
with headphones on Audible, but to be discipled or mentored was originally
understood as an investment of one's entire life. The underlying concept of the

---

2. Rick Warren, "Foreword" in Craig Ott and Gene Wilson, *Global Church Planting: Biblical
Principles and Best Practices for Multiplication* (Grand Rapids: Baker Academic, 2011), viii.

two words "study" and "mentorship" is actually "learning" ("discipline," in the original sense of the word). Discipline means to pay attention, keep focused, or lock onto something. In discipleship, we are modeling Jesus to others, but we are ultimately asking them to look beyond us and see him. According to Brad Brisco, the word *apprenticeship* is the best English translation of what discipleship means, and he compares the process to learning a trade, such as plumbing or working with concrete where one studies under a master craftsman. "This is accomplished under the guidance of a skilled worker. The apprentice learns from observing and being in the presence of the one who has experience and wisdom in a particular trade."[3]

Mentorship is hardwired into the fabric of the universe, and you experience it anytime you desire to learn something: working on cars, painting, or becoming a doctor. To truly master something, you must study under a master, exercising great discipline.

Our neutered definition of learning does not do justice to the biblical concept of discipleship. We think if we memorize or recite chunks of information, we've learned it, but biblically speaking, unless something changes our lives, resulting in transformed thoughts generating new actions and behaviors, learning has failed to take place. Listen to Paul's use of the word *learn*:

> But that is not the way you learned Christ!—assuming that you have heard about him and were taught in him, as the truth is in Jesus, to put off your old self, which belongs to your former manner of life and is corrupt through deceitful desires, and to be renewed in the spirit of your minds, and to put on the new self, created after the likeness of God in true righteousness and holiness. (Eph. 4:20–24 ESV)

> For the grace of God has appeared that offers salvation to all people. It teaches us to say "No" to ungodliness and worldly passions, and to live self-controlled, upright and godly lives in this present age. (Titus 2:11–12)

Therefore, discipleship involves transformation. You wouldn't watch a YouTube video of a guitar lesson, then tell people you could play guitar. To "learn" guitar, we pick one up and start practicing until playing guitar is so ingrained into our minds that we become proficient and our fingers maneuver fluidly across frets and strings. Until we've learned Jesus like an instrument,

---

3. Brad Brisco, *Covocational Church Planting: Aligning Your Marketplace Calling & The Mission of God* (Alpharetta, GA: SEND Network, 2018), 12.

and people around us can see and hear him in our words and lives we've not "learned Christ," according to Paul, because *you don't act or sound like him to others*. Everyone knows that the most effective way to learn guitar is to take guitar lessons from somebody else.

The Jews daily turned toward Jerusalem and prayed the Shema, a prayer quoted from Deuteronomy 11:13–21 that commanded them to holistically love God with all their heart, soul, and strength. Discipleship was the equivalent of guitar lessons for those who wanted to love God, involving all that you did, thought, said, and valued. Such holistic faith is more caught than taught. Alan Briggs calls this the Shema-centered approach, or "4D discipleship," applying heart, soul, mind, and strength in the following ways:

- *Heart:* Our passion and will. What are you creating or striving after?
- *Soul:* Our connection with the eternal, our spiritual imagination. What are the God-inspired dreams you are thinking about and praying for?
- *Mind:* Our pursuit of knowledge and depth. What are you hungry to learn about and investigate?
- *Strength:* Our rhythms of expending time, energy and talent. What do you spend time and energy on in your life?[4]

Westerners approach cultivating these aspects of their lives in an individualistic, "self-help" fashion. The Jewish community of Jesus, however, was intensely relational. Extended families lived together, and the roots of the Jewish nation were found in a mobile, sojourning, camping community that bonded as a tribal society, leaving no room for individualism. Even the roots of the atonement were found in togetherness. Because they thought as a relational people, the individual's sins represented the sins of the nation and vice versa. Relationships were key to them because they were a relational community designed by a Trinity who exists in an eternal relationship. As Richard Plass observed, "We are relational beings because we are created in the image of a relational God. By definition the Christian God exists in relationship as Father, Son and Spirit. While existing in three distinct persons, they share one divine essence that is described as love (1 John 4:8). God can be love only if God exists as community."[5] Discipleship therefore was embedded in the fabric of parental and societal relationships.

---

4. Briggs, *Guardrails*, 78–79.
5. Richard Plass and James Coffield, *Relational Soul* (Downers Grove, IL: InterVarsity Press, 2014), 13.

THE DISCIPLESHIP PATTERN OF JESUS

Jesus modeled the pattern of discipleship in the New Testament that planters should incorporate into the lives of their church plants. Jesus's endgame was to train twelve disciple makers who went beyond him in discipling many others, imitating the same care and intention that Jesus poured into their development. We often make the mistake of thinking that leaders disciple leaders, but Ralph Moore's testimony, contemporary church planting movements, and the trajectory from Jerusalem to Antioch all tell a different story. When every believer is discipled into a disciple maker, a leadership lifestyle is passed on from generation to generation.

The three elements of discipleship that Jesus used to train his team were:

- Time
- Teaching
- Tactics

Where these three circles overlap you find biblical discipleship. Remove one circle and its elements and you will be left with something that stagnates multiplication.

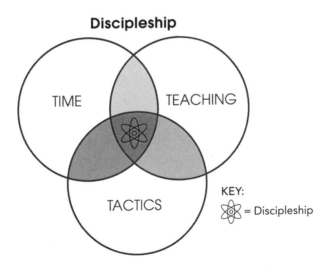

Teaching

Teaching is the low-commitment item found in most groups. In Acts 5:42 (ESV), teaching was central to the small groups of the early church: "And every day, in the temple and from house to house, they did not cease teaching and preaching that the Christ is Jesus." Like today, houses and small groups were central to the growth and spread of the church (Rom. 16:5). The small group conveniently serves as a discipleship vehicle or tool where the exchange of scriptural principles, thoughts, and ideas lead to the essential renewing of a disciple's mind.

Time

Next level discipleship involves spending time together outside of meetings, building relationships, and practicing what some call "life-on-life." This level of commitment requires a higher personal investment but gives us time to develop practical applications of what we've learned. Rubbing up against the sins, mistakes, and attitudes of others becomes a means of honing groups and individuals alike. An individual can disciple a group as much as the group can disciple the individual.

Time provides opportunity to practically apply the twenty-three "one another" passages of the New Testament.[6] Larry McCrary holds up Christ as the example, "His name 'Emmanuel' sums up His missionary heart better than any other word—'God with us.' And when was Jesus with the people? Everyday. And what did he do when he was with them? Eat. Drink. Serve. Converse. The rhythms of daily life."[7] It should not surprise us that the missional movement has experienced deeper levels of discipleship by adding this second circle into their discipleship process.

Tactics

Teaching is the norm, and time is increasingly on the rise, but how many groups have you been part of that don't merely direct each other to get outside the church walls, but actually go there together? We all know the answer to the rhetorical question. Leaders make a decent living pretending to be experts, pontificating about things they never practice. For all our talk about reaching the world, few actually venture out with intentionality. If leaders aren't careful, small groups can become a breeding ground for Christians who become experts on inactivity. Jesus counteracted this tendency by deploying his disciples into the villages of Judea before they were ready. The Gospels record two tours of duty, once with the Twelve and once with the seventy-two. Jesus was instilling a rhythm to their discipleship that was as natural as breathing.

If this were a biology textbook, the chapter on the Holy Spirit would be the chapter on the respiratory system, but the chapter on discipleship would be the circulatory system. Disciples take in knowledge, fellowship, and encouragement in one giant breath, and then exhale faith, risk, and mission with the same regularity. In the same way that the blood carries the oxygen to the rest

---

6. For a full list of the "one anothers," see pages 299–300.

7. Larry E. McCrary and Caleb Crider, *Tradecraft: For the Church on Mission* (Portland, OR: Urban Loft Publishers, 2013), 9.

of the body's tissues, so the Spirit flows more powerfully and is carried through the practice of discipleship more than anything else. More transformation happens in community than anywhere else.

Jesus took a bunch of recruits, the dirty dozen, and trained them into gospel commandos. He spent the bulk of his limited public ministry pouring himself into twelve people for three years, demonstrating the importance of discipleship. With only three brief years to accomplish his mission, the majority of his time was spent discipling others. Even when we see him preaching and doing miracles, it was largely for the benefit of the Twelve, who were watching and often participating. They were apprenticing, in order to "do even greater things than these" (John 14:12).

Jesus knew that you can't teach somebody how to fly a rocket ship using cardboard controls. Eventually they have to practically experience the law of aerodynamics. Therefore Jesus commanded them to heal, perform exorcisms, and even feed the five thousand. Remember that Jesus used a shock tactic by telling them, "You give them something to eat." The miracle of the loaves literally multiplied out of the disciples' hands as they passed out the bread, making them the dispensers of the miracle. Jesus wants all of us to participate, letting God use and work through us in ways we never imagined possible.

If I only spend time teaching my team, they become archaeologists of the academic type. To transform them into jungle-slashing, whip-cracking temple raiders like Indiana Jones, they had to be turned loose in an urban park to share Jesus with others instead of attending another stadium crusade. The disciple who only spends time in the teaching circle will become a know-it-all mockery of a disciple doing nothing to lift a finger to reach or help those around him. The disciple who only goes out on mission in the tactics circle eventually burns out. The person who only treasures the time circle and spends time with believers only becomes the "hostess with the mostest" at the best cookout where nobody ever heard the gospel.

LEVELS OF DISCIPLESHIP

Discipleship will naturally bottleneck at the level of your personal capacity. Deeper levels of discipleship will require deeper levels of commitment. Thankfully, the capacity of Jesus's discipleship reflects various levels of intimacy and investment. Despite gathering crowds of hundreds and thousands, Jesus discipled groups ranging from three to five thousand. The greater the intimacy, the smaller the group. Examining the various sizes of groups Jesus interacted with will assist the planter in strategizing the appropriate level of interaction according to the size of the group being discipled.

The Five Thousand

These were crowds made primarily of spectators who listened to him preach and watched him perform miracles. It is simply impossible to spend quality time with five thousand people. There was no real commitment to the group, only sporadic gatherings that varied in size and seem reminiscent of the fickle Christmas and Easter crowds modern churches experience. Nevertheless, members of this crowd sometimes funneled into the next grouping.

The Five Hundred

This bracket consists of regular attendees. The crowd of five hundred gathered with the disciples after the resurrection (1 Cor. 15), indicating a commitment to Jesus even after his death. There was an identity and bond between them, but they probably weren't that active . . . yet. Jesus had regular attendees and, despite what "discipleship experts" assert, every planter has them, no matter how intentional their discipleship strategy. Jesus's answer for his literal *consumers* (they came for bread) wasn't to bone up on discipleship but to gross them out. If Jesus experienced spurious conversions, we should not be shocked by 75 percent rate of attrition as asserted by the parable of the sower.

Crowds happen. Crowds only become a bad thing when you think they're the main thing and refuse to ask for a deeper level of commitment like Jesus did by asking them to eat his flesh and drink his blood. The missional community model aims to weed attendees out but may overshoot at times; attempting to deepen people's commitment externally sometimes venturing into practices bordering on cultish, controlling, compulsive, and manipulative. Dictating how people should attend, give, and spend time together is not necessary. Your capacity will only allow you to focus appropriately at each level, trusting that discipling those closest to you will result in them discipling others.

The Seventy-Two

When their time of theological sparring was over, and it was time to draw first blood and drip a few drops of their own, Jesus sent the seventy-two out on mission. In your group, these are the ones who are gung-ho to go on mission. It will not be the entire congregation, despite the desire to see everyone mobilized. The mobilized missionaries will return rejoicing like the seventy-two as they transition from spectators to participants. When they do, their contagious zeal will effectively infect portions of the five hundred. Jesus sent the seventy-two on mission, and despite following him closely, they weren't yet a part of the inner circle, yet from out of these ranks, Matthias replaced Judas and eventually entered the ranks of the Twelve (Acts 1:21–26).

The Twelve

Jesus picked twelve of the most unreliable, unpredictable recruits to be his platoon. He spent three years with them, mentoring them nonstop. Few would have picked those twelve to go into battle, or even to be on their football team, but Jesus wasn't picking them for battle; he was picking them as models of transformation. Jesus picked a ragtag, misfit group of leaders to model the principle that those who are discipled well, regardless of their origins, always emerge as leaders who become agents of change in others. That principle alone is the most profound lesson I've learned in the past two decades of ministry: leaders are simply people who have been discipled well.

Growing up, I watched a show called *Kung Fu*, starring David Carradine. It centered around the adventures of a Shaolin monk who had trained in the Tibetan monastery under his Shaolin master. Each time he would face a challenging circumstance, his mind flashed back to a moment of training in which a failure had been turned into a transformative lesson.

Refuge Long Beach was my transformative lesson of failure. I trained up too many planters but not enough people to leave behind, resulting in us struggling to find people to stay. Everybody wanted to go. That church changed how I trained leaders, but more important, it changed how I believe leaders are made. After the third church planting strike team was sent out, there was nobody with leadership potential left behind, or so I thought. Under the real threat of being left hopelessly trapped and unable to pursue my personal calling to leave and plant again, I asked God to show me how to solve my dilemma.

Disclaimer: No brilliance exists in the next few sentences. The resulting epiphany was that I should disciple the people directly in front of me to the best of my abilities, despite the fact that none of them were currently ministry candidates. At the risk of insulting those who were there, I confess that I obediently started discipling those in front of me, despite their apparent lack of potential. As a result of that experiment, leadership emerged from whomever I discipled. Chain-link fence salesmen became gospel animals. Ex-cons became elders. Perhaps what C. S. Lewis said in *Weight of Glory* is most fitting: "There are no ordinary people. You've never talked to a mere mortal."[8]

Winfield Bevins observed that the secret to John Wesley's genius and the making of the Methodist movement was the "importance of creating disciple-making systems."[9] He organized people into three interlocking discipleship groups: societies, class meetings, and bands. Societies were larger gatherings of

---

8. C. S. Lewis, *The Weight of Glory and Other Addresses* (San Francisco, CA: Harper, 1980), 45–46.

9. Winfield Bevins, *Marks of a Movement: What the Church Today Can Learn from the Wesleyan Revival* (Centreville, VA: Exponential, 2017), 44.

fifty to seventy people that provided worship and teaching (much like a new church). It was in the smaller, more intentional class meetings, however, where deep discipleship happened. Class meetings numbered about twelve people, and bands included five people. D. Michael Henderson says, "It could be said metaphorically that the society aimed for the head, the class meeting for the hands, and the band for the heart. Wesley would take new converts and place them into class meetings, which were much like small groups; they were designed to meet spiritual needs. These class meetings met weekly for prayer, instruction, and mutual fellowship. Each group had a designated male or female leader. The leaders served their group with a kind of pastoral oversight."[10]

Wesley himself described these societies in the following way:

> The design of our meeting is to obey that command of God, "Therefore, confess your sins to one another, and pray for one another, that you may be healed" (Jas. 5:16 ESV). To this end, we intend:
>
> 1. To meet once a week, at the least.
> 2. To come punctually at the hour appointed, without some extraordinary reason.
> 3. To begin (those who are present) exactly at the hour, with singing or prayer.
> 4. To speak each of us in order, freely and plainly, the true state of our souls, with the faults we have committed in thought, word, or deed, and the temptations we have felt since our last meeting.
> 5. To end every meeting with prayer suited to the state of each person present.
> 6. To desire some person among us to speak his own state first, and then to ask the rest, in order, as many and as searching questions as may be, concerning their state, sins, and temptations.

In doing this, Wesley provided an observable track of discipleship for believers who met the simple qualifications of elders and deacons, and he built a discipleship movement from it. Preaching alone could not do the trick, as Whitefield demonstrated, and confessed later that due to the neglect of a discernable discipleship process he had "built a rope of sand."[11] Wesley possessed the other half of the sword of power, and when the two components of evangelism and discipleship were combined, the impact still reaches even to the present day.

---

10. D. Michael Henderson, *John Wesley's Class Meeting: A Model for Making Disciples* (Wilmore, KY: Rafiki, 2016), 100.

11. George Whitefield, "Life and Times of Whitefield," *The Christian Review*, vol. 3, (1838), 281.

The Three

We know Jesus had a special relationship with three of his twelve apostles that was exclusive: Peter, James (son of Zebedee), and John. Jesus brought these three closest to himself, as demonstrated by Peter's special walk with Jesus down the beach, or by John leaning on the chest of Jesus, identifying himself proudly as Jesus's best friend, "the one whom Jesus loved." James claimed nothing special, but as a member of the inner circle, he would be the first to be martyred. Each was special in his own way, and Jesus poured into them with the luxury of special encounters reserved only for best friends with access into the circle of trust.

We see numerous examples of Jesus training these three men together on a deeper level:

- During the healing of Jairus's daughter (Mark 5:37)
- On the mount of the transfiguration (Matt. 17:1–2)
- In his final moments before captivity in the garden of Gethsemane (Mark 14:33)

Interestingly, these three events centered on death. The healing of Jairus's daughter demonstrated Jesus's power over death. The transfiguration included God's greatest servants, Moses and Elijah, who were seen to be very much alive. The final event happened in the shadow of the cross. Perhaps these three men would need to remember Jesus's lordship over death in the coming years. Since they would be living under the shadow of death, obedience was a necessity as they testified before kings and emperors. Two of the three became network leaders as the church expanded outward and as the narrative of Acts unfolded. James the son of Zebedee may have become the lead in Jerusalem (as James the Lord's brother was [Gal. 1:19, 2:9] years after Herod martyred James the son of Zebedee in Acts 12:2) overseeing the vast network of Jewish believers throughout Israel as Peter traveled. Either way, James's death might have catalyzed the others during the persecution. Peter became the network leader in Rome, and John became the network leader in Ephesus. Each of these cities functioned as a sending hub in a larger network and became vital and strategic to the missionary enterprises of the early church. Perhaps for this reason, Jesus invested in the three more than the others. When Paul visited Jerusalem, he noticed that John and Peter stood out from the others, and wrote, "James, Cephas, and John seemed to be pillars" (Gal. 2:9). Paul refers to James the brother of Jesus here, since James son of Zebedee had been martyred by this time, yet the argument can be made that Jesus poured into his brother his entire life as James's older brother. James the brother of Jesus would have been the natural choice of a leader in Jerusalem to replace James the son of Zebedee, because he knew Jesus like no one else, and earned the moniker "James the Just." In the case of both Jameses, the principle stands: Jesus reserved his most intimate mentoring for his network leaders.[12]

One to One Mentorship

When discipleship enters the 1:1 ratio as it did, at times, with the three, it becomes mentorship. Mentorship is the most powerful form of discipleship, and this is why Jesus reserved it for the three network leaders of the New Testament. Lawless writes, "Indeed, the best mentoring has the informality of a strong relationship coupled with the formality of intentional goals toward spiritual growth."[13] Mentorship will take mentees beyond principles and mix the experience of the mentor into their developing practices. In the discipleship relationship, you are not just studying somebody else. They are also studying you. This two-way process of study is present whether the mentorship is driving, golfing, guitar playing, or becoming a doctor. A mentor should help the one being mentored to "discover strengths and ministry function, develop character, determine focus, discern blind spots, and close the gap between potential and performance."[14]

Perhaps the most terrifying thing leaders ever realize is that they and their entire congregation are constantly making disciples, whether they realize it or not. Churches unconsciously portray a concept of "what being a Christian is" at all times. The real question is whether the portrayal of following Jesus resembles the sobering truth that most parents realize as they witness the embodiment of their strengths, values, failures, and mistakes running around on short, stubby legs. Proverbs reinforces the principle that what is caught may be more powerful than what is taught, "Whoever walks with the wise becomes wise " (Prov. 13:20 ESV). Consider Paul's awareness of his own lifestyle "osmosis" process of discipleship:

- "Therefore I urge you to imitate me" (1 Cor. 4:16).
- "Brothers, join in imitating me, and keep your eyes on those who walk according to the example you have in us" (Phil. 3:17 ESV).
- "Follow my example, as I follow the example of Christ" (1 Cor. 11:1).

---

12. The idea of a network leader, centered on mission and multiplication in a geographic area gave rise to the role of bishops (lit. overseer in 1 Peter 5:1), which appear as network leaders as early as in the writings of Ignatius. Clement of Alexandria wrote, "Even here in the Church the gradations of bishops, presbyters, and deacons happen to be imitations, in my opinion, of the angelic glory and of that arrangement which, the scriptures say, awaits those who have followed in the footsteps of the apostles and who have lived in complete righteousness according to the gospel" (*Miscellanies* 6:13:107:2 [AD 208]). In this sense, Patrick also called himself a bishop in his letter to the soldiers of Coroticus. Patrick was a church planting movement network leader.

13. Chuck Lawless, *Mentor Member Book: How Along-the-Way Discipleship Will Change Your Life* (Nashville: Lifeway, 2011), 53.

14. Lawless, *Mentor Member Book*, 53.

- "And you became imitators of us and of the Lord, for you received the word in much affliction, with the joy of the Holy Spirit" (1 Thess. 1:6 ESV).

Paul learned this imitation methodology firsthand through his mentorship under Gamaliel, a prominent rabbi, who is still quoted in Jewish circles today. This effective mentorship style was passed down to Timothy and those who catalyzed multiplication movements. Not surprisingly, during the Celtic Missions Movement, the missionary monks practiced spiritual discipleship in the model of Jesus, the lead missionary monk viewing his guiding role as that of a spiritual father raising spiritual sons, nurturing them in spiritual learning.[15] Whereas unintentional discipleship breeds lethargy, intentional discipleship produces multiplication movements.

TYPES OF MENTORSHIP

There are various types of mentorship relationships. A *formal* mentorship is deliberate, and both parties understand the nature of the mentoring relationship. J. Taliaferro outlines five types of mentors:

1. Foundational mentors, who establish you in the faith
2. Building mentors, who help you establish your gifting and purpose
3. Skilled mentors, who hone a particular craft necessary to your ministry
4. Weathervane mentors, who interpret the world around you and assist you to speak into it
5. Situational mentors, who assist you in dealing with people, circumstances, and conundrums.[16]

There were times I formally asked others to mentor me in the following areas:

- Family: I asked someone to mentor me on how to be a good husband.
- Spiritual gifts: I asked someone to help me develop my spiritual gifts.
- Leadership: I hit a leadership ceiling and asked someone to lead me to become a better leader.

An *informal* mentorship takes place indirectly through spending time with someone. For example, I informally mentored a new convert every Monday night for eighteen months at my house. We talked, prayed, and worked alongside each

---

15. Jennifer O'Reilley, "Adomnán and the Art of Teaching Spiritual Sons," in *Adomnán of Iona: Theologian, Law Maker, Peacemaker*, ed. Jonathan M. Wooding (Dublin: Four Courts Press, 2010), 69.

16. J. Taliaferro, *Letters to an Apprentice: A Culture of Mentorship* (Houston: Lucid, 2020), 6–9.

other crafting a garage project together. The relationship was undefined, and mentorship unfolded between discussions about measurements, types of glue, and how many screws to use. At some point, we cracked 1 John, discussing it together.

When it comes to mentoring those on your team, remember that despite all leaders being equals on a team, all team members do not possess equal experience. Sometimes your team is made up of Barnabases who equal your gifting, and abilities. Sometimes, however, your team is made of Timothys who look to you as their Paul. When you serve alongside a Barnabas, your relationship is more of a partnership; when training a Timothy, it is more mentorship. Therefore, it needs to be understood by both parties what the nature of the partnership is. If you fail to ask permission to mentor, or don't define the nature of the relationship it risks resulting in resentment. At times my unintentional presumption and arrogance were to blame. Other times, it may have been theirs. Without a mutual understanding of the expectations of the relationship, frustrations are inevitable. Finally, the more formally you intend to mentor someone, the more clearly the mentoring relationship must be defined by both parties. Otherwise, it may not be clear that your mentees have granted you sufficient permission for the role you are offering to play in their lives. Giving permission does a few things for the person receiving advice:

1. Permission postures them to receive it in a nondefensive manner. They asked to be mentored, and gave permission for you to speak into their life.
2. Permission establishes the advisor as somebody who is, in fact, more qualified or experienced and, therefore, able to speak into the situation of the mentee.
3. Permission establishes a respectful boundary. Although the time of both parties is valuable, it establishes a climate of respect for the mentor's time and knowledge. It is healthy for mentees to recognize that the time spent is for them, specifically, rather than for the mentor. Despite friendship being a part of the relationship, the time spent is sacred, and designed for the strategic development of the mentee.
4. Permission produces gratitude, the necessary attitude of any student, whether being mentored in martial arts, carpentry, or church planting.

DON'T MAKE DISCIPLES, MAKE DISCIPLE-MAKERS

When you are training your team and discipling people in various stages, remember that you are seeding the future DNA of the church. You have not discipled people effectively if their discipleship stops with themselves. They must disciple others. Paul exhorted Timothy to "entrust to faithful men who will be able to teach others also" what he had heard from Paul (2 Tim. 2:2 ESV). This passage includes four generations involved in discipleship:

- Paul—the sender of the message
- Timothy—the one he discipled
- Able men—the ones Timothy will disciple
- Able to teach others—the ones these able men will disciple
- Paul wasn't content to make a disciple in Timothy. Timothy had to be able to make disciples who made disciples. Any planter who makes that their goal will accomplish so much more than merely planting a church.

REFLECT

- Many Christians are not, and have not, been involved in a personal discipleship relationship. The Barna report found that most Christians don't practice discipleship. Have you been involved in formal discipleship? (Solo study does not count.)
- How have you been discipled?
- How have you practiced discipleship?
- Do you have disciples?

DISCUSS

- The author provides a simple but practical model of discipleship based on time, teaching, and tactics. This model includes ideas such as, "This is how Jesus did it, this is how you do it, this is how you'll train them to do it." Where do time, teaching, and tactics overlap? Where are they distinct?
- From this bare-bones model of discipleship, where would you expand the model with greater information and detail?
- A general truism of learning is that the best approach is direct instruction with deliberate practice and feedback. A disciple is a learner. How does your model of discipleship incorporate direct instruction, deliberate practice, and feedback?

CHALLENGE

- There are entire libraries of books and materials on discipleship. Articulate a workable model of discipleship for your present circumstances and then commit to expanding your knowledge and practice by studying some of the vast resources available.

CHURCH PLANTING MODELS

The Church exists for nothing else but to draw men into Christ, to make them little Christs. If they are not doing that, all the cathedrals, clergy, missions, sermons, even the Bible itself, are simply a waste of time. God became man for no other purpose.

—C. S. LEWIS

FORMS AND FUNCTIONS

When I train planters, I train them to reframe their thinking about planting like a reverse negative of film. In the 1970s, when dark rooms were part of developing film, a photographer could develop pictures in a way that reversed the light exposure, making teeth black and pupils white. This effect literally provided an opposite perspective of the same image. I train planters to plant a church that is a reverse negative of the Sunday gathering with the following assignment: "Design a strategy for your church plant with the only prohibition being that your plant cannot convene a Sunday service." There are two reasons for this assignment:

1. Once you've grasped the answers, you've cracked the nut of missional engagement.
2. Church starters use the Sunday service as a crutch and focus on it to the exclusion of missionally engaging their communities.

Most of this book has focused on planting from a "back-to-front" approach, or the reverse negative of a Sunday gathering, but this chapter will focus on the form and function of Sunday gatherings. Have you ever wondered why the same jack-in-the-box church model keeps popping up? Church history doesn't remember the planters who unpacked an Ikea prefab church service in the middle of another neighborhood, but those who innovated on mission, such as J. Hudson Taylor, Nikolaus von Zinzendorf, or John Wesley. Because there is not a single outline of a church service in Scripture, leaders are not merely allowed to innovate, they are invited to.

Despite an absence of church service outlines, there are various models presented in Scripture. Most of the models we observe today are represented in Acts with the same overlapping witnessed today:

- House churches—Jerusalem hybrid, Rome, Corinth, Ephesus
- Churches in public space—Philippi, Ephesus
- Mega-micro hybrids—Jerusalem, Ephesus (Temple and Hall of Tyrannus)
- Network of Microchurches—Rome[1]

We get the church's functions in Acts 1–2 (prayer, preaching, breaking bread, fellowship) and catch glimpses of the church's forms.[2] The Jerusalem church was a hybrid between the missional house church and churches in public space as evidenced by Acts 5:42 (ESV): "And every day, in the temple and from house to house, they did not cease teaching and preaching that the Christ is Jesus." The church in Jerusalem is the closest description the New Testament comes to providing a glimpse of worship gatherings. We get snippets from the epistles about the exercise of spiritual gifts as part of worship and Lord's table from Paul's Corinthian letters. We can conclude from this fact that there is relative freedom in crafting our gatherings based on the culture surrounding the church. Christianity is a contextualized faith that has the ability to fill whatever container it is poured into.

All the models listed above have pros and cons depending upon what setting they are in. The New Testament only has different options because different approaches were needed for different contexts on mission. One size does not fit all. Mission always trumps models. Strategy eats structure for breakfast. John Calvin states that each age should be flexible based on the needs of that generation in regard to rejecting old traditional forms and adopting new ones. Jesus's ministry allows for this, according to Calvin:

The Master did not will in outward discipline and ceremonies to prescribe in detail what we ought to do because he foresaw that this depended on the state of the time, and he did not deem one form suitable for all ages . . .

---

1. Graham Beynon, *Planting for the Gospel: A Hands-on Guide to Church Planting* (Ross-shire, UK: Christian Focus Publications, 2011). Beynon adds additional models such as re-plants, and start up, and mother-daughter that have more to do with the methodology than the form.

2. Aubrey Malphurs, *Developing a Vision for Ministry* (Grand Rapids: Baker, 2015), 55.

because he has taught nothing specifically, and because these things are not necessary to salvation and for the upbuilding of the church ought to be variously accommodated to the customs of each nation and age, it will be fitting (as the advantage of the church will require) to change and abrogate traditional practices and to establish new ones.[3]

MISSION IS THE MOTHER OF INVENTION

There are traditional existing structures and models in Western society when it comes to church. The network or denomination the planter is from may determine what type of church is planted. For example, church governance will be largely decided if the planter belongs to a denomination such as the Lutherans or Presbyterians. Independents will find themselves planting very similar structures to the mother ship. We either choose our convictions, inherit them, arrive at them through critical thinking and analysis of Scripture, or forge them out of our knowledge and experiences.

Your tribe is the biggest factor in determining what structure you will inherit, and the body of Christ is nothing if not tribal. Seth Godin defines tribes as "a group of people connected to one another, connected to a leader, and connected to an idea."[4] Within the church planting world, tribes such as NAMB, Acts 29, Soma Communities, and the Assemblies of God all differ from one another and bring a different set of assumptions, attitudes, and actions to the table. Contemporary church planting is therefore tribal in nature, where members of one tribe attempt to multiply their tribal communities. To one tribe, church planting means going multi-site, and when they multiply their tribal customs involving multi-sites, values multiply with it. To the house church tribe, multiplication happens from house to house, and tribal customs, including house church assumptions, attitudes, and actions, follow suit.

Therefore, one planter's church plant may be nothing like the next. One tribal failure may look like success to another tribe. The bride of Christ's wardrobe contains a vast array of dresses, and beauty is found in the eye of the beholder. Because our idea of what a church plant is differs, we may find that our definitions of church planting differ as well, causing us to echo Inigo Montoya's infamous refrain, "You keep using that word. I do not think it means what you think it means."[5] For example, if Rick Warren utilized a purpose-driven model of planting churches, then I've employed an accident-driven one.

3. John Calvin, *Calvin's Institutes*, IV.10.30, https://www.ccel.org/ccel/calvin/institutes.iv.xvii.html.
4. Seth Godin, *Tribes: We Need You to Lead Us* (New York: Penguin, 2014), 13.
5. *The Princess Bride*, Buttercup Films Ltd., directed by Rob Reiner (Twentieth Century Fox, 1987).

The churches I've planted have been much like Bob Ross's "happy accidents," where he makes a tree from an accidental brush stroke in the wrong place.

The most innovative models will be where the mission naturally dictates the model. This may be why the Holy Spirit provided freedom to planters to innovate dynamically when he chose not to supply us with a cookie-cutter model in Luke's Acts narrative. Bob Logan quotes Dave DeVries, "Some planters get excited about the cookie jar. . . . Jars are not an end in and of themselves. A lot of churches are more interested in the cookie jar business, as opposed to the cookie-making business. Yet the reality is—if you are making disciples, you do need somewhere to put them."[6] In conclusion, church planters make cookies. Church starters are focused on making better cookie jars. The Great Commission pointedly told us to focus on making disciples, not churches to put them in. Therefore mission trumps models.

CRAFTING YOUR GATHERING

It's not that we shouldn't put care into crafting our times of gathering—quite the opposite. Stealing another form or model is the lazy option for someone who isn't carefully crafting their gatherings, assuming the DNA of another form fits their plant. In *Shop Class as Soul Craft*, the author leaves the field of data analysis to build motorcycles for a living. He muses that there is something about creating, putting your hand to something, and leaving for the day knowing that something was physically there that you built and crafted that is different from conceptual work, like data analysis. He quotes Alexandre Kojève, "A man who recognizes his own product in the World that has actually been transformed by his work: he recognizes himself in it."[7] When we craft a gathering, we want others to recognize God in the design. By ignoring the ability to shape our "liturgy" on Sunday, we deprive ourselves of one of the greatest gifts: to shape how people will experience God. Edison challenged his team of engineers with, "There is a better way boys, find it!" In the same way church planters should be challenged to craft gatherings for greater illumination.

When we create, we imitate God in his first act in redemptive history. God designed us to create as demonstrated in a compelling study that contrasted the brains of pianists as they played either a new piece of music that they personally improvised on the spot, or a piece of music previously rehearsed. The study found

6. David DeVries, "Cookie Jars and Church Planters," Missional Challenge, https://www.missionalchallenge.com/cookie-jars-and-church-planters/, quoted in Robert Logan *The Church Planting Journey* (Logan Leadership, 2019), 6

7. Matthew Crawford, *Shop Class as Soul Craft: An Inquiry into the Value of Work* (New York: Penguin Press, 2010), 23.

that during the rehearsal of a pre-set piece of music, the prefrontal cortex, responsible for self-checking and regulating thoughts and actions was highly active. When the musicians were asked to "jam" or improvise, the prefrontal cortex was less active, allowing for a greater breadth of exploration and creativity.[8] Have we practiced the same rote formulas for worship that have limited our spiritual imagination? Another study measured the same phenomenon in the brain as rappers free-flowed. The theater director for *The Lion King* confessed that most of her strangest ideas come from early morning sleep, when her brain is less regulated by the pre-frontal cortex, as is true for most of humanity.[9] What did the designer of our brains intend us to with our cognitive functionality of creativity and innovation if not to enhance our worship of himself with it? Famous commentator Frank Gaebelein wrote, "Our capacity to make and enjoy art—to look at it and find it 'good'—is a condition of our very humanity. As G.K. Chesterton said, 'Art is the signature of man.' No animals practice art any more than they worship. Subhuman creatures may make beautiful things, but only by instinct. The things they make—such as coral or honeycombs, spider webs or multicolored shells—are not their own conscious deliberate creation but an expression of God's thoughts."[10]

Church starters typically cherry pick someone else's model from a book because of the pragmatic approach to having a church. If it works, and gets them funded, and gathers a crowd, then they consider their mission accomplished. In these services the boredom of the attenders is matched only by the careless lack of innovation of those who lead them. Thirty minutes of lackluster singing followed by thirty minutes of hip monologue may not be the most inspiring or engaging way to convey spiritual truth. Neurologists tell us that info dumps don't produce breakthroughs or change behavior, yet leaders still persist adhering to forms that are not biblically prescribed in the least, or how God designed us to engage at best.

In his book *The Church in Exile*, Lee Beach cites Nehemiah and Ezra as exiles who returned to the prevalence of God in the land at an all-time low. With God's worship and Israel's influence in tatters, they sought to rebuild the walls and the temple under Zerubbabel, but not exactly like Solomon's before. So, the church in exile needs to creatively rebuild the worship of God in this post-Christian, post-exilic return to glorifying God in an age of exile.[11] The mission is to glorify Jesus, not produce a worship playlist. Warren Wiersbe stated that

8. Jeffrey Kluger, "This Is Your Brain on Creativity," *Time, Special Edition: The Science of Creativity* (August 3, 2018), 16.

9. Claudia Kalb, *The Science of Genius* (Washington, DC: National Geographic, 2018), 34.

10. Frank E. Gaebelein, *The Christian, the Arts and the Truth: Regaining the Vision of Greatness* (Portland: Multnomah, 1985), 73.

11. Lee Beach, *The Church in Exile: Living in Hope after Christendom* (Downers Grove, IL: InterVarsity Press, 2015), 147.

when he attended church, the primary drive was not to passively enjoy a sermon, praise, or fellowship but to "bear witness that Christ is alive and worship Him."[12]

We find ourselves in a challenging time in the church because society is shifting so rapidly with technology and social media. As Paas observed in his study of church decline in Europe, "Old recipes do not work so well anymore, but new ones are still to be found."[13] If planters are bold enough to think outside of the box, the Holy Spirit may inspire them with his unique brand of creativity leading to the next breakthrough instead of their vain attempt to live someone else's story. All scientific breakthroughs teach that necessity is the mother of invention, and missional breakthroughs are no different. When C. S. Lewis hit the airwaves in war-torn Britain, the radio was the chief means of communicating with the populace, therefore Lewis broadcasted his Mere Christianity lectures innovatively to the masses. This was an apostolic move, crossing frontiers, and using his gifting as an apologist and teacher in an apostolic way. This is the frontier work that church planters excel in, and Lewis entered the conversation in a new way and took church to people who would not take themselves to church.

After training planters for many years and personally planting on three different continents, I subscribe to a "by any means necessary" approach. All the models hold value up to a certain point. If the majority of models and approaches glorify Christ, stay true to divine revelation as communicated by Scripture, and are effective at reaching the lost in its unique context, they hold value. That said, a "by any means necessary" approach should not be confused with an "anything goes" mentality. There may not be one right way to plant a church, but there are certainly many wrong ways. Failure to reach your community with the gospel results from importing blueprinted forms, structure, styles, and models that are divorced from your local mission and context. Think of the difference between Jerusalem and the Gentile churches. Each was a right model that would become wrong if forced into the other's context.

So what is the right model? Building on the progression of work from our previous chapters, models should form naturally from these determining factors:

- APEST functions determine drives.
- Drives determine burdens.
- Burdens determine mission.
- Mission should determine models.

---

12. Charles W. Colson and Ellen Santilli Vaughn, *The Body: Being Light in the Darkness* (Nashville: W Publishing Group, 1992), 71.

13. Stefan Paas, *Church Planting in the Secular West: Learning from the European Experience* (Grand Rapids: Eerdmans, 2016), 201.

Therefore, your model, style, approach, and liturgy (or order of service) should be contextualized from your mission. Planting in an urban context requires learning a new set of rules if the planter comes from a suburban context. In white, evangelical circles, the church attenders typically drive within a fifteen-mile radius to attend a middle-class suburban gathering, yet businesses in urban areas understand that people in the inner city will typically remain within a five-minute walking radius to shop, eat, and attend. Therefore an urban church will need to concentrate on the neighborhood in their immediate surroundings. Attractional websites and service imported from a suburban model fall flat. In a rural area, a new flashy building is viewed with suspicion, and trust is earned through generations. Therefore, a replant in a traditional building better fits the context of a rural community where long-standing trust is a factor.

STYLE

Planters from every denomination or tribe inherit or innovate a particular style of gathering. Anglican, Southern Baptist, Presbyterian, and Assemblies of God plants are nothing alike. Planters must balance how much form, structure, tradition, and interaction they will include in their gatherings.

What we aim to accomplish determines our order of service. In evangelical Britain, the "hymn sandwich" is favored (prayer, hymn, reading, hymn, sermon, hymn) to achieve proclamation of the gospel. In American evangelicalism, the inherited form is twenty-five minutes of song and a similar-length sermon connected by a little knot of announcements in the middle to complete the evangelical "bow tie" to attract through music and highlight a speaker. Referring to the New Testament as the sourcebook of how to craft gatherings reveals the early church's highly interactive nature that neither form expresses: Communion, corporate prayer times, and the gifts are all conspicuously absent, in spite of Paul referring to them as normal practices of Christian worship.

To avoid the problems of Corinth, it seems we've removed the interactive elements altogether, but in doing so we've stripped away the awe and wonder of interacting on a more spiritual level. Planters must balance various factors to craft a gathering that dovetails with their mission, burden, and gifting their team to fit the context of their community.

The churches I've planted incorporate interaction, and our leadership team chanted the following mantra for Sunday, "Only three things need to happen." Those three things were:

1. We need to hear from God—through the Word, communion, and prophecy.

2. God needs to hear from us—through worship, prayer, and communion.
3. We need to hear from each other—through discussion, ministering the gifts, and all of the above.

As long as those three things happened, we counted our gatherings a success. These were born out of many years of reducing church down to the three essential functions of any liturgy or service. Our assorted backgrounds meant that our experiences of gathering lacked differing elements of these three, yet we were convinced that all three were present in the New Testament gatherings. Discussion helped us accomplish hearing from one another. Once we'd experienced that level of participation, it meant that we could no longer sit staring at the back of people's heads in rows. We organized the our gathering space into semi-circle small groups, giving birth to the joke, "O's before rows."

Traditionally churches have called their gatherings worship services despite stripping the core elements of worship, such as prayer, communion, and participation out of them. Paul strongly emphasized the regular rhythm of communion, saying, "as oft as you come together," yet we save it for special occasions like the red "Somebody's Special" birthday plate. In our attempt to eliminate anything confusing, we have oversimplified our liturgical forms so that the transcendent reverence present in ancient gatherings is replaced by emotionalistic mood manipulation during the music.

If we replace engaging the invisible God with something tangible, or an atmosphere to create a mood, we've swapped true spiritual worship for the idol of an emotional experience. Swaying to the movement of the music and being emotionally touched can make praise a façade of an idolatrous appeal to the senses. Have we unwittingly allowed ourselves to be awed and overwhelmed by the semblance of Oz the great and powerful, even though we know that an eternal God does not dwell in the lights, pyrotechnics, and booming noise?

In medieval times, religious leaders felt the need to overawe the people with God's majesty, so they simply created it with ornate carvings and mystical smells and bells.[14] Call it a little industrial light and magic, but those primitive medieval savages drank it up. Instead of cathedrals today, we have warehouses. Instead of the cloudy fumes of incense, we have smoke machines. Spotlights shine instead of candles, and the sound system delivers a boom that rivals the ginormous pipe organs that made the stones vibrate. All this can become a cheap substitute for the true substance.

---

14. Truth be told, I first learned to worship in an Episcopal church that practiced a sung liturgy. To this day, this is my preferred way of worshiping. The comments here should in no way be taken as a critique of high church practices. In many ways, I have more respect for high church liturgy than most of what many nondenominational evangelicals practice on Sundays.

Maybe people like standing in a room for thirty minutes chanting the same words over and over. C. S. Lewis was such a nonfan of the worship practices of his day that he reportedly waited in church to receive the communion and immediately left when the deed was done, slamming the side door behind him in frustration as he left the church every week. Noble describes our "high-production church services that feel more like a concert and TED talk than a sacred event. High-quality video clips interrupt the sermon. The pastor paces the stage with a headset mic, skillfully weaving facts, stories, and dramatic pauses. The young, fashionably dressed worship band puts on a performance at center stage. The lighting and volume make it clear who the congregation should be paying attention to." His conclusion is that the church is designed to be a motivational conference.[15]

Gordon T. Smith, in his book *Evangelical, Sacramental & Pentecostal: Why the Church Should Be All Three*, argues that each component in the title is necessary to abiding in Christ, and therefore should be an essential aspect of gathering as a church.

- Evangelical—Jesus defined his disciples as those who would abide in his word, and asked Peter to feed his sheep (John 8:31–32; John 21:15–17).
- Sacramental—There is a physical aspect to our faith as demonstrated in the physical presence of baptism and the Lord's Table, grounding the church in the incarnational presence of Christ through his body.
- Pentecostal—It is the Spirit who leads us into understanding of the truth and glorifies Christ within us (John 15:26; 16:12–14).

Through a blend of all three, believers may abide in the vine, bearing fruit like a cluster of grapes together. Sacrifice any aspect of this in your gatherings, and it is like strangling part of the vine that is intended to supply life to the bunch.[16]

LITURGY

Liturgy means "the work of the people." It doesn't refer to candles or high forms of church, even though it has come to be associated with those things. The etymological root of liturgy refers to participation and interaction. The planter must ask, how can Christ best be glorified during our time together? If Christ's APEST functionality has been deposited to the church, how can the ministry of Christ best be embodied during our time together? Are we

---

15. Alan Noble, *Disruptive Witness* (Downers Grove, IL: InterVarsity Press, 2018), 122.

16. Gordon T. Smith, *Evangelical, Sacramental & Pentecostal: Why the Church Should Be All Three* (Colorado Springs, CO: IVP Academic 2017), 16–19.

guilty of making our time together focused only on the teaching functionality at the expense of the others? How would a prophet operate in our gathering? How can the shepherd function be expressed in our gathering? How can all the APEST functions operate to equip others in our gathering?

Church planters have the unique opportunity to craft a gathering that incorporates *every aspect* of the APEST functionality:

Apostolic liturgy—The gathering has an aspect of mission and mobilization.

Prophetic liturgy—The gathering has a deeply spiritual atmosphere. There is margin to create a controlled atmosphere where the gifts can operate. Confession, prayer time, and prophetic ministry are welcomed.

Evangelistic liturgy—The gathering mimics the preaching in Acts, calling unbelievers to believe, and emphasizing surrender, repentance, and baptism.

Shepherding liturgy—The gathering focuses on communal activity, such as corporate prayer, communion, singing, and discussion.

Teaching liturgy—The teaching of the Word is honored, but people are also able to rotate into the pulpit. People can share what they've learned in groups and teach one another.

Here is a sample of an APEST-sensitive liturgy I might craft for my context:

- Communal arrangement: We sit at tables, eating breakfast together and spending time catching up with each other's lives. We've set the tone straight out of the gate: This is no show, but a show-and-tell for all as we strip gathering down to the bare bones of interacting with one another (*shepherding, evangelistic*).
- Communion serves as the transition of the meal to the beginning of worship, fixing our hearts upon the grace and glory of Jesus (*prophetic, evangelistic*). Additionally, as a sacrament, communion teaches us to take something ordinary and common, such as bread or wine (or common water in baptism), and put it to sacred use. Teaching people to approach life this way demolishes the secular-sacred divide.[17]

17. This is elaborated on in Andrew M. Greeley, *God in Popular Culture* (Chicago: Thomas More, 1988), chapter 7, "Empirical Liturgy: The Search for Grace."

- Communion leads to a time of open prayer (guided or free-form) so people can respond to Christ and his great love. If guided, our people would be taught the various forms of prayer, such as adulation or confession. Free-form people spontaneously read a Scripture, break into song, or share a prophecy. To conduct this in a gathering "decently and in order" (1 Cor. 14:40 ESV) requires skilled leadership and faith to trust Paul that it's possible. We would read a creed to remind ourselves of the guardrails of historic Christianity. It might rotate, but we would come together around the revealed truths of Scripture before coming to a time of teaching (*prophetic, teaching*).
- Finally, we would have preaching after some public reading of Scripture (*teaching, evangelistic*).
- There would be a deep discussion in small groups, allowing people to use their gifts, evangelize, pray for one another, or minister from their gifts. In this way the people are actively mobilized in our gathering through hands-on ministry (*apostolic, prophetic, evangelistic, shepherding, teaching*).
- Finally, we close with announcements, and exhortation (*apostolic, prophetic*).

This would take a few hours. Every church that I've led incorporates meals, extended fellowship, and a rounding up of the APEST functions. Even if our gatherings last closer to two hours, people don't seem to want to leave. I haven't figured how to make disciples who know how to worship, pray, share their faith, and use their spiritual gifts by running an hour-long show. Perhaps I'll learn one day. For now, I'll cling to Brad Brisco's conclusion: "Missional engagement is best done as a communal activity."[18]

BALANCING QUALITY AND QUANTITY

In order to ensure that a model fits the mission, planters must weigh the balance between quantitative and qualitative factors (Q-factors).

Quantitative: The Q-factor that measures quantity
- What size do you want to reach before you multiply outward?
- How big of a gathering will you allow?
- How will size determine how you interact or where you gather?

---

18. Brad Brisco, "Disciple-Making Environments and Church Planting," SEND Network, November 6, 2018, https://www.namb.net/send-network/resource/disciple-making-environments-and-church-planting/.

Qualitative: The Q-factor that measures quality
- o What do you value, how will you disciple, and how will the gifts be used?
- o What do you believe are the essential things that need to happen during a gathering?
- o Will your church be missional, attractional, incarnational, or interactive?

Each of these factors must be carefully weighed in whatever model of church is planted. *Missional/incarnational* churches imagine themselves to be a qualitative plant and unconcerned about numbers, but as we will see, this is misleading. People who are concerned with qualitative metrics gravitate towards missional and incarnational models adopting the forms and structures of microchurches, house churches, or cell churches. Missional/incarnational models also emphasize discipleship, the priesthood of all believers, and intimacy.

Attractional churches by contrast, are accused of being obsessed with quantitative measures, and whoring after numbers. People who are concerned with quantitative measures tend to be drawn towards the megachurch model emphasizing growth and programs.

These oversimplified conclusions ignore the crossover between the Q-factors across all models. No model will ever fully get away from a quantitative metric despite many claims that "we aren't into numbers." Numbers will still exist, and in some way they are being used to measure something. For example, incarnational models such as house churches may focus on quantitative metrics by establishing a multiplication pathway and celebrating the numbers of churches planted outward. Steve Timmis's *Crowded House* network of house churches in Sheffield, England, practiced a multiplication system called *Crazy 8s* that started missional communities with eight people. Once the missional community grew by adding twelve more, the group of twenty split into a team of eight and a team of twelve.

Quantitative metrics will determine when you will multiply or have reached your pre-determined capacity. Leaders may imagine such factors as qualitative decisions, but they remain quantitative factors. The Dunbar number limits the capacity of one individual to retain relationships with a maximum of 150 people. This natural growth barrier is both a quantitative and qualitative factor. The raging debate between missional and attractional approaches ignores that both are represented in Scripture.

The attractional model was born out of the church growth movement started by Donald McGavran, author of *Church Growth Principles*. Churches who read *The Purpose Driven Church* and were inspired by it felt they could grow beyond their means if they simply followed the formula. The plan was simple: rent an industrial building, renovate the sanctuary, plan a bunch of programs, hire a dynamic youth pastor, cater to families, and watch the people pile in. Place the emphasis of church upon meeting needs, running programs, and excellent teaching, and the church becomes a one-stop shop for everything people need to enhance their spiritual life. In short, the *Field of Dreams* methodology was applied, "If you build it, they will come." Despite applying the best wisdom that Hollywood fictional characters could offer, many adherents of the attractional model still have numerically small congregations, never growing beyond the growth barriers. Despite courses, conferences, and coaching that promised to deliver the secrets to explosive growth, churches that attempted to borrow Rick Warren's church model, simply look like a *failed version* of Rick Warren's church. Sadly, the attractional model defines success by attracting people to itself, so a small church equals a failed church. This has led to an existential crisis in many leaders who realized they should adopt a different model, or be content being the small church they are.

Despite the criticism that attractional churches suffer, it could be argued that Paul strategically used a mixture of the incarnational and attractional models when engaging synagogues, knowing that preaching there would cause controversy and attract a crowd of hearers. In Jerusalem, the apostles rode the middle line between the two extremes by combining public meetings in the temple courts, blended with house gatherings in a missional-attractional rhythm, "And day by day, attending the temple together and breaking bread in their homes" (Acts 2:46 ESV). This is repeated in Acts 5:42, "And every day, in the temple and from house to house, they did not cease teaching and preaching that the Christ is Jesus." The Gospels testify to Jesus blending public ministry to the masses with small intimate settings. After Jesus's ascension, the Spirit came at Pentecost and attracted a crowd with the sound of a rushing wind. The Spirit stirred up tongues of fire over the heads of the apostles, gave them supernatural language abilities, and filled them with so much joy that they appeared drunk . . . and it drew a large crowd of thousands. Three thousand joined the church that day, and a few days later, thousands more joined when a public miracle attracted even more at the temple gate.

Charles Spurgeon was so attractional that he asked the congregation to limit their attendance to the Metropolitan Tabernacle to three out of four Sundays so the massive crowds in London could be accommodated. There was even a special ferry crossing the Thames on Sundays whose conductor would yell, "Over the water to hear Charlie!" Similarly, Whitefield and Wesley used a combined approach of the missional and attractional models. In the fields, they attracted crowds of thousands, broadening the Methodist movement. Wesley recognized the need to gather the converts into house groups where discipleship would be fostered, and the "Experience Meeting" was born. These "societies" became future church plants after Wesley and Whitefield rode away on their horses and into the sunset.

Some argue that the house church is the only model of church that should be observed based on the evidence of house churches in nearly every community in the first century:

- Jerusalem: Acts 2:2; 2:46; 5:42
- Corinth: 1 Corinthians 16:19
- Colossae: Colossians 4:15; Philemon 1:2
- Rome: Romans 16:1–27

Additionally, Jesus mentioned gatherings of two or three in his name, indicating smaller gatherings. He valued small gatherings and promised to join them.

If a balance of both was utilized by Jesus, Paul, Whitefield, and Spurgeon in the past, then why must planters choose today? Models are a tool to accomplish the mission. If a blended approach of missional and attractional models helps accomplish the mission, then both quantitative and qualitative metrics are acceptable measures. Therefore if the model is an obstruction to mission in a particular context, that model must be sacrificed. After nearly thirty years pioneering the missional community movement in Sheffield, the Crowded House network of house churches spread throughout Sheffield to reach thousands. They realized, however, that they had missed swaths of people who'd never be reached simply because they'd never feel comfortable entering a stranger's home. Recognizing a cultural barrier to the gospel, they sought to leap the hurdle by crafting a large gathering once a month. It was evangelistic in nature and intended to draw those untouched by the missional community model. These larger gatherings served as the front porch to the church, allowing many more to cross the threshold and step into the metaphorical living room (house gatherings) of the church. Crowded House allowed the mission to change their model and became all things to all men in order to win some.

Context is king, and the most important metric of success for church planters is making disciples. Contrast that with church starters who value making crowds from converts, or what I call the art of moving Christians around in an ecclesiastical game of musical chairs. Dai Hankey, the cofounder of New Breed Network and church planter in Cardiff, Wales, started a coffee roasting company that rescues people out of sex trafficking, employing them at the roaster to give them a new start. Not only are slaves freed, their own personal transformation also help transform their neighborhoods. Rather than rapid growth, transformation on this level requires going slower to penetrate deeper.

Jesus took thirty years to go public. Transforming twelve men's lives took three years until they launched out. When I planted in downtown Long Beach, many of the missional models that were in vogue weren't missional enough for the inner city. Urban Long Beach ate church plants for breakfast, so we planted in a park in the open air specifically because we witnessed more people joining the community outside rather than cloistering ourselves inside a building. That approach may not fit a suburban context where meeting outside would be seen as a sort of fanaticism, but it bore substantial fruit in our urban context. In Wales, we planted a church in a coffee shop, because like our urban context, mission dictated models bear more fruit.

CENTRALIZED AND DECENTRALIZED STRUCTURES

Last of all, every planter must determine at some point what will be centralized and what will be decentralized. "Centralized" refers to what is gated behind leadership and done officially by a paid staff worker. "De-centralized" refers to what can be accomplished by all people within the church. Hugh Halter observed, "You really only need to pay for what you centralize."[19] Think about that. Centralization provides governed and controlled outcomes, which often makes leaders feel more secure, but centralized structures are also harder to reproduce and multiply. They are also expensive. Hugh Halter lays out what he centralizes:

- worship
- corporate community gathering
- vision
- training/equipping
- children's ministry

---

19. Hugh Halter, *BiVo: A Modern-Day Guide for Bi-Vocational Saints Leveraging All of Life into One Calling* (Littleton, CO: Missio Publishing, 2013), 92.

I assume that the last one is for safety more than anything else. There is very little that needs to be centralized.

Here is his list of what is decentralized:

- community
- cultural engagement
- evangelism
- teaching
- accountability
- crisis management
- youth ministry
- sheep herding
- mission to the "poor"

In decentralizing those activities, planters not only save money, but mobilize their congregants in their gifts, equipping them for kingdom impact outside the walls of the church. There is no prescription of the right or wrong way, simply the combination that best accomplishes your mission. Allow mission to drive the inspiration, or as Willy Wonka chided, "Invention, my dear friends, is 93 percent perspiration, 6 percent inspiration, 4 percent evaporation, and 2 percent butterscotch ripple."[20] In this case, however, it should be 100 percent mission.

CONCLUSION

A planter begins with their drives and ends with a model. Along the way, the development of a good model makes the following stops:

- APEST functions determine drives
- Drives determine burdens
- Burdens determine mission
- Mission should determine models

Anything that fails to connect with all the determining factors in the list will contribute to the failure of the church plant itself. Models are not irrelevant if they are informed by the right things. The only irrelevant models are those which are irrelevant to their missional context.

---

20. *Willy Wonka and the Chocolate Factory,* directed by Mel Stewart (Paramount Pictures, 1971).

REFLECT

- The author argues that all the forms of church we have today exist in the Scriptures, from megachurches to house churches to microchurches. However, we become attached to our particular model of gathering. Think about your gathering. Why does it take this form? Is this how you would have designed it?
- Consider crafting a service based on multiple forms of church. How would it look?
- Ben Ingebretson shares four criteria for guiding you to a right model:
  1. Will the model help you reach the underserved?
  2. Will the model leverage the resources you have?
  3. Will the model fit the gifts and calling of your team?
  4. Will the model align with where God is leading you?[21]

DISCUSS

- The author argues that we become attached to our particular model of gathering. However, models should form naturally from the exercising of spiritual gifts (e.g., apostle, prophet, evangelist, shepherd, teacher). Models are last in the progression from drive, to vision, to mission, and finally to models. Is your mission faithfully reflected in your model? Have you been practicing what you've inherited?
- Discuss appropriate models for various contexts and communities. Consider how the church planters' drive, vision, and mission leads to a model for:
  - A prison ministry
  - An inner-city house church
  - A rural community church
  - A suburban college church

CHALLENGE

- Examine your gatherings in light of the model of church they represent, the mission they serve, and the vision they reflect. Are the gatherings consistent with the vision, the mission, and the model? What parts of your gathering are overvalued? How would you temper your devotion to a model or elements of your gathering that you prefer when your vision and mission aren't faithfully represented and advanced?

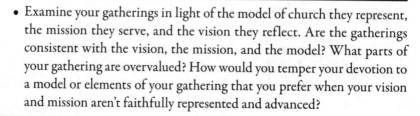

21. Ben Ingebretson, *Missional Moves: A Field Guide for Churches Planting Churches* (Grand Rapids: Faith Alive, 2012), 110–11.

REDISCOVERING THE SPIRIT'S EMPOWERING

From Fake Bravado to
Spiritual Power

SPIRITUAL DYNAMICS OF CHURCH PLANTING

14

We cannot create movements, only the Spirit of
God can. But we can align ourselves, raise the sails
of Kingdom-oriented ministry, so that when the
Spirit does blow we are ready to move forward.

—STEVE SMITH, *T4T*

The world is perishing for lack of the knowledge of God,
and the Church is famishing for want of His Presence.

—A. W. TOZER

TACTICAL RETREATS

Sir Ernest Shackleton led a failed expedition to cross Antarctica in 1914. He
endures as a hero despite the failed attempt because of the miraculous survival.
For almost two years, the twenty-eight men aboard the *Endurance* struggled to
survive when their ship became trapped and crushed by ice floes. After freeing
their emergency boats, they made it to Elephant Island. Shackleton then sailed
nearly eight hundred miles to South Georgia Island. Crossing the island by
foot, he was able to return and rescue the other twenty-two men left behind.
During the three-month ordeal, Shackleton wrote in his diary:

> When I look back at those days I have no doubt that Providence guided us,
> not only across those snowfields, but across the storm-white sea that sepa-
> rated Elephant Island from our landing-place on South Georgia. I know that
> during that long and racking march of thirty-six hours over the unnamed
> mountains and glaciers of South Georgia it seemed to me often that we
> were four, not three. I said nothing to my companions on the point, but
> afterwards Worsley said to me, "Boss, I had a curious feeling on the march

that there was another person with us." Crean confessed to the same idea. One feels "the dearth of human words, the roughness of mortal speech" in trying to describe things intangible, but a record of our journeys would be incomplete without a reference to a subject very near to our hearts.[1]

Do not mistake the placement of this chapter as an indicator of its importance. The Holy Spirit has been laced into every chapter, even if invisibly behind the scenes, as he is in our everyday lives and mission. This chapter has been placed strategically before we shift into missional engagement because this is the order of Luke's narrative in Acts:

Prayer (Acts 1:4–11; 2:1)
Empowerment (Acts 2:2–4)
Missional engagement (Acts 2:5–47)

If the Twelve weren't ready without the empowering of the Spirit, despite being trained daily by Jesus for three years, planters today don't stand a chance without it. Jesus's public ministry began at his baptism by John, when the Spirit fell upon him, and he was given the Spirit without measure (John 3:34). Much of ministry is a long tug of war between our wills and God's, until we finally surrender, completely depending upon him. As it was for Shackleton, the result is the sense that we are not alone, that someone is with us in the furnace, during our trials and tribulations, during our agonies and ecstasies. Leaders who have been truly used of God are aware of this power, and aware that it was not of themselves. They join Peter in saying, "Fellow Israelites, why does this surprise you? Why do you stare at us as if by our own power or godliness we had made this man walk?" (Acts 3:12).

There is a mission principle at work that the more front-line advancement you make, the more of the Spirit's power will be required.[2] Being dropped unexpectedly into an exorcism or witnessing a supernatural healing can quickly reveal how out of our depth we are, and our need for immediate dependence upon the power of the Holy Spirit.

Theologically speaking, the two bookends to the atonement are the cross and the resurrection, the two events that delivered God's grace and power to us.[3] At the cross, Jesus fulfilled the law's demands, and at his resurrection,

1. Ernest Shackleton, *South: The Last Antarctic Expedition of Shackleton and the Endurance* (London: Bloomsbury, 2014), 199.
2. I elaborate more on this in my book *Reaching the Unreached: Becoming Raiders of the Lost Art* (Grand Rapids: Zondervan, 2017).
3. Jerry Bridges, *The Bookends of the Christian Life* (Wheaton, IL: Crossway, 2009), 15.

he was declared the son of God with power, explaining why Moses, representing the law, and Elijah, representing power, appeared to him leading up to the cross on the mount of transfiguration. Having atoned for our sin and risen from the dead, Jesus made possible the indwelling of the Spirit within us as the temple of God. Therefore the filling of the Spirit was a condition of leadership in the early church when the apostles chose seven men who were "full of faith and of the Holy Spirit" (Acts 6:5).

John Wesley believed that "the filling of the Holy Spirit (and accompanying gifts) is for all believers in all ages and looks to God's ultimate victory at the end of the present age."[4] The empowerment of the Holy Spirit was given for the proclamation of Jesus as King in attestation to his reign and rule. This was the key to the New Testament church's effectiveness, the Wesleyan movement, and any subsequent movements since.

Church starters focus on the external activities of starting a church, but the church planter knows that fools rush in where angels fear to tread. Jesus told the apostles to wait in Jerusalem to preven the casualty of running out to complete the mission in their own strength like Samson shorn of his hair. Planting a church is a long internal process of painful surrender. Planting serves as both the anvil upon which God hammers out the impurities of our good and wrong desires, and the crucible burning away the mixed motives of spirit and flesh. Planters take a beating in their bodies, and souls, their expectations dying a hundred deaths through blessed crucifixion.

When a first-time church planter launches the vague expectation that the lost will flock to the plant with unanswered questions is met with the doors opening to few numbers as the church begins to do the downward spiral from day one. Every week is perceived as a circling of the drain, the skid mark of the planter's heart rubbing itself a bit more raw with every revolution on the descent.

At the end of the first year, most planters are doing well to be left with twenty-five people in their gatherings. If the deceptive metric of numbers determines success or personal fulfillment, a planter's soul is headed for trouble. The love of success is the root of many evils, and few have the character to whether the temptations it brings. Numbers provide no support for an ego that feeds only on Christ, and planting breaks our hearts until we finally take that soul-restoring walk with Jesus down the beach and get back to the heart of the matter. On the beach, Peter knew what he wanted: just Jesus. It took three years to get there and to answer the first question Jesus asked him, "What are you seeking?"

---

4. John Hucks, *John Wesley and Eighteenth century Methodist Movement: A Model for Effective Leadership* (PhD diss., Point Loma Nazarene University, 2003), 74.

(John 1:38 ESV). I'm convinced it takes most planters that long to determine what they really want; to glorify his name or make a name for themselves.

This conversation with Jesus can stretch out for years, until sick of ourselves, we finally surrender, confessing, "Lord, you know all things." The fig leaf drops, wrestling the angel finished, a slow death of crucifixion, the long defeat. We realize it was worth the pain and bewilderment because perhaps for the first time we see Christ again, and in his light, we see ourselves—not our self-infatuated fantasy of who we could become, but who we truly are in front of him. We regain our missional clarity and the understanding that loving him and knowing his love were the fuel for making him known.

God is more concerned with what he can do *in* his servants than what he will ever do *through* them. Perhaps our church plants do the planter's soul more good than anyone else. Perhaps the planter was the one who needed reaching more than anyone else. Therefore, the planter must ensure that they are not the only one who isn't reached when planting the church. Planters must look to their own souls first. In his book *Relational Soul*, Plass identifies four disciplines that will help restore a weary, worn-out soul at the feet of Jesus[5]:

- Solitude
- Silence
- Contemplative reading of Scripture
- Contemplative prayer

In all the hustle and bustle of church planting, these things can be edged out, yet our true source of power comes not from frenzied flurries born out of restlessness anxiety from the restfulness from his grace and peace. Spirit-filled ministers exude a calm, quiet confidence. Spirit-bereft ministers bleed anxiety and stress. What you become, more than what you preach, will be powerfully modeled to your church, shaping the DNA. Isaiah's warning echoes, "In returning and rest you shall be saved; in quietness and trust shall be your strength. But you were unwilling, and you said, 'No! We will flee upon horses'; therefore you shall flee away; and, 'We will ride upon swift steeds'; therefore your pursuers shall be swift" (Isa. 30:15–16 ESV). Many planters flee from rest, dogged by even swifter anxieties.

Into our neurotic frenzy, God interjected the concept of sabbath, or rest, setting time aside from work, any work, to focus upon God. Scripture reading

---

5. Richard Plass and James Coffield, *Relational Soul* (Downers Grove, IL: InterVarsity Press, 2014), 134.

and prayer may be done in a rush, but solitude and silence prove more of a struggle and must be fought for like Abraham chasing the buzzards off his sacrifices. When we are walking with God daily, we do ministry with Jesus and not for him.

THE REAL WORK OF MINISTRY

The work of the Holy Spirit is central to the work of church planting. Despite our love of the church in Acts 2:42, a church can only experience Acts 2 results by engaging in the activities of Acts 1.[6] In a hushed upper room, a motley crew determined to go on mission resisted the urge to hit the open road and burn rubber, choosing to heed Jesus's words to wait and fill up the car with fuel. At the core of any forward movement of the kingdom hums an engine that runs on spiritual fuel.

At Refuge Long Beach, we engaged in frontline, sometimes even dangerous, mission on a weekly basis. But we constantly prayed in our home groups during the week. We broke bread, prayed, and talked. And stuff happened. A saying attributed to William Temple goes, "I believe in coincidences. When I pray, coincidences happen. When I don't, they don't."[7]

If there was anything that Luke wanted the readers of Acts to know, it was the primary importance of the power of the Holy Spirit in connection with mission. E. M. Bounds asserted that "prayer and mission are bosom companions"[8] The first orchestrated advancement of a church planting movement in Acts 13 testifies to this fact. George Miley outlines some key spiritual factors in Acts 13:2-3 that can be overlooked for those merely looking for methods:

1. We discover worship—"They were worshiping the Lord."
2. We discover fasting—"and fasting."
3. We discover the Holy Spirit speaking—"The Holy Spirit said . . ."
4. We discover being set apart—"Set apart for me."
5. We discover a team—"Barnabas and Saul."
6. We discover a mission—"for the work to which I have called them."
7. We discover prayer—"So after they had fasted and prayed."
8. We discover the laying on of hands—"They placed their hands on them."[9]

---

6. Brian Nickens, *The Little Church That Will: Crossing Over into the Coming Reformation* (Redding, CA: self-pub., 2011), 7.

7. David Watson, *Called & Committed* (Wheaton, IL: Harold Shaw Publishers, 1982), 83.

8. E. M. Bounds, *The Complete Works of E. M. Bounds on Prayer* (Grand Rapids: Baker, 1990), 142.

9. George Miley, *Loving the Church . . . Blessing the Nations: Pursuing the Role of Local Churches in Global Missions* (Downers Grove, IL: InterVarsity Press, 2003), 82–91.

It becomes glaringly clear that the power chronicled in Acts doesn't derive from a leadership course, a podcast about maximizing your effectiveness, or the myriad of things distracting leaders today from the "one thing is needful" (Luke 10:42 KJV). Consider the implications of Jesus holding the apostles back from the mission to pray ten days for power from on high as a confession of their inadequate weakness. Prayer is often born out of the desperation from realizing the enormity of the task before us and preparing to step out of our comfort zones. Nothing gets you on your knees like stepping out of your comfort zone. The confession of inadequacy is the first step toward dependence upon the Holy Spirit.

Like missional breathing, you inhale the presence of and power of God as you pray, and then exhale it out as you take action. Taking action without prayer is presumption, and praying without taking action is idleness. Prayer and action are two sides of the same coin. In the following prayer journal examples, the first entry chronicles somebody who prays but never takes action. If you were to combine action with prayer the entries might sound like the second entry.

Actionless Prayer Journal:

Neighbor across the street—provide an excuse for me to talk to them. Give me an opportunity to introduce myself.

Or, combined with action:

The Johnsons—provide something that we have in common so we can build a solid friendship with them and share our lives (dinner, CrossFit, our street adopting a refugee family together?).

Each time the Spirit meets a planter on the other side of obedient faith-filled evangelism, the planter's faith increases in size and substance like a muscle. Our evangelistic prowess grows over time through regular use, yet does not replace dependence upon the Spirit. As we take action, our dependence on God grows the more we observe him doing the heavy lifting. God is seeking faithful messengers who will deliver the right mail to the right people, giving him the credit when they win the sweepstakes. Any planter feeling out of their depth as they wade into the crashing waves is in exactly the right place, feeling exactly the right things. The power of the Holy Spirit was given to pioneer new frontiers, and new frontiers involve the unknown.

POWER IS FOR THE FRONTIERS

Whenever the early church advanced the kingdom across frontier boundaries, their mission was accompanied by the power of the Holy Spirit. Remember the four frontiers from Acts 1:8: Jerusalem, Judea, Samaria, and the ends of the earth? As long as the Jerusalem church continued to posture itself leaning forward into mission, it thrived. As Roland Allen asserted, "the coming of the Holy Spirit at Pentecost was the coming of a missionary Spirit."[10] The power that accompanies every example of outward expansion between Acts chapters 1 and 28 provide readers with a link between mission and the supernatural empowerment across every frontier of gospel advancement:

- THE FIRST FRONTIER—JERUSALEM: Jews were scattered away from Israel, but from all over the Roman Empire, devout Jews made the annual pilgrimage to Jerusalem to observe Passover. The feast of Pentecost, or the "Feast of the First Fruits," was Israel's early harvest festival designed to give God thanks for the first fruits of the crops. In faith, worshipers offered thanksgiving to Yahweh for what was to come later when the full harvest was brought in. Thus, the thousands who came to faith as a result of Peter's preaching became a picture of "the first fruits" of a much greater harvest. Luke trusts that the worshipers originating from every part of the Roman Empire provide a glimpse of a greater global harvest from every nation. Due to the missionary nature of the events at Pentecost, there was an outpouring of the Spirit, and hence, the "power" that Jesus promised in Acts 1:8.

- THE SECOND AND THIRD FRONTIERS—SAMARIA AND JUDAH: The miracles performed in Samaria are enough to warrant the claim that the closer you get to the front line, the more supernatural things become. Philip visits Samaria and they receive the baptism of the Holy Spirit in another Pentecost outpouring unique to the Samaritans. "When the apostles in Jerusalem heard that Samaria had accepted the word of God, they sent Peter and John to Samaria. When they arrived, they prayed for the new believers there that they might receive the Holy Spirit, because the Holy Spirit had not yet come on any of them; they had simply been baptized in the name of the Lord Jesus. Then Peter and John placed their hands on them, and they received the Holy Spirit" (Acts 8:14–17).

---

10. Roland Allen, *Pentecost and the World in The Ministry of the Spirit: Selected Writings of Roland Allen*, ed. David M. Paton (Grand Rapids: Eerdmans, 1960), 59.

- THE FOURTH FRONTIER—THE GENTILES: Philip the evangelist, one of the deacons chosen alongside Stephen, was told by an angel to travel the desert road out of Jerusalem that leads to Gaza, and by divine appointment intercepted an Ethiopian official who happened to be reading Isaiah 53. After baptizing the eunuch, Philip is supernaturally transported like Elijah the prophet (Acts 8:26–40). Cornelius, a Roman centurion of great standing, received an appearance from an angel who told him, "Your prayers and gifts to the poor have come up as a memorial offering before God" (Acts 10:4). Sending for Peter in Joppa, unbeknownst to Cornelius, Peter had his own supernatural visions of unclean animals. Immediately upon waking, the messenger from Cornelius arrived at that moment. When Peter accompanied him, the Spirit was poured out identically upon Gentiles as it was on Jews at Pentecost, prompting Peter to baptize them with water after seeing that God had baptized them already with the Holy Spirit. Cornelius represents all Gentiles and serves as a turning point for the gospel.

Each of these ventures to take the gospel to new frontiers were surrounded by supernatural activity. This pairing of supernatural power is intentional in Luke's narrative because it fulfills Jesus's promise that when they were clothed with power, they would be his witnesses. The two are inseparable.

This connection continues throughout Acts. The promised power accompanies Paul's expansion into Macedonia. His ministry to Achaia is broadened out westward as he receives a supernatural vision of the man of Macedonia begging the team to "Come over to Macedonia and help us" (Acts 16:9). In the midst of a difficult season of ministry that is interpreted by Luke to be the Holy Spirit preventing them from preaching the gospel in areas they'd previously visited (such as Galatia), this symbolizes another shift into a completely new field. Acts continues to link power and expansion, leading to the conclusion that mission is where the power of the Spirit is truly found.

At the time of writing this book, Francis Chan announced his family's intention to move to Asia based on the supernatural he experienced on front-line mission in Myanmar. Speaking at Azusa Pacific University at a morning chapel, Chan stated, "For the last few years I have believed in miracles . . . recently, while sharing the gospel with people in Myanmar . . . every person I touched was healed. I have never experienced this in 52 years."[11] A deaf boy had his hearing restored,

---

11. "Francis Chan Says Every Person He Touched in Myanmar Was Healed," *Relevant Magazine*, Relevantmagazine.com, February 2018, https://relevantmagazine.com/podcast/francis-chan-says-every -person-he-touched-in-myanmar-was-healed/_written; Caleb Parke, "Christian Pastor Francis Chan

among other miracles. Chan stated that as a result of that trip, he and wife had made the final decision to move to Hong Kong and serve as missionaries there.

In *Reaching the Unreached*, I argue, "The front lines of outward expansion are where Jesus promised that the Holy Spirit would be with us in power. Without the risk inherent in the mission of Jesus, we would have no great need for his power."[12] Famous missionary and wife of martyr Jim Elliot, Elisabeth Elliot said "There is no need for faith where there is no consciousness of an element of risk."[13]

SPIRITUAL WARFARE

With every advancement of the kingdom into enemy territory, a counterattack can be expected. Typically, spiritual warfare gets filed away into the "things we don't ever talk about" folder. Despite Paul writing about it in light of mission work, few train planters for engaging the enemy's "welcoming committee" when they arrive. In World War Two, Hitler's German forces readied themselves by erecting telephone poles called "Rommel's Asparagus" to stop low-flying planes. The enemy peppered the countryside with pillboxes equipped with mounted machine guns, and covered the beachhead with tank-stoppers, mines, and barbed wire.

The enemy presses a leader's defenses until finding a weakness, and then waits to find opportunity. Planters should ask themselves what they would use to stop themselves if they were the enemy and seek to bolster that area of their lives. Paul had met this enemy head-on repeatedly and knew he was no match, so he exhorted the Ephesians to don spiritual armor to brace for the fight. Armor is borrowed strength, a second skin, worn because yours isn't strong enough to last the attack. At best, Paul hoped they could make a stand. Repeating the word *stand* seven times in Ephesians 6, Paul is telling them to dig in against the coming blow.

When people have joined my strike team over the years in the churches I've planted, my welcome included a backhanded apology. "Welcome" I'd say, then quickly add, "And I'm sorry . . . your life is about to fall apart." In my first church plant ever, everybody's lives fell apart rather quickly. The same happened in my second. This is the protocol of pressing kingdoms into each other, and occurs every time a church planter attempts to cross the frontiers with the gospel.

---

leaving US to be international missionary in Hong Kong: 'Why wouldn't I go?' Fox News, November 8, 2019, https://www.foxnews.com/faith-values/christian-pastor-francis-chan-missionary-hong-kong.

12. Jones, *Reaching the Unreached*, 95.

13. Lavonne Neff, *The Gift of Faith: Short Reflections by Thoughtful Anglicans* (Seattle: Morehouse, 2003), 60.

Dave Earley points out four of the most commonly used the stratagems Satan employs against those who put their toe to the line:

- Condemnation (1 Pet. 5:8; Zech. 3:1; Rev. 12:10; Job 1:9–11)
- Deception (John 8:44)
- Temptation (1 Thess. 3:5; Matt. 4:1–11; Gen 3:1–6)
- Distraction (Mark 8:31–33)[14]

Planters who are not ignorant of Satan's devices ready their team for spiritual skirmishes and train their hands for warfare (Psalm 144:1). Equipping your team to do battle by fasting and prayer ahead of time will prevent bewilderment when they begin to set foot on the mission field. The rhythm of stand . . . pray . . . advance will be on constant repeat as the planter's battle cry, battle stance, and battle tactic. Prayer is akin to calling in air support, clearing the way for the troops on the ground. Therefore the prayer life of the team is critical before setting out. It is worth pointing out that in addition to advancing, you must sometimes retreat in prayer. This is why all my training involves prayer retreats for the team.

PERSEVERING IN PRAYER

Luke introduces his parables on prayer with the following epigraph, "And he told them a parable to the effect that they ought always to pray and not lose heart" (Luke 18:1 ESV). Jesus knew us intimately, aware that we would struggle in prayer and need to persevere in it like an Olympic athlete striving for the gold.

After a season of extraordinary mission accompanied by miracles, I was determined to increase the amount of spiritual power in my life. I'd been in an intense exorcism, one that left me physically injured for about nine months. Nothing shows you your spiritual weakness more than experiences with the supernatural, so I determined to ensure that I was stronger for the next round. Had I known then what I know now, I would have cautioned myself about the journey I was about to go on, because by the end of it, I'd be left a broken crumpled heap of weakness and insufficiency.

During that time, I began to fast, pray, and meditate. Deep down I was seeking to become spiritually stronger and more competent, but I was unaware

14. Dave Earley and David Wheeler, *Evangelism Is . . . How to Share Jesus with Passion and Confidence* (Nashville: Broadman & Holman, 2010), 160.

that this desire was an undermining of my dependence upon the Holy Spirit. True strength comes from being weak, and I was attempting to become strong in myself, and was inadvertently creating my own thorn in the flesh. Rejecting God's Plan A, I had invented my own Plan B. The journey was mapped out with good intentions but executed with bad ideas, and it began with an inability to link any thoughts together to pray. Putting it down to spiritual attack, I doubled down and read all eight volumes of E. M. Bounds on prayer. Rather than helping me kneel, it left me writhing on the floor, a helpless mess.

I knew better than to make prayer a legalistic task, but what I'd set out to do was prideful. The purpose of prayer is dependence on the Spirit and his power. Anything that leads us away from dependence upon God himself is a subtle deception. Satan is a superior strategist. He is a master tactician. David wrote about being hidden in the secret place of the Most High, buried deep within a royal pavilion, but I felt thrust outside the camp. The heavens remained like a bronze shield between us, the arrows of my prayers bouncing off and clattering around my feet.

Six months in, I simply prayed the Lord's Prayer in a gesture of defeat. Slowly a trickle of God's presence filled the parched, arid desert. I experienced a breakthrough after praying the Lord's Prayer when my own prayers were powerless. Upon thinking that, the Holy Spirit arrested me mid-thought like a spiritual traffic cop. Paul's epiphany was that God's strength was made perfect in his weakness, but my breakthrough was that I had believed that my words and their length and effort would equal the words of God's beloved Son. In my spiritual pride and arrogance, I thought my prayers had value in themselves.

God had broken me down, emptied me of myself, and taught me that I couldn't even pray without his strength in me. I had been praying for power, but the lesson was my own powerlessness. Had my efforts led to greater power and strength, I would have started believing in my own efforts and would have been more spiritually sick than ever. God's love for us is so strong that he may withdraw his presence from us slightly as part of our discipleship process, as even Jeremiah experienced when he complained, "You have wrapped yourself with a cloud so that no prayer can pass through" (Lam. 3:44 ESV).

GROWING IN PRAYER

Intimate prayer will become a lifelong personal pursuit, and as planters grow in prayer individually, they will also develop in corporate prayer. Rather than allowing prayer to devolve into the transition between songs or Sunday morning speeches, it will evolve into a wartime tactic, a survival strategy that mobilizes your troops to present a front line.

Planters should track their growth in prayer in the following three areas:

- Personal prayer—Am I learning vibrant lessons about prayer?
- Corporate prayer—Is my team learning to pray together?
- Leader prayer—Are the leaders around me seeking to develop a deeper prayer life like Jesus's disciples as a result of my influence?

It is worth pointing out that when Jesus's disciples asked him to teach them to pray, he gave them an advanced breakdown of the consisting of the essential components of prayer by revealing the Lord's prayer to us in Matthew 6:9–13:

- Adoration—Our Father in heaven (v. 9)
- Contemplation—hallowed be your name (v. 9)
- Petition—Your kingdom come (v. 10)
- Surrender—Your will be done (v. 10)
- Intercession—On earth as it is in heaven (v. 10)
- Dependence—Give us this day our daily bread (v. 11)
- Confession—forgive us our debts (v. 12)
- Listening—as we also have forgiven our debtors (v. 12)
- Warfare—and lead us not into temptation, but deliver us from evil (v. 13)[15]

If our people are to grow in prayer, it can be tracked by the presence of these components. Rather than merely asking for things, prayer will become a tug-of-war, give-and-take affair that the Lord's Prayer so beautifully outlines. John Eldredge wrote a book that I would recommend you work through with your entire church at some point called *Walking with God: Talk to Him. Hear from Him. Really*. In it, he describes how to have a conversational relationship with God as your Father. He outlines busyness as one of the reasons we don't make seeking God as our greatest priority:

Every age has a certain spirit or mood or climate to it. Ours is busyness. We're all running like lemmings from sunup to way past sundown. What's with all the energy drinks? There must be dozens now. Rocket Fuel. Crank You Up. Not to mention the coffeehouses on every corner. Why do we

---

15. David M. Lloyd-Jones, *Studies in the Sermon on the Mount* (Grand Rapids: Eerdmans, 1984), 202.

need all this caffeine? And why do so many of us now need sleep aids to rest at night? Our grandparents didn't. We thought the age of technology would make life simpler, easier. It has us by the throat. We need to operate at the speed of computers. Seriously, I'm irritated that my email takes four seconds to boot up now, when it used to take ten. I realize I'm not the first to put this down on paper. People have been making this observation for a long time. We are running around like ants do when you kick their hill, like rats on a wheel, like Carroll's Mad Hatter. And for some reason, we either believe we can't stop, or we don't want to.[16]

CONCLUSION

C. S. Lewis wrote *The Screwtape Letters* about a demon named Wormwood who writes to his nephew about how to thwart "the patient." If the metaphorical demon plaguing the modern church would identified itself by name, it might introduce itself by saying, "My name is Later . . . for you can always seek God later." Later never comes, of course. Later has never come. Waiting for your ship to come in looks a lot like missing the boat as you watch the boat sail away from the docks. There are many wrong ways to pray according to Jesus, but the best way to pray is to simply show up. And pray.

REFLECT

- The author uses military terms and imagery in this chapter. The military operates under the authority of its leadership. Church planters must operate under the authority of Jesus Christ by the power of the Holy Spirit. What does this look like for your church planting ambitions? For example, the power of the Holy Spirit is unleashed where God is working. How do you know that your plans are consistent with where God is working?
- Read Ephesians 6:10–20. The military terms and imagery also reinforce the fact that church planting involves entering a spiritual war. Although our plans involve the people, communities, and institutions of this world, there are also spiritual forces involved that we cannot see. How are you and your team using the tools and tactics of spiritual warfare?

---

16. John Eldredge, *Walking with God* (Nashville: Thomas Nelson, 2008), 116.

DISCUSS

- Prayer is the foundation of church planting. How would a church planting team ensure that they are not neglecting the ministry of prayer at multiple levels of the fellowship?
    - The planting team and leadership
    - The workers
    - The body of Christ involved in the church fellowship
    - Individual believers

CHALLENGE

- How have you been spiritually transformed by the process of aspiring to be, becoming, or being a church planter?
- If you agree that part of your transformation involved a transition from human plans and self-effort to greater reliance on the Holy Spirit and appreciation of the spiritual dynamics of Christian ministry, what were the key events, experiences, and relationships that contributed to this understanding?

15

DISCOVERING, DEVELOPING, AND DEPLOYING THE GIFTS

You have never met a mere mortal.

—C. S. LEWIS

The secret to kingdom work is mobilizing everyday believers through their gifts. If you still think you're the main player in the church you plant, you will never tap into the apostolic genius of Paul. A Barna study in 2017 found that Christians who believed they had a responsibility to share their faith had dropped from 89% to 64% since 1993, a 25% difference of those polled. Further, the study reported that in 1993, 10% believed it was the church's job to convert people, contrasted with 29% who believed that in 2017.[1] This is because for the past twenty-five years, we've trained Christians to sit back and leave the job to the "professionals." But in the New Testament, the professionals would leave. Therefore, equipping believers to operate in their gifts was paramount.

When the COVID-19 virus hit America, leaders scrambled to get their faces back in front of the people who'd come to depend upon them. Pouring all their energy into the Sunday show remotely as if spiritual input was a streaming service like Netflix or Disney+ exposed the weaknesses of the Western church. For too long we've allowed religious entertainment to replace infiltrating our

---

1. Barna Group, *Spiritual Conversations in a Digital Age: How Christians' Approach to Sharing Their Faith Has Changed in 25 Years* (Ventura, CA: Barna Group, 2018), 18.

communities. In *Reaching the Unreached*, I wrote about mobilizing a church on mission,

> Stories have piled up about communities changed by small unassuming everyday believers discovering new and innovative ways of connecting with individuals as they blunder into mission. Big doors turn on small hinges. Tugboats turn tankers. Splinter cells can win wars. We're in a different kind of battle, where individual guerilla tactics make you a fast moving, light footed, low-to-the-ground reconnaissance weapon of witness. You won't be effective in big numbers in the future. You won't need the heavy artillery. You're perfect for the job in a way that your church never will be. No matter what we do, no matter how many programs we launch, stadiums we fill, or outreaches we put on, statistics from Lifeway Research tell us that sixty percent of the un-churched American populace will *never* come to church. Period. It's up to you. There is no cavalry riding over the hill, no big guns, no backup ground support, no rescue team coming.
>
> Just you.[2]

Ministry according to Ephesians 4 says that gifting of the church with apostles, teachers, evangelists, prophets, and shepherds is "to equip the saints for the work of ministry" (Eph. 4:12 ESV). That means that when something like the coronavirus crisis broadsided the church, it served as a pop quiz to measure how effectively leaders had been discipling their congregations. Lockdown was an opportunity for the church to shine, to display peace in the midst of panic, to model sacrifice in contrast to the survival instincts of the hoarders, and to serve as a contrast to those who were panicked by every wave of social media madness.

If leaders kept church attenders too busy watching the show all these years, they found themselves panicked, unable to leave a church at a moment's notice as Paul did in the case of Thessalonica and other churches he planted. If there isn't an arsenal of discipled team members waiting to take to the skies to plant and others to hold down the fort, it's because the leader has neglected his duty to train up able people who are also able to train up others (2 Tim. 2:2). When the church fixed its eyes upon leaders as the Corinthians did—"'I follow Paul,' or 'I follow Apollos,' or 'I follow Cephas'" (1 Cor. 1:12)—Paul diagnosed the Corinthians as carnal instead of the dynamic spiritual force with its collective eye focused on Jesus.

---

2. Peyton Jones, *Reaching the Unreached: Becoming Raiders of the Lost Art* (Grand Rapids: Zondervan, 2017), 136.

ONE ANOTHERS

That there are over fifty "one another" statements and commands in the New Testament should be a sign that we are called to a special kind of life together. Planter, take the time to read them here and envision what a church practicing these would look like. The "one another" statements and commands are:

- "Be at peace with each other (Mark 9:50).
- "Wash one another's feet" (John 13:14).
- "Love one another" (John 13:34; Rom. 13:8).
- "Be devoted to one another in love" (Rom. 12:10).
- "Honor one another above yourselves" (Rom. 12:10).
- "Live in harmony with one another" (Rom. 12:16).
- "Stop passing judgment on one another" (Rom. 14:13).
- "Accept one another, then, just as Christ accepted you" (Rom. 15:7).
- "Instruct one another" (Rom. 15:14).
- "Greet one another with a holy kiss" (Rom. 16:16; 1 Cor. 16:20; 2 Cor. 13:12).
- "When you come together to eat, wait for one another" (1 Cor. 11:33 ESV).
- "Have equal concern for each other" (1 Cor. 12:25).
- "Serve one another humbly in love" (Gal. 5:13).
- "Let us not become conceited, provoking and envying each other" (Gal. 5:26).
- "Carry each other's burdens" (Gal. 6:2).
- "Be patient, bearing with one another in love" (Eph. 4:2).
- "Be kind and compassionate to one another" (Eph. 4:32).
- "Forgiving each other" (Eph. 4:32).
- "Speaking to one another with psalms, hymns and songs" (Eph. 5:19).
- "Submit to one another out of reverence for Christ" (Eph. 5:21).
- "In humility value others above yourselves" (Phil. 2:3).
- "Do not lie to each other" (Col. 3:9).
- "Bear with each other" (Col. 3:13).
- "Forgive whatever grievances you may have against one another" (Col. 3:13).
- "Teach [one another]" (Col. 3:16).
- "Admonish one another" (Col. 3:16).
- "Make your love increase and overflow for each other" (1 Thess. 3:12).
- "Love each other" (1 Thess. 4:9).

- "Encourage one another" (1 Thess. 4:18; 5:11).
- "Build each other up" (1 Thess. 5:11).
- "Encourage one another daily" (Heb. 3:13).
- "Spur one another on toward love and good deeds" (Heb. 10:24).
- "Encourage one another" (Heb. 10:25).
- "Do not slander one another" (James 4:11).
- "Don't grumble against one another" (James 5:9).
- "Confess your sins to each other" (James 5:16).
- "Pray for each other" (James 5:16).
- "Love one another deeply, from the heart" (1 Pet. 1:22).
- "Live in harmony with one another" (1 Pet. 3:8).
- "Love each other deeply" (1 Pet. 4:8).
- "Offer hospitality to one another without grumbling" (1 Pet. 4:9).
- "Each one should use whatever gift he has received to server others" (1 Pet. 4:10).
- "Clothe yourselves with humility toward one another" (1 Pet. 5:5).
- "Greet one another with a kiss of love" (1 Pet. 5:14).

When in your gatherings is there actually time to do any of these things? Making your way from the parking lot or to the bathroom or getting donuts and coffee is the only time you're not stuck staring at the back of somebody's head. Someone needs to hit the reset button.

SET THE STAGE

Set the stage. Pentecost. People. Power. Puzzlement.

The people are confused as to what they're witnessing, telling Peter, "Go home, you're drunk," to which Peter replies, "This is what was spoken of by the prophet Joel" (Acts 2:16):

> In the last days it shall be, God declares,
> that I will pour out my Spirit on all flesh,
> and your sons and your daughters shall prophesy,
>   and your young men shall see visions,
>   and your old men shall dream dreams;
> even on my male servants and female servants
>   in those days I will pour out my Spirit, and they shall prophesy.
>   (Acts 2:17–18 ESV)

Analyzing Peter's approach to the assembled crowd, at first glance it's not clear why he referenced Joel's prophecy, an obscure lesser prophet's discourse on a plague of locusts, to explain what was happening. Yet the passage focused upon God pouring out his Spirit upon everyone, activating their spiritual gifts. Peter emphasized that people of all types, sexes, and social strata would use their gifts, and explains that that was what they were witnessing, and that "this promise is for you" also (Acts 2:39). Peter is proclaiming that the Spirit desires to fill each of them, activate them, and mobilize them to evangelize in the same way. The key to unleashing powerful movements is to deploy everyday believers in their gifts. Peter linked evangelism to spiritual gifts in this passage. How tragic, therefore, that the contemporary church spends so little time assisting our people to discover who they are!

Acts 2:42–47 describes what it looks like on the ground when the Holy Spirit is "poured out" and believers are activated.

They devoted themselves to the apostles' teaching and to fellowship, to the breaking of bread and to prayer. Everyone was filled with awe at the many wonders and signs performed by the apostles. All the believers were together and had everything in common. They sold property and possessions to give to anyone who had need. Every day they continued to meet together in the temple courts. They broke bread in their homes and ate together with glad and sincere hearts, praising God and enjoying the favor of all the people. And the Lord added to their number daily those who were being saved.

These activated believers became scattered through Paul's persecution so that the gospel went throughout all the region in Acts chapter 11:19–21 (emphasis mine):

Now those who had been scattered by the persecution that broke out when Stephen was killed traveled as far as Phoenicia, Cyprus and Antioch, spreading the word only among Jews. Some of them, however, men from Cyprus and Cyrene, went to Antioch and began to speak to Greeks also, telling them the good news about the Lord Jesus. *The Lord's hand was with them, and a great number of people believed and turned to the Lord.*

What happened in Antioch was the direct result of the effective discipling in Jerusalem chronicled in Acts 2:42–48. The "one anothers" were in full swing in

Jerusalem. Acts 11:19–21 describes the activity of those same people in Jerusalem who migrated Northward to Antioch during Paul's persecution. What Paul witnessed when he arrived was a powerful group of believers with no discernable leadership who were killing it in ministry. When Paul penned that the APEST functions were to "equip his people for works of service" he was emphasizing what he had personally witnessed as the norm when believers become activated in their gifts. Ephesians 4:11–12 says (emphasis mine), "So Christ himself gave the apostles, the prophets, the evangelists, the pastors and teachers, *to equip his people for works of service*, so that the body of Christ may be built up."

What Paul is describing is what I term *Gift-Driven Ministry*. Most of our ministry today is vision driven, where we align members to perform church chores around the five-year plan thought up in a board room by ecclesiastic executives, Alpha males, and yes men. Most church starters gravitate towards this business model, and the church feels like a well-oiled machine as it plots religious activity and profit margins. Gift-driven ministry as witnessed in the New Testament harnesses Spirit-empowered believers to naturally work out their supernatural gifting as star players on the field. In church starting, the body serves leadership. In church planting, leadership serves the body. Leadership exists to equip believers to discover, develop, and deploy in their gifting, driving them out into the community.

SPIRITUAL GIFTS

Like the APEST functions, the gifts serve an inward and outward function as the church is driven forward and into the community. In the early church, prophecy, encouragement, and other gifts functioned as people ministered to one another and the presence of God was revealed to unbelievers. The presence of the gifts provide witness to his reality as "a sign not for believers, but for unbe-lievers" (1 Cor. 14:22) Prophecy allows God to enter the room, ushering in his felt presence. When was the last time at one of your gatherings "an unbeliever or outsider enters, he is convicted by all, he is called to account by all, the secrets of his heart are disclosed, and so, falling on his face, he will worship God and declare that God is really among you." (1 Cor. 14:24–25 ESV). Surely some-thing is missing in modern churches that the early church regularly experienced.

Stifling the gifts quenches the Spirit and bars God from breaking in. As E. Stanley Jones explained,

> The very setup of the ordinary church tends to produce the anonymous. The congregation is supposed to be silent and receptive, and the pastor is

supposed to be outgoing and aggressive. That produces by its very makeup the spectator and the participant. By its very makeup it produces the recessive, the ingrown, the non-contributive, and the parasite. Men and women who during the week are molders of opinion, directors of large concerns, directors of destinies are expected to be putty on Sunday, and are supposed to like it. They have little responsibility, hence make little response, except, perhaps, "I enjoyed your sermon." They have little to do, hence they do little.[3]

As the gifts have been relegated to the back seat in the Western church, multiplication has been bottlenecked. Tozer diagnosed the Western church's absence of the spiritual gifts in these terms: "Satan knows that Spiritless evangelicalism is as deadly as Modernism or heresy, and he has done everything in his power to prevent us from enjoying our true Christian heritage. A church without the Spirit is as helpless as Israel might have been in the wilderness if the fiery cloud had deserted them. The Holy Spirit is our cloud by day and our fire by night. Without Him we only wander aimlessly about the desert."[4]

WHAT ARE THE GIFTS AND WHAT IS THEIR PURPOSE?

Ephesians 4 outlines the anatomy of the gifts: Christ defeated the enemy, ascended to the Father, showered us with the spoils of war, leaving us to minister and display the fruits of his victory through the exercising of the gifts. Displaying the gifts displays Christ and his victory. In 1 Peter 4:10–11 (emphasis mine), Peter tells us that the gifts we exercise are for Jesus's glory, and similarly, "Each of you should use whatever gift you have received to serve others, as faithful stewards of God's grace in its various forms. If anyone speaks, they should do so as one who speaks the very words of God. If anyone serves, they should do so with the strength God provides, so that in all things God may be praised through Jesus Christ. *To him be the glory and the power for ever and ever.*" Because the gifts are linked to God's glory, Paul affirms that without the Holy Spirit, nobody acknowledges Jesus as Lord. Therefore, Timothy is exhorted not to neglect his gift because to neglect them is to neglect to glorify Jesus in the unique way he has sovereignly chosen to display himself through a believer.

3. E. Stanley Jones, *The Reconstruction of the Church—On What Pattern?* (Nashville: Abingdon, 1970), 109.
4. A. W. Tozer, *Keys to the Deeper Life* (Pioneer Library: First edition 1959, Kindle edition 2014), loc. 310 of 392, Kindle.

The gifts also display God's grace, bringing him more glory still. In 1 Corinthians 12:4 the word *gifts* is translated from the Greek word *charisma*, hence, our term "charismatic." The root word (*charis*) means "grace." "Now there are varieties of *graces* [*using the literal translation*], but the same Spirit." Gifts aren't earned, nor are they rewards for being holy, but are extra graces bestowed out of the abundance of God's grace itself. For this reason, Paul calls them *graces*. Gifts are *not* given in relation to holiness, but supplied at his discretion according to God's bottomless well of grace. Paul shatters the illusion that people who exercise spiritual gifts are more spiritual than others. Paul introduced the topic of spiritual gifts in 1 Corinthians 12:1: "Concerning spiritual gifts . . ." According to Gordon Fee, "concerning spiritual gifts" is actually "concerning spirituals" in the original language.[5] By sarcastically labeling the individuals who were abusing the gifts as "spirituals" he mocked those who passed themselves off as "spiritual people" and equated spiritual gifts with spirituality itself.

Today the existence of "spirituals" or people who abuse the gifts drive sincere believers away from attempting to experience them. Many within the charismatic movement do bizarre things, such as pray for the resurrection of dead children, or bounce Gandalf-like staffs on stage to "end racism." That said, the abuses of some should not erase the legitimacy of those who practice the gifts biblically. Thomas R. Schreiner, a continuationist, summarized J. I. Packer's assessment of the strengths and weaknesses of the charismatic movement that help to identify the blessings and potential dangers of ministering the gifts.[6]

Positive

- Spirit-empowered living
- Emotion finding expression
- Prayerfulness
- Every-heart involvement in the worship of God
- Missionary zeal
- Small-group ministry
- Communal living
- Joyfulness
- Belief in Satan and demons
- Belief in the miraculous

---

5. Gordon Fee, *The First Epistle to the Corinthians: The New International Commentary on the New Testament* (Grand Rapids: Eerdmans, 1987).

6. Thomas R. Schreiner, *Spiritual Gifts: What They Are and Why They Matter* (Nashville: Broadman & Holman, 2018), 7–14.

Negative
- Elitism
- Sectarianism
- Anti-intellectualism
- Illuminism (Gnosticism)
- Super-supernaturalsim
- Eudaemonism
- Demon obsession
- Conformism
- Experience centered

Despite the existence of abuses of the gifts, they should not be feared or neglected. Paul exhorted believers in the same breath to maintain the balance of discernment and openness: "Do not quench the spirit. Do not despise prophecies, but test everything; hold fast to the good" (1 Thess. 5:19–21 ESV). Unpacking the types of gifts and their functions sheds light on how they glorify Christ and therefore why they are sorely needed by planters.

CATEGORIES OF GIFTS

What kinds of gifts have been given and how are they categorized? The five main passages where spiritual gifts are listed are Romans 12:6–8 (seven listed), 1 Corinthians 12:8–10 (nine listed), 1 Corinthians 12:28 (eight listed), 1 Corinthians 12:29–30 (seven listed), and Ephesians 4:11 (five listed). Nowhere are we given a comprehensive list. Each of these lists has repeated gifts, and some include gifts that the other lists do not. Eliminating the repeated gifts leaves nineteen distinct spiritual gifts. Perhaps there are other gifts not listed in these passages, such as the gift of hospitality, a prerequisite activity for the role of an elder. The "most desirable" gift of prophecy that "edifies all" is listed in all five passages.

The gifts are categorized into three sections according to the members of the Trinity. 1 Corinthians 12:4 speaks of them as from "the same Spirit," as already noted. But verse 5 speaks of them as from "the same Lord" (Jesus Christ) and verse 6 as from "the same God" (the Father). The three different classifications of gifts are:

1. Ministry Gifts—The Lord (vs. 5)
2. Manifestation gifts—The Spirit (vs. 7)
3. Motivation gifts—God (vs. 6)

Each of them has a different function, but gifts might also have a different strength, anointing, or energizing. For example, you may have somebody with the gift of preaching; they are able to preach, yet another person may excel at it.

1. Service Gifts (Ephesians 4:10–11)

Gifts of the Son, given to the church in the form of the APEST functions so that they can equip the body to serve:

- Apostle—Equips the body to be on God's mission.
- Prophet— Equips to the body to hear God's voice.
- Evangelist—Equips the body to proclaim God's message.
- Pastor—Equips the body to care for God's family.
- Teacher—Equips the body to teach God's Word.

2. Manifestation Gifts (1 Corinthians 12:8–10)

Gifts of the Spirit:

- Utterances—prophecy, speaking in tongues, interpretation of tongues— for edification of believers and witness to unbelievers (when interpreted).
- Messages—of knowledge, wisdom—can be used in preaching and counseling.
- Discerning of Spirits, and revelations—these gifts reveal things that the church needs to see.
- Miracles—healings and signs such as the feeding of five thousand, slipping through a crowd, and the raising of the dead—these gifts are signs validating the authority of the gospel message.
- Faith (listed in Romans 12)—supernatural faith to risk, dare (Wesley, Whitefield, and frontline missionaries), and trust for provision (George Müller, J. Hudson Taylor)—these gifts empower the church to cross frontiers

3. Motivational Gifts (Romans 12:3–8)

Gifts of the Father:

- Serving/Helps
- Teaching
- Giving
- Exhortation and encouragement
- Administration/Leadership

THE PHASES OF GIFTING

There are three phases involved in gifting:

1. Gift discovery
2. Gift development
3. Gift deployment

Gift Discovery

D. L. Moody was passed over by multiple church leaders who thought him useless as a Christian and lazy because he fell asleep during the church service. John Farwell wrote, "The recollection that I thought him lazy as a Christian haunts me still, for I ascertained afterwards that he came in after spending all morning in getting poor children into a Mission Sunday School." Moody later spoke of the years he sat in the pew being overlooked, "For years I really believed I could not work for God. No one had ever asked me to do anything."[7] He would go on to lead hundreds of thousands to Christ and inspire Billy Graham as an evangelist. How many Moodys sit in the pews for years being untapped and inactive?

How does a planter equip the team to discover their spiritual gifting? When I plant a church with the intention of reaching the unreached, it occurs to me that *I've got a room full of people strategically gifted by the Holy Spirit for such a neighborhood and time as this.* This means that rather than bearing the burden alone, we share the burden, and the load lightens as many hands make light work.

My peculiar gift in church planting is making contacts and building relationships with strangers. Apostles create community, penetrate frontlines, draw people in, and engage them meaningfully. My church planting partner was gifted at leading a room of unbelievers to faith. Our ministerial tag team involved me getting them into the room for him, a skill he lacked. I set up the play, he dunked the ball. This collective team approach allows each member of a team to naturally function in their lane with intentionality, which naturally bears fruit.

The moment believers awake to their unique spiritual gifting, they tap into and leverage what makes them tick. Most people believe that they don't like evangelism because they are presented with it in a narrow, intrusive, socially awkward form. Forcing round pegs into square holes ignores how God sovereignly and naturally (or supernaturally) hardwired them as individuals. People often don't recognize their own spiritual gifts because they have become second

---

7. Kevin Belmonte, *D. L. Moody: A Life* (Chicago: Moody, 2014), 59, 78.

nature to them. However, they still hunger for biblical evangelism in the way they were divinely wired for it.

One of our activities to help people discover their gifting is to ask them to remember the "big audacious idea" they had when they first believed. The idea typically died when smacked down by a leader with a "We don't do that here" response. "That is probably what you should be doing," we tell them, but the way many churches are set up doesn't allow for the harnessing of their gifts. This is why Jesus chose his words carefully in Acts 1:8, saying we'd be his witnesses. Note that he did not use the word "evangelists." There are those called to be evangelists, and they equip people for evangelism according to Ephesians 4:10–11. Nonetheless, although we may not all be called to be an evangelist, being a witness is something much more natural. Being a witness is an unconscious thing. It oozes out of you. It also involves the Holy Spirit part-nering with you in your everyday rhythms of life. Civil Rights activist Howard Thurman once said to Gil Bailie, "Don't ask what the world needs. Ask what makes you come alive, and go do it. Because what the world needs is people who have come alive."[8]

What if being a witness is as simple as doing what makes you feel alive? What if you love to bake or entertain people at cocktail parties? What if you love to barbecue? What if you like to immerse yourself in nerdy tabletop board games or MMORPGs? What if you love to help people who are less fortunate? What if you are the ultimate fighter in the octagon but an ambassador in the gym? What if you could take the things that naturally flow out of you and harness them toward evangelism? What if all these things are connected to your spiritual gifts and provide an opportunity for you to connect with people? I think we'd find that people are actually excited to share their faith because it's sharing their lives—what makes them feel alive—with others.

Our urban plant met in a park in central Long Beach and had sent multiple teams to plant out. After asking my small group to pray for God to raise up laborers for the harvest, Steve, a chain-link fence salesman, said, "I can run a barbecue." His wife nudged him with a reality check and said, "For two hun-dred people?" He just smiled a smile that I came to know as the *"I'm going on an adventure"* smile. That Sunday, hundreds turned up to our barbecue in the inner city, and as I looked over at the grill, Steve was grinning like the Cheshire Cat—that is, whenever his mouth wasn't moving! Steve, ordinarily a reserved, quiet man, was animated, talking, smiling, and patting people on the

---

8. Howard Thurman as quoted in Gil Bailie, *Violence Unveiled: Humanity at the Crossroads* (New York: Herder and Herder, 1996), xv.

back as he handed them cheeseburgers, tacos, and ribs. I had never seen him so energetic. Steve had found his gift of serving, and once that was unlocked, the Spirit coursed through him. We couldn't shut the guy up. People came to faith. It was the reawakening of our church, and it started with unleashing the gifts of ordinary people. Perhaps what C. S. Lewis said in *Weight of Glory* is most fitting: "There are no ordinary people. You've never talked to a mere mortal."[9] The Holy Spirit within Steve was manifesting Christ that day in a way that was unique to Steve and our church plant got a second wind.

Discovering Your Team's Gifts

Leadership can get fired up about something that leaves their church ice cold. Therefore, leadership teams must discover what their people care about and what they're burdened for. When the church is gathered as a core team, break them into groups, and slap a few local newspapers down on the table in front of them. A newspaper serves as a city's roadmap for navigating brokenness, needs, and pain. One newspaper can provide a hundred more needs than any one church plant can address.

Step one of this exercise is to ask each table group to identify every need in the community by circling the newspaper headlines with a black pen—"Kids Aging Out of Foster Care Fall Prey to Sex Trade" or "Mayor Says Crime Is Out of Control Downtown." After they discuss their findings about what surprised them about the city, have them revisit the newspaper with a red marker, circling what they feel passionate about. Ask, "If you were going to allow the church to serve two or three needs—no questions asked, no budget restrictions, no manpower limitations—which ones would they be?"

What emerges from this is their burdens.

And people's burdens point to their passions.

And people's passions point to their gifts.

As you allow the core team to talk about their burdens, you'll witness their passions expressed through tears. If someone is burdened for the homeless population, they may be fitted with the gift of compassion, helping, and giving. Although people on your core team won't be equally burdened for kids aging out of foster care, the homeless, young families, orphans, ex-cons, addicts, sex trafficking, or slavery, when ten people on a team of thirty possess the same gifts, a strategic apostolic planter acknowledges that the Holy Spirit has sovereignly engineered the team and equipped them for a need in this place at this time. If enough people possess gifts oriented towards mobilizing on issues of

---

9. C. S. Lewis, *The Weight of Glory and Other Addresses* (San Francisco: Harper, 1980), 45–46.

poverty, that determines what direction our church plant takes. Gift-driven ministry allows the gifting of the people in front of you to lead the way with passion, purpose, and power. Gift-driven ministry follows the philosophy that it's much easier to ride a horse than to drag it by the reigns to somewhere it doesn't want to go.

Developing Your Team's Gifts

Branson warns that the APEST conversation commonly "turns gifts inward and makes them into offices," bottlenecking the adventure that the entire church is called to embark on together.[10] Gift-driven ministry allows for the APEST team to equip people for the work of the ministry. People who are developed in their gifts naturally deploy them on mission.

Any five-year plan on a whiteboard involves lines spreading out from the present and branching out into various goals during that timeframe. Because ministry involves both people and the Holy Spirit, you're dealing with unprecedented unpredictability that renders your white board useless. Dealing with people is like herding cats, so I draw circles instead of lines.

Imagine that your team's influence is represented by a circle. Your team members are represented by dots within that circle. As your members begin to use their gifts to minister to others, they begin to cross over into the realms of their normal influence and outside of the circle. When they do this, they begin reaching people with the gospel. As your sphere of influence grows, the circle of influence expands, and new dots are added to the expanding circle as people come to faith. New dots equal new gifts.

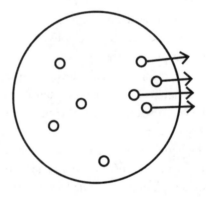

---

10. Mark Lau Branson and Nicholas Warnes, *Starting Missional Churches: Life with God in the Neighborhood* (Downers Grove, IL: InterVarsity Press, 2014), 45.

It's possible that the addition of new gifts brings new direction. For example, if the plant was mobilized towards serving poverty-stricken areas because a significant ratio of the team was gifted for compassion, helping, and serving, the influx of new gifts might lead to new passions and burdens. Therefore, the church may additionally expand outside of the circle of influence in another direction, broadening the circle in a new direction. As this process repeats, the circle continues to grow, encapsulating new people who bring new gifts:

New people = new gifts
New gifts = new directions of mission
New direction = new people

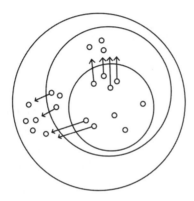

When mission is facing out in various directions, people are leading out, rather than being driven out like cattle. After equipping people like this in Europe, our plant had two chefs and answered the mayor's call to teach single unwed teen mothers how to cook for their malnourished children because they were uneducated, raised on welfare, and buying the cheapest junk foods available.

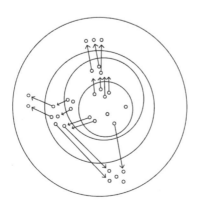

Believe that the Holy Spirit has equipped your plant for effective ministry. The task of a gift-driven leader is to discern what direction to point them in by allowing the Spirit to take the lead. The best leading always begins with careful following.

Deploying Your Team's Gifts

For centuries, the church has been staring for hours at a solitary preacher who works hard to master one gift while the gifts of thousands remain underutilized in the crowd, reinforcing that their gifts don't matter (unless they point back to the gifts of that preacher). Those believers sit weekly in silence completely unaware that the Holy Spirit has supercharged them for ministry by equipping them with spiritual gifts that lay dormant. If, however, you take that same believer on a short-term mission trip to Haiti or Thailand on the front lines of mission, their dormant gifts awaken. Having tasted the adventure, they've broken free from the mundanity of spectator Christianity. Like the apostles returning from their Judean mission with the seventy-two, they are amazed and filled with joy at what miracles they were a part of. But mission has ruined them for sitting, and they can't fall back in line. This holy discontent is the first stage of mobilization that births movements and helps a church become what Exponential calls a "level-5 multiplying church." Without the awakened gifts of individuals in a church there will be no movement, no matter how gifted the church's "leader."

When the church becomes a theater, the attendees become an audience of spectators. Hence the tension pastors face trying to mobilize the audience to move like missionaries. Church was designed to be a participatory sport where all leave the bleachers and take to the field. E. Stanley Jones spoke about leaders as coaches, equipping the saints to do the work of the ministry:

> If the laity only listen they will produce only listeners, but no leaders. If the pastors are the coaches of a team they will produce players. Out of those players they will produce coaches. Out of our present setup is produced increasingly empty pews. If the church is pastor centered, then the output will be rhetoric; if it is lay-centered, then the output will be action. It will be the Word became flesh instead of the word became word."[11]

---

11. Jones, *The Reconstruction of the Church*, 109.

Inhabiting homes, working alongside people in their places of employment, and resting in the places of their recreation is how a church planter's entire life becomes mission. Conversely, church starters speak of reaching critical mass, fancy marketing, and applying business models. What would happen if, instead of starting with a core team, bags of cash, and a sexy website, you tried an experiment?

- Get out into the city and identify its needs.
- Serve the community based on your gifts.
- Build relationships that lead people to God.

Any planter who does this for one year prior to your church's launch will witness the crucial difference between renting a public space and crossing their fingers that unchurched strangers will come; they will have already been witnessing first century mobilization on the ground. The apostles mixed in the marketplace, trafficked with people, and shared the good news about Jesus. What is trendy among leaders is often a cheap substitute for sharing the gospel. Substitute evangelism with anything that isn't evangelism, and eventually the temple crumbles. Halter has what he calls "Wild goose Sundays" where they break people up into training rooms and equip them to serve, and then send them out for a week to engage in local mission.[12] He says later, "It's not that I don't want to sing. It's just that I don't want to sing with people who *just* sing."[13] Church starters might, but church planters won't.

REFLECT

- The author argues that the gifting of the Holy Spirit is often apparent in the burdens people have. What are you burdened to do? What spiritual gifts might this indicate?
- The author argues that the progression from discovering, to developing, to deploying spiritual gifts is rooted in the mission for which the Holy Spirit gave people those gifts. How has the Holy Spirit provided the needed gifting to accomplish the mission you and your team are on?

---

12. Hugh Halter, *BiVo: A Modern-Day Guide for Bi-Vocational Saints Leveraging All of Life into One Calling* (Littleton, CO: Missio Publishing, 2013), 81.
13. Halter, *BiVo*, 89.

DISCUSS

- The APEST gifts in Ephesians are often discussed in relation to church leaders and church planting teams. How can leaders use their gifts to equip others to use those gifts? How do spiritual gifts go beyond the minister being gifted to include the minister being able to equip others in that (or other) gifts?
- How do church planters and leaders help people discover their spiritual gifts at a deeper level than the use of their preferences (e.g., paper-and-pencil spiritual gift inventories)?

CHALLENGE

- Memorize as many of the "one another" statements and commands listed in this chapter as you can. Commit to obeying these commands in your fellowship or church plant to nurture authentic fellowship.

REDISCOVERING CHURCH AS MISSION

From Scattering on Mission
to Gathering on Mission

16

SCATTERING ON MISSION

Do something every day that scares you.

—ELEANOR ROOSEVELT

Your homework this week is to go back to your communities and win one person to Jesus." Most of the heads in the church planting class snapped up and stared at me in wide-eyed disbelief. Half of them expected me to smirk and relieve them by indicating that I was only joking, so I put it in perspective: "Listen, I've read so many church planting newsletters over the years and, in each one of them, you guys always talk about how you're going to transform this city or take this city for Jesus. Okay rock stars, all I'm asking is that you lead one soul to Jesus this week, and you're looking at me like I asked the impossible. Well, I'm not buying it. You're going to expect your people to be on mission, but it won't happen unless you model it."

Leaders have unwittingly been attempting to mobilize their people to do something that they themselves aren't doing. No wonder their Sunday morning motivational speeches fall flat! If we don't model discipleship and evangelism, then it's no surprise that pep talks won't produce action. Leaders should not be surprised that they've discipled their congregations to be like themselves; people who don't take action. We've discipled what Paul called "empty talkers" (Titus 1:10 ESV). If leaders dislike what they see in the pews, it's time to take a hard look at the pulpit. Church planters don't have to be awesome organizers of a Sunday service, but they do need to be able to speak with lost people and share the gospel fluently because they are missionaries before all else. When criticized for his methods of evangelizing, an undocumented quote reports that Dwight L. Moody responded, "It is clear you don't like my way of doing evangelism. You raise some good points. Frankly, I sometimes do not like my way of doing evangelism. But I like my way of doing it better than your way

311

of *not* doing it." Moody understood that the wrong way to evangelize was not to do it at all. After all, there are many different examples of evangelism approaches in Scripture.[1]

- Testimonial approach—The Samaritan woman, the man born blind, Paul before Felix and Festus
- Intellectual reasoning—Paul in Athens
- Confrontational—Peter on Pentecost
- Service—Dorcas
- Interpersonal approach—Andrew inviting Peter and Philip inviting Nathaniel
- Teaching—Paul in the synagogue and the Hall of Tyrannus
- Discovery approach—Nicodemus, Jesus at the well with the Samaritan woman
- Bible study—Paul and the Bereans
- Prayer and the supernatural—The apostles in Jerusalem and Paul in Philippi with the demoniac fortune teller

Many of our modern-day ministries wouldn't be worth writing about if Dr. Luke decided to write the Acts of the Twenty-first Century Western Church. Reading the Acts of the Apostles exhilarates risk-averse Westerners who avoid activities they fear. Overcoming fear requires faith. For faith to actually be necessary, risk must be a present challenge. Evangelism is an extreme sport that was never intended to be easy. Easy is overrated. Many leaders are bored with their cushy careers as clerical pencil pushers for Jesus, their souls longing for the adventures that Paul inhaled with the salty spray on the Mediterranean Sea. Consider the following statistics from the book *The Unchurched Next Door*:[2]

- One person in five among the unchurched is seeking God and would respond if the gospel were presented.
- Only one in twenty people are antagonistic to Christians talking about their faith.
- In one survey from the Barna Group, 25 percent of the unchurched said they would come to church if invited by a friend.

---

1. Craig Ott and Gene Wilson, *Global Church Planting: Biblical Principles and Best Practices for Multiplication* (Grand Rapids: Baker Academic, 2011), 215.

2. Barna Group, *Is Evangelism Going Out of Style?*, December 17, 2013, https://barna.org/barna-update/faith-spirituality/648-is-evangelism-going-out-of-style.

Paul reminds us of the universal principle that "whoever sows sparingly will also reap sparingly, and whoever sows bountifully will also reap bountifully" (1 Cor. 9:16 ESV). What are we not doing that, if we actually did it, could result in more people coming to faith in Jesus? What if that were to be the next chapter in your life, church planter? What if after all the study you've invested into the lives of missionaries, saints, and preachers, God was calling you out to live the adventure that, heretofore, you've only read about? Wouldn't *that* be something?

GOING ON MISSION AS A TEAM

People hunger for biblical evangelism because the Holy Spirit hardwired them for it. Paul said, "For Christ's love compels us, because we are convinced that one died for all, and therefore all died. And he died for all, that those who live should no longer live for themselves but for him who died for them and was raised again" (2 Cor. 5:14–15). Planters whose hearts break for the people in their communities see them as souls for whom Christ died, leading to their "drivenness" or "compulsion," resulting in gospel activity that leads to the planting of a church. Ed Stetzer and Philip Nation remind us that biblical compulsion is more than mere emotion, for compulsion drives love into action.[3]

HOW TO MOBILIZE YOUR CONGREGATION

Being compelled is what separates Christians who reach people from those who don't. Leaders labor from the front in an attempt to externally compel good Christians to reach the lost, when a lack of internal compulsion is the chief obstacle planters face in mobilizing people. Wesley recognized that attempting to manipulate, cajole, or motivate people with a sense of duty always falls flat, because Christianity grows fastest when it is, as Wesley remarked about the early Methodists during the Great Awakening, "a religion of the heart."[4]

The chief reasons we lack an inward compulsion are:

1. We don't know the gospel for ourselves.
2. We don't know God's heart for others.
3. We don't know how to contextualize the gospel for others.
4. We are afraid to step out in faith and risk for others.

---

3. Ed Stetzer and Philip Nation, *Compelled: Living the Mission of God* (Birmingham, AL: New Hope, 2012), 15.

4. John Wesley, *The Sermons of John Wesley – Sermon 50* (Wesley Center for Applied Theology, 1999).

The solutions, therefore, are that we must:

1. Understand the gospel.
2. Gain an understanding of God's heart for others.
3. Learn to contextualize the gospel in conversation.
4. Recognize opportunities for stepping out in faith and risking for the sake of lost people.

1. Understanding the Gospel

The method for gospel sharing that is presented in Scripture isn't a straightforward, one-size-fits-all message. The New Testament largely portrays evangelism in fluid, unpredictable, two-way conversations. John's Gospel is almost exclusively gospel conversations, which is why we present it to people who are considering Christ. In the book of Acts, the key characteristics of the gospel message are told differently in various contexts. Jesus told stories to illustrate the gospel, confront the rich young ruler, threaten the Pharisees with judgment, or soothe the woman caught in adultery with love and grace. In each situation, the Spirit knows what is called for, and as Moody reportedly said, "The Holy Spirit is the best evangelist." In addition, the gospel has to be the *the gospel according to . . . you*. It's not by accident that Paul's testimony is recorded in full three times in the book of Acts! The Holy Spirit is giving us a message; personal testimony is one of the most powerful weapons in the evangelistic arsenal. We must train people to use theirs; but they have to know it first.

Evangelism cannot be an activity performed out of duty; it must become a lifestyle that flows from a heart overflowing with gratitude. Therefore you must work hard to stress the gospel as the central message and preoccupation of believers.

2. Gaining God's Heart

According to Jesus, those that are forgiven much love much (Luke 7:37). We must first be broken ourselves by our own sin and become conscious of the flood of God's grace toward ourselves. The good news won't be good news to anybody unless it's the good news to us first! John Wesley preached the gospel as a missionary to America and witnessed conversions happening to others, yet he confessed to feeling like an outsider looking in before being flooded with God's grace at Aldersgate. From that day forward, he was compelled. Similarly, Whitefield came to the end of himself and threw himself on his bed in desperation and cried out, "I thirst!" All great soul winners have agonized over their own souls before agonizing over the souls of others. It's no accident that Peter was rocked by grace prior to rocking the mic at Pentecost and reaping a harvest of souls. The great soul winner Spurgeon said, "If a man has a low opinion of himself, it is very possible that he is correct in his estimate."[5]

Once we know God's grace for ourselves, we begin to see how it can apply to others. Jesus bemoaned the disciples' lack of compassion on the people who were harassed and helpless, like sheep without a shepherd, and he instructed them, "open your eyes" (John 4:35). Jesus saw their lack of compassion as a vision problem. Gaining God's vision for people until it breaks our hearts begins when we pray for the Lord to send workers into the harvest (Luke 10:2).

3. Learn to Contextualize the Gospel in Your Own Words

Evangelism is the gospel according to you, for everyone you meet. Contextualizing the gospel means communicating it in a way that can be understood by somebody without using excessive explanation or theological jargon. I frequently refer to films that people know, such as *Raiders of the Lost Ark* when illustrating atonement through the ark of the covenant, or *The Matrix* when speaking to people about the reality of their existence in an unseen yet very real spiritual realm.

When training people to contextualize the gospel, I give them an assignment over a one-week period, asking them to partner with a friend who will randomly call them every day and ask what the gospel is. The twist is that every day they have to get creative and pretend to be a different person and present the following scenarios:

- The gay hairdresser who strikes up a conversation about spiritual things
- The guy at the gas station who asks about your sticker
- Your neighbor who asks why you go to church
- The guy on the surfboard next to you waiting for the next wave
- The Starbucks barista who asks why you're always so nice
- The mom who is overwhelmed with her kids and struggles with depression

Afterward, debrief and invite your friend to critique you on how understandable, compelling, and relevant you were.

4. Step Out in Faith and Take Risks for Others

If evangelism is a little scary, you're doing it right. There are strong psychological factors hindering us from sharing the gospel, so we often hide behind

---

5. Charles H. Spurgeon, *The Soul Winner* (Springdale, PA: Whitaker House, 1995), 47.

theological or missional platitudes (like God's sovereignty or excusing ourselves based on APEST gifting), wrinkling our noses at anything challenging. We must identify what holds us back if we are to be effective in evangelism. Is it fear? Insecurity? Rejection?

Paul, the grizzled, veteran missionary, frequently requested that his churches pray for him to be given boldness. Westerners place a huge value on bravado, yet the fear of rejection and fear of failure hold them back. The only failures at evangelism are the ones who never share the gospel at all. An anonymous call for a nugget of wisdom can be applied to evangelism: "I've learned that you shouldn't go through life wearing a catcher's mitt on both hands. You need to be able to throw something back." Many Christians have woken up to the sobering reality that their throwing arm hasn't seen action for ages, and while they have caught the gospel in one hand, they've never tossed it to anyone else with the other. We've been handpicked to be on his team, and he's given us the ball. If we don't throw it to somebody, points won't be scored in this part of the match (at least not by us), and we are attempting to rob God of the glory he deserves. Besides, there are no star players in the game. Paul knew that evangelism is a team sport where one sows, another waters, and another reaps.

REMEMBER THE AUTHORITY AND POWER

The fiery darts of fear are what keep an army from advancing within the range of the enemy archers and delay our entry into the fray. The shield of faith, however, allows us to advance in the face of fear and defy the enemy's threats. God promised that when his word is sent out, it will always accomplish whatever he sent it out to accomplish; the sovereign God can sway any heart, push anyone's buttons, and stir any soul. This should instill confidence in *his* abilities when we doubt our own.

Sometimes you must fight fire with fire. As Satan attempts to lodge fearful thoughts into our minds to keep us from advancement, we must act with "with minds that are alert" (1 Pet. 1:13) and arm ourselves with equally powerful thoughts to combat them. The truths of God center our minds on the object of our faith and infuse us with confidence to push through the fear. In Matthew 28, Jesus hardwired seven powerful truths that should aid us to overcome any obstacles of anxiety in our missional engagement.

1. *We have been sent on Jesus's authority.* "All authority in heaven and on earth has been given to me . . . " (v. 18)
2. *We have a new purpose.* "Therefore go . . ." (v. 19)

3. *We are tasked with making disciples.* "Make disciples of all nations . . ." (v. 19)
4. *We are tasked with preparing the way for physical and spiritual baptism.* "Baptizing them . . ." (v. 19)
5. *We are tasked with sharing about Jesus, his Father, and the Holy Spirit.* "In the name of the Father and of the Son and of the Holy Spirit . . ." (v. 19)
6. *We are tasked with teaching others about the life and commands of Christ.* "Teaching them to obey everything I have commanded you." (v. 20)
7. *We aren't alone. The Spirit of God goes with us.* "And surely I am with you always, to the very end of the age." (v. 20)

PRACTICAL STEPS TO STAY SHARP

Nothing on earth brings Jesus more glory than the message that a God of such purity and power would freely offer his grace and love to a scandal-filled and shameful human race instead of simply just wiping us out with the blink of his eye. In our appeal to the armchair athlete who has only participated in the spectator sport of evangelism, we must insist that this message demands more than screaming in a stadium. The Great Commission is an invitation to get in the game. Every athlete must practice, and home, school, workplace, and places of recreation are the practice field. Here are some principles to get your core team started:

- **Take one step**—You may find yourself paralyzed by fear, but the key is to take the first step in the right direction. Find one tangible area where you can grow and act this week. Identify a community hub and prayerfully visit. Invite somebody to dinner. Begin praying for somebody. Spurgeon said, "Do something. Do something. Do something. While committees waste their time over resolutions, do something. While so many are making constitutions, let us win souls. Too often we discuss, and discuss, and discuss, while Satan only laughs in his sleeve."[6]
- **Keep dropping gospel seeds**—Work the gospel into everyday conversations, dropping comments and testimony. Pepper a conversation with, "Sometimes in my life, God gives me peace through hard times like you're going through." Talking about faith and engaging people in a meaningful way usually uncovers some major fears and insecurities and begins to erode our unwillingness to engage with others.

6. C. H. Spurgeon, *An All-Round Ministry* (London: Banner of Truth, 1960), 55.

- **Read or listen to gospel sermons**—The internet is filled with gospel preachers who can provide clarity in how to deal with someone's soul as carefully as a surgeon. Hearing the gospel regularly is not only good for your soul, but church history is packed with evangelists like Charles Spurgeon or D. L. Moody from whom you can learn. Spending time with evangelists in person or print has an infectious result.
- **Pray intentionally**— When Jesus encountered sluggish hearts in the twelve, he instructed them to pray God would send workers. Pray that the Lord opens your eyes to places and people you should become intentional about reaching.

FOUR AREAS OF MISSIONAL ENGAGEMENT

When Jesus passed his team the ball at the end of the Gospels, in the beginning of Acts, he also told them the play. From Jerusalem to the ends of the earth, Jesus outlined concentric circles of mission that would ring in the ears of the apostles until they breathed their last in accomplishing it, most of them spilling out their blood. Each of these circles has something to teach us, and each should be a focus of your church as a whole as well as individuals.

The four concentric circles of mission are:

1. Jerusalem—Your neighborhood and work where you always go.
2. Judea—Public spaces where you don't normally go.
3. Samaria—The marginalized areas where you never go.
4. Ends of the earth—The rest of the world where it's hard to go.

Jesus promised his followers that they'd be his witnesses in these four areas. Therefore, part of your task as a planter is to encourage and equip your church to engage in mission on these fronts.

Jerusalem

Your Jerusalem is your immediate contacts as you traffic through everyday life. How do you begin to sow gospel seeds into familiar settings? Within your Jerusalem (your home), you have your house, your neighborhood, and work. It's your first place (home) and your second place (work). Imagine that you've invited a family over for a meal to practice gospel hospitality. The food is the picture of excellence, the atmosphere superb, the company splendid. Then a perfect night becomes ruined by a forced conversation about Jesus as the obligatory gospel conversation is pulled out and dusted off to justify the existence of a night on "mission." Have you ever had that experience, being left to scratch your head wondering how it all went wrong? Have you laid your head on your pillow at night, wondering if it would have gone down differently if you'd have picked a better moment?

Or, perhaps you've been on the other side of the fence. You've been socializing with a couple or individual for months, or maybe playing on a sports team, and nobody knows you're a Christian. You don't know how to bring it up, so you wait, anticipating the perfect moment that never seems to come. After so much time has passed, it now seems embarrassingly awkward to share about Jesus out of left field.

Timing is everything. In both situations, a little more faith was required. At the dinner table, faith was needed to allow God to open up the right opportunity. And even though it seemed to be taking a while on the basketball courts, God was at work. Sometimes people take a lot longer to talk about deep things, but God is always wooing them behind the scenes. He who believes will not make haste (Isa. 28:16) but will trust God's perfect timing. As we get to know people, they open up and share things that invite us into their lives on a deeper level, and our times to reciprocate will come.

When I was working in a factory or a firehouse, I observed that people were intermittently unreserved and cautious depending upon the individual or situation. One night, while sitting on the fire truck monitoring the radio for incoming alerts, I was approached by a young man telling me his marriage was on the verge of breaking up. I listened, and we talked and prayed. Often, we've been taught to share the gospel like a slick salesman, quickly laying out our pitch and then closing the deal on the spot, but people are worth the time and patience it takes for us to sit and listen thoughtfully to them without us imposing our agenda on them. The sovereign God you are telling them about cares more for them than you do. He is radiating his glory and presence out of you more than you realize. You were placed in that situation for a reason, and sometimes the most evangelistic thing you can do is be a good friend, neighbor, and coworker.

DON'T BE SLICK

"God loves you and has a wonderful plan for your life" has opened many a gospel conversation over the years due to the gospel pamphlet *The Four Spiritual Laws.*[7] Despite many people coming to faith through

---

7. "Would You Like to Know God Personally?," Cru, accessed September 1, 2020, https://www.cru.org/us/en/how-to-know-god/would-you-like-to-know-god-personally.html.

the nondescript, unassuming booklet over the years, its true power was not in the content; it was in the confidence that holding it was able to instill in those who felt they needed training wheels. What might happen if believers were able to depart from the letter of the four spiritual laws and depend upon the Spirit himself sharing the gospel? What did the church do before the invention of this publication? What have been the negative effects that might have resulted from using it? Many have sounded like a vacuum cleaner salesman going through a carefully prepared script, "Mrs. Jones, I have the answer to all your problems. If you can give me the next brief minutes, I can change the rest of your life." Whether someone is trying to unload a used car or salvation, the slick, packaged presentation has led many customers (and salesmen) to feel that they want nothing to do with the sales process.

Any call to action may also prematurely press people to make a commitment to Jesus within minutes of hearing the gospel, though the Holy Spirit may be bringing them into a more gradual recognition of who Jesus is. This may leave the impression that they have closed the book on the gospel and locked that in as their final answer, when perhaps they were simply not ready or needed more time to consider the implications. Sometimes people simply need more time to reflect on the real costs and benefits of following Jesus. When Paul preached at Mars Hill, there were three key responses; some of them believed, others mocked, and some said, "We want to hear you again on this subject" (Acts 17:32).

I am a free-spirited evangelist who feels that methods are helpful tools to have in the box, but each tool should be uniquely pulled out at the appropriate time to be the right solution for the right problem. I tend to talk to people, listen, and ask thought-provoking questions. I've found that by asking questions in the spirit of the Socratic method, people are less sure of themselves as they hear themselves speak. They may claim to know much, or have life, God, and the universe figured out, but a few well-placed questions can expose a massive chink in their armor or even provide a hole the size of a truck that permits the evangelist to drive the gospel on through.

What Are the Major Areas of Growth You Should Focus On?
- Identify your Jerusalem (neighbors, shops, and coworkers).
- Develop a prayer life that incorporates your immediate surroundings.
- Develop a missional, gift-based engagement strategy for your neighborhood.
- Develop a family-based action plan for missionally engaging your neighborhood.

Identifying Your Missional Rhythms

It's important to identify what your rhythms are as a family, because when you have kids, you need to primarily engage on mission as a family or it will never happen at all. Even if your neighbors are single, inviting them around to a family meal will have a deep impact. Your rhythms can be broken up into daily, weekly, and monthly categories:

Daily

What do you do on a daily basis? There is a street in the beach community of San Clemente, California, that is known for front yard dinners during the summer months. The neighbors on the street enjoy an ocean view from the vista that their street rests on. Therefore, the neighbors formed a tradition of eating in their front yards and throwing a localized potluck dinner with each other. Somebody initiated these nightly dinners into a daily rhythm of shared meals. In other neighborhoods, the parents barbecue after work at the apartment pool and hang out in the hot tub while their children swim. In yet another neighborhood, the parents stand and talk while the kids skateboard in the cul-de-sac. Want to create a community hub? Put a basketball net at the end of the street, or build a neighborhood half-pipe, and create the rhythms if they don't exist naturally.

Weekly

Family dynamics require time as a unit, so it can be easier to start with a weekly window where you minister to someone as a family. It can involve hospitality or the local skate park. Wherever you can engage in gospel conversations alongside natural activities as a family, it will provide an opportunity for mission. Statistically speaking, 90 percent of people who have had a spiritual life change as a result of discussions state that it was somebody they knew well or very well. Seventy percent state that it was over the course of multiple conversations.[8]

---

8. Barna Group, *Spiritual Conversations in the Digital Age: How Christians' Approach to Sharing Their Faith Has Changed in 25 Years* (Barna, 2018), 47.

Monthly

My favorite place to engage people is in discussion groups at reading clubs where I feel engaged and in my element. My dream for years has been to start a local film or reading club with my neighbors to bring us together around some element of pop-culture. I love to hear the opinions of others and to hear how they think about and process their lives.

Where can you enter into a monthly rhythm of mission that excites you and takes into account what you enjoy? Attempt to come up with at least five items to include in each column.

	Benefits	Challenges	Church Planting Application
Places			
Hobbies			
People			

Reaching Your Judea

Judea is represented by public places (or third spaces) where we take mission beyond our first frontiers of Jerusalem. We have a saying at New Breed Church Planting, "If you want to reach the ones nobody is reaching, you need to go where nobody is going, and do what nobody is doing." You can't change the world behind a desk. The apostles were masters of ministry in public spaces, and the next chapter will unpack that concept further. The first rule of missional engagement in public space is that it should not feel unnatural. If Paul preached in the open air, it was because it was what was natural or expected, such as at the Areopagus at Mars Hill in Athens. If he reasoned in the synagogues, it was because such debates were normally had there. If Jesus spoke spiritual wisdom to multitudes, it was because they were following him to hear more teaching.

I once started a church in a Starbucks in Wales. It rained every day, and because of that, the community hub was in a warm, dry bookstore. The store boasted a large Starbucks to warm the body with coffee, and its wares promised to warm the soul with books. In a culture where it rains every day, sports are a pipe dream at best. Therefore, reading groups were the hot ticket. The reading group we formed provided the perfect opportunity to discuss Jesus, because that's what you would naturally do in a book reading group when it came time to read the bestselling book *The DaVinci Code* by Dan Brown. On the back of that reading group, a church was planted; unbelievers came to profess faith in Christ, and a multiplying movement was born.

Whether you are joining team sports, reading or walking groups, film clubs, philosophy think tanks, or science discussion groups, you will find that all of these will open up discussions that allow you to contextualize the gospel in modern groups.

5 Key Relationship-Building Opportunities in Your Judea

- **Recreational Activities**—There are sports teams, CrossFit groups, and individual fitness plans that people like to partner up on. People who take their kids to dance, gymnastics, and soccer games form a type of community. There are play groups for parents, sewing groups, sculpting classes, yoga classes, and an endless list of diverse possibilities. Church planters think like missionaries when it comes to strategic engagement, but at the end of the day, they need recreational breaks as much as anybody. Recreation is there to help you relax from the pressures of life, blow off steam, and have fun with other people. Let your enjoyment of life become part of the mission on which God has sent you.

- **Intellectual Pursuits**—Art class. Reading groups. Cooking classes. Night school. Many people are always trying to learn more, feed their minds, and stimulate deeper thinking. Public libraries provide opportunities to teach writing workshops or to speak on an area of personal expertise. Going to art exhibits with your neighbors and engaging in discussions about an artist's work can provide amazing gospel conversations. One of my favorite outreaches was a film club where the group watched a film and somebody presented a ten-minute talk on why they chose it for the group. Then everybody got to speak about the themes the film dealt with. Morality. Mortality. Such themes abound in movies! Movies are windows into the human experience, and many films feature themes of redemption. If that's not a gospel conversation waiting to happen, nothing is. After all, everybody's a critic!

- **Social Causes**—Unbelievers today are socially aware of the conditions in their world and socially awakened to do something about it. Nothing speaks so powerfully about grace as a group of people sacrificially serving others. Often, when unchurched people witness the love of God in action, they are moved to join in and help. Planters may "pick a fight" with one area of darkness in their city such as homelessness or sex trafficking and engage in meaningful mission in those areas. You earn the right to speak to a culture when you serve a culture.

- **Hospitality**—Inviting someone over to eat seems like a big ask, but since you'd already planned to do eat anyway, it's not a huge investment of time. Instead of an hour around the table, you might spend two hours in conversation with your neighbors.

- **Proximity Spaces**—Frequenting a particular place of business like a pub, skate park, coffee shop, or shared community garden can foster a sense of belonging. These places are all what Alan Hirsch calls "proximity spaces," or places where the people congregate and establish an unspoken relationship and foster a sense of community. There is something sacred about shared geographic space, as T. Desmond Alexander observes about Genesis: "There is hardly an episode in the entire Bible which does not in one way or another mention the land."[9]

To ignore these five areas of outreach is to ignore the way that Paul operated when he entered a city. He practiced them all by setting up a booth in the marketplace, participated on Mars Hill, visited the synagogue, and ate with the Gentiles. All of this was strategic.

Practical Tips for Reaching Your Judea

Once you've determined to take it to the streets and master the lost art of ministry in a public space, how do you know where to go? You'll need to assess your daily, weekly, and monthly rhythms like you did in the last section, but this time add another layer. Everything discussed in this chapter applies to both individuals and groups. Let's take something as simple as enjoying a hot cup of java in a local coffee house and draft a brain-stormed list of benefits, challenges, and church-planting applications to examine if it's the proper Judea mission.

Example: My Local Coffee House

Benefits: I like coffee. Coffee houses can be places to chill and relax, or a public space to work. Locals come here. It's a hub of the community. Work, recreation, and family all come together in places like these.

Challenges: I'm busy. I don't have much time to simply chill or read a book at a coffee shop. I have family pressures that make it hard for me to justify a trip like that and prevent me from hanging out for too long.

Church-planting application: Perhaps once a week, I could go solo. Another time, my wife and I could grab an hour for a chat, building our relationship together through talking. Lastly, the family could go there for hot chocolates for the kids and coffee for the adults. Three times a week makes us a fixture there. We'd surely build relationships with both employees and regulars, and

---

9. T. Desmond Alexander, *From Paradise to the Promised Land: An Introduction to the Pentateuch* (Grand Rapids: Baker Academic, 2002), 19.

we'd have the opportunity to get to know the people in our community who use the coffee shop as a community hub. We'd also spend some money on coffee! But again, it's for the kingdom (wink).

	Benefits	Challenges	Church Planting Application
Places			
Hobbies			
People			

Samaria—The Marginalized

When it comes to the marginalized people in our society, the words of Jonathan Swift ring true: "We have just enough religion to make us hate, but not enough to make us love one another."[10] Your Samaria is the part of town that you don't think about. Identifying this opportunity requires asking the intentional question, "Who am I forgetting?" The Samaritans were half-breeds born of intermarriage between Jews and Assyrians, and they served as a reminder to the Jews of God's judgment upon the nation for idolatry. Marginalized people live on the fringes of every society due to ethnic prejudice, socio-economic status, or shame-based subcultures, such as communities of prostitutes or addicts. Jesus intentionally targeted the marginalized during his ministry, "spilling over" from ministering to the house of Israel and into the fringes of Judaism, such as the Phoenician woman, the Samaritan woman at the well, the Centurion, numerous lepers, tax collectors, and prostitutes, among others. Planters who are worth their salt will not neglect this important aspect of mission in their city. Nor will they ignore the marginalized around the world. When Count Zinzendorf heard the plight of the slaves in the Caribbean, and learned that one had been converted, he included the slaver hubs in his missionary itinerary. The very first two missionaries of the Moravian mission movement moved to the Port of St. Thomas and established trades there to reach the slaves, resulting in thirteen thousand converts among them, and churches planted "on the islands of St. Thomas, St. Croix, Jamaica, Antigua, Barbados, and St. Kitts."[11]

---

10. Quoted without reference in Duane Elmer, *Cross-Cultural Servanthood: Serving the World in Christlike Humility* (Downers Grove, IL: InterVarsity Press, 2006), 57.

11. Steve Addison, *Movements that Changed the World: 5 Keys to Spreading the Gospel* (Downers Grove, IL: InterVarsity Press, 2011), 42. Addison mentions Jacob Young, a circuit rider who also ministered among the slaves (88). Also see Jon Tyson and Heather Grizzle, *A Creative Minority* (self-pub., 2016), 23.

	Benefits	Challenges	Church Planting Application
Places			
Hobbies			
People			

Ends of the Earth

This final ring covers the entire world. This is perhaps the most honest type of mission you can be involved in, simply because there is little return on investment for your church plant. This mission is engaged in simply proclaiming the name and fame of Jesus abroad. Consider that in 1900, one-third of the world's population was Christian, but 80% were North American or European. By 2050 the church will gain on the growth of the world's population to occupy one-third of it again, but the difference today is that 60% of the church "are citizens of Africa, Asia, and Latin America," and there is every reason to believe that the global trajectory will continue.[12]

For far too long the church in the West has believed itself to be at the epicenter of God's activity like the Jerusalem church, when in fact, it has been largely left behind like the second half of the book of Acts as God continues to advance his kingdom beyond the borders. As you continue to branch out into the broader concentric circles, you will find that God has already been at work there, waiting for the Western church to join him.

Ends of the Earth

For your church plant to be effective when gathering for mission, you must first be effective at scattering on it. The leaders of your church must model reaching their Jerusalem, Judea, Samaria, and the ends of the earth, so that the church plant can follow them into gathered mission when they assemble, and scattered mission when they disperse.

Both the individual and the church as a whole must ask:

1. How will I reach my Jerusalem?
2. How will I reach my Judea?
3. How will I reach my Samaria?
4. How will I reach the ends of the earth?

12. Ralph Moore, *How to Multiply Your Church: The Most Effective Way to Grow* (Grand Rapids: Baker, 2009), 57.

REFLECT

- Do you see the people in your community as people for whom Christ died? How does this compel your missionary efforts?
- How can your daily routine help you engage in mission in daily life?

DISCUSS

- The author provides four "big ideas." Discuss each of them in turn, expanding on the explanation in the text.
  - Evangelism cannot be an activity performed out of duty, but must be a lifestyle of love. How does a lifestyle of love fuel evangelism in your life?
  - Evangelism comes from genuinely caring for people as God does. When was the last time your heart broke with compassion for a specific person who doesn't know God?
  - Evangelism is the gospel according to you and everyone else. What does this mean? Practice sharing the gospel in ways that would resonate with your community.
  - Evangelism should be a little scary. If you're scared, you're doing it right. Which of these is the biggest emotional barrier to evangelism for you—fear, insecurity, or rejection?

CHALLENGE

- Meditate on Acts 1:8 and Matthew 28:18–20 one phrase at a time. What are all the indicatives and imperatives in these passages? Pray through these verses, asking for illumination to fully understand how they apply to you in your specific context.
- Craft a personal plan for how you will reach your Jerusalem, Judea, Samaria, and the ends of the earth. (Do the hard work of spending time in the detail of incorporating it into your rhythms, relationships, benefits, and challenges).
- Craft a plan for how your church will reach your Jerusalem, Judea, Samaria, and the ends of the earth.

17

GATHERING ON MISSION

The present is theirs. The future from where I've primarily worked is mine.

—NIKOLA TESLA

Many churches are still prepping themselves for a future that isn't coming. Our strategies rely upon utilizing tomorrow the buildings we've built today. But if Europe is any indication of where things are going, yesterday's ornate church buildings are going to be converted into tomorrow's nightclubs, mosques, and carpet warehouses. It is disheartening to stand in an intricately carved gothic stonework church, from which the gospel once thundered forth, where the pulpit now serves as a DJ booth in a swanky nightclub. The bastions of religion will serve as barriers to the culture around them and endure as lifeless monuments to a wasteful age of opulence and misguided priorities. Inevitably, America will follow suit with our large buildings pastored by leaders hoping, despite their dwindling megachurch attendance, that there will be enough money to see them through retirement. Many leaders are in a holding pattern, and they know it. They're just hoping their congregations don't.

Every epoch of church history that catapulted the church forward was preceded by a time of shrinking and desperation. In every case, when the Spirit began to move in revival, the church responded by leaving the building. At the dawn of the church, when the Spirit fell in the upper room, he drove the apostles outside! The tongues of fire above their heads, combined with the wind, meant that the fire was going to spread, and spread it did.

A similar spark caught when Whitefield revived open-air preaching because he realized that the Kings Colliery coal miners would never darken the doors of a church. Bible in hand and sermon in heart, Whitefield mounted a tree stump and preached the crucified Christ. When he told Wesley, the future

Methodist leader was scandalized, told George that it was evil, and instructed him not to do it again. At the dawn of the Welsh revival, Seth Joshua pitched a boxing ring in the midst of a South Welsh town and advertised the fight of the century. When people turned up, Joshua announced that the devil was about to get a beating. Souls were saved after the Spirit-driven gospel preaching delivered the knockout punch.

These fearless ministers of the gospel braved the world outside the double doors of their churches and blazed new trails. It wasn't long before the miners themselves functioned as Methodist preachers down the mineshafts, "in the pits," creating churches underground. A mine seemed almost built for a house of worship, and as the men sang hymns and preached to one another, their sermons and praises echoed up the mine shafts and the revival began to spread.

This was gospel innovation, created by necessity and modeled by Jesus, who preached in fields, boats, and public courts. Consider that the Son of God ministered for three years and barely set foot inside the temple. Our building-centric models often hold us back and keep the kingdom from expanding, like the old wineskin that's lost its ability to be flexible and expand. Over the years, I've noticed that, whether it's planting in a Starbucks or planting in a CrossFit that doubles as church space, we aren't as original as we thought. Jesus and Paul beat us to ministry in public space. We are now rediscovering what the apostles already did, from Paul at Mars Hill to the streets of Jerusalem. Kanye just made it popular again.

MARS HILL MINISTRY

When the Bible describes the temple courts, it is speaking of the public square, the center of society in Jerusalem. The normal rhythm of the church was that "in the temple and from house to house" (Acts 5:42 ESV). Meeting house to house is the hallmark of the missional movement today, but unless it's also meeting in temple courts or public space, it's not missional enough for the apostles' taste. When the church can't take it into the public arenas like the temple courts, it hasn't earned the name missional. What most people consider "temple courts" is a big box with expensive speakers. I maintain that the temple was merely the city center, the place where the majority of people trafficked: the watering holes, the proximity spaces, the marketplace, the cultural hub. The question is, are you willing to go there and set up shop? Or would you rather hunker down in the bunker? There's nothing that tells you that God is on the move quite like the person who's weeping with you after the open mic night in the gay coffee house, asking what the gospel means.

The disciples left the upper room on Pentecost because *they wanted to go where the people were.* Although buildings are helpful, in that they serve as a gathering hub, the difference between our church plants and first-century church plants is that the crowds gathered outside of the four walls in the New Testament, not behind them.

After we began to meet in the open air in urban Long Beach, we decided to stay outside after mistakenly trying a few weeks back inside. Inside just wasn't the same. When we went back outside, we had twenty or thirty people every week standing around the edges of our meetings listening in noncommittal fashion, safely stationed at the meeting's perimeter. Some never returned, while others inched in from the perimeter over the weeks, moving deeper into our gathering. One of them heard me mentioning Anthony Kiedis, the lead singer of the Red Hot Chili Peppers, and Jesus in the same sentence and had to stop to see what they had in common. Originally, he was going to kick the crap out of me if I was begging for money in the inner city. Instead, he heard the gospel that day, came to faith, and now serves on our leadership team. If we'd been inside, we would have never reached him; but by being present in his space, we simply made ourselves vulnerable and available. This quote from Charles Spurgeon applies:

> No sort of defense is needed for preaching out of doors; but it would need very potent arguments to prove that a man had done his duty who has never preached beyond the walls of his meeting house. A defense is required rather for services within buildings than for worship outside of them.[1]

Of course, it's not just Sundays that provide opportunities to do this. If the community had hubs, the people in our church would join them. If it didn't, we created them. We've formed film clubs, book clubs, community runs, and relief projects.

You don't have to stand and preach in the open air to master public space ministry. Mastering ministry in context is the key to reaching third spaces.

MASTERING THIRD-SPACE MINISTRY

We have already discussed ministry in the first places (your home) and second places (your workplace), but in this chapter we'll focus more on innovative ministry in the third spaces. The first place is where you lay your head at night; the second place is where you work, where you *have to be* to earn the money for your first place, but your third space is where you *want* to be.

---

1. Charles Spurgeon, *Lectures to My Students* (1816, repr. Grand Rapids: Zondervan, 1954), 254.

The apostles in the early church did three things regarding public space:

- They established a rhythm of prayer and activity.
- They got out where the people were (second and third spaces).
- They engaged those people in a meaningful way.

Our culture has forced the church to rethink how it meets. Twenty years ago the writing on the wall stated that the church's obsession with buildings was unsustainable. Mel McGowan writes, "Between 1993 and 2000 the dollars spent on church construction increased by 100%. During the same timeframe the US population *increased* 40%, while US church attendance *decreased* 40%."[2]

How to Kick Off a Discussion Group in Public Space

The first time I planted a church, I didn't know I'd done it. In fact, it took me years to realize that I'd actually planted a church. I was twenty-eight years old, and I didn't know a lot. I did know that if you wanted to reach students, you needed food. I gathered all the college students around and confessed, "Look, I don't know what British students want besides food. What do YOU think would be effective?" Their answer was, "Let us talk. Nobody ever lets us talk."

So those were the three rules:

1. Let them talk.
2. Feed them.
3. Don't meet in a place associated with church.

We rented a room upstairs at the local sports center and set up about five tables with chairs in small groups. Food would bring the students, but what would engage them? The conversation itself had to be engaging. We wrestled with finding a subject with which a student with absolutely no religious experience could engage? We found it by identifying what *brings humanity together across all stratospheres; humor.* Laughter is the great unifier, bringing us together and dispelling our defenses, easing tensions, and creating a shared experience in a room. When we laugh, for a brief moment, we let our guard down and demonstrate to the world that we're not as sophisticated as we'd like everyone around us to believe. If people were uptight that first evening, we could set the atmosphere right away by making them laugh a bit and relaxing them. Food, like laughter, is also an equalizer, a confession of our mortality, making them

---

2. Mel McGowan, *Design Intervention: Revolutionizing Sacred Space* (self-pub., 2008), 21.

perfect fertilizer for sowing the gospel. C. S. Lewis once observed that the tug of two worlds in humans could best be inferred by our (often crude) sense of humor and our sacred approach to death.[3] The two are not mutually exclusive, despite what many Christians think. G. K. Chesteron wrote, "Mr. McCabe thinks that I am not serious but only funny, because Mr. McCabe thinks that funny is the opposite of serious. Funny is the opposite of not funny and nothing else."[4]

So how would we get from humor to heaven? I carefully crafted my topic for the first night with the intention of progressing weekly into a bigger and deeper revelation of who God was. Studying my systematic theology books, I discovered that theologians always started with the revelation of God—both natural and supernatural. Natural revelation is how God shows the aspects of his character that can be universally known. Therefore, I would start with the theology of man being made in God's image; if God had hardwired humor into the world, then he himself must also possess a sense of humor. The topic for the night was set: "Does God have a sense of humor?" We made up flyers advertising the time, location, and offer of free food, and our first night was a hit.

The golden rule of public space evangelism is, "Eat first, ask questions later." After eating, I opened up the discussion for them to hammer it out, letting them know that *all* opinions were received with respect. Then I came and gave a brief, ten-minute talk that was a veiled discussion on what theologians called "natural revelation." That led into "supernatural revelation." The outline of that ten minutes went something like this:

- The universe is funny; nature is funny. (Specimens: goats and monkeys.)
- Humans are funny: I talked about the universality of farts being funny and discussed the Darwin awards (facetious honors given to people who were foolish and clumsy in a tragic way, thus removing themselves from the gene pool and ironically proving Darwin's theories of natural selection). If I did it today, I might use memes and the Ted Talk *Lessons from Naked Dancing Guy*.
- The Bible is funny: Balaam's donkey makes the point that before DreamWorks thought Eddie Murphy was funny as a talking donkey, God had beaten them to the punch. We walked through various other humorous biblical examples.

---

3. Referenced in Philip Yancey, *Rumors of Another World: What on Earth Are We Missing?* (Grand Rapids: Zondervan, 2003), 38.

4. G. K. Chesterton, *Heretics* (Grand Rapids: Christian Classics Ethereal Library, 2002), 72.

- Jesus was funny: We mapped out some of the funny things Jesus said and did. His nicknames for the apostles were particularly funny. Thaddeus meant "child of the breast" or "milk baby," and he probably got that name because he had a baby face. As a firefighter in the town, I assured them that twelve men could not hang around each other for any length of time without huge chunks of laughter. Plus, Jesus said a bunch of things that were comical, like walking around with a plank in your eye.

After that, we turned it back over to them to discuss, asking, "What other things do you think are funny that might point to the existence of a God who has a sense of humor?" For the next twenty minutes, there were eruptions of laughter all over the room. It was working. People were not only talking about God, but they were enjoying it. Finally, we wrapped it up with some concluding thoughts. I asked some of the groups to share with the room, and some hilarious things were shared, and other things were shared that probably shouldn't have been. This is an occupational hazard of working with nonreligious people. If you're going to have people as fragile as Humpty-Dumpty who get their shells cracked easily, you may want to get them to go sit back up on their wall.

Finally, we rounded out the night with a concluding thought. I said something like:

Well, we've obviously seen countless examples of things that are funny. Now, if we're made like the Bible says in the image of God, then it means that the things that are a hardwired part of our humanity are true of him. Humor didn't have to exist, but it does. Even from a naturalist point of view, humor is an extra luxury; but, as I think we would all agree, humor is really an essential quality that makes everything that's good better, and everything that's bad endurable. I think tonight that we made a great case for God having a sense of humor with the world he made, and the existence of monkeys, goats, and farts. But there's something even cooler. Who knew God was funny? We have to ask the question, if God is funny, and we didn't know it, what other things might shock and surprise us about God?

Join us next week where we ask the question: Who is God?

Now remember, I had a strategic plan of where I was going. By the third night, I was going to unpack who Jesus was, and this is how I got there. So when they returned on night two, the topic was "What Is God Like?" Asking them to discuss among themselves for ten minutes, and following the same format as the first night, I gave another ten-minute talk. This time, I opened with a sort of postmodern monologue about how do we know what or whom to believe when everyone seems to think something different about God? Eventually, I worked around to saying,

> The best record I have is from people who say that they've met God. There is some history here, and the person who seemed to know the most about God was Jesus. And I think he was on to something, because the religious people didn't like him. In fact, they killed him. And there's one thing I've learned about God—it's that you can't always trust religious people to tell you what God is really like. But Jesus wasn't religious. He actually said things that were so nonreligious that they were shocking. Some of those things got him killed. That tells me that he was striking a nerve. He was saying things that people knew were true but didn't want to hear. Here's an example of something he said . . .

I read the parable of the prayer of the sinner and the tax collector. I asked the room how shocking they thought that was, even by today's standards, and epic conversation followed. Lastly, I shared about the prodigal son. Before I released them to the next round of group discussions, I said,

> Okay, in some of these things, some of us aren't sure if we could actually believe that God would be that good. I mean, we hoped he would be, but there's something in us that seems to struggle with the idea of getting close to God. But we read about Jesus and, intrinsically, we realize that if God is real, He *has* to be the way Jesus described him. Like there are things that our souls are intrinsically telling us. These are what are known in the branch of philosophy as reformed epistemology (the study of how you know what you know). Reformed epistemologists discuss something called core beliefs. Core beliefs are things we know intrinsically without being told, like fairness. Nobody told us that, but we know it's real and true. What other things do you think would be true of God that we intrinsically know?

Then, after that twenty-minute discussion in groups, I called their attention once again for a final brief monologue, which brought them to Jesus.

> So, we can see that there are things about God we just know. But here's the weird thing: The most shocking thing Jesus ever said may have been when

his disciples said, "Show us God," and Jesus said, "If you've seen me, you've seen the Father." That means if you really want to know God, you have to look closely at Jesus. So next week, our third question is going to be, "What was Jesus like?" I'll see you next week, same food, same people, and same great discussion.

By the third week, people were hooked. Obviously, we dug into Jesus on the third night. But by week four, we were on to sin and grace. We were talking about the Holy Spirit, but by then, we had a room of saved people, some of whom had already encountered him directly. On that night, discussing the Holy Spirit, somebody turned up who'd had an amazing encounter of being filled with Spirit the day before. It was some pretty deep water, and I was out of my depth because it was out of my hands; but, like anytime God acts on frontline mission, I found myself to be merely a spectator.

In summary, here's roughly what our schedule looked like:

1. Opening and intro of topic—5 minutes
2. Discussion question 1—12 minutes
3. Asking people to share—5 minutes
4. Summary of second point—7 minutes
5. Discussion question 2—20 minutes
6. Summary and wrap up—3 minutes

How to Do an Open Mic Night

What about infiltrating a room you don't have control of? Have you ever thought about doing an open mic night in the local gay coffee house? Me neither. All I can remember is being scared out of my mind leading up to it, wondering why on earth I'd ever agreed to do it in the first place. Afterward, I remember thinking that I'd come as close to Paul's style of evangelism as I ever would in my life. It went well, but we made the following mistakes:

- We had too many people with us.
- We couldn't help feeling that we interrupted the night for people who weren't there for the event.
- We talked first.

I learned some important ground rules from it that I have since learned to take with me anytime I do public space ministry:

1. Buy everyone a drink before the night kicks off. Buying a round is the best way to say, "Sorry for the interruption," show good will, and bring everyone into your family, so to speak.
2. Apologize for the interruption. You've bought them a drink, but you still didn't earn the right to butt in on their evening. The owner let you host open-mic night, but you still may have ruined their patrons' plans.
3. Don't stack the deck. Less is more. If you have too many people with you, it's going to feel staged and awkward. Your herd mentality will be quickly discerned, and people will clam up for fear of going against the party line.
4. Let them talk first. Out of everything we did wrong that first night, it was this mistake that set the tone. Always let the crowd speak first so you can set the tone as an interactive, discussion group. If you start talking and giving your opinions first, you've just set the trajectory, and the key to good evangelism is good listening.
5. Announce the next time. There should always be a next time. Don't just plan a one-off night. Make sure that you're there multiple times with relevant topics. That means you need to craft a series of interesting topics, woven together to draw people deeper in.

The Conversations the World Is Having

The key to harnessing ministry in public space is to enter the conversations that the world is having. Sam Chan's *Evangelism in a Skeptical World* has a chapter on "How to Give Evangelistic Topical Talks" that reinforces this principle. The subtitle of the chapter is "Beer, Sex, and Santa Claus."[5] "Every good conversation starts with good listening" goes the anonymous saying. Conversations are a two-way street and, in Acts 19, prior to talking, Paul was listening. He listened to the unspoken conversations by walking around the city and noticing their superstitions and fears, and finally locked on their FOMO tendencies, seeing that they had even covered their rears by sculpting a statue to the "Unknown God."

The church counteracts the postmodern apathy and the existential despair that grips the media. The church, in its purest form, stands for grace and grates against hypocrisy instead of harboring it. The church embraces absolutes, preaches purpose, champions dignity, and announces a higher calling for humanity as God's image-bearers. All of this has resulted in a wave of

5. Sam Chan, *Evangelism in a Skeptical World: How to Make the Unbelievable News about Jesus More Believable* (Grand Rapids: Zondervan, 2018), 187.

orphanages, hospitals, universities, homeless shelters, rehabs, leper colonies, and charities, like Habitat for Humanity. The world would be poorer without the voice of the church. It has always had, has now, and will continue to have, something to say to the world around it.

For the purpose of this chapter, I've included some topics with the *Harness, Redeem,* and *Transform* Framework from chapter 11 for your groups to engage with and even practice talking about with unbelievers. Many of the conversations we avoid as Christians are the low-hanging fruit that have prepped people for the gospel. For example, Philip Yancey asks, "On what grounds do we feel outrage if we truly believe that morality is self-determined or scripted in our genes?" He quotes Nietzsche's philosophy of nihilism, and ends with Hitler's conclusion, "Nature is cruel, therefore we too can be cruel."[6] Therefore, a discussion on where morality comes from is a springboard for leading people to understand man as created in the image of God.

Interaction

There is a lot of talk about being relevant, which comes from the word *relate.* Can we relate to people? Can we relate to our times? When you read the Gospels, you quickly realize that Jesus knew how to relate to people and, as an even greater compliment to his way of witnessing, they could relate to him.

If we're going to relate to people, that means we're going to have to learn to talk to people. John's Gospel is the most evangelistic book of the New Testament. Have you ever noticed that it's a collection of discussions between Jesus and people? The entire thing. What does that tell us about evangelism?

Sometimes I think the church has always believed in drone strikes. For most of the history of military campaigns, armies have had to set foot onto enemy territory if they want to take it. Drone strikes are initiated from bases far away from their targets. Nonetheless, the church sets up a base of operations and never leaves it. They hope that the enemy will simply walk in and surrender to them, or they can drop some evangelism on people from a distance. I have bad news for you: the drones aren't coming.

When John Wesley and George Whitefield rode the wave of the Holy Spirit during the Great Awakening, they established small groups throughout the country called "societies." They were convinced that life change happened in circles, not in rows. They found conversions in the field and discipleship in

---

6. Philip Yancey, *Rumors of Another World: What on Earth Are We Missing?* (Grand Rapids: Zondervan, 2003), 22–23.

the living room. There were churches. Lots of them. But the churches weren't reaching people, so Wesley and Whitefield went outside.

This took huge faith and gumption. They had to exegete their culture. Whitefield went to the coal fields because the miners worked seven days a week and couldn't hear the gospel at church. The Methodist preachers were soon down the mineshafts, taking church to the people "in the pits." Their gambit payed off and the revival spread.

Wesley originally thought it "a sin to preach in the fields" when he heard of Whitefield, but within a few months, he was preaching to crowds of 20,000 people. Our models often hold us back and keep the kingdom from expanding. In the Great Awakening, and in most times of revival, what God was doing happened *outside* the church walls. So did Jesus's ministry. Did you realize that? He wasn't found where religious people were. He didn't have a church. The Son of God came and barely set foot inside the temple for three years. His ministry was *outside* of the church. My first church plant was in a Starbucks. My second was in in a public park. My third is getting ready to plant in a gas station in the inner city.

What the Youth Already Know about Your Sucky Church

Churches have largely lost the youth, due to a failure to facilitate the important conversations they were having outside the church. According to a study, 86% of unchurched people say that they can have a good relationship with God without belonging to a church.[7] In my book *Church Zero*, I included a conversation entitled, "Why your Church Sucks," which was written from the perspective of a young person in today's interactive world. The discussion was intended to highlight the dilemma that faces us as a church trying to play an 8-track version of good news to a Spotify world:

> Perhaps you've overheard someone saying the following, "I don't need to go to church. I can still have a relationship with God at home. If I want to listen to a sermon, I'll download something from the internet. If I want to worship, I'll hit my favorites off of iTunes. I'm not really missing out on anything by staying at home. Watch the show at church or watch it at home—what's the difference?" How do you answer that?
>
> Do you tell such a person that he should go to church because the presence of God is there and he'll miss it if he stays at home? I'll tell you

---

7. Cathy Lynn Grossman, "Survey: Non-Attendees Find Faith Outside Church," *USA Today*, January 23, 2008.

what he'll say: "Why would the Holy Spirit refuse to meet with me just because I wasn't physically sitting in the building? I can spectate just like anybody else from the comfort of my own home. I can be blessed in the worship and be edified from the Word and save gas, all at the same time." Of course, you'll be quick to talk about Hebrews 10:25: "Don't forsake the gathering of the saints together." He'll be quick to respond with, "Well, I do meet with other Christians for coffee like we're meeting now. We're talking about Jesus."

But the truth is that he's getting more fellowship with you as you are speaking into his life in an attempt to get him to church than he would if he came to church! He definitely won't starve from missing out on the chitchat he'd get drinking coffee in the lobby after the service, talking with the few people who actually stick around instead of burning rubber during the final song. You might even answer that he needs pastoral leadership, but we've already established that he's not really going to get pastoral care at most of our churches. Unless he can fit into the pastor's schedule, or he's lucky enough to have penetrated the iron curtain of secretaries and receptionists, he'll never see the great and powerful Oz.

As long as the church is set up as an audience on a Sunday morning, there's little to say to the departing youth. There's nowhere for them to get involved. They sit at home in the neon light of their monitors because all they need in church is ears, eyeballs, and legs. All we ever ask them to do is sit. We never ask them to use their mouths. And they've got so much to say.[8]

Synagogue-Style Evangelism

When we say synagogue, we mean dialogue. Synagogue-style teaching was when the rabbi sat in the middle of a group and asked questions designed to engage the learners to think on a deeper level. I discovered this accidentally but have since become very intentional about it. Reinforcing this drive to engage people in group interaction is the way Jesus taught in the Gospels. Did you know that he asked 308 questions, was asked 187, and only answered three directly?

I want you to think for a second about how much of Jesus's teaching in the Gospels is actually in dialogue form. Many of the things that we think Jesus spoke as a sermon were actually responses to a question or an observation and were part of an ongoing discussion.

---

8. Peyton Jones, *Church Zero* (Colorado Springs: Cook, 2013), 177–79.

Observe how Jesus, the master of conversation, handles a question about fasting:

> Then John's disciples came and asked him, "How is it that we and the Pharisees fast often, but your disciples do not fast?" Jesus answered, "How can the guests of the bridegroom mourn while he is with them? The time will come when the bridegroom will be taken from them; then they will fast. No one sews a patch of unshrunk cloth on an old garment, for the patch will pull away from the garment, making the tear worse. Neither do people pour new wine into old wineskins. If they do, the skins will burst; the wine will run out and the wineskins will be ruined. No, they pour new wine into new wineskins, and both are preserved." (Matt. 9:14–17)

Observe that he asked a question in response. He also did this when told about his mother and brothers waiting for him outside, and also when he was asked by the rich young ruler how he could obtain eternal life. The list could go on with nearly thirty examples in Matthew's Gospel alone.

Monological or Dialogical

Dialogical preaching is a two-way conversation between a speaker and an audience. Contrast this with monological preaching, where the speaker takes the entire time to speak at the audience. Dialogical preaching is fast becoming popular. In 2005, we lucked our way into this approach by hosting a reading group around *The DaVinci Code*, but it added to our monological practice, rather than subtracting from it.

People with strong opinions so often attempt to force us to choose between two options, as if they are the only two choices in front of us. This staged either/or scenario is known as a false dilemma, or a false dichotomy, and is considered an informal fallacy. We shouldn't have to choose between monological or dialogical preaching. Both have their uses and are prevalent in society. They've also been prevalent in Scripture. Paul entered the synagogue to engage in conversations "as was his custom ... and on three Sabbath days he reasoned with them from the Scriptures" (Acts 17:2). Paul knew that conversations equal conversions.

In my experiences with the churches I've planted, striking a balance between proclamation in short bursts followed by discussion in short bursts was best. In the same way Ezra read the law from the platform and also sent his priests into the crowd to dialogue and explain teachings with which the crowds had difficulty, so we set up our church for both.

Practical Tips

Furnishings were the first consideration in facilitating interaction in our gatherings. Like the reformers moving the altar aside and thrusting the pulpit to the center of the room to teach that the Word of God was at the center of their functionality, we had to reorganize the chairs to function for interaction. In our "O's Before Rows" configuration, eight to twelve people sat around Ikea coffee tables in a horseshoe formation. The tables were cheap, but the conversations were priceless.

Second, we had to adopt a third-space concept. I was a barista when I got started, so it was in my blood to provide a positive environment through food, good coffee, and an inviting atmosphere. Remember the intense temple incense recipe in the Pentateuch? God wanted it to be special, spiced, and of high quality so it would create "a pleasing aroma" (Lev. 2:12). And while I'm not concerned at all about "excellence" when it comes to running a Sunday morning show, I've come to believe that good cakes facilitate better conversations and make people want to stay. It's science! A travel writer for *Westways* wrote about this when reporting on the Irish pubs littered across Ireland, "Sure, the pubs in Dublin serve booze—and plenty of it—but they're also serving up something else, something that has made the Irish pub legendary, and much imitated around the world. The warm welcome, the sense of community, and camaraderie help to ensure that the vibrant oral history of a people is relived and renewed each night. It's a history that gathers to create a unique culture centered around 'the chat' and a common sensibility. And that's what I'm after, and with my clear head, I won't quit till I find it—in its purest form."[9] Its purest form is the church.

Third, and because I can't stand it when churches "run a show," it pains me to say that I had to design a choreography of maneuvering the cakes, coffee, and teas to the groups after a message. During the final song, the group leader delivers it to the Ikea coffee table. Once the music stops, the worship leader shuts up, and the small group leader kicks off the first question after welcoming the group.

Fourth, the format of the entire gathering had to be thought through. The first church I engaged in dialogical preaching, it looked like this:

Pillar

1. Worship—25 minutes
2. Sermon—40 minutes
3. Discussion (three questions)—25 minutes
4. Closing—5 minutes

---

9. Andrew McCarthy, "The Crawl," *Westways* (Jan/Feb 2020), 32.

The second church that I engaged in dialogical preaching looked like this:

Refuge
1. Worship—10 min
2. Discussion question 1 (Thought provoking)—7 min
3. Worship—10 min
4. Discussion question 2 (Exploration)—7 min
5. Sermon—45 min
6. Discussion question 3 (Application)—7 min

We called Refuge's approach the *Question Sandwich*. Each of these can be modified and played with endlessly. The first thing you'll notice about both formats is that our services go longer than yours. In fact, they went longer than what I'm portraying. If you tell a Christian in an established church that services last longer than an hour, they burn rubber out of the parking lot. If you allow unchurched people to talk, however, they'll complain that you didn't give them long enough. Therefore, we learned to ignore any Christians who felt the service was too long. The Doctor was in, and as the good physician, he was healing their souls, and we had all the time in the world for that.

As noted in an earlier chapter, there are fifty-nine "One Another" passages in Scripture. Paul's instructions to "instruct one another" (Rom. 15:14), "carry each other's burdens" (Gal. 6:2), and speak "to one another with psalms, hymns, and songs" (Eph. 5:19) imply a highly interactive congregation. Where would you see this unfold in your gatherings? My suspicion is that you wouldn't on a Sunday. But you could. The brief time of interaction would allow for it. If the service goes past one hour but enriches you beyond your expectations, you would ditch the sixty-minute time limit you've given to church gatherings. Interaction, like discipleship, takes time. Anything that brings transformation is time consuming.

Fifth, the questions had to be planned and put into the overheads so people could read them. At first, this was done ahead of time, but over time, the leaders realized my sermons got blown off course if I felt liberty or a prophetic burden on the spot. In such cases, things shifted, leading to more applicable questions. Therefore, the person running the overheads also had the task of writing searching questions. Generally, questions should not be able to be answered with "yes" or "no." There should be layers to them. There should always be a progression. This is typically how it goes:

1. A thought-provoking icebreaker question: Let's say I was preaching on the woman at the well. I would use the metaphor of sending a message

in a bottle. The woman may never have sent a message in a bottle, but every prayer uttered is heard by God, every message read. Jesus coming to where this woman was and sitting next to her was like him picking her bottle out of an ocean and responding to all her groans and silent prayers. So, during the first question, as an icebreaker, I might ask, "If you could send God a message in a bottle, knowing you would get an answer, what would it be?"

2. An exploration question: I'd go deeper here. Now this one would require a little bit of my trust in the group. It would be, "What is something that you think people are ashamed of, and with which we don't think God can be trusted?" We could either draw up a list via a brainstorm, or we could speak personally from our own experiences. Our team would, of course, be trained to be more relational and tell brief stories about their own lives to facilitate transparency and trust.

3. Lastly, we'd have an application question. In fact, in this case, we might combine the final question with an activity or exercise. I may ask my leaders to bring eight empty water bottles for their group and eight slips of paper. We would challenge everyone to write something personal on that piece of paper—some wound, some deep shame, or something that was equivalent to what the woman at the well was carrying. It needs to be something they'd like God to change, something with which they have been struggling. We'd ask them to keep that water bottle and remember to pray about it daily and to meet with Jesus and discuss it all week.

In the short term, you'll train your leaders to handle these groups, however, over time, each of your members will also learn to lead these groups and facilitate discussion and what, in his *Transformational Training Theory*, Mac Lake calls Holy Spirit breakthrough moments. The long-term view is that each member who leads these can lead a small group in the week, which becomes a core team, which becomes a church plant.

Lastly, the overarching thing to remember in evangelistic conversations is that the goal is not for you to preach but to listen. Consider what counselor Larry Crabb wrote: "You must not make it your goal to tell your story, share your secrets, and make known your struggles to a listening ear. . . . Rather, determine to lead with your ears, so that others will tell you their stories, share their secrets with you, and make known their struggles to your listening ears."[10] This universal principle applies to evangelism. Once you discipline yourself to

---

10. Larry Crabb, *SoulTalk: The Language God Longs for us to Speak* (Nashville: Integrity, 2003), 161.

become a good listener, you will become a good gospel preacher as you naturally respond.

The Benefits

The benefits of allowing your people to minister to one another in these groups is that almost any pastoral issue known to humankind will come up in those groups, and it will accelerate ministry training in the following areas:

- People learn to disciple others.
- People learn to evangelize.
- People lead others to faith in Christ.
- People use their gifts.
- People learn to pray for one another.
- People learn to apply the Word of God to various circumstances and situations.
- People learn to walk in the supernatural.

Identity Issues as a Sample Topic of Conversation

There is neither space nor time in this chapter to cover the vast range of issues society is having, but utilizing the three-pronged approach of *harnessing*, *redeeming*, and *transforming*, we could address issues such as the environment, sexuality, social justice, mental health and addiction, or epistemology. To guide the planter in crafting a conversation this section will focus on the hot topic of sexuality.

Sexuality, gender confusion, and the LGBTQ movement have brought issues that were previously on the fringes of society to the center stage. Unfortunately, the church has been ill-equipped to deal with this conversation, other than to condemn society for discussing it in the first place. When most Christians converse about it among themselves, the term *agenda* will be inserted into the discussion. Yet we forget that behind this issue are brokenness, victimization, and trauma. People are clearly confused on issues of sexuality and, despite the church assuming it is not confused, the actions of the church speak of panic birthed out of confusion, rather than the calm confidence of someone with answers.

Clinical psychologist Dr. Juli Slattery predicts that the current narrative on sexuality in the West will cause a dramatic increase in abuse, addiction, and trauma in our society. She writes, "Although sexuality presents an enormous challenge to Christians and the world at large, *it is not a problem to be solved but a territory to be reclaimed. . . .* Philip Yancey stated, 'I know of no greater failure among Christians than in presenting a persuasive approach to sexuality.'"[11] Citing notable Pew Research studies and data collected from Christian dating sites, she relates the following results:

- 41% of Christians believe cohabitating is a good idea.
- 60% of Christians on a Christian dating site say that they would openly engage in premarital sex.
- 54% of Christians believe that homosexuality should be accepted rather than discouraged.[12]

Slattery concludes that the sexual revolution in the 1960s worked because it tapped into the postmodern hunger for defining one's own truth, and consequently, one's own morality. Rejecting all traditional boundaries or institutions, such as marriage, individuals were prompted to do what felt right, regardless of the consequences.[13] This has resulted in the abuse that necessitated the MeToo movement decades later; people acting on what felt good to them has led to consequences like misogyny, rape, victimization, and sexual harassment. It seems that you can't have it both ways. She continues, "The transgender movement is the ultimate expression of postmodern thought, denying even the biological constraints of male and female."[14] Let's try using the *harnessing, redeeming,* and *transforming* approach to respond to this difficult topic.

Harness

The Bible points to our sexuality as being central to the core of our beings. In the mysterious way that a husband and wife "become one," so an individual and a prostitute become united, according to Paul (1 Cor. 6:15–16). For all other sins are committed "outside our bodies" (1 Cor. 6:18), indicating that sexual acts are more than just external. As people know from the morning-after awkwardness, something more than bodies has been shared between two individuals engaging in sexual intercourse. There has been a connection of the soul and psyche on an intimate level. This is why sexual violation causes mental disequilibrium and suffering. This is why violating the sexual expectations of monogamy ends relationships. If sex were merely recreational, it would be viewed as no different from surfing or playing a board game with someone of the opposite sex.

11. Dr. Juli Slattery, *Rethinking Sexuality: God's Design and Why It Matters* (Colorado Springs: Multnomah, 2018), 7.
12. Slattery, *Rethinking Sexuality*, 29, 30.
13. Slattery, *Rethinking Sexuality*, 21.
14. Slattery, *Rethinking Sexuality*, 22.

Paul harnesses this spiritual connection in his exhortations about marriage in Ephesians 5 and speaks of the mystery of the intimate relationship that we can share with God. Hirsch sees orgasms as a foretaste of heaven, unrivaled by any pharmaceutical high and interwoven with our spiritual longing for connection. It is not unnoticed that the zenith of human ecstasy is intended to be experienced with others for, as Hirsch observes, "Sexuality can be described as the deep desire and longing that drives us beyond ourselves in an attempt to connect with, to understand, that which is other than ourselves. Essentially, it is a longing to know and be known by other people (on physical, emotional, psychological and spiritual levels)." She continues, "Defined in these ways the similarities become obvious. It turns out that sexuality and spirituality are in fact two sides of the same coin."[15] Along these lines, Bruce Marshall wrote that "the young man who rings the bell at the brothel is unconsciously looking for God."[16]

Redeem

There are many sexually broken individuals in our society. Our sexuality has been affected by our fallen nature, and yet, as the title of Debra Hirsch's book *Redeeming Sex* rightly indicates, it can be redeemed by Christ. The question is how. For such a complex issue, there are no simple answers, but the LGBTQ movement has rightly identified that this is an issue of identity. Sadly, however, this movement has presented sexuality as the defining characteristic of one's identity, whereas it is truly only one aspect of it.

The Christian finds his or her identity in Christ and is being remade into the image of God, namely into the image of Christ himself. Those who grapple with these issues will have something to offer the LGBTQ community; those who don't will fail to reach them. My mentor, Dan, used to take my youth group Christmas caroling to gay bars back in the 1980s. If you're younger, the degree to which this was radical for its day will be completely lost on you. Gay men would stand at the door and weep as they heard the songs from church; many of them had probably grown up singing these songs, believing that Jesus would want nothing to do with them due to their feelings of same-sex attraction.

Christians mistakenly enter the fray by arguing whether or not somebody was born LGBTQ. How we got here is irrelevant. Where Jesus wants to take us is the focus. We can prove that alcoholics possess a genetic predisposition

---

15. Debra Hirsch, *Redeeming Sex: Naked Conversations About Sexuality and Spirituality* (Downers Grove, IL: InterVarsity Press, 2015), 26.

16. Bruce Marshall, *The World, the Flesh and Father Smith* (Boston, MA: Houghton Mifflin, 1945), 108.

to alcohol by proteins that have been encoded on their DNA, but nobody in recovery would ever justify taking a drink with a genetic argument. An alcoholic simply knows that they need to stop drinking.

Transform

When it comes to transforming culture on the issue of sexuality, there is more hope for society than we may realize. Although the addiction to pornography works by releasing dopamine, our DeltaFosB proteins can build up with enough dopamine release to actually bind themselves to our DNA sequence, thereby passing down the addiction. In *The Brain That Changes Itself,* Norman Doidge observes the following about the porn addicts he studies: "The male patients I worked with often craved pornography but didn't like it. . . . Addicts take drugs when there is no prospect of pleasure, when they know they have an insufficient dose to make them high and will crave more even before they begin to withdraw. Wanting and liking are two separate things."[17]

Sexual tolerances build up as the brain becomes less excited and easily bored. As individuals reinforce the dopamine release through addiction, people find themselves spending hours on the internet per day, sometimes every waking moment, hungrily searching for images that will arouse the pleasure centers in their brains. To put this in biblical terms, people are becoming enslaved to their sexuality. Unlike their fantasies online, real women are not available 24/7 and prostitutes are expensive. Therefore, many today opt for a fake sexual encounter where they control everything. The problem is, they're out of control. To put it biblically, they've become slaves.

As neuroscience chronicles the effects of pornography, the church may lead the way in educating people about the dangers it poses to them personally, and the harm it causes as abuses against women and children are perpetrated through the industry. Once pornography is truly seen as harmful through the evidence of neuroscience, the church may be in a position to see free porn become a thing of the past, and to see our children protected. The fact that it has been allowed to run so rampant at the expense of the innocence of children is something of which a civilized society ought to be ashamed.

Imagine hosting a conversation around these issues armed with these talking points. A myriad of topics such as human origins, science and God, social justice and reconciliation, and others await those brave enough to tackle topics of this gravity.

---

17. Norman Doige, *The Brain that Changes Itself* (Weisbaden, Germany: Scribe, 2010), 107.

Guidelines

During the discussion, it may be helpful to hide the bones of the Harness, Redeem, and Transform paradigm underneath the flesh of your gathering. You will need to remember that this is a journey for the unchurched, and many who attend will need multiple conversations, like the Athenians who said, "We will hear you again about this" (Acts 17:32 ESV). After Christ is clearly presented, you may call the listeners to faith, and some may even come to faith prior to that, but you will need to be sensitive to the leading of the Spirit in these gatherings. They are as much spiritual as they are cerebral. People will laugh, cry, and raise their voices at times in anger, frustration, and pain.

Through it all, you will need to teach people to respect one another's views, and that is best done by modeling it yourself. When somebody gets out of line, humor goes a long way in diffusing the situation. Threatening to put an adult on time-out usually makes everybody laugh if said with a wry grin and a compassionate heart. As you navigate through these tempestuous waters, one thing is certain: people will change. The one who will change most of all is you.

REFLECT

- Where are the "third spaces" in your community?
- What public spaces in your community would be best for a public meeting?

DISCUSS

- Plan a gathering for the following public spaces:
  - A college campus
  - A suburban high school
  - The mall where people used to shop, but that is now mostly frequented by senior citizens walking indoors and high school students in the food court
  - An outdoor mall where people shop, eat, and wait for their movie time
  - A local park with lots of playgrounds for children

CHALLENGE

- Gather in a public space for your next Bible study or small-group meeting.

REDISCOVERING REPRODUCIBLE SUSTAINABILITY

From Fully Funded to Apostolically Agile

FUNDING CHURCH PLANTING

18

Make all you can, save all you can, give all you can.
—JOHN WESLEY

VARIABLE MULTI-SOURCE FUNDING

No planter should have to choose between feeding their family, paying the bills, and reaching the lost. Paul trained his fellow workers, providing them with the versatile skills that would make them mobile ronin, gospel ninjas able to traverse the map and take the gospel anywhere, to anyone, at any time. This is why Paul's team was able to move rapidly from town to town. Anyone who had a versatile way of making a living could do the same.

After living twelve years overseas and seventeen years as a bivocational missionary planter, I find it amusing to hear theorists insist that planters should be bivocational, despite the fact that they, themselves, have never worked a bivo day in their lives. Continuing to draw a full-time paycheck from Christian institutions with healthy benefit packages, they thumb their noses at those who raise support from the front lines. Yet there are more verses in support of receiving a paycheck for ministry than against it. The disciples in Jerusalem were fully supported by the ministry. Personally, I've only received a full paycheck for a total of two years for my entire twenty-one years since embarking as a missionary. Opting not to burden the churches, I was bivocational most of my years until I finally settled comfortably into tri-vocationalism, or variable multi-source funding.

Variable multi-source funding (trivocationalism) consists of:

1. Vocational employment
2. Bivocational employment[1]
3. Outside funding

Variable multi-source funding means balancing those three sources of income at various levels based on the needs of the mission at the moment. At times, the mission mandated that I work more hours to keep food on the table. At other times, the mission dictated that I shift to an intense concentration on fundraising. Or, if the church required me to invest more discipleship skills in order to multiply, I sacrificed my outside employment and accepted more pay from the church as it purchased more of my time.

Paul also operated from this variable multi-sourced funding approach known as trivocationalism:

1. Paul's vocational employment: At some point in Ephesus, Paul was paid by the church. He never claimed otherwise, and the elders there were funded (1 Tim. 5:17).
2. Paul's bivocational employment: Paul said, "we worked night and day, that we might not be a burden to any of you" (2 Thess. 3:8 ESV).
3. Paul's outside funding: Paul raised support from believers, as evidenced by Romans 15:24, "I hope to see you while passing through and to have you assist me on my journey there."

This chapter will explore the first two components of variable multi-source funding: vocational employment and bivocational employment. Chapter 19 will explore establishing outside funding through financial partnerships and missionary funding principles. As the mission dictates, the planter shifts in response adjusting the components of trivocationalism.

1. VOCATIONAL EMPLOYMENT

Jesus frequently broached the subject of money before establishing his missionary enterprise known as the church. His predetermined plan of evangelism would require funding for furthering the mission, and the source of those funds would be variable depending on the need and circumstance. Although

1. Brad Brisco, *Covocational Church Planting: Aligning Your Marketplace Calling & The Mission of God* (Alpharetta, GA: SEND Network 2018), 89.

the apostles briefly fell back on fishing, Jesus instructed them about receiving support from others while on mission:

And remain in the same house, eating and drinking what they provide, for the laborer deserves his wages. (Luke 10:7 ESV)

Paul re-enforced this by reiterating,

For if it written in the law of Moses, "You shall not muzzle and ox when it treads out the grain." Is it for oxen that God is concerned? (1 Cor. 9:9 ESV)

Elders who do their work well should be respected and paid well, especially those who work hard at both preaching and teaching. For the Scripture says, "You must not muzzle an ox to keep it from eating as it treads out the grain." And in another place, "Those who work deserve their pay!" (1 Tim. 5:17 NLT)

Paul appealed to a fully sustained priesthood when referring to financial remuneration for elders, and repeated Jesus's directive that the worker is worthy of his wages (Matt. 10:10; Luke 10:7). Further, Scripture teaches the obligation and adequacy of supporting those who work for the gospel. In Corinth, and also at Thessalonica, Paul worked at making tents to meet his needs, allowing him to boast:

Don't you remember, dear brothers and sisters, how hard we worked among you? Night and day we toiled to earn a living so that we would not be a burden to any of you as we preached God's Good News to you. (1 Thess. 2:9 ESV)

For in what were you less favored than the rest of the churches, except that I myself did not burden you? Forgive me this wrong! (2 Cor. 12:13 ESV)

Besides working with his hands, Paul also supplemented his partial income by receiving funds from other congregations.

I robbed other churches by accepting support from them in order to serve you. And when I was with you and was in need, I did not burden anyone, for the brothers who came from Macedonia supplied my need. So I refrained and will refrain from burdening you in any way. (2 Cor. 11:8–9 ESV)

You Philippians yourselves know that in the beginning of the gospel, when I left Macedonia, no church entered into partnership with me in giving and receiving, except you only. Even in Thessalonica you sent me help for my needs once and again. Not that I seek the gift, but I seek the fruit that increases to your credit. I have received full payment, and more. I am well supplied, having received from Epaphroditus the gifts you sent, a fragrant offering, a sacrifice acceptable and pleasing to God. (Phil. 4:15–18 ESV)

However, the general principle and expectation is:

Let the one who is taught the word share all good things with the one who teaches. (Gal. 6:6 ESV)

Despite this being the norm, front-line mission rarely provides a sustainable wage. One single method of support may not be sufficient to meet the immediate needs of the planter or the mission. Paul's tri-vocational approach permitted him to shift and maneuver according to the needs of the team and the needs of the church. Don't allow anyone to con you into thinking full-time vocational ministry is a remnant of Christendom; it's a remnant of first-century Christianity.

Despite Paul's practice of renting the hall of Tyrannus in Ephesus, supporting the mission usually meant supporting the minister, not paying for a building. The church met at convenient places, such as homes or rented accommodations. Buildings are cash-demanding, and they also reduce the money available for supporting people who go and tell the gospel. Buildings slow the expansion of the church because it takes time to assemble the necessary cash and build them. The advantages of Paul's methods were that church could be done cheaply and multiplication happened quickly because churches were light on their feet, rather than being the strange contradictory "evangelism centers" separated from where the masses meet.

Church Planter Funding

Chaucer's *Canterbury Tales* ridicules the fat friar as a man who talks about God and feigns concern for the souls of the poor, but who is actually motivated by maintaining a lavish lifestyle. The parson, the humble minister who works hard with his hands, is one of four clergymen on the journey, along with the friar, the monk, and the pardoner. The parson alone is sincere and in ministry for the love of God and others. Even in Chaucer's day, the majority of ministers were viewed as self-serving hirelings. When the world looks back one hundred years on the ministers of today, what will be remembered? Paul was motivated to work with his hands, specifically because of the bad example set by the pagan philosophers who demanded coin before dispensing enlightenment.

Ministers suckling at the teat of the mother church for the milk of a paycheck need to stay latched on, at least if they want more milk. Church planting on the cheap, however, is a rare but necessary skill. Planting for free is an even rarer superpower. The standard practice for church planters and missionaries to be fully funded before they're released into the mission field, was a luxury I never had. Like the old-school fundraising thermometer, the red line has to reach 100 percent funded before we'll allow people to launch out; but Paul didn't wait around for Christians to fund him, or he'd probably be waiting still. Paul worked with his own hands to purchase his mobility. The overreliance on funding holds planters back from going when they should have already been gone. I imagine that some pastors reading this feel trapped by the very church they planted. After all, the money is finally good and the church is thriving, but what really holds them back from venturing out again and fulfilling the apostolic call to venture out is the comfort of a guaranteed paycheck.

The basic principles of funding in the New Testament were:

1. If a Christian wants to start a church as an unpaid volunteer, they may do so.
2. If a church sends out planters, then it has a responsibility to support them —at least partially.
3. A planter may be a volunteer, a part-time earner, or partially funded and, at any time, may move from one status to another.

In Methodism, the local societies were asked to provide sustenance for their leaders. When they did however, it was often inadequate. Many itinerants turned to pastoral arrangements in response because established churches provided the basics when itinerant situations failed to do so. Wesley desperately tried to solve the problem but failed to find a solution. After his death, the Methodist Church gradually abandoned itinerant ministry altogether. There were some who wanted to continue, and they formed *The New Connection*, but the pastoral pull proved too strong when they failed to fund the mission.

Francis Asbury, the first Methodist bishop in the US, faced a widening frontier. He oversaw approximately eight hundred itinerants who were not so much circuit-riders as wanderers migrating Westward, seeking out settlers to convert. These circuit-riders were self-sufficient, often living off the land, and they died young because of it. John Chrysostom, witnessed itinerant apostolic preachers traveling outside of Antioch in the late fourth century:

You might see each of them now yoking oxen to the plow, and cutting a deep furrow in the ground, at another time with their word cleaning out sins from men's souls. They are not ashamed of work, but ashamed of idleness, knowing that idleness is a teacher of all wickedness. And while the philosophers walk about with conspicuous cloak and staff and beard, these plain men are far truer philosophers, for they teach immortality and judgment to come, and conform all their life to these hopes, being instructed by the divine writings.[2]

Such "good and useful men," Broadus notes, "have abounded . . . in every period, country and persuasion in which Christianity was making any real and rapid progress."[3]

Support for gospel work from the generosity of individuals or churches is biblical, but history testifies all too clearly than an overreliance on it will dramatically slow the pace of kingdom expansion. If the only reason we're not going fast is that we proffer the excuse of poor funding, then we'll have a heck of a time explaining that to our impoverished brothers and sisters in developing nations where the gospel is spreading faster than it did in the first century.

Either Western planters are using models that are too expensive, or something is wrong with our model of expansion. Expansion doesn't have to be expensive; neither do our missionaries. According to David Garrison, "Building a movement on foreign funds is like running a machine with an extension cord that stretches across the ocean. When the movement meets the end of the cord's length, it will abruptly stop. A Church Planting Movement must have an internal engine and internal fuel if it is going to flourish."[4] In Haiti, a Nazarene missionary has helped the church develop an indigenous method of funding church multiplication by breeding sheep. The church breeds a sheep, then carefully selects someone in the community to act as a steward of one of the sheep's lambs. That individual gives every other sheep to the church to further fund multiplication and keeps the alternate sheep to sell for themselves. In Haiti, selling a sheep is the equivalent of selling a car.

Funding Multiplication

For my first three years planting, I worked with my hands as a firefighter, factory worker, registered nurse, clinical trainer, or barista. By the fourth year

2. John Broadus, *Lectures on the History of Preaching* (Charleston, SC: Bibliolife, 2009), 50, 51.
3. Ibid.
4. David Garrison, *Church Planting Movements: How God Is Redeeming a Lost World* (Midlothian, VA: WIGtake Resources LLC, 2004), 249.

of my church plants, the church could pay my full ride but, unfortunately, apostolic planters operate on a three-year mission cycle.[5] When it was time to leave, I had to start over from zero by handing my paycheck over to my replacement. As I began to have kids, I felt a different pressure and wondered if I was treating my family right to ask them to move frequently and embrace a return to poverty every three years. Therefore, I designed a funding system for sequential planting called the Ninja Planting System.

Let's imagine that I've planted a church bivocationally. Employing variable multi-source funding, I'm able to increase my pay by $12,000 annually ($1,000 per month). In year two I make $2,000 per month. In year three I make $3,000 per month. But then, as my mission cycle kicks in and it's time to move on, I begin to start funding my replacement. Every year, I go down by $1,000 per month, while my replacement goes up by that same amount so the church is never burdened. The church I planted sends me on my way, funding the strike team and, as my support diminishes, my replacement's support increases.

For the purpose of this chapter, the sequential planter is referred to as the *Ninja Planter*. Here is how the Ninja Planting System works:

Plant	Ninja Planter	Replacement Worker / Fist team leader
Plant 1—Year 1	$1,000 per month—Church plant 1	0
Plant 1—Year 2	$2,000 per month—Church plant 1	0
Plant 1—Year 3	$3,000 per month—Church plant 1	0
Plant 1—Year 4 Plant 2—Year 1	$2,000 per month—Church plant 1 $1,000 per month—Church plant 2	Replacement Worker 1 —$1,000 per month
Plant 1—Year 5 Plant 2—Year 2	$1,000 per month—Church plant 1 $2,000 per month—Church plant 2	Replacement Worker 1 —$2,000 per month
Plant 1—Year 6 Plant 2—Year 3	$0.00 per month—Church plant 1 $3,000 per month—Church plant 2	Replacement Worker 1 —$3,000 per month
Plant 2—Year 4 Plant 3—Year 1	$2,000 per month—Church plant 2 $1,000 per month—Church plant 3	Replacement Worker 2 —$1,000 per month
Plant 2—Year 5 Plant 3—Year 2	$1,000 per month—Church plant 2 $2,000 per month—Church plant 3	Replacement Worker 2 —$2,000 per month
Plant 2—Year 6 Plant 3—Year 3	$0.00 per month—Church plant 2 $3,000 per month—Church plant 3	Replacement Worker 2 —$3,000 per month

5. Paul never stayed in a region for more than three years, and neither have I. The only time I stayed longer was when I was figuring out the apostolic call and was trying to figure out how to leave.

The salary value in my example may vary, but the simple numbers above help communicate the concept. This program provides a cushion and ensures apostolic mobility by reducing the financial tension that bottlenecks itinerant ministry. Churches could fund this type of system to foster multiplication and mobility. Some might criticize a lead planter who collects money from two church plants at the same time, particularly when one is a church at which the planter is no longer serving. To this, I respond:

1. The sequential planter is never taking more than a consistent amount in the above model ($3,000 in the example, but the amount is inconsequential). This prevents money from hindering kingdom expansion.
2. The planter who took all the risks in the beginning, making nothing or very little, is compensated after three years. The replacement fist-team member must make the same sacrifices as the lead planter. Only hirelings complain about making sacrifices on mission, and planters should never hand over to hirelings.
3. Supporting the apostolic planter allows the existing church to support church planting by continuing with an apostolic planter with whom they are already in relationship.
4. Within three years of leaving, the planter no longer makes an annual wage from the sending church. They may choose to support the apostolic planter as a missionary, as Paul asked the Philippians and Corinthians to do.

We await a rude awakening regarding the future of full-time ministry. If you expect to disciple the next generation, they'll need training in mission funding like Jesus and Paul gave. I'll continue to minister at no cost to churches if that's what it takes; however, attempting to rewrite the New Testament's teaching on funding will not help advance mission.

2. BIVOCATIONAL MINISTRY

A job is what you're paid for. A vocation is what you're made for. Bivocational ministers are called to employment both inside and outside of the church, and both can be ways of ministering "as unto the Lord." This balancing act is riddled with challenges but rife with opportunity. It can be the most freeing and rewarding lifestyle a minister experiences. In operating bivocationally, planters have tapped into a plan that provides answers to these three questions:

1. How will I provide for my family?
2. How will I penetrate my community?
3. Where will we meet and how can I afford to pay for it?

Balancing Three Factors

Maintaining a bivocational lifestyle requires wisdom and skill, and it's important to understand how to balance the various financial factors involved. The first order of business is what type of work will allow you to effectively maintain a sustainable and scalable life. Specifically, there are three factors to consider when choosing a career path that will greatly affect your quality of life as a bivocational planter: time, money, and exposure.

Balancing the three factors of time, money, and exposure to your target community in different combinations will produce different results in your personal life and your ministry. It could be argued that one can never have enough of all three, but sometimes the bivocational planter must prioritize one over another in order to accomplish something different.

For example, working forty hours a week as a barista at a popular coffee shop won't put much money in the bank account. It will also demand much of your time for little financial return. Therefore, a barista job fails to maximize your income or your time. One thing it does do, however, is maximize your exposure to people. In a barista job, you are encouraged to talk to customers and build relationships with them as you make their drinks.

On the bivocational maximizer scale, your life looks like this:

Job	Income	Time	Exposure
Barista	-	-	+

My dilemma as a barista was that the trade-off for maximum exposure to the community was making minimal income, and my time wasn't optimized. This isn't usually ideal. I was poor, but I reached tons of people . . . and every month my debt grew just a little bigger. Having previously lived debt-free most of my life, this was not a sustainable situation.

Therefore, when considering a job that requires a maximum amount of time, you must ask two questions:

1. Will this job pay me what I need to sustain my household?
2. Will this job expose me to the people I'm trying to reach?

If the answer to question one is "Yes, it will provide me with enough income to support a family," then the second factor to be considered is whether or not it will put you around the people you're trying to minister to. If the answer is no, then perhaps the job may not be a good fit. For example, a job tucked away in the back of a warehouse sitting at a computer screen may not be the best place for an apostolic leader who is gifted at creating community. He or she will now have very little time left in which to do it and will meet very few people with whom to do it.

In the case of the barista job, the bivocational planter is sacrificing money and time for exposure to the target community. Another way to say this is that the planter is sacrificing economic margin for evangelistic reach. Thankfully, this does not always have to be the case. There are jobs that will maximize the planter's time, money, and exposure to the target community.

Consider the job of window cleaning in a community that has lots of inclement weather. People usually neglect cleaning their windows and will gladly pay somebody else to do it. Contrasting the window cleaning job with a barista position, we will see that the window cleaning job will require more physical labor, but the payoffs in the three areas of time, money, and exposure are very different.

A window cleaner works far fewer hours than a barista does to make the same amount of money. If the window cleaner really hustles, he can work two days a week instead of five, and make double the income he would as a barista if he lives in an area that has wet weather. The bonus is that, although he works two days a week, he has an excuse to knock on every single door in the city to acquire clients. There aren't many businesses that can boast that opportunity! Thus, the job of a window cleaner maximizes time, money, and exposure to the target community. The drawback, however, is that the window cleaner may find that the conversations he used to have as a barista were more meaningful because, as a barista, he wasn't selling something while he was talking. Therefore, some planters may still opt to become baristas instead of becoming window cleaners.

All these factors must be weighed and considered. Consider the contrast of the two jobs discussed.

Job	Income	Time	Exposure
Barista	-	-	+
Window Cleaner	+	+	+

One additional factor to consider is the health of your family. Some families require more time than others, and some spouses may resent a bivocational lifestyle if the planter is always absent from the home, especially with little return on the investment. If there is little money coming in to pay the bills and little time for emotional connection, a spouse will soon begin to resent the sacrifices being made and the small reward the planter has to show for it. Wise planters will discuss these things with their spouses in order to establish expectations and will be clear about what is being sacrificed in pursuit of which end. A spouse will frequently sacrifice one of these factors (emotional availability or return on investment) at any given time to accomplish the mission, but not both. Not for long, anyway. Therefore, the emotional temperature of the home must be well-maintained.

Types of Employment

That leads to the next set of factors to consider. Bivocational work can take many different forms, based on the type of employment the planter chooses. This will greatly affect the degree of freedom the planter will have under which to adjust the work/life balance. The three different types of employment are:

- Employment by others
- Self-employment
- Entrepreneurship

Being employed by others often provides a feeling of stability and security. The typical employee turns up and gets paid, regardless of customers or sales. The employee is not responsible for building a business, administering at a corporate level, or dealing with IRS compliancy issues. This provides a measure of freedom, but other freedoms are sacrificed. Planters so employed are not able to dictate when they will be free, or when they can take time off. They must operate within a limited set of parameters and sacrifice a degree of their freedom. For planters who require security over freedom, this is a good option.

Self-employment is an option for those who value freedom in their schedule and are willing to shoulder all the responsibility of providing their own income. This involves starting a business, dealing with the IRS on a regular basis, entering the world of workman's comp, and complying with other federal and state regulations. There is a lot of freedom, but that freedom comes at a price. If the self-employed worker doesn't hustle, there is no money. Self-employment can be skill-based, such as being a marketer, business consultant, or social media manager. A company can also be formed around a product or a service, such as a landscaping business. Each of them has advantages and drawbacks, and each must be considered.

Business as Mission

In his book *The Art of Nonconformity*, author Chris Guillebeau reveals how he works remotely from cities all over the world: Singapore, London, Mexico City, and Moscow, among others. Instead of a massive house payment, insurance, maintenance, and utilities, he stays mobile by investing the same amount of money into flights, hotels, and Uber lifts. He mathematically works out that he actually spends less on the cost of living than the average American. He lives a mobile lifestyle simply by thinking outside the box. Untethering mission from the trappings of our buildings will enable churches to send out their best rather than only sending our untested, untried, and unwanted leaders to start from scratch.

Brad Brisco has raised awareness that being bivocational shouldn't be seen as second best, and Paul certainly saw it as a strategic first choice.[6] Paul approached mission as shrewdly as he approached entrepreneurial business. Successful businessmen are wise, shrewd, careful, and hard-working, and Paul inherited his father's strategic mind along with the successful family tent-making business. Had Paul's father not been financially well off, he'd never have been able to afford studying at the feet of Gamaliel.[7] When Paul left his occupation as a Pharisee, he returned to Tarsus and learned to excel using the same business principles that made his father rich.

To the prosperous trade town in Ephesus, Paul wrote, "Make the most of every opportunity" (Col. 4:5). The word Paul used paints the picture of a merchant "buying up" bargains to shrewdly turn a profit, and Paul applied those same principles to expanding the kingdom. It's possible that Paul learned the family trade during the eight years he spent post-conversion in Tarsus after leaving Syria and Cilicia. The education he received at the feet of Gamaliel may have impressed people at the temple, but that wouldn't do squat on mission. One can imagine this apostle's frustration during the decade he spent in such pursuits after Christ had charged him with reaching the Gentile world. Perhaps Paul didn't know where to start, but during those eleven years learning to make tents, feeling held back from mission, God was establishing Paul's sustainability for mission more than he could have ever realized. When planters work with their hands, it may not seem like history is being made, but eternity may be breaking in.

---

6. Brad Brisco's book *Covocational* is highly recommended.
7. Eckhard J. Schnabel, *Early Christian Mission: Paul and the Early Church* (Downers Grove, IL: InterVarsity Press, 2004), 926.

Like most Pharisees, Paul had been trained for a life aloof from others, walking through the crowds with an air of superiority. Tent making, on the other hand, taught him to talk with everyday people. The ivory tower of religious studies taught him about the workings of men's souls, yet it disconnected him from them. Working until his hands were raw, burning the midnight oil, and conversing with everyday people for a decade provided insight into people that Paul needed in order to reach them. Further, it provided the means to support himself. Paul could travel to any marketplace, make money, and develop connections quickly. Further, he could boast to the Ephesian elders on the docks of Miletus that his tentmaking directly funded the living expense of his fellow missionaries: "You yourselves know that these hands of mine have supplied my own needs *and the needs of my companions*" (Acts 20:34, emphasis mine).

Paul's career change transitioned him from Pharisee to tentmaker and not only provided skills that paid the bills but also, in God's providence, opened up a crucial link with Priscilla and Aquila as missional business partners. Down the road, that bond would transform not only his ministry, but also that of the fellow workers he trained.[8] Devenish says, "And when he was in Ephesus, his tent-making business financed not only his own ministry but that of his team as well. Paul seems to have had entrepreneurial and practical skills which enabled him to finance his mission himself."[9] Therefore, when Paul reproduced himself by training church planters, he didn't simply train them to plant churches—he trained them how to make a living.

Funding Others

Priscilla and Aquila's multi-city business venture supported Paul's team abroad and the ministry in Rome as they'd done for Paul personally in Corinth (Acts 18:1–3). They hosted the church in their home in the Roman imperial capital (Rom. 16:3–5). Paul had worked and lived with the couple in Corinth and, after setting up their business in Ephesus, where they began to train Paul's missionaries to make a living. Priscilla and Aquila became an integral part of establishing the three mission hubs set in important cities on massive trade routes; Corinth, Ephesus, and Rome. The result of their support is portrayed in Acts 18:5 (ESV): "When Silas and Timothy arrived from Macedonia, *Paul was occupied with proclaiming the word*" (emphasis mine). Ben Witherington III observes that the original language "refers to Paul's devoting himself

---

8. Ryan Lokkesmoe, *Paul and His Team: What the Early Church Can Teach Us About Leadership and Influence* (Chicago: Moody, 2017), 101.

9. David Devenish, *Fathering Leaders, Motivating Mission: Restoring the Role of the Apostle in Today's Church* (Milton Keynes, England, UK: Authentic Media, 2011), loc. 4306, Kindle.

exclusively to the sharing of the word once Silas and Timothy came to town. We may deduce, from 2 Cor. 11:19 and Phil. 4:14–15, that Timothy and Silas brought not merely good news with them from Macedonia but also funds, which allowed Paul to forgo working with his hands, at least for a while, and concentrate on ministry in the synagogue and elsewhere."[10] What may have seemed like initial chance meeting in the marketplace in Corinth, changed the trajectory of mission in the first century. Paul expanded Priscilla and Aquila's business by training his fellow gospel workers, like Timothy, and Titus, thus franchising their tent-making business abroad, and with it, the gospel.

Titus, Timothy, Silas, and Apollos were empowered to scratch out a living for themselves and bankroll their journeys to new cities with pop-up businesses in the form of a trade. Paul could even ask Titus to help fund the others, "Do everything you can to help Zenas the lawyer and Apollos on their way and see that they have everything they need" (Titus 3:13).

The single-funding model of most missionaries and planters not only removes them from the culture they're attempting to reach, it also bottlenecks mission through insufficient funds and often misplaces the livelihood of the missionary as the central concern of missionary work. Timothy Tennent says, "The collapse of Christendom has left Western Christians in an uncomfortable position because most have no real preparation or precedent for how to live on the margins, counter to the culture. For the most part, we don't know how to think about missions without ourselves being at the center (including sending structures, personnel, money, and strategic planning)."[11] Yet planters continue to hole up in the hovel of their church office, imagining how good it would be to take their city, yet staying safely sequestered away from the people they are attempting to reach.

Entrepreneurial Enterprises Today

Guy Pfanz was a revitalization pastor who needed to pay the bills when the majority of his tithers walked out the door, lobbing curses over their shoulder, and leaving the coffee shop they started in the lurch. "Good luck without our money!" they threatened upon exiting. To make ends meet in the church's failing coffee shop, Pfanz started selling cappuccino machines, and started a coffee-roasting business. There was one problem. Coffee roasters aren't cheap and he didn't have the funds to purchase one. Pfanz had a vision of roasting coffee by day and training church planters by night. Shortly thereafter, an envelope came

---

10. Ben Witherington III, *The Acts of the Apostles: A Socio-Rhetorical Commentary* (Cambridge, UK: Eerdmans, 2001), 548–49.

11. Timothy Tennent, *Invitation to World Missions: A Trinitarian Missiology for the 21st* Century (Grand Rapids: Kregel Academic, 2010), loc. 156 of 7178, Kindle.

in the mail containing a check amounting to more than Guy's annual salary. Emboldened by evidence of God being behind his coffee/church planting venture, Pfanz continued to invest in more roasters with the proceeds from his quickly growing coffee business. Every morning, Pfanz trained planting interns to be coffee roasters, reserving the afternoons to train them in ministerial skills. When they launched out to other neighborhoods and cities in America, they left with a coffee roaster into which they'd invested through a partnership arrangement, fully ready to plant a church. They had enough money to support themselves and their church plant. In training them both for ministry and in a skill, he empowered them to go anywhere at any time.[12] By merging entrepreneurial start-ups with their plant, they immediately had an instant income and instant space to meet.

Moving from San Diego to Portland, a planter opted to start a CrossFit gym in combination with raising support. Franchising a CrossFit gym created a community, provided an income, and established a central place for their church to gather. When I asked him what mistakes he'd be sure not to repeat next time he planted, he turned the question around without missing a beat. He responded that the one thing he would never do is to plant without developing an independent income stream.

The business as mission, or the entrepreneurial combination of church planting with establishing a business in the local community, immediately provided the planters above with instant income, instant community, and instant places to meet.

Pitfalls of Bivocational Planting

Becoming bivocational does have its pitfalls, however. After a few years of training bivocational planters with Peter Mitchell, we discovered that some ministers who'd been poor for the majority of their ministries suddenly left ministry to engage in a midlife second career. We struggled for a bit, wondering if we'd put too much temptation in the way of planters by transitioning them from just surviving financially to thriving. Paul reported that Demas deserted him because he loved this present world (2 Tim. 4:10). Scholars struggle to say why or how he left, and why Thessalonica was a temptation, but it may be that Demas struck out to make as much money as he could once he'd learned the skill, abandoning his first calling to minister the gospel. Ministers who take their hand off the plow at the first green flash were most likely shabby ministers in other ways as well.

---

12. Guy Pfanz and Monica Hoover, *Stacking the Deck: What Happens When We Believe God Wants It More Than We Do* (Muncie, IN: Small Voice Publishing, 2010).

If you're earning your crust pumping gas while holding out the Bread of Life, you're already more like the apostle Paul than you realize. Learning to pay your bills while reaching the lost is about as first century as it gets.

REFLECT

- The author introduces a model of funding that he terms "trivocational." This means combining three streams of funding: (1) raising funds, (2) working at a job, (3) accepting some support from the church. Do any of these surprise you?
- Why would a church planter keep all three streams of funding active at all times?

DISCUSS

- What are the pros and cons of each stream of funding: (1) raising funds, (2) working at a job, (3) accepting some support from the church
- Suppose a church planter says, "I'll never take money from a church!" Why would he or she say that? What is potentially wrong with that?
- Suppose a church planter says, "I don't want to raise support like a missionary!" Why would he or she say that? What is potentially wrong with that?
- Suppose a church planter says, "I'm a professional minister and don't have time for a 'day job'!" Why would he or she say that? What is potentially wrong with that?

CHALLENGE

- This funding model is a major paradigm shift and a challenge to the Western concept of professional ministry. How would developing three balanced streams of funding "hard wire" the planter for *serial* church planting?
- Are you less of a minister if you aren't a paid professional on staff with a church?
- How will you provide for your family, penetrate your community, and secure a gathering space and the funds to pay for it?

19

GOSPEL PATRONS AND PARTNERSHIPS

The last part of a man to be converted is his wallet.

—JOHN WESLEY

Michael Cheshire once said, "Money and church planting . . . It's hard to get those two in the same room." No matter how much funding you have been promised for your church plant, it often doesn't materialize. Church planting saps a planter's time, rendering fundraising a luxury few can afford. When they're a part of advancing the kingdom of God, however, planters often have to soldier up to accomplish the mission. Paul said, "Who serves as a soldier at his own expense?" (1 Cor. 9:7 ESV). Every conscientious sending church provides funding, but planters should be careful to not approach them as a missionary ATM. There is a depth of potential in relationship, mentoring, and sincere kingdom partnership. Four questions every planter should ask himself before setting out are:

1. Who is sending me? (Finding a sending church)
2. Who is supplying me? (Supplying the equipment)
3. Who is going with me? (Building your team)
4. Who is supporting me? (Funding the mission)

Answering these questions before setting out does not mean that a planter won't be faced with financial dilemmas, but Jesus warned that, "Or what king, going out to encounter another king in war, will not sit down first and deliberate whether he is able with ten thousand to meet him who comes against him with twenty thousand?" (Luke 14:31 ESV). Keeping the supply lines open is essential. For every church that Paul planted, however, there was the backing of Antioch. He wasn't a maverick or a lone ranger operating under his own authority. He'd been sent. In between each of Paul's missionary journeys, he returned to Antioch as his mission station. Captain Kirk had the Starship Federation, Wesley was still an Anglican, and Paul had the ordination from the risen Lord, the blessing of Jerusalem, and the backing of Antioch. Author, planter, and visionary Brian Sanders, who has championed the model of micro church networks, raises millions of dollars per year to make it possible. Hugh Halter also raised funds and established partnerships to establish Post Commons in Alton, Illinois—one of the most innovative outposts of missional endeavors at the time of writing, emphasizing that mission and funding are intimate bedfellows.

WHO IS SENDING ME?

The most important asset a sending church provides is the relationship with a seasoned leader who can send you. Unfortunately, some planters just go on their own without allowing anybody the privilege of propelling them out into the field. Planters often need the wisdom, support, and encouragement of a sending pastor, and dark days will arrive when planters, with their tails between their legs from a beating, will need spiritual and emotional restoration.

My sending pastor regularly visited me in the field, both stateside and abroad. He acted as my confessor when I felt confused, alone, or wanted to quit. His veteran wisdom and experience supplied vision in areas where I'd lost perspective. He bandaged up my wounds, loved me no matter what, and inspired me to keep marching. And when I was overseas, he gave me a home to come back to and a homecoming when I did. Such a leader will be your medic and field chaplain while you're charging the gates of hell.

That said, a sending church may unwittingly also be the biggest factor in killing a church plant that had good potential. A sending church that is bent on controlling the church plant is the fastest way to send it to an early grave. Sending churches are there to support a plant, not to control it. The sending church is tempted to control the plant because, if the plant fails, it reflects poorly on those who sent the planter. The sending church must recognize that they released the planter into the hands of God, and therefore no longer bear the burden of success or failure. If they fail to understand this biblically from the book of Acts, they will prove more of a hindrance than a help to the planter. More than likely, the rules and regulations they impose will be the reason the church failed, because they stifled the planter and quenched the Spirit.

It's crucial that you have the support of your sending church. After all, you're going to be asking permission to "fish" your support base from out of "their pond." Your sending church has the money, resources, and manpower you need. Church planters tend to be daredevils and cowards simultaneously. What puts fear in the heart of a church planter is being held back, and for that reason, most planters fear sharing their plans with their sending pastor.

With hat in hand, and the humblest three-piece suit of humility with which you can cover yourself, you're going to need to put yourself in the sending pastor's shoes. As a result of your recruiting efforts, sending pastors stand to lose some of their best people. From your pastor's perspective, losing those people could be very disheartening, especially if they're as valuable to the sending pastor's work as they are to yours. Stay cool and try to understand the reaction of the sending pastor if they are less than gracious in the first meeting. Taking bullets in your back from friendly fire comes with the territory.

Over the years, New Breed asked a bunch of planters if they could do something different, what would it be? Without any hesitation, almost all of them said they wished they'd reached out better to the pastors of established churches before they'd launched. In dealing with criticism from other pastors, I've found this to be the case as well. I've unintentionally hurt pastors whom I've respected and who were like fathers to me. I've scoured an area and absent-mindedly missed a leader there who later started a campaign against me, complete with effigies and piñata sticks. Don't be surprised if there are arrows in your hide and knives in your back when you invite friendly fire by unfriendly behavior.

WHO IS SUPPLYING ME?

Your sending church has resources. Because you don't have bags of money, resources are at a premium. The sending church's serviceable but outdated sound system sits in a storage closet collecting dust while the church planter agonizes over how to raise the funds to pay for a new one. Don't raise the funds, raid the storage closet! Most churches have enough old gear laying around to kit out two or three church plants. Recycled projector screens, LCD projectors, offering boxes, and coffee machines will save thousands of dollars.

Gear isn't all you're going to be asking your sending pastor for, though. You're also going to ask them to pay your salary for two years. It's always best to ask high. Ask for two and you stand a chance of getting one. Originally, they hadn't been thinking along those lines, but since you asked big, now they are entertaining a six-or twelve-month paycheck coverage. This is how it works. Ask for nothing and you're guaranteed to get what you asked for. So, after you ask, and they pause and reply, "Sorry, we just can't do that," you counter with, "What would be reasonable?" Then wait. Don't talk. In the sales world, there is a saying that the first person to speak after an offer has been laid out is automatically the loser in the deal. When they answer, you're going to ask for more:

- Health benefits
- Use of their insurance and their accounting staff to run your finances
- Their constitution and bylaws
- Their legal team (for 501c3)
- A bank account
- Permission to give a pitch and appeal on a Sunday morning
- A sound system
- Access to all their graphics and media (videos, music, licenses)
- Some interns (They have them and usually don't know what to do with them to keep them busy.)

If you're afraid of asking, consider the worst that could happen. They could say no, and you could come back and ask again at a later date—but we'll come back to that.

WHO IS GOING WITH ME?

You will also ask for people. Your sending church is packed with people who are bored with being part of an audience. This is a target-rich environment for core team builders looking for unused gifts, undeveloped potential, and congregants with that half-crazed gleam in their eyes. If your pastor trusts you and you're being sent, he'll throw you in front of them to announce your crazy exodus in hopes that you'll take the weird and difficult ones off his hands. When Pillar was forming its core team, God brought us everybody else's rejects. In 1 Samuel 22:2 (ESV), God brought David those who were "in distress, in debt, or discontented." That sounds like most church planters! No offense to my team, but we were really a motley crew; but in the end, they proved themselves to be like David's mighty men of lore.

WHO IS SUPPORTING ME?

Your plant may not be the budget priority of your sending church, but they should be supplying some degree of financial contribution toward it. Despite mission funding being a biblical concept, most planters are as uncomfortable raising the issue of money with their sending church as they are raising funds from individuals. Patrick Mclaughlin observes,

> The Old and New Testaments have 1,189 chapters with 31,163 verses. Around 2,300 verses in the Old and New Testaments concern money, materialism, and stewardship. That's 7.4 percent, a bunch for a book primarily about redemption! According to a variety of sources, 1,441 verses just in the New Testament clearly address or touch on the areas of stewardship (money, materialism, time, talent, and treasure). The New Testament has more verses about stewardship than the 550 verses on prayer and 680 verses on love combined.[1]

Part of my job in training planters is to help them understand fundraising. Fundraising is a key component of planting churches, at least biblically. Paul worked with his hands when he was present with them, sharing the gospel, but his pattern was to ask churches he'd planted to fund him to plant the next one once he moved on. The cool thing about Paul was that he asked for it directly—he didn't manipulate or beat around the bush.

Here's the advice I often give to church planters: Don't ask for prayer when what you really want is money. When you want prayer, ask for prayer. When you need money, ask for money. Neither is wrong. But when you mistakenly equivocate the two terms or make prayer support simply a euphemism for money, you undermine the value of asking for each of them.

Years ago, I was shy about asking for money. I was a missionary, but I would never do the "missionary thing." My mission board followed me around and, when I walked off the stage, they scratched their heads and asked me, "Why didn't you ask for support? You know you need it!" There was a reason I was very thin during my first years as a missionary.

Every year America spends $1 billion on missions. Sounds good, right? Until you realize that's also how much they spend on chewing gum. They spend seven times that on dog food. The IRS figures reveal that Americans give 1.6 to 2 percent of their income to charity. Marijuana sales are predicted to rise to $21 billion in 2021, higher than the amount it would cost to end world hunger. When I returned to American soil and witnessed waste as we spent on everything else but mission, I grew angry and something shifted within me. I felt justified robbing the rich to give to the poor in the neighborhoods in which I planted. One of New Breed's taglines was, "We go where the need is, not where

---

1. Patrick G. McLaughlin, *Major Donor Game Plan* (Grand Rapids: The Timothy Group, 2010), 45.

the money is." Churches didn't want to venture into those neighborhoods and, as I scanned the faces that the church had forgotten, I started asking for them, not myself. If you think your mission is worth embarking on, someone else thinks it's worth giving to. They're making decisions on what causes to fund, and if you'll let them, they'll fund yours. Think of fundraising more as giving permission to others to partner with you, rather than as begging for money.

Randy Alcorn once wrote, "Like piano playing, giving is a skill. With practice, you get better at it."[2] In the same way, the skill of inviting others to partner in mission can also be improved. One of the greatest transformations happens when missionaries realize that by asking others to fund mission, they are actually helping their donors to develop as disciples. Talk is cheap, but so are Christians. I've noticed a pattern. Those who say that all believers are missionaries seldom give to those who have left their nets and traveled to the frontlines where Christ is not named. A research group looking back at the past forty years of church giving determined that the average amount that Christians give to their churches is 2.58 percent of their income. Unfortunately, the Christian church can't even out-give the Mormons. Give us some freedom, and we'll rip God off simply because he asks and doesn't force us.

GOSPEL PATRONS

In his excellent book *Gospel Patrons*, John Rinehart chronicles how the major advances of the gospel in the Western world, starting with the early church, can be traced back to the partnership with a wealthy patron who funded the work. Tyndale's translation of the Bible into English was financed by Monmouth, a merchant whose money, ships, and printing presses made it happen. Whitefield had Lady Huntington to fund his evangelism and raise money for multiple church plants throughout England, resulting in twenty-eight churches planted. Newton had John Thornton, who funded gospel preachers to occupy pulpits controlled by wealthy landowners. Paul had Priscilla and Aquila, Phoebe, and Erastus.

Erastus is one of the most surprising discoveries in Paul's missionary strategy. In 1929, archaeologists uncovered a slab that had the inscription "Erastus, in consideration of his aedileship, laid this pavement at his own expense." Erastus, according to Acts 19:22, Romans 16:23, and 2 Timothy 4:20, was a fellow worker and patron of Paul. He'd been so successful that, when he was promoted to aedile (curator of public works), he commemorated the laying of

---

2. Randy Alcorn, *The Treasure Principle* (Colorado Springs, CO: Multnomah, 2005), 67.

the road with the plaque that was discovered. Erastus helped Paul furnish his missionary journeys. Theophilus commissioned the accurate account of Luke's Gospel and Acts.

No stranger to raising funds (1 Cor. 16:1), Paul asked the Romans to support him as slingshots from Rome to Spain, "I hope to see you in passing as I go to Spain, and to be helped on my journey there by you" (Rom. 15:24 ESV). Jesus was supported by three wealthy women: ". . . and also some women who had been healed of evil spirits and infirmities: Mary, called Magdalene, from whom seven demons had gone out, and Joanna, the wife of Chuza, Herod's household manager, and Susanna, and many others, who provided for them out of their means" (Luke 8:2–3 ESV). As a planter, never be ashamed to have a wealthy friend undertake for you as a patron or partner.

Unless you change your perspective from fund-raising to mutual partnership, it will continue to feel weird. Fund-raising is charity. Partnership is a two-way street that benefits both parties. Scott Morton, author of *Funding Your Ministry*, advises a missionary to "focus on the giver, not the amount" and quotes Paul in Philippians 4:17 (ESV), "Not that I desire your gifts; what I desire is that more be credited to your account." Paul knows that their partnership will benefit them spiritually. Therefore he exhorted the Corinthians to up their game in 2 Corinthians 8:7, "But since you excel in everything—in faith, in speech, in knowledge, in complete earnestness and in the love we have kindled in you—see that you also excel in this grace of giving." Admittedly, Paul's Greek in 2 Corinthians 8 and 9 is, according to N. T. Wright, "very labored and tortured," saying something about Paul in a mix of passion and awkwardness.[3]

RULES FOR ROOKIES

Rookie fundraisers try to take the easy way of funding by making calls or asking for funds via email. Those are good tools, but not great ones. They will help to firm up your funding strategy, but they are not the goal. Always ask for funds in person, if possible. The Navigators organization did a study of 7,401 appeals from 100 Navigator staff in which they discovered that 46% of the face-to-face appeals resulted in monthly pledges. Telephone calls resulted in a 27% response, personal letters garnered 14%, and group meetings like church services resulted in a 9% response.[4]

---

3. N. T. Wright, *Paul: A Biography*, 308.
4. Scott Morton, *Funding Your Ministry* (Colorado Springs, CO: NavPress, 2007), 76.

Therefore, the goal of any fundraiser should be to get someone in a room, to sit face-to-face at a table with them, and have a meal. Food is an informal way to meet that dispels the awkwardness of fundraising conversations. If you don't have any mashed potatoes to focus on during the awkward silence or a cup of coffee to reach for, you'll be wondering what to do with your hands. Plus, eating a meal together is an essential part of developing a relationship, and developing a relationship with your donors is the most crucial element. If you approach your donors as people to whom you can minister, rather than banks from which you withdraw, it will change your entire perspective regarding the partnership.

If it is a church, rather than an individual, to whom you are appealing, it is important to identify the type of donors they are and the relationship they will want with your church plant. Besides sending churches, there are also supporting churches. Supporting churches don't necessarily take the full burden of your support or sending, but they have attached themselves to your mission, champion your cause, and proudly "own you" as one of their missionaries whom they support, even if it's partial. They may send you only one or two hundred dollars a month, but that money is invaluable to helping you keep the lights on.

BUDGETING FROM MISSION AND VALUES

Before you can ask someone to give, you should know how much you need. The first thing a large donor will ask about is your budget. The bigger the donor, the more detailed your budget needs to be. People who possess more money also know how to invest wisely. Therefore, it's important that you become as clear as possible when making and presenting a church budget.

Tasked with making up a budget for New Breed years ago, I didn't have a clue where to start. The church planting concierge at an organization named *Evangelical Christian Credit Union* removed the mystique from making a budget by instructing me to start with New Breed's values and mission and working backward from there.

What are your values?
What do you feel God calling you to do?

He explained that people will give to your values more than to your needs. Therefore, fundraisers must communicate the unique and specific ways God has called you to mission. Once you know your values, you can set goals. To make a good budget, you have to start with the goals that your values are driving you to accomplish.

New Breed's goals in 2021:

- Ensure that our planters are the best cared for on the planet.
- Plant twenty team church plants.
- Identify four hub cities in every quadrant in the US.
- Train two hundred church planters.
- Find twenty partner churches and organizations to collaborate with.

The next step is to break down what it would cost the organization to accomplish these goals. What training, staffing, coaching, and resources would each step require? Without those elements, there's no tangible way for a donor to feel that they've contributed to real kingdom impact on the ground. These results are what you'll report on regularly to keep your donor base informed. Therefore start with your values, define your mission, list your goals, and determine from there what it would cost to accomplish those goals. One word of caution: Don't cheap out on funding the mission. Remember that it's your butt in the chair, as John Glenn, the first astronaut to orbit earth, reportedly expressed: "As I hurtled through space, one thought kept crossing my mind—every part of this rocket was supplied by the lowest bidder."[5]

PERSISTENCE WINS THE DAY

Every rookie fundraiser dreads making that first call, but your demeanor matters. You're not asking for welfare, but for a partnership that will change lives. Asking them to partner with you on God's mission is not asking them to do you a favor; it's you paying them the respect of considering them partners. As an inspiration, consider that the author of *The God Ask* profiles a staff member who followed his instructions and raised 100 percent of her support in ninety-two days (from June 29th to October 1st). She sent 180 letters or emails, then spent thirty-nine hours on the phone making follow-up calls. Twenty-nine people she called said no to a follow-up appointment, whereas 101 said yes.

---

5. "Remembering John Glenn," NPR, December 9, 2016, https://www.npr.org/2016/12/09/5049 30256/remembering-john-glenn.

- Sixty became monthly supporters.
- Twenty-two gave a one-time gift.
- Nineteen said no.

Vince Antonucci planted a church called *The Verve* just off the Vegas strip where fundraising was essential to his survival. Antonucci reports that most church planters send out a few letters to people they think will support them and then wonder why nobody does. The problem is that they did it wrong.

Antonucci advocates the following steps for raising church plant funding from *individual* donors:[6]

1. Start with a spreadsheet and list every person you know, including people you haven't spoken to in years. Include the people you think would *never* support you and people who don't have faith. People you never imagined would support you will surprise you.
2. Begin by phoning every individual on that list, asking if it's okay to send them a letter about your church plant. Say, "I don't know if you've heard, but this is really cool . . . I'm starting a church." If you're not enthusiastic about it, why it's important, and how it's going to reach and impact people, they won't be either. They will donate to the missionary who inspires them.
3. Send the letter.
4. Call them a few days after they get the letter to follow up. Antonucci warns that you "have to rescue the letter from the fruit bowl." He tells the story of somebody who completed the first three steps but failed to follow up. After nobody responded, she thought about her successful lawyer brother who believed in her and believed in mission, wondering why he hadn't supported her. Antonucci pressed her to call after weeks went by. When she called, she asked why he wasn't going to support her, and he responded, "Of course we're going to support you." She pressed him, "Well, then why didn't you send back the commitment card and tell me 'yes'?" "Oh—it's in the fruit bowl," he replied. "When we got that letter, we threw it in the fruit bowl on the table to discuss later how much we wanted to support you for. We threw it in the fruit bowl and we just totally forgot about it. Thanks for reminding us!" Whether or not your donors have a fruit bowl that mail goes into, you must always rescue your letter from the fruit bowl.

---

6. Taken from an interview with Vince Antonucci with the author and Pete Mitchell on the *Church Planter* podcast, episode 69, aired May 11, 2014.

For raising funding with churches, Antonucci suggests:

1. Write down every church with which you have a connection.
2. Call them like you did the individuals on the first list and have a similar conversation.
3. Write the letter. The letter for churches is different, because the letter for an individual focuses more on you and your family raising support. The letter to the church is focused on the church you will plant, instead of on you.
4. Call and follow up on the letter within a few days. Make the phone call to the person on staff with whom you have the best relationship, but who also has the most authority. Be aware that a positive response is usually pending, based on an upcoming missions meeting where they might submit your request for approval. Your response should be to ask for the date and then ask if you can call the next day to find out the result of the decision. A "no" response will sound more like, "Things are tight right now," or, "We already are supporting two church plants, so we don't really have more room in our budget." When you receive this type response, it is not a final "no" answer. Respond by saying, "I totally understand. Could I call you back within the year just in case that circumstance changes?" People seldom tell you "no."
5. Call back in six months if a time was not specified. Some churches will tell you that they have an annual meeting where they decide these things. If this is the case, call before that meeting or ask when the best time would be to call in anticipation of the meeting; you want to allow them to get ready and actually consider your proposal.
6. Call again. When you call back, change your request. You don't want to seem pushy or stubborn. If you asked for a certain amount (i.e., $50,000 over three years), when you call back, ask for half that amount. If they say that they can't do that, ask if you can call back again in a few months.
7. Call again. When you call back you could say, "I know I asked you to consider giving $25,000 over three years—maybe part of your thought process is that you don't know where you're going be in three years; I understand that. But right now, I have to buy equipment, I'm going to be doing whatever it is, and it's going to cost $10,000. Could you just give me $10,000 right now?" If they take it to the committee, follow up. If the answer is no, ask if you can call back again.
8. Call again. When you call back you could say, "Would you send a mission team with enough money for them to do the things they're going

to do? We're going to send this team out, and they're going to serve the community in these kinds of ways. It's going to cost about $1,500 for their week of serving. Would you guys be willing to send a mission team for $1,500?" I know of people who have asked a church for $50,000 and called repeatedly, getting no for an answer to $25,000, $10,000, and right down to $500. Then about a year later, the planter received a call from that church saying, "We are going to give you $64,000 over the next three years. We just did a financial campaign and we prayed and we felt like we should tithe what we brought in, and so we' re going to give it to you because we've talked to you so much and know what you're doing is really important. We didn't have the money before, but now we do." If they see you're persistent and on fire for the mission, it instills confidence in them.

WRITING A LETTER

Your letter should reflect who you are. Don't just speak to the mission and dismiss the relationship. Share what your family has been up to, what you've been feeling, and a miniature version of your vision. End by telling them that you'll be contacting them soon to get together with them for a cup of coffee, or, if they live far away, you'll be making a phone call to talk with them. You will notice a difference between the older and younger generations in response. Hugh Halter observes,

> Culturally, those under forty have shifted their value sets. Fifty years ago, one of the highest virtues was "loyalty," and people would give faithfully to the church, trusting the institution and the leaders to use the money wisely. And even if they didn't agree with a building fund or focus, or the corporate finances, they would continue to give simply because they trusted the spiritual hierarchy. Not anymore. Today's believers are not loyal or blindly trusting. One of their highest values is "meaning," and they will only give to what they see is making a visible difference, or what they perceive will. Bring them meaning at a personal level. You may argue with this at a philosophical level, but you will not be able to fight it at the street level.[7]

---

7. Hugh Halter, *BiVo* (Denver, CO: Missio Publishing, 2013), 11.

After the initial greetings, tell them what God has been doing in your life personally, then share the vision. Share about the community and what you think God's calling you to do there. Tell a story. Share needs, but don't beg. Ultimately, this isn't an asking letter. It's a telling letter. You're not asking for their money; you're asking for their ear. Your goal in this letter is to schedule another meeting. Therefore, you're to make this letter the most exciting thing in the universe. Pray over it, pore over it, read it, re-read it, edit it, and bounce it off others. Remember that you aren't looking for benefactors; you're looking for gospel partners.

THE FOLLOW-UP CALL

Make two separate lists, one for people who live near you, and one for people far away. For now, don't worry about those who are nearby, just start contacting the people who live far away. Phone conversations are the best you can do in that case.

1. Begin by asking if they received your letter.
2. If they say yes, pause and allow them to talk.
3. If they say no, then just run through the content with them.
4. Afterward, ask them what they think about what you've said.

It's always good to get some feedback. Don't be surprised if people don't understand what you're saying, or if the idea to plant a church sounds strange to them. Before you end the conversation, ask them if they'd be willing to support you by praying for you. To that end, you should ask them if they'd mind receiving a monthly, bi-monthly, or semi-annual support letter that will update them on everything you are doing. Paul included a detailed account of his plans in almost every letter that he wrote, sharing where he'd been and where he was going. He also closed every letter with a request for prayer. Before you get off the phone, ask them if there is anything about which you can pray for them. Remember that you are ministering to their spiritual needs as part of your partnership.

THE SIX RS

Patrick McLaughlin, author of *The Major Donor Game Plan,* is responsible for fundraising at the famous Carnegie Hall. In his book, he outlines the six Rs of fundraising. They are:

Research

Finding out what makes your partners tick helps you report to them. One donor might want to hear about new ground taken, while another might want stories of personal life transformation. One might just want the results. Mclaughlin admonishes that "the quality of your ministry vision will impact the quantity of major/mega donor participation."[8] In other words, the more money you need to raise, the more refined your vision presentation needs to be.

Romance

You will have raving fans. Eighty percent of your income will come from twenty percent of your donor base.[9] Romance is the long-term relationship you're going to build with people. Otherwise, people are simply tipping you.

Request

This is where you meet, talk, advocate for your ministry, and eventually ask for a commitment in terms of financial partnership. Once you've done your research and built the romance of relationship, you need to ask strategically. You should not use a cookie-cutter formula like asking each giver to give $25; rather, you should know your audience. If you're meeting with a millionaire, you might say, "John, I'm looking to raise $125,000 by the end of the year and was hoping you might be willing to give $25,000." This is specific, and not a small amount, but you've been strategic, clear, direct, and not presumptuous. You've shared your hope and have not pressured. You've also not embarrassed yourself or your donor by asking for $100. You've demonstrated that you understand who you're talking to and that you value the contribution they can make.

Recognition

Once somebody gives, it's important to thank them. The bigger the gift, the more you should thank them. Thanking somebody who gives twenty dollars will mean the world, but how far that money can stretch will make it seem like overkill and part of your "process" if you keep waxing on too thick. The larger the gift, however, the more you should massage the gratitude. Send a handwritten note. Have a recipient do the same. Text a picture to them of what their giving has made possible. Meet with them to give an update mid-year or even quarterly, full of stories about how it helped you reach your goals.

---

8. McLaughlin, *Major Donor Game Plan*, 84.
9. Scott Morton, *Funding Your Ministry* (Colorado Springs, CO: NavPress, 2007), 38.

Recruitment

You'll need a pit crew to help with newsletters, making deposits, preparing financial statements, organizing fundraising events, and recruiting new donors.

Reporting

"Like cold water to a weary soul is good news from a distant land" (Prov. 25:25). McLaughlin shares four steps for reporting to donors.[10] First, as he does with everything else in these steps, he asks that you aim for face-to-face meetings. From there, the steps are as follows:

1. Be genuine.
2. Focus on what God is accomplishing.
3. Share stories.
4. Give a prayer update.

Now, let's apply those four principles about reporting leads to the practice of writing follow-up newsletters.

FOLLOW-UP NEWSLETTERS

After your initial letter, you'll need to start sending follow-up newsletters. Paul modeled how to write a follow-up support letter in his letter to the Corinthians,

"Because of the service by which you have proved yourselves, others will praise God for the obedience that accompanies your confession of the gospel of Christ, and for your generosity in sharing with them and with everyone else. And in their prayers for you their hearts will go out to you, because of the surpassing grace God has given you" (2 Cor. 9:13–14 ESV).

McLaughlin deconstructs the passage, identifying that it demonstrates four things that happen "when someone makes a sacrificial gift: (a) the gift meets a need, (b) the gift causes the receiver to praise God, (c) the gift proves that the giver genuinely loves God, and (d) the receiver is prompted to pray for the giver."[11]

Newsletters are one of the most powerful tools in the church planter's arsenal when it comes to raising funds. Marketers swear by them. Entrepreneurs attend conferences costing thousands of dollars to learn to master their use because so many things can be accomplished with a newsletter. Newsletters

---

10. McLaughlin, *Major Donor Game Plan*, 143.
11. McLaughlin, *Major Donor Game Plan*, 143.

allow you to communicate anything you want to: ministry news, needs, prayer requests, family stuff, and useless trivia. Consider the care that Nehemiah poured into the response to King Artaxerxes's question before he penned it in Nehemiah 2:4–10. Nehemiah's appeal was deliberate, directive, and distressed. If you write it well, people get to know you and your mission better, which is valuable in the process of getting people to connect with you.

The first thing to consider is the format. Experts argue that a four-page spread (two-pages front and back) is the best format. The rationale for the four-page spread is so you can have various "articles." For the millennial-aged reader, four pages seems too long. Know your audience. With regard to print versus email newsletters, online communication provides instant links to online donation platforms, but it also makes it easier to delete.

Whatever format you have chosen for your newsletter, it should possess the following elements:

1. featured news
2. a story of life change
3. a testimonial from someone who has been impacted by your ministry
4. upcoming events to pray for or participate in
5. a featured resource that has been blessing you
6. contact information
7. a link to your donation portal

CONCLUSION

Although I have worked at no cost to the churches I've planted, these projects have not been free. They have always cost somebody, somewhere, something significant. Planters need the backing and finances of kingdom partners to establish an outpost, but trying to fund the war all by oneself is foolish, according to Jesus. Wise planters will train themselves to battle with the necessary equipment, backup, and leadership; although these advantages do not guarantee victory for the mission, they can help even up the odds.

REFLECT

- What is your plan for making gospel partnerships and recruiting patrons?
- Why would a church planter keep all three streams of funding active at all times?

DISCUSS

- What feelings emerge when you think of building gospel partnerships?
- Describe what receiving a rejection for your invitation to partner on mission would feel like?
- Suppose someone you know says, "I don't want to support a missionary!" Why would he or she say that? What is potentially wrong with that? What would your response be?

CHALLENGE

- Draw up a list of your top two hundred people to contact and implement a plan to call them in the next two months.
- Draft up a list of all your needs and assign names next to each of them.

REDISCOVERING KINGDOM COLLABORATION NETWORKS FOR MULTIPLICATION

From Building Upward to
Spreading Outward

20

FORMING NETWORKS FOR RAPID MULTIPLICATION

Well, you're either part of the problem, part of the solution . . . or you're just part of the landscape.

—ROBERT DE NIRO AS SAM IN *RONIN*

What do you consider the end game of church planting? Beginning with the end in mind will help you to plant beyond your church plant, accelerating you toward multiplication from day one. Rick Warren said, "Our churches are growing, living organisms, and therefore will naturally produce. If we're not reproducing, it's a sign something is unhealthy in our congregations."[1] The New Testament model was built upon principles of expansion from Jerusalem to the ends of the earth. One of the leaders I greatly respect, Vance Pitman, has sent out sixty-eight churches from Las Vegas in the past ten years. Vance asserts that everything changed when he stopped focusing on establishing his own church and started focusing on his city. His church is now a multiplication hub planting world-wide, and echoes Wesley who once stated, "All the world is my parish."[2]

Alan J. Roxburgh, in his book *Structured for Mission*, observes that the telling conversations happen after the denominational meetings at the restaurants and cafes where delegates informally debrief. In Protestant circles, denominations are chiefly organized around issues of orthodoxy and orthopraxy, but in the present time, younger leaders are forming affinity groups that center

---

1. Rick Warren quotation taken from Gene Wilson and Craig Ott, *Global Church Planting: Biblical Principals and Best Practices for Multiplication* (Grand Rapids: Baker Academic, 2011), vii.

2. John Wesley, *The Journal of John Wesley* (Grand Rapids: Christian Classics Ethereal Library, 2000), chapter 3, Journal Entry Monday, 1.

around mission. This is where networks seem to be proving more valuable to modern society. Roxburgh points to the popular television series *Downton Abbey* to illustrate that in all organizations form determines function. He notes, "Downton Abbey revolves around a structure that shaped a whole way of life. It's more euphemistic description was 'upstairs-downstairs.' Behind structures lie these deeper cultural values."[3] The show depicts the younger generation abandoning the older traditional structures, in favor of ideals. That is exactly what the younger generation of ministers is doing today. Roxburgh asserts, "The possibility that is emerging is for denominations to remake themselves in the form of a distributed network in relationship with multiple local contexts generating experiments and responses to the challenges of mission and ministry at this time. This doesn't require these denominations to start with major organizational or structural change."[4] John Wesley established a mission-centric structure when he organized networks of preachers who rotated within the circuits. When the old attitudes prevailed in Dublin, he wrote them a letter instructing them "to forget past problems, to focus on the remedy to problems that he had helped them work through, told them 'let each wheel keep its own place.' He cautioned them not to encroach on each other's work, but to strive for expansion and challenged them to 'move together in harmony and love'."[5]

In 2014 a Baptist church in Washington planted an Anglican church. Barry Crane, the pastor of the church, asked a group of leaders, "What would it look like if instead of a traditional church-planting model—planting our denomination in a different geography—we looked at it from a missiological viewpoint? What if we saw the unreached people groups in our area? Who in our community is not being reached by existing churches?" After doing an unreached people group study through Percept Group, they found 17,000 people within a three-mile radius who said that they would prefer a more liturgical, "high church" worship experience. Because they were a part of the Converge network, they had seen them "give money and people away." So they contacted Bishop Todd Hunter and discussed how to plant an Anglican church within their church space. Along with a lease, they provided mentorship to the young couple planting the church. This has spawned other partnerships, as well.[6] Collaboration formed around mission is the future of the church today as it was in the past.

---

3. Alan J. Roxburgh, *Structured for Mission: Renewing the Culture of the Church* (Downers Grove, IL: InterVarsity Press, 2015), 21.

4. Roxburgh, *Structured for Mission*, 132.

5. John Hucks, "John Wesley and Eighteenth Century Methodist Movement: A Model for Effective Leadership" (PhD diss., Point Loma Nazarene University, 2003), 78.

6. "The Peculiar Tale of an Anglican-Baptist Church Plant: Why Would Two Distinctly Different Denominations Work Together? and What Have They Learned?" Interview by Kevin Miller and Kyle

FIRST-CENTURY NETWORKS

Every time multiple churches were planted within a geographical area in the first-century, a local network of churches in relationship was formed. Networks, in turn, lead to greater levels of multiplication because networks mean strength in numbers, shared common goals, and pooled resources. Every church planting movement starts with a local network, as Paul discovered on his first mission. He planted a series of churches throughout the region of Galatia (Iconium, Lystra, and Derbe), and penned a circular letter addressing them as a network of churches known as the letter to the *Galatians*. The Galatian cities were Lystra, Iconium, and Antioch. "They preached the gospel in that city and won a large number of disciples. Then they returned to **Lystra, Iconium and Antioch**" (Acts 14:21). Each time Paul grouped them together, he was acknowledging a local geographic network.

Paul came to **Derbe** and then to **Lystra**, where a disciple named Timothy lived, whose mother was Jewish and a believer but whose father was a Greek. The believers at **Lystra** and **Iconium** spoke well of him. (Acts 16:1–2)

. . . what kinds of things happened to me in **Antioch**, **Iconium** and **Lystra**, the persecutions I endured. Yet the Lord rescued me from all of them. (2 Tim. 3:11)

Similarly, Jesus addressed the seven churches of Asia as a local network in Revelation 2 and 3. Paul wrote the epistle to the Romans and addressed it to multiple churches in the massive city (Rom. 16). Similarly, he wrote the circular letter to the Ephesian network, to be circulated among the seven churches of Asia, which explains why personal greetings are absent from it, unlike Paul's letters. This also explains why Tertullian called it the letter to the Laodiceans.[7] Local networks were how the early church spread outward. To see the same spread and gospel saturation of Christianity today, planters must think beyond their own church plants and imagine networks of churches. If this was natural to them, why does it seem novel to us?

If one traces Paul's movements during his first missionary journey, two networks can be identified:

Rohane, Christianity Today, November 12, 2019, https://www.christianitytoday.com/pastors/2019/november-web-exclusives/peculiar-tale-of-anglican-baptist-church-plant.html.

7. Mike Breen, *The Apostle's Notebook* (Eastbourne, England: Kingsway, 2002), 153.

- Tarsus to Antioch (Acts 11)
- Antioch to Cypress (Acts 13)—The Cypriote Network
- Cypress to Turkey (Acts 14)—The Galatian Network
- Turkey back to Antioch (Acts 14)

We have no evidence of a network surrounding Antioch, but Antioch grandfathered networks as Paul and Barnabas's sending church. His first missionary journey to Galatia had taught him that heresy spread quickly, whereas his second journey taught him that networks caused the gospel to travel faster. On Paul's second missionary journey, the Macedonian network was spawned. Besides clocking up the miles on the odometer and scoring frequent planter miles, he also spent significant time in jail for "bad behavior." Paul realized that he'd probably not be hanging up his harmonica anytime soon and that the likelihood of future incarcerations meant he needed to clone himself. Even if he was chained, the gospel wasn't. If he could train an army of planters, a city hub would become a more strategic command headquarters than a jail cell. Therefore, for the first time since embarking on mission, Paul stayed in one place for somewhere between two and three years (Acts 19:10).

Creating the Ephesus network was so effective at fostering multiplication that, after his third missionary journey, he could write, "But now that there is no more place for me to work in these regions" (Rom. 15:23). As Paul penned these words, he was on his way to Spain via Rome. He equated the establishment of multiplication networks with a "mission accomplished" status in the Mediterranean. He greeted over thirty people in chapter 16, despite having never been to Rome himself. This proves his aptitude at creating interchangeable strike teams who could work within local networks. Priscilla and Aquila were there, among others. They had once been a part of both the Corinthian and Ephesian networks. Therefore, Paul had no need to minister in Rome, since a local network was in place and would naturally foster multiplication.

As Paul departed Ephesus three years later, he knew that wolves would come and tear that flock, yet he also knew the Ephesian elders would be able to hold their own against them. If Galatia was a failure, it was a failure because it couldn't function without Paul's constant presence. However, by establishing networks of churches under apostolic ministers, Paul was able to leave knowing that others would continue the work of training, preaching, and multiplication, which would lead to kingdom expansion. Independent networks focus on reproducing and training leaders so the network can function without its founder. He had fostered a network that had graduated beyond him; this is the most desirable goal for every church planter.

To start a local network, therefore, a planter can observe and follow these Pauline practices:

1. Plant your church with the intention of creating a network.
2. Determine that your church will become a hub of church planting.
3. Hardwire the conviction that the church plant itself will not be the main focus of the future.
4. Focus on your region instead of your church.
5. Train teams of leaders who will not be content with the idea of staying in one place.
6. Constantly seed the message that today's church plants should be tomorrow's sending churches.

When Paul wrote to the Romans that there was "no more work left" for him in the region because "from Jerusalem and all the way around to Illyricum I have fulfilled the ministry of the gospel of Christ" (Rom. 15:19 ESV), he was describing the fruit of his network of networks. If one traces the geographic outline comprised by these words, one sees that Paul defined the entire region around the north rim of the Mediterranean as reached because he had set multiplying networks in place. No one would claim that the city of New York was reached by the planting of a single church, but if the goal was to catalyze a movement of reproducing churches there, all that would be necessary is to place the multiplying DNA into a local network in that region as Paul had in Thessalonica.

Further, Paul was convinced that Illyricum, which was the westernmost part of the empire, was also being reached by others he'd deployed. Paul had not been everywhere in the Roman Empire, but he had established six networks, each branching out from a strategic hub. Every time Paul deposited a hub in an area, he considered it a fulfillment of his missionary responsibility there. Thus, Paul defined a region as reached once he had established networks of churches there.

Consider the networks Paul founded on his successive journeys between Jerusalem and Illyricum:

- First missionary journey—The Isle of Cypriote Network (Paphos and other towns), and the Galatian Network (including Iconium, Derbe, Lystra)
- Second missionary journey—The Macedonian Network (Philippi, Thessalonica, Berea, Athens, and Corinth)

- Third missionary journey—The Asian Network (The Ephesus Network consisting of the seven churches of Asia) and the Cretian Network
- Bonus network—The Roman Network of churches (house churches within the city)

Paul's seven networks are pictured here:

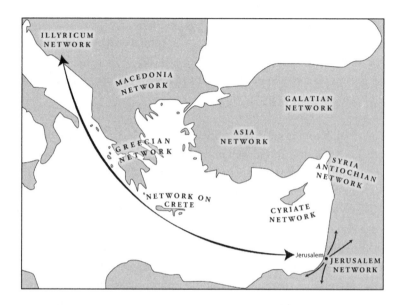

Paul writes of his fourth and undocumented missionary journey to the Romans, making note that, during his brief years on the field, he had followed the existing nautical and overland trade routes and formed familiar circuits for his followers. In so doing, he had formed what the Methodists would name a "Connexion" 1,700 years later. Admittedly, the church can be a bit slow to catch on. What if, instead of remaining stationary at one plant, we ministered to multiple churches within a local network?

Contrast our method of multiplication with that of Paul's first-century methods:

First-Century Ministry	Twenty-First-Century Ministry
Rapid deployment	Slow to plant
Cheaply funded	Expensive to plant
Strong networks	Shortsighted regarding other churches
Greater multiplication	93% not multiplying

The goal of this chapter is to present a network paradigm that will foster more effective training, as well as intentional models for greater multiplication. First, we must recognize that there are various types of networks.

Networks are generally centered around a church planting hub that constitutes the center of operations. *The Underground Network* in Tampa, Florida, is centered around the hub that Brian Sanders has established. Vance Pitman's Hope church in Las Vegas as well as the Summit Church in Raleigh, North Carolina, welcome planters from outside the area to intern and plant out. Regardless of how hubs are founded, they function like Antioch, Ephesus, or Corinth. These churches, however, were not the same types of hubs. There are a few different types of hubs described in the New Testament:

1. Affinity Hubs—Jerusalem
2. Catalyst Hubs—Antioch
3. Collaboration Hubs—Lystra and Derbe
4. Training Hubs—Ephesus

Affinity Hubs—Jerusalem

An affinity hub is a type of network that focuses on reaching a particular type of person. Jerusalem was led by twelve apostles bent on reaching the twelve tribes of Israel. This was the model Rick Warren used for his network of plants throughout Orange County, California, aimed at converting yuppies in the 1990s. Despite their local focus (the Jerusalem church was focused exclusively on the Jewish population), these churches pushed the mission beyond their own borders by transplanting church plants afar.[8]

Jerusalem spread the gospel throughout Judea, becoming a mothership of church planting under the persecution of Saul, accidentally sending exiles northward and sparking new mission outposts. As people were converted throughout Judea, Samaria and, eventually even Antioch, they lent support by sending others to help; yet, they kept their focus upon reaching the Jews. Jerusalem sent Barnabas up to Antioch when word reached them that there was a burgeoning gospel work.

Without Jerusalem hubs, the kingdom of God would not expand. They raise up and release leaders on their ministry team that they are willing to catapult outward. Not only did they send Barnabas early on to Antioch, but they continued releasing leaders to advance the kingdom: "Then it seemed good

---

8. Some would actually argue that the Jerusalem church was doing exactly what was necessary to reach the Jewish community in Jerusalem. Paul's arrest there seems to indicate that any move towards reaching out to the Gentiles in Jerusalem would have resulted in more barriers to the gospel.

to the apostles and the elders, with the whole church, to choose men from among them and send them to Antioch with Paul and Barnabas. They sent Judas called Barsabbas, and Silas, leading men among the brothers" (Acts 15:22 ESV). In the Acts 1:8 schema, they appear to be focusing primarily on their local Jerusalem, but not at the expense of the ends of the earth.

Catalyst Hubs—Antioch

Catalyst hubs take the forward missional momentum that their church plants have created and multiply themselves outward. They possess strong leadership (fist) teams, but also send strike teams. As a gateway city, Antioch's open door faced the open sea of the Mediterranean, the jumping-off point for missionary endeavors to the rest of the Gentile world.

Once Paul and Barnabas cut their teeth in ministry there for a year, they agreed to be sent out by the Antiochian elders. Antioch initially funded them, laid hands on them (ordination), released them to plant multiple churches, and received them back again to hear their missionary reports. When somebody debates whether individuals plant churches or churches plant churches, it's good to remind them that apostles plant churches, and Antioch released Paul and Barnabas, yet maintained no direct oversight of the churches they planted. In this way, Antioch church hubs released apostolic leaders to catalyze networks elsewhere. They may not be level-5 churches (or churches that multiply to the fourth generation), but they have reached level 4 (a reproducing church that has planted out of itself a minimum of one time), simply by caring enough to send their very best.

They also fund mission. Prior to meeting Priscilla and Aquila, Paul may have been funded from Antioch to engage in frontline mission work, only falling back upon tent making if he was in dire straits. Upon returning to Antioch, Paul gives a missionary report: "On arriving there (Antioch), they gathered the church together and reported all that God had done through them and how he had opened a door of faith to the Gentiles. And they stayed there a long time with the disciples" (Acts 14:27–28 ESV). It may be that when Paul says, "I robbed other churches," (2 Cor. 11:8–9 ESV) he spoke of Antioch.

Today, these types of networks may support mission by funding and sending. If you attended their churches on a Sunday, you'd draw the conclusion that they were insular and feel sorry for them; but, if you analyzed their mission budget, you'd feel sorry for planters who weren't on their list. As Antioch served as an internship for Paul and Barnabas to witness ministry among the Gentiles prior to embarking on mission, Antioch churches tend to produce internship programs.

Collaborative Hubs (Iconium, Lystra, and Derbe)

These churches were of note among the Galatian region. Collaborative churches are typically small, but together they form a network of encouragement with other small churches. On their own, they are unable to properly fund, train, and support a planter, but they want to see planters raised up and sent out.

Timothy came from the Galatian network of Iconium, Lystra, and Derbe, which operated as a type of farm system for future leaders and church planters. These churches work together to plant out from themselves. Today these networks may be a citywide collaboration that bands together to fund, train, and coach a planter. The New Breed Network provides *citywide* training to help collaborative churches work together to further multiplication.

Ephesus Hubs

Every multiplication network possesses a hub, a point of origin, out of which the other churches have been planted. Ephesus was *the* hub of Macedonia, but one could argue that it was the model hub of the New Testament. Not only did Paul spend more time there than anywhere else, the apostle John resided there along with Mary, the mother of Jesus. Patmos was an island prison colony accessed by boat from the Ephesus harbor, making it John's home church even when he was in exile. Ephesus was clearly one of the epicenters of apostolic activity in the first century. By the time the writing of the New Testament closed, it was the primary center for mission operations.

The importance of Ephesus as a strategic hub was demonstrated by the fact that Paul sent his best partner, Timothy, to pastor them for a time (Timothy was stationed in Ephesus when he received 1 and 2 Timothy as letters). He boasts of Timothy to the Philippians: "For I have no one like him, who will be genuinely concerned for your welfare" (Phil. 2:20 ESV). Timothy was nearly a carbon copy of Paul, which is why he provides such high praise of him, "For though you have countless guides in Christ, you do not have many fathers. For I became your father in Christ Jesus through the gospel. *I urge you, then, be imitators of me.* That is why I sent you Timothy, my beloved and faithful child in the Lord, *to remind you of my ways in Christ*, as I teach them everywhere in every church" (1 Cor. 4:15–17 ESV, emphasis mine). To emphasize just how strategic Ephesus was to Paul's ministry, two of the pastoral epistles were written about how to deal with Ephesus (The Pastoral Epistles to Timothy), and the letter of Ephesians, of course, had been written directly to the Ephesian church itself. It is the only city in the New Testament to have three letters written to it. One could argue that it was addressed a fourth time in Revelation by a letter from Jesus recorded by John.

Perhaps this special attention given to Ephesus was because it was there that the apostolic genius of Paul's missional strategy reached its zenith. After preaching the gospel in the synagogue at Ephesus for three months, arguing persuasively, Paul left the unresponsive Jews and "took the disciples with him and had discussions daily in the lecture hall of Tyrannus." The hall of Tyrannus (literally the hall of the "tyrant," "absolute ruler," or "despot") was probably a nickname given by one of his students, much like the moniker "The Great Knock" bestowed by C. S. Lewis on his tutor because he could give you an intellectual bashing if you weren't on your toes. "[Tyrannus's] pupils evidently attended his lectures in the cooler hours of the day and then teacher and pupils alike went home towards noon for their siesta;" then, during the middle of the day, Paul likely had the use of the hall and held public debate there."[9]

"This continued for two years, so that all the residents of Asia heard the word of the Lord, both Jews and Greeks" (Acts 19:10). During that tenure, Paul was training those disciples to reach their community as missionaries. The training that went on in the lecture hall (Acts 19:9) resulted in the entire province of Asia hearing the gospel, "So that all the Jews and Greeks who lived in the province of Asia heard the word of the Lord" (Acts 19:10).

Luke amplifies this effect of establishing a hub in the region by repeating it two more times:

. . . the name of the Lord Jesus was held in high honor. (Acts 19:17)

. . . the word of the Lord spread widely and grew in power (Acts 19:20)

These verses most likely refer to this spread of the gospel by strike teams that were sent out of Ephesus into the surrounding mountainous regions to plant the other six churches. If you trace the order of churches addressed in Revelation 2 and 3, Jesus addresses them in a northward ascending order, listing Ephesus, Smyrna, and Pergamum, and then in a southward descending order, hitting Thyatira, Sardis, Philadelphia, and Laodicea.

If you traced the order of churches addressed with a red pen, you would roughly draw a letter "n" on the map. The order of the letters follows the geographic direction one would take to navigate around the finger-like mountain ranges separating the first three churches listed from the final four. If you were to deliver the letters to the seven churches, you would naturally leave Ephesus,

---

9. N. T. Wright, *Paul: A Biography* (San Francisco: Harper One, 2018), 245–46.

go up to Smyrna, and carry the letters in the order in which they are addressed. It's therefore likely that this was also the chronological order in which those churches were planted. From Ephesus, the churches would have been planted outward in a geographical ring, spiraling outward into a wider ellipse with every successive church plant.

It is my belief that Paul intentionally sent missionaries out from Ephesus to plant the network of the seven churches of Asia as the next step of strategic mission deployment during the two to three year stint we read about in Acts 19. As Paul trained them in mission, Priscilla and Aquila trained the missionaries bivocationally to franchise their tent-making business, like Guy Pfanz's coffee-roasting empire in the Midwest. Priscilla and Aquila owned homes in which the churches met at Rome, Corinth, and Ephesus, the three most significant church planting hubs outside of Antioch, demonstrating that they served a missiological function in each of them. When they encountered Apollos in Corinth, it is likely that they employed him after Paul left to carry on the work, facilitating future funding for himself as an emerging missionary. Perhaps they trained in the shops until Paul arrived in the hall of Tyrannus. Their bivocational tentmaking empire that supported missionaries to bring the gospel to new frontiers may explain why Paul wrote of Aquila and Priscilla that "*all* the churches of the Gentiles are grateful to them" (Rom. 16:4, emphasis mine).

During Paul's tenure time in Ephesus, his tentmaking directly funded the living expense of his fellow missionaries: "You yourselves know that these hands of mine have supplied my own needs *and the needs of my companions*" (Acts 20:34, emphasis mine). This was the antithesis of Paul's team supporting him financially, freeing him to preach in Corinth, for in Ephesus, Paul became the sender.

If this is an authentic church plantology principle, then it should be repeated throughout church history whenever multiplication movements have arisen. Movement scholar Steve Addison notes that the Moravians established a business in Herrnhut as a "center for prayer and worship" but also as a mission funding powerhouse much like Ephesus.[10] The Celtic Monastics in Ireland and Wales established "monasteries" that doubled as powerhouses of prayer and training hubs from which missionaries were sent out. In *The Celtic Way of Evangelism*, George G. Hunter III noted, "In broad outline, the emerging strategy of Aidan and his people looks familiar. First, they multiplied monastic

10. Steve Addison, *Movements that Changed the World: Five Keys to Spreading the Gospel* (Downers Grove, IL: InterVarsity Press, 2011), 41.

communities. We have no way of knowing how many such communities the movements spawned by Patrick, Columba, Aidan, and others established in the British Isles alone. John Finney cites evidence showing thirty-two monastic communities in the area of Worcester; that density would indicate many hundreds of monastic communities across the British Isles," that "sent apostolic teams to reach settlements within the region."[11]

Similarly, John Wesley, largely influenced by the mission hub of Herrnhut and his great respect for the Moravians, designed his chapel "The New Room" to be a three-story building with stables on the ground floor, a chapel on the second, and accommodations for circuit riders on the third. Wesley established a similar mission hub known as "The Foundry" in London years later, mirroring Paul's strategy in Ephesus. From these bases, Wesley strategized a preaching circuit, manned by circuit riders, to cover the whole land in evangelism and discipleship under the name "connectionalism."[12] At the Foundry alone, their base of operations from April to June 1739, the number of disciples grew from twelve to three hundred! Out of this burgeoning growth "lay preaching evolved more out of necessity than by design."[13] Of course, Wesley had already discovered what Jesus had demonstrated by sending the seventy-two, that the best way to train missionaries is to send them on mission.

Field Training in Ephesus

Over the years he spent locked in prison, Paul must have been convinced that he couldn't truly train church planters from a distance, from behind a desk, or even in a classroom. Therefore, he would need to provide *field training*, sending them out from Ephesus, as Jesus had sent the seventy-two, to get their hands dirty.[14] There is a saying in the world of martial arts training: "You can only fight the way you practice."

When I founded the New Breed Network in Europe, I was committed to training planters on the ground. We called sequential planting "ninja planting," and our Ephesus training hub was termed a multiplication dojo. In martial arts training, the dojo serves as a place to test the skills that one has learned in

---

11. George G. Hunter III, *The Celtic Way of Evangelism: How Christianity Can Reach the West . . . Again* (Nashville: Abingdon, 2010).

12. Richard P. Heitzenrater, *Wesley and the People Called the Methodists* (Nashville: Abingdon, 1995), 108.

13. Heitzenrater, *Wesley and the People Called the Methodists*, 113.

14. When I trained as a Starbucks barista, almost all of my training was learning by doing in a hands-on mentorship on the bar. In addition to a half day of training off-site in a classroom, I was allowed to take the store handbook home for two nights. The rest was getting my hands dirty and learning by doing. Starbucks has built a coffee empire training baristas like this.

the study of the discipline. I have purposefully used the term dojo to describe the type of training that Paul gave in the training hub in Ephesus. When you train in a dojo, there is immediate application. Whatever the Sensei trains the student in must be immediately put into practice, or the result is a fist punch to the head, or a swift foot to the solar plexus. So it is with front-line mission. Planter training should occur outside the church walls, with planters engaging in front-line mission until it becomes a reflex. What we teach them needs to become subconsciously absorbed as they "paint fence," "polish floor," and "wax on, wax off." Paul didn't just intern planters in Ephesus by lecturing them in the hall of Tyrannus. He sent them to plant the other seven churches of Asia.

Paul's Ephesian student Epaphras most likely planted the church in Colossae during his training in Ephesus. Originally a part of the "eight churches of Asia," Colossae had been destroyed in an earthquake by the time that Revelation was written, providing a last chance to those who would meet the same fate as the doomed citizens of Pompeii and reducing the number of Asian churches to seven after the disaster. Nevertheless, Epaphras was sent to plant there according to Paul's letter: "In the same way, the gospel is bearing fruit and growing through the whole world—just as it has been doing among you since the day you heard it and truly understood God's grace. *You learned it from Epaphras*, our dear fellow servant, who is a faithful minister of Christ on our behalf, and who also told us of your love in the Spirit" (Col. 1:6–8, emphasis mine). Epaphras was a serial planter who moved in strike teams with the other students. Thus, Paul's Ephesus hub was literally planting out of itself by means of his students deploying, as Paul sent them ahead to train in the field like Jesus sent the twelve and the seventy-two. N. T. Wright observed, "How much safer Paul would have been had he founded a seminary in Tarsus or Antioch and required future church leaders to sit at his feet day by day!"[15] Rather than caving to the temptation to stagnate mission by centering it around himself and his own brilliance, Paul chose to stay put so that he could better send out.

If we're going to train effectively, however, the seminary model that we are currently using will not suffice. Spurgeon, ever politically incorrect, described most ministers as hydrocephalic, declaring that their heads were out of proportion to the rest of their bodies.[16] Our training has been producing men and women who, despite their seminary degrees, are not able to do what we read

---

15. N. T. Wright and Michael F. Bird, *The New Testament in its World: An Introduction to the History, Literature, and Theology of the First Christians* (Grand Rapids: Zondervan Academic. 2015), 79.

16. Charles Spurgeon, *Lectures to My Students* (Pantianos Classics ebook edition, first published 1875), 751.

about in Acts. They *know* things, but they can't *do* things. More aptly, they know things about what they can't do. They will exposit all the passages about miracles, while never actually performing any. Leaders with letters behind their names lack spiritual power and prowess.

We produce leaders who can navigate fashion and church politics, gain social media followings, and discuss the finer points of theology over coffee. They know nothing of what Paul and his companions described on the front lines: "To this very hour we go hungry and thirsty, we are in rags, we are brutally treated, we are homeless" (1 Cor. 4:11). As someone who has both been beaten and gone hungry on mission, I can testify that these things have a way of providing a type of initiation into ministry from which you never completely return. Tozer preached so he wouldn't be invited back, and once remarked to Lloyd-Jones that he'd preached himself off every major stage in the country.[17] Whereas B. B. Warfield noted wryly that "the staple of Paul's preaching was God and judgment," today's generation of preachers wouldn't want the negative blow back on social media.[18]

Training must occur in stages, in a real-life church planting context, just as it did in Ephesus. It concerns me that we send planters out on their own before they have ever accompanied a seasoned church planting veteran on mission as the Twelve had accompanied Jesus prior to being sent out. Paul expressed that some types of ministry must be caught, not taught, when he wrote, "I long to see you so that I may impart to you some spiritual gift to make you strong" (Rom. 1:11). Ancient craftsmen and artists required years of apprenticeship, and church planting is not the exception to the rule. As Paul trained his students, he modeled gospel conversations as they worked in the marketplace making tents alongside him. Perhaps he would observe them as they took the lead with the next customer, quietly making tents in the background, storing his feedback away for the appropriate time when they were alone once more.

BENEFITS OF NETWORKS

Training is the essential key to building a planting network. By now you may have pieced together that I am advocating building your own network within your city by raising within, training up, and sending out to create local planting networks. Besides the obvious benefit of network hubs spreading the gospel exponentially, there are other benefits of networks:

17. James L. Snyder, *The Life of A.W. Tozer: In Pursuit of God* (Ventura, CA: Regal, 2009), 107.
18. Iain H. Murray, *David Martyn Lloyd-Jones: The First Forty Years 1899–1939* (Edinburgh, UK: The Banner of Truth Trust, 1983), 325.

1. A central multiplication strategy
2. Easier strike team formation
3. Greater funding
4. Shared personnel
5. Shared assessment
6. Shared training
7. Funding
8. Recruitment
9. Support
10. Identification and informed, intimate data regarding a target area
11. The shared best practices of different tribes and denominations
12. Kingdom collaboration
13. Wisdom in the multitude of counselors
14. Resourcing—centralized banking, bookkeeping, and equipment of multiple churches
15. Greater range of options regarding the type of relationship with sending churches
16. A wider base from which to build a core team
17. Greater prayer support
18. Greater fundraising capacity

Churches that work within a local planting network will find it easier to multiply. The shared resources of people like Epaphras make it easier to interchange personnel in and out of local congregations or new plants. For example, when I served as the evangelist at Lloyd-Jones's church, I assisted a shepherd who planted in the next town over. I was able to visit once a month for six months on Sundays, preaching the gospel, seeing a shower of new conversions every week that I visited, and thereby helping to grow the church. It is nearly impossible to maintain the rate of multiplication that Paul did if leaders try to stay at their post. But what if their post was to move around between six churches?

It might look something like this:

- A church is planted with a strike team of eight members.
- Within six to twelve months, half the team breaks off and moves on to plant again, taking some of the newer disciples with them.
- Within a similar timeframe, that team breaks off again, but this time newer strike team members have been trained, and some of the original team members from the first church plant come and join the third wave of churches after establishing a secure fist team.

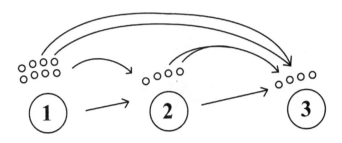

Paul specialized in teams that planted together in Ephesus. If the seven other churches of Asia churches were all planted during the three years that Paul was in Ephesus, that means that, starting with Ephesus, churches would have had to be planted at three-to-four month intervals, which was Paul's normal speed on his other missionary journeys; a time frame he was comfortable with.

Accompanying them may have been a team of equally gifted, qualified, experienced church planters, like Silas, Timothy, or Titus, who banded together for impact so they could spread out quicker once the foundation was adequately laid.

If we planted in teams like this, we'd see:

1. Stronger launches
2. Better-supported teams
3. Less loneliness for the planter
4. Greater impact
5. Faster multiplication
6. Greater pooled resources
7. A shared strategy of multiplication

This would be a stark contrast to how many denominations and networks are currently approaching planting.

The goal of strike teams planting within a localized network would be to reproduce sustainable church plants at an increased rate, while minimizing wasted time, wasted resources and, worst of all, wasted people who become busted up and broken-hearted when they fail. Instead of deploying five separate planters, the hub sends one planting team made up of five planters, like a rocket that will break up in stages when the time is right. Each of the five planters that plant the first church together are all hardwired for multiplication, and ready to deploy once the first church is established.

PLANTERS	YEAR 1	YEAR 2	YEAR 3	YEAR 4	YEAR 5	NET GAIN
PLANTER 1	O	⊗	X	X	X	1 CHURCH PLANT
PLANTER 2	O	O	⊗	X	X	
PLANTER 3	O	O→O	O→O	O~⊗	Q⊗	O
PLANTER 4	O	⊗	X	X	X	
PLANTER 5	O	O	X	X	X	

In the first diagram, we see five planters all shot out separately over a five-year period, according to the current practices of church planting in the West. According to statistical data only 20% of churches survive into the fifth year. Further, only 7% of churches actually reproduce themselves. Within five years using that model, the net result is one church planted despite thousands of dollars and man hours. Thus, there is a net loss of four churches after those five years of multiplication and mortality.

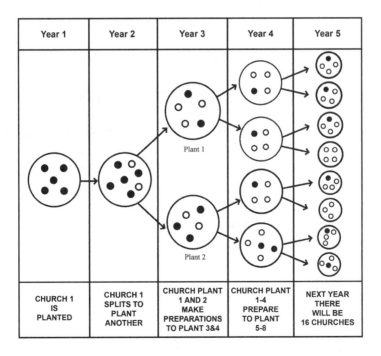

Year 1	Year 2	Year 3	Year 4	Year 5
CHURCH 1 IS PLANTED	CHURCH 1 SPLITS TO PLANT ANOTHER	CHURCH PLANT 1 AND 2 MAKE PREPARATIONS TO PLANT 3&4	CHURCH PLANT 1-4 PREPARE TO PLANT 5-8	NEXT YEAR THERE WILL BE 16 CHURCHES

In the second diagram, the strike team approach sends five top leaders together, who plant a solid hub, and focus on their second church plant in the second year. In other words, the first church plants the second. By year three there is a net total of four church plants, and by year five, if each has reproduced in the fourth year, resulting in sixteen churches. The four previous years would provide more than enough time to develop and disciple enough strike and fist teams to sustain the movement. Even allowing a 25 percent attrition rate, which is unlikely given the strong teams put in place, you would still have a net gain of eleven churches at the end of the fifth year due to the local network approach's ability to provide greater support through shared funding, training, and assessment.

In summary, consider this formula of how a network can quickly reach sixty-four churches within a seven-year period by committing to one church plant per year:

Year 1: The prime planter plants a church. Now you have one church.
Year 2: Plant one church out of the original plant. Now you have
     two churches.
Year 3: Each one plants out. Now you have four churches.
Year 4: Each one plants out. Now you have eight churches.
Year 5: Each one plants out. Now you have sixteen churches.
Year 6: Each one plants out. Now you have thirty-two churches.
Year 7: Each one plants out. Now you have sixty-four churches.

NETWORKS IN CHURCH HISTORY

As stated at the beginning of this book, John Wesley was the closest thing to the apostle Paul that the Western world has witnessed. Over the course of Wesley's ministry, he rode on horseback over 250,000 miles to share the gospel; this is enough distance to circle the earth ten times! But during his lifetime, the Methodist movement grew from four people to 132,000 people across two continents (72,000 in Great Britain, and 60,000 in the U.S.)!

Because he applied the plantology principles laid out in this book, Wesley's skill in networking also rivaled the apostle Paul's. Wesley unearthed these principles, studying and poring over the actions of Paul. Wesley was desperate to rediscover some of Paul's apostolic secrets in hopes of recovering the apostolic DNA of the early church that would become the beating heart of the early Methodist movement. Wesley desired to see a revival of what he called "scriptural Christianity" in his day. Wesley's vision was clear: "Not to form any new sect; but to reform the nation, particularly the church; and to spread scriptural holiness over the land."[19] By scriptural holiness, and "scriptural Christianity," he meant a return to the power and mission witnessed in the first century. It is fair to say that he accomplished his objective. Winfield Bevins comments: "Only a few years after his death, Methodism in North America grew from twelve hundred to two hundred thousand strong with more than four thousand preachers. By 1830, official membership reached almost half a million people, and attenders numbered six million. Then, from 1850 to 1905, American Methodism planted more than seven hundred churches per year on average."[20] Like Paul depositing networks in Asia, Galatia, and Macedonia that exponentially overflowed into multiplication in Rome, Wesley created a similar effect during his lifetime and, more important, after his death. Erwin McManus reminds us, "Two thousand years ago God started a revolt against the religion he started (through Jesus). So don't ever put it past God to cause a groundswell movement against churches and Christian institutions that bear his name. If he was willing to turn Judaism upside down, don't think for a moment our institutions are safe from a divine revolt."[21] He did it during the Methodist revival, and he may do it again.

SEQUENTIAL PLANTING

We must relearn the ancient ways, or what Alan Hirsch calls *The Forgotten Ways*, but it would be naive to think that there are no obstacles to this. For the remainder of the chapter, we will examine Paul's strategy of sequential planting out from a network hub to outline the skills we must master to see our church plants multiply:

1. Shift from a stationary to a mobile mindset.
2. Operate from Jesus's missional principles.
3. Craft a timeline multiplying outward.
4. Set expectations that you're leaving the church plant.
5. Retrain your team before your exit.

1. Shift from Stationary to Mobile

Have you ever noticed that all the jumps in technology are about being mobile? From the invention of the wheel to the progress of trains, planes, and

---

19. Winfield Bevins, *Marks of a Movement* (Centreville, VA: Exponential, 2017), 34.
20. Bevins, *Marks of a Movement*, 17.
21. Erwin McManus, *The Barbarian Way* (Nashville: Thomas Nelson, 2005), 114.

automobiles, all our huge innovations that changed the world we live in focus on mobility from iPhones to driverless cars. When the church has learned to rediscover mobile ministry, the church will truly be innovating again and gaining ground once more. Gating ministry behind stationary structures however, slows us down. For example, the circuit riders took America by storm throughout the eighteenth and nineteenth centuries, until, being chided by other denominations for being unschooled, they gated ministry behind seminaries. From that moment, the movement ground to a halt, and the circuit riders faded from history.

2. Operate from Jesus's Missionary Principles

Jesus trained his apostles to hit the road without taking extra provisions, telling them not to return until they had gone throughout all the towns of Judea, preaching the gospel of the kingdom. There are those who are doubtful about whether this passage is a universal set of rules or if it was just intended for the ones Jesus sent out. I would venture a few observations:

1. 1. The instructions in Luke 9 and 10, Matthew 10, and Mark 6 were given to the apostles for this specific mission, yet it is significant that all three synoptic Gospels record it for us as if these principles necessary reading. If it had no universal missionary application, it is doubtful it would have been important enough to transcribe three times for emphasis.
2. Paul repeatedly implements the principles in Matthew 10 in Acts. Paul regularly utilized the person of peace who is the gateway, or open door into reaching a community. Crider and McCrary quote Thomas Wolf defining the person of peace: "'Person of peace' is a Hebraism meaning 'one inclined to peace.' A person of peace is someone or some group sovereignly prepared by God to receive the gospel."[22] In the Gospels, Jesus utilized the persons of peace strategy with Zacchaeus, Matthew the tax collector, and the woman at the well during Jesus's ministry. In Paul's mission, they were Sergius Paulus (Cyprus), Lydia (Philippi), Aquila and Priscilla (Corinth), and Jason (Thessalonica). Peter was welcomed by Simon the tanner and Cornelius as gateways into the community.
3. In most parts of the undeveloped world, these instructions are still very relevant and strategic missional practices.

---

22. Larry E. McCrary and Caleb Crider, *Tradecraft: For the Church on Mission* (Portland, OR: Urban Loft Publishers, 2013), 107.

4. John Wesley fashioned his circuit riders using this passage to great effect as already demonstrated.[23]

There is a reason they were not to take extra provisions. They were to rely on God to provide everything they needed, including the very words they would speak. The overriding principle of the passage is dependence upon the Holy Spirit, particularly for:

1. Preaching (Matt. 10:7)
2. Miracles (Matt. 10:8)
3. Provision (Matt. 10:9–10)
4. Open doors (Matt. 10:11–13)
5. Response to the message (Matt. 10:14–15)
6. Wisdom in persecution (Matt. 10:16–20)

Such dependency is a far cry from people who think that a literal reading of Matthew 10 means we must become homeless missionaries. A few years ago, I met a young couple who were from the *International House of Prayer* (formerly known as IHOP, until litigation ended their use of the acronym). They started coming to our church plant as it met in homes during the week. At first, we fed them and gave them some money, but when somebody offered them a job at their company, they refused to work with their hands, stating that they were living out Matthew 10 and "taking no bag or tunics." Their plan was to be homeless missionaries in an affluent Southern California culture, completely missing the passage's principle of provision by the Holy Spirit, so when God provided them with jobs, they wouldn't take them. Paul lived according to these principles, but certainly didn't interpret Matthew 10 to mean he would refuse to work with his hands and would eventually turn up somewhere in Asia Minor as a homeless person.

As you plant your church, ensure that you are studying the principles Paul learned from Jesus and laid out for us in the above-mentioned chapters. It will save you time, energy, and frustration.

3. Craft a Plan for Multiplying Outward

There are a few factors involved in crafting a plan for multiplication.

The need: J. D. Payne attempted to answer how many churches should

---

23. Robert R. Witten, *Pioneer Methodism, Or, Itinerant Life in Missouri* (Vernon, CA: Hannibal Print Company, 1881), 42–43.

be in a network, concluding that one church per every one thousand people in urban areas is necessary to keep up with population growth, which is outpacing the number of churches planted annually.[24] To convince a reluctant sending pastor of the need to plant churches, I phoned every Christian church within the city and asked what its membership was. I subtracted that number from the population of that city, to reveal the number of unchurched, concluding that to merely reach 10% of the population of the city, would require twenty-eight churches the size of a megachurch of two-thousand plus.

The Total Population in your city
(-) The Total Attendance of churches in your city (google)

(=) The unchurched
(/) 1,000

You can further examine the population density in a given area to determine how many people reside within a certain area. If you have three thousand people per square mile, you'd be looking to plant three churches per mile. In the city where I grew up, the population density is nearly eight thousand people per mile, meaning eight churches within a square mile would be required.

The capacity: The capacity of your multiplication plan is determined by the mission cycle, or the length of time an apostolic leader stays in one location. Paul's mission cycle depended upon what he was trying to accomplish, but his average mission cycle was between three months when planting rapidly (Galatia) and three years when establishing a hub (Ephesus). Corinth was settled at approximately 18 months as he was focused on establishing a bivocational base of operations.

Similarly, Jesus modeled a three-year mission cycle training the Twelve and preparing them for the Jerusalem hub. Alan Hirsch suggests that apostolic mission cycles should last approximately three years, when an internal alarm clock rings inside the apostle's spirit.[25] On a personal note, my own tenures

---

24. Steve Nerger, *BiVo: Planters and Pastors: Mobilizing the Next Generation* (Alpharetta, GA: North American Mission Board, 2012), 8.

25. Daniel Sinclair, *Vision of the Possible* (Downers Grove, IL: InterVarsity Press, 2012), 39. Daniel Sinclair notes with astonishment that a year and half of Paul's work in Corinth is summarized by, "He settled there a year and six months, teaching the word of God among them" (Acts 18:11). He continues by stating that the following should be a life verse for all pioneer planters: "Be diligent to present yourself approved to God as a workman who does not need to be ashamed, accurately handling the word of truth" (2 Tim. 2:15). Sinclair, *Vision of the Possible*, 242.

have lasted three years with a few exceptions. (One even lasted three years to the day without my realizing it.) Knowing that the apostle carries an internal ticking time clock set to go off, they must prepare for their inevitable departure from day one.

4. Set Expectations for Leaving

While most established churches are seeking to avoid splitting, apostles believe that all healthy churches will eventually split. Therefore, apostolic planters learn to build two teams to facilitate a hasty retreat:

- A fist team to replace you
- A strike team to go with you

As you build your strike team to head out, the fist team will be made up of elders and deacons. An effective fist team will be highly specialized. Some leaders will be good for frontline evangelism, like Apollos who filled that gap in Corinth after Paul's departure. Others on the fist team will focus on discipling believers and counselling. Others will train others to teach, seeding future strike teams to be harvested, as Paul did with Timothy on his second rotation through Lystra and Derbe.

Equally important to prepping the fist team is preparing the congregation for the departure of the strike team.

People must be prepared to accept that:

- Some of their leaders will soon be leaving (strike teams).
- Some of their leaders will be staying longer (fist teams).
- Some of them will soon be leaders (fist teams).
- Some of them will soon be going too, hopefully planting churches (strike teams).

Shared leadership, the rotation of teachers in the pulpit, and constant messaging about the above points will help to prevent dependence upon the leader and will help eliminate the Corinthian dilemma: "I follow Paul, I follow Cephas, I follow Apollos" (see 1 Cor. 1:12). The apostle John commends first-century strike teams deployed for planting in 3 John 1:7–8 (ESV), "For they have gone out for the sake of the name, accepting nothing from the Gentiles. Therefore we ought to support people like these, that we may be fellow workers for the truth." We too must support them if we desire the same traction in the West, but we must structure our forms to fulfill this function.

TIPS FOR RAPID MULTIPLICATION

1. Set elders in place *as well as* transient, mobile workers.
2. You need to have someone who will commit to staying there for a time, even though they may want to move out with a strike team. Paul left Timothy and Titus behind so that he could move on and do more front-line planting.
3. Create a culture of kingdom expansion. Too many churches model empire building instead of kingdom expansion. You can only mentor kingdom expanders if you've shifted from the "my church" mentality to a "Christ's church" mentality.
4. Set a time based on development. You will be able to roughly plan for the cell division to take place, but you will never be able to come up with a fool-proof system. Each person's training will take a different amount of time based on their gifting, abilities, and previous experience.

5. Retraining the Team

Paul stood on the docks with the Ephesian elders addressing them for what he knew would be the last time. Paul retrained the team in Ephesus when he gathered them at the docks of Miletus and addressed them in Acts 20:18–35. He retrained them how to be a fist team by giving them the following three points:

1. Watch out for yourself.
2. Watch out for each other.
3. Protect the flock against wolves.

For a man on the move, he prioritized giving the Ephesian elders their final instructions. In the same way, sequential planters must retrain their teams before departing. Here is why:

1. When you first trained your team, they didn't understand 50% of what you said.
2. Of the remaining 50%, they only believed half of that, leaving you with 25% of what you trained into them.
3. Because your team had never experienced what you were training them to do, they only remembered half of what they believed, leaving you with

12% of what you taught them. In other words, they need to be retrained for approximately 88% of the original training.

When you trained them, they couldn't visualize it, but they trusted you enough to move forward with your vision. Now that they have seen what was built and established, they know *experientially* what they failed to grasp *theoretically*. Putting into words what people think, feel, or know intrinsically is powerful, and Paul did this for the Ephesians. He also left behind Timothy and others who would continue to disciple and train. To the Corinthians, Paul wrote, "That is why I sent Timothy, my beloved and faithful child in the Lord, to remind you of my ways in Christ, as I teach them everywhere in every church" (1 Cor. 4:17 ESV). Like Paul, when I've returned to churches I've planted, it wasn't just doctrine, but "my ways" that they needed to be reminded of. For example, I trained my team that the Sunday announcements weren't a laundry list, but the most powerful time to cast vision. I trained people before I left by modeling it, but they failed to train others. When the next round of people were picked for announcements, they reverted back to the laundry list because those who stayed behind were never taught the principles that the first wave were. Principles can't be transferred to others unless they can first be articulated. Therefore, you must articulate to future leaders the intentionality behind what you have modeled to them as a church when you were still among them.

There were other things, simple things like not breaking down the chairs and tables for ten to fifteen minutes after the service, or people will hustle out of the building. In our churches, the conversations would often spill out over the groups, and we'd have people hanging out for one or two hours after the gathering had officially closed down. After I'd left a church plant, the teardown crew eventually adopted the practice of breaking down immediately, killing the atmosphere the church previously enjoyed. When I took the teardown crew aside and gently shared my observations, they were horrified, and acknowledged that this had caused a significant regression in the atmosphere in the church. Big doors often turn on small hinges. Retraining those left behind will give them the theory that they missed the first time around and marry it to their practice so that they can pass it on to others.

Lastly, Jesus retrained the Twelve for forty days when he walked with them in Galilee after his resurrection. He took that time to train them retroactively; since they now possessed all the pieces, he helped them put it all together. They needed retraining for the next step of ministry, when they would stand on their own in Jerusalem. The sending of the seventy-two was just a drill. Acts was the real thing.

Four generations

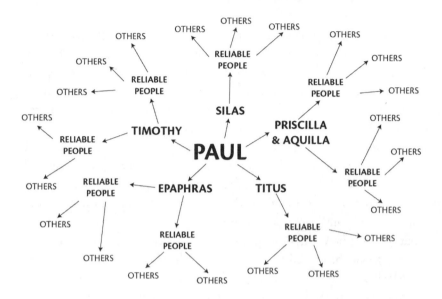

When I started as a church planter, a newly planted church was the end goal. By my second plant, I was already thinking of training others. Consciously making this shift in focus meant not taking myself too seriously while treating the training of tomorrow's leaders with a deadly seriousness. Nothing drives home the importance of prepping the next generation of leaders quite like handing off a church into which you've invested your blood, sweat, and tears. Years ago, I handed off my first church plant with all the awkwardness of a bride's father at the altar. I could only hope that the next leader could take care of that particular church. Since then, I've learned to ensure they do by training the leaders myself, following the apostolic pattern of committing "them to the Lord, in whom they had put their trust" (Acts 14:23). Dave Ferguson calls the process of training others hero making. Paul was instructing Timothy to make heroes he could move on from Ephesus and rejoin him on the field: "The things you have heard me say in the presence of many witnesses entrust to reliable people who will also be qualified to teach others" (2 Tim. 2:2). Thus the key to multiplication is discipleship, which sheds light on why Jesus invested the majority of his time during his three years of ministry to it. Once discipleship was a part of the DNA of the disciples, multiplication was hardwired into the church yet to be. Rippling thousands of years down from the epicenter of Jesus's ministry, multiplication has diminished. As those ripples continue thousands of years into the future, multiplication will be key to moving forward.

Sustainable and Unsustainable Multiplication Strategy*

Sustainable Strategies	Unsustainable Strategies
Fully fund every church planter	Train church planters to raise funds or become tentmakers
Require seminary training for planters	Multiply trainers in the field
Start a church	Multiply churches
Denomination takes power for recruiting and training planters	Every church planter trains and apprentices planters on the field
Centrally coordinate and plan where churches are planted	Expect churches in the field to determine where the need is and follow the leading of the Spirit
Tight organizational control	Led by mission and relationships
Long-term sponsorship from churches	Plants take responsibility for long-term sustainability

* This table has been modified from Steve Addison, *Movements that Change the World*, 110.

REFLECT

- The author argues that the church growth crisis in America is rooted in the leadership multiplication bottleneck. How are leaders reproduced in your fellowship? How will they be reproduced in your church plant?
- The author states that every church planting movement starts with a network. How would the ambition to plant a network of churches affect your vision and plans?

DISCUSS

- Most people consider church planting networks to be the nonprofit parachurch organizations that support church planters. This is not what the author means by network. Whether or not your team has joined a 501 (c)(3) nonprofit church planting network, have you considered creating a network of churches?
- Compare and contrast networks with denominations.
- Discuss the following obstacles to kingdom expansion:
  - Sacrificing size for reach. Why do we prefer larger fellowships?
  - Sacrificing impact for ego. Why do we persist in the "super pastor" model of ministry?

- Sacrificing penetration for pay. How can we eliminate our dependence on a paycheck from the fellowship?
- What are some advantages of planting from a network? Do you have a training center for your church planters?

CHALLENGE

- If you were working toward a church plant, what would it mean for your plans to think in terms of church multiplication, sequential planting, and reaching your state or region, instead of planting a single church?
- The author argues that starting a local network involves these practices:
  - Start with your church as a planting training center.
  - Determine that your church will be a hub of church planting.
  - Convince your fellowship that their church isn't the main focus of the future.
  - Focus on your region instead of your church.
  - Effectively communicate that today's church plants become tomorrow's sending churches.
- How are these practices reflected in your fellowship or church plant?

CONCLUSION

The lesson is ended.
The wastebasket is full.
The dress rehearsal is over!
Carpe Diem!

It's time to stand on the desk like Ethan Hawke at the end of *Dead Poets Society* and stand on the *Church Plantology* principles laid out in Scripture, church history, and global mission practices. As you stand on your desk, awkwardly at first, remember that I have merely served as Mr. Keating—a guide who has opened the door to the equivalents of Byron, Tennyson, and Wordsworth. Only we have read from Wesley, Spurgeon, and others. The wise and master planters have spoken. The apostles, and those who have followed in the way of the apostles, are those who should be heeded and heard; my aim has simply been to bring you under their tutelage, for ultimately, we embark on mission under the tutelage of Jesus, in apprenticeship to the One for whom you may boldly stand against conventionality. As you stand on your desk nervously, looking around but standing in faith nonetheless, you make me proud. More importantly, you make God proud. As you stand in the power of these principles that will transform yourself and others, may your words echo into eternity with his glory, "Oh Captain, My Captain!"

ACKNOWLEDGMENTS

As with any work of this size, there are many people to thank.

First, I thank my wife, who became my ministry and life partner long before we tied the knot. We kindled the beginnings of a best friendship at seventeen years old when I had the providential hand of God causing me to sit in front of her in college-prep English class my senior year. Since I was normally in the class with the bad kids, it was providential that I sat in that classroom at all, but God knew that my ministry would start young and that from an early age I would require a ministry teammate. As on the mission field, and in our life, she has made many sacrifices to see this book become a reality, releasing me from many aspects of being a husband for the better part of a year.

With that, I thank my two beautiful girls, the best gifts God has ever given to me. They too have unwittingly made sacrifices from times Dad couldn't be at the beach, build a bonfire in the back yard, or play with them. They will never have to make that sacrifice again, because writing a book is not worth paying that price.

I would also like to thank my mother, Linda Jones. My mom was not alive to see this work, but she bought my books no matter how many copies I gave her, handing them out to her friends and telling them it was one of the best books she'd ever read. That's moms for you. Without my family cheering me on, it would not be the same.

To my brother, and best friend, Trey Jones, who aside from my wife and Mom, has always been among my greatest writing cheerleaders. My brother (the handsomer, manlier, taller, smarter version of me) is also a much more gifted writer than I am, and inherited it, I believe, from our grandfather, who was a best-selling civil war author.

To my writing collective, The Inklings, for looking over the manuscript, Andrew Terry, Andy Froiland, Robert Frazier, and most of all Dr. Joel Hughes, who kindly crafted all the questions at the end of every chapter.

My friends who understand that a low-maintenance friendship with a guy like me is still a real one. Mark Convoy, Dave Perrigan, Dai Hankey, Pete

Mitchell, Kris Langham, and Beau Moffatt—it's an honor to know each of you and to have been able to call you friends over the years. You are each men I admire for various reasons.

To my friend and senior by thirty-seven years, Len Gibbs. I knew the last time I saw you in Wales that it would be the last time we'd ever speak face to face, and I knew I would need to tell you that you were like a father to me. You were a friend, mentor, and great encourager. Your wisdom about a great many things has stayed with me over the years, and much of your wisdom is laced within the pages of these books. You were a true influencer, and the church should have made you drink poison like Socrates to stop your influencing of young reformed minds as a Methodist circuit preacher. Thank you for everything, from lectures about crafting ale, the ministry of the Holy Spirit, Wesley as a model, marriage advice, to life hacks on nearly anything. You are greatly missed . . . at least by me.

I would also like to thank all those who saw ministry potential in me at a young age and took a chance on me, especially Eric Fulmer, Dan Berg, and Peter Jeffery. Without each of you I would not be where I am today, and I have often thought that this book and all I do is my way of paying forward what you did for me.

My posse, the network of apostolic leaders I travel with, the New Breed planters spread across the globe, this book is for you. I mean, it's for everybody. (But it's really for you . . . shhh.)

The New Breed Pit Crew through the years—Stephen, Nancy, Jason and Nicole, Joe, Lee, Don and Val, the entire Olson family, and all the New Breed supporters: Where would I have been all those years if you hadn't held the rope for us as we rappelled down some dark holes with the gospel candle?

My training partners Mac "Yoda" Lake, Charles "Siri" Campbell, Armando "second Peyton" Barraza, and Rick "the Beast" Duncan. My time with you boys greatly impacted how I train planters and informed much of this book.

I thank my podcasting co-hosts: Andrea and Barry Waters from the Ministry Ninja Podcast, Pete Mitchell from the Church Planting Podcast (the longest running church planting podcast on earth, baby! "Oklahoma!"), and Daniel Yang from the Exponential Frontlines podcast. Together we have been more about influence than impact. We have been able to stand aside and influence others who will surely accomplish great exploits for the kingdom. Eternity alone will display the fruit from the seeds of our partnerships together.

My Through-the-Word compadres: Kris Langham, Ryan Farrar, and Jonathan Ferguson, who have assigned me the toughest books in the Old Testament not as a challenge, but because they don't want to walk teens through 2 Chronicles. You're welcome, but also, thank you. It has enriched me more than you will ever know and allowed me to kick out my preaching jams in the time of my exile, in "the land between" my church planting ventures.

To the team at Exponential for all the incredible work they've done to move the number of churches that reproduce in North America closer to the 10% goal. Todd Wilson and the Wilson family, Dave Ferguson, Jason Stewart, Manservant Brook Hamon, Terri Saliba, Larry Walkemeyer, Ralph Moore, Grace, Jan, and the rest of the team.

To the crew at Zondervan, thanks for placing your faith in me to deliver this book. (Ahem . . . I still have another textbook on the cutting room floor . . . Plantology 201?) I am grateful for my acquisitions editor Ryan Pazdur, my friend and champion of this book, not to mention my work and writing in general—words fail me. You truly get church planting, and without your willingness to shift the paradigm slightly, this work would not be available to planters. They have you to thank. My marketing director Nathan Kroeze for making sure my cover and title are rad, and all the other things you do. Lastly, my editors, Kim Tanner, who is a wizard and makes me look gooder than me write, and Josh Blunt, who greatly encouraged me that I didn't completely suck at this.

I am blessed to have the best literary agent on the planet, who is what you'd want in an agent. He can make you laugh, teach you about the Bible, punch you in the face (metaphorically, although we've never met face to face—maybe I could take him), and peel you off the pavement when you need it. When we first spoke on the phone in 2010, he asked me, "No offense, but who would want to read a one-thousand-page book about church planting written by an unknown like you?" I've since discovered the answer. Nobody. I tried submitting an eight-hundred-page manuscript, and Zondervan asked me to chop it in half. Let's see how they do with four hundred pages. You've gotta start somewhere. I will leave it to Steve to discover if I've used his name for an acronym, buried an Easter Egg about him murdering people somewhere, or footnoted him as a pariah somewhere in this manuscript.

David had his thirty-seven mighty men. When I lost my footnotes and half of my bibliography at the eleventh hour, many mighty men rallied around me to manually help me recover them. The people who stepped up were Gabe Berg "Cowabunga," Shane Beauvais, Billy Mills, Ben Biscoe, Keaton Smith, Travis Currin, Luke Baumstark, and Joseph Slamoiraghi.

But among those mighty men, there were three: Don Stoner, Mark Convoy, and Dave Perrigan. Don Stoner was a constant companion, working in my office on a steady diet of walnuts, Slim Jims, and cheese. I offered him more, but he insisted that was the only fuel his body tolerated for such feats. "He was the mightiest among the three." This book has now reached across the continent and even been worked on by people in other parts of the world. You will never know how much it has meant to me that you reached out. I have never felt so utterly defeated by anything in my life . . . eleven months of blood, sweat, and tears seemed gone . . . and then the mighty men showed up. For as long as I live, I will never forget the calming voice of Doc Mark, one of my nearest and dearest friends, on the other end of the line, saying, "What do you need? I'm here." That was the first moment I knew it was going to be okay. That was when I realized I wasn't in this alone. That was the moment that my eyes misted up and I was reminded of what true friendship is. Dave Perrigan, thanks for volunteering to jump in after not seeing each other for years and being that same steady friend on the other end of the line. As I'm somebody who trains in team planting and was working on a book about team planting, it's fitting that this book was a team effort at the final stretch.

BIBLIOGRAPHY

Addison, Steve. *Movements That Change the World: Five Keys to Spreading the Gospel.* Downers Grove, IL: InterVarsity Press, 2011.

Addison, Steve. *Pioneering Movements: Leadership That Multiplies Disciples and Churches.* Downers Grove, IL: InterVarsity Press, 2015.

Addison, Steve. *What Jesus Started: Joining the Movement Changing the World.* Downers Grove, IL: InterVarsity Press, 2012.

Alcorn, Randy. *The Treasure Principle: Unlocking the Secret of Joyful Giving.* Colorado Springs: Multnomah, 2001.

Alexander, T. Desmond. *From Paradise to the Promised Land: An Introduction to the Pentateuch.* Ada, MI: Baker, 2002.

Ambrose, Stephen E. *D-Day, June 6, 1944: The Climactic Battle of World War II.* New York: Simon & Schuster, 1995.

Barna Group. *Spiritual Conversations in the Digital Age: How Christians' Approach to Sharing their Faith Has Changed in 25 Years.* Barna Group, 2018.

Barnett, Paul. *The Second Epistle to the Corinthians: The New International Commentary on the New Testament.* Grand Rapids: Eerdmans, 1997.

Beach, Lee. *The Church in Exile: Living in Hope after Christendom.* Downers Grove, IL: InterVarsity Press, 2015.

Beale, G. K. *The New International Greek Testament Commentary: The Book of Revelation.* Grand Rapids: Eerdmans,1999.

Belmonte, Kevin. *D. L. Moody: A Life.* Chicago: Moody, 2014.

Bennardo, Tom. *The Honest Guide to Church Planting: What No One Ever Tells You about Planting and Leading a New Church.* Grand Rapids: Zondervan, 2019.

Beynon, Graham. *Planting for the Gospel: A Hands-On Guide to Church Planting.* Ross-shire, Scotland: Christian Focus, 2011.

Bloye, Brian and Amy. *It's Not Personal, Surviving and Thriving on the Journey of Church Planting.* Grand Rapids: Zondervan, 2012.

Bonhoeffer, Diedrich. *The Cost of Discipleship.* New York: Macmillan, 1963.

Branson, Mark Lau, and Nicholas Warnes. *Starting Missional Churches: Life with God in the Neighborhood.* Downers Grove, IL: InterVarsity Press, 2014.

Breen, Mike. *The Apostle's Notebook.* Eastbourne, England: Kingsway, 2002.

Breen, Mike. *Leading Missional Communities: Rediscovering the Power of Living on Mission Together.* Pawleys Island, SC: 3 Dimension Ministries, 2013.

Briggs, Alan. *Guardrails: Six Principles for a Multiplying Church.* Colorado Springs: NavPress, 2016.

Briggs, Alan. *Staying is the New Going: Choosing to Love Where God Places You.* Colorado Springs: NavPress, 2015.

Brisco, Brad. *Covocational Church Planting: Aligning Your Marketplace Calling & The Mission of God.* Alpharetta, GA: SEND Network North American Mission Board, 2018.

Bruce, F. F. *Paul: Apostle of the Heart Set Free.* Grand Rapids: Eerdmans, 1996.

Buchanan, Mark. *The Rest of God: Restoring Your Soul by Restoring Sabbath.* Nashville: Thomas Nelson, 2006.

Carter, Stephen L. *The Culture of Disbelief: How American Politics Trivialize Religious Devotion.* Alpharetta, GA: North American Mission Board, 2012.

Chan, Sam. *Evangelism in a Skeptical World: How to Make the Unbelievable News about Jesus More Believable.* Grand Rapids: Zondervan, 2018.

Cheshire, Michael. *How to Knock Over a 7-Eleven and Other Ministry Training.* Denver: Cheshire Publishing, 2012.

Christopherson, Jeff, and Mac Lake. *Kingdom First: Starting Churches that Shape Movements.* Nashville: Broadman & Holman, 2015.

Clifton, Clint. *Church Planting Thresholds: A Gospel-Centered Guide.* Chattanooga, TN: The New City Network, 2016.

Cole, Neil. *Primal Fire: Reigniting the Church with the Five Gifts of Jesus.* Carol Stream, IL: Tyndale, 2014.

Colson, Charles W., and Ellen Santilli Vaughn. *The Body: Being Light in the Darkness.* Nashville: W., 1992.

Crider, Caleb, Larry McCrary, Rodney Calfee, and Wade Stephens. *Tradecraft for the Church on Mission.* Louisville, KY: Upstream Collective, 2017.

Devenish, David. *Fathering Leaders, Motivating Mission: Resotring the Role of the Apostle in Today's Church.* Milton Keynes, UK: Authentic, 2011.

Deyoung, Kevin. *The Hole in Our Holiness: Filling the Gap between Gospel Passion and the Pursuit of Godliness.* Wheaton, IL: Crossway, 2012.

Doidge, Norman. *The Brain that Changes Itself: Stories of Personal Triumph from the Frontiers of Brain Science.* New York: Penguin, 2007.

Driscoll, Mark and Grace. *Real Marriage: The Truth About Sex, Friendship, & Life Together.* Nashville: Thomas Nelson, 2012.

Eldridge, John. *Walking with God: Talk to Him. Hear from Him. Really.* Nashville: Thomas Nelson, 2008.

Eldridge, John & Staci. *Love and War: Find Your Way to Something Beautiful in Your Marriage.* Colorado Springs: WaterBrook, 2009.

Eusebius. *The Ecclesiastical History.* Grand Rapids: Baker, 1989.

Fee, Gordon D. *The First Epistle to the Corinthians: The New International Commentary on the New Testament.* Grand Rapids: Eerdmans, 1987.

Ferguson, Dave, and Warren Bird. *Hero Maker: Five Essential Practices for Leaders to Multiply Leaders.* Grand Rapids: Zondervan, 2018.

Frost, Michael. *Exiles: Living Missionally in a Post-Christian Culture.* Grand Rapids: Baker, 2006.

Frost, Michael. *The Road to Missional: Journey to the Center of the Church.* Grand Rapids: Baker, 2011.

Frost, Michael, and Christiana Rice. *To Alter Your World: Partnering with God to Rebirth Our Communities*. Downers Grove, IL: InterVarsity Press, 2017.

Godin, Seth. *Tribes: We Need You to Lead Us*. New York: Penguin, 2014.

Green, Keith. *Keith Green's Final Message: Why You Should Go to the Mission Field*. Lindale, TX: Pretty Good Printing, 1984.

Green, Melody, and David Hazard. *No Compromise*. Eugene, OR: Harvest House, 2000.

Greig, Pete. *How to Pray: A Simple Guide for Normal People*. Colorado Springs: NavPress, 2019.

Grudem, Wayne A. *The Gift of Prophecy in 1 Corinthians*. Lanham, MD: University Press of America, 1982.

Halter, Hugh. *BiVo: A Modern-Day Guide for Bi-Vocational Saints, Leveraging All of Life into One Calling*. Golden, CO: Samizdat, 2013.

Hammond, Mark, and Don Overstreet. *Gods Call to The City*. Arlington, TX: Touch, 2011, 2015.

Hansen, Collin. *Young, Restless, Reformed: A Journalist's Journey with the New Calvinists*. Wheaton, IL: Crossway, 2008.

Henderson, Michael D. *John Wesley's Class Meeting: A Model for Making Disciples*. Wilmore, KY: Rafiki, 2016.

Herron, Fred. *Expanding God's Kingdom through Church Planting*. Lincoln, NE: iUniverse, 2003.

Hiestand, Gerald, and Todd Wilson. *Tending Soul, Mind and Body: The Art and Science of Spiritual Formation*. Downers Grove, IL: InterVarsity Press, 2019.

Hirsch, Alan. *5Q: Reactivating the Original Intelligence and Capacity of the Body of Christ*. Columbia, SC: 100 Movements, 2017.

Hirsch, Alan. *The Forgotten Ways*. Grand Rapids: Brazos, 2006.

Hirsch, Alan, and Tim Catchim. *The Permanent Revolution: Apostolic Imagination and Practice for the 21st Century Church*. San Francisco: Jossey-Bass, 2012.

Hirsch, Alan, and Tim Catchim. *The Permanent Revolution Playbook: APEST for the People of God: A Six Week Exploration*. Denver: Missio, 2014.

Hirsch, Debra. *Redeeming Sex: Naked Conversations About Sexuality and Spirituality*. Downers Grove, IL: InterVarsity Press, 2015.

Hucks, John. *John Wesley and the Eighteenth-Century Methodist Movement: a Model for Effective Leadership*. San Diego: Point Loma Nazarene University, 2003.

Hunter, George G. III. *The Celtic Way of Evangelism: How Christianity Can Reach the West Again*. Nashville: Abingdon, 2010.

James, Christopher B. *Church Planting in Post-Christian Soil: Theology and Practice*. New York: Oxford University Press, 2018.

Karr, Allan, and Linda Bergquist. *The Wholehearted Church Planter: Leadership from the Inside Out*. Nashville: Chalice, 2013.

Keller, Timothy. *Center Church: Doing Balanced, Gospel-Centered Ministry in Your City*. Grand Rapids: Zondervan, 2012.

Köstenberger, Andreas J., and Peter T. O'Brien. *Salvation to the Ends of the Earth: A Biblical Theology of Mission*. Downers Grove, IL: InterVarsity Press, 2001.

Lawless, Chuck. *Mentor Member Book: How Along-the-Way Discipleship Will Change Your Life*. Nashville: Lifeway Press, 2011.

Lewis, C. S. *The Weight of Glory: And Other Addresses*. New York: HarperCollins, 2009.

Lewis, Dhati. *Among Wolves: Disciple-Making in The City*. Nashville: Broadman & Holman, 2017.

Lloyd-Jones, D. Martin. *Healing and the Scriptures: The Power of Faith as a Healing Element*. Nashville: Oliver-Nelson, 1988.

Logan, Robert E. *The Missional Journey*. Bloomington, MN: ChurchSmart Resources, 2013.

Logan, Robert E., and Tara Miller. *Becoming Barnabas: A Ministry of Coming Alongside*. Bloomington, MN: ChurchSmart Resources, 2014.

Logan, Robert E., and Tara Miller. *From Followers to Leaders: The Path of Leadership Development in the Local Church*. St. Charles, IL: ChurchSmart Resources, 2007.

Lokkesmoe, Ryan. *Paul and His Team: What the Early Church Can Teach Us about Leadership and Influence*. Chicago: Moody, 2017.

Mancini, Will. *Church Unique: How Missional Leaders Cast Vision, Capture Culture, and Create Movement*. San Francisco: Wiley, 2008.

Malphurs, Aubrey. *Developing a Vision for Ministry*. Grand Rapids: Baker, 2015.

Malphurs, Aubrey. *The Nuts and Bolts of Church Planting: A Guide for Starting Any Kind of Church*. Grand Rapids: Baker, 2011.

McDaniel, Chris. *Ignite Your Generosity: A 21-Day Experience in Stewardship*. Downers Grove, IL: InterVarsity Press, 2015.

McKinley, Michael. *Church Planting Is for Wimps*. Wheaton, IL: Crossway, 2010.

McLaughlin, Patrick G. *Major Donor Game Plan*. Grand Rapids: The Timothy Group, 2010.

McNeal, Reggie. *The Present Future: Six Tough Questions for the Church*. San Francisco: Jossey-Bass, 2003.

Medearis, Carl. *42 Seconds: The Jesus Model for Everyday Interactions*. Colorado Springs: NavPress, 2018.

Metcalf, Sam. *Beyond the Local Church: How Apostolic Movements Can Change the World*. Downers Grove, IL: InterVarsity Press, 2016.

Meyer, F. B. *Paul: A Servant of Jesus Christ*. London: Morgan & Scott, 1897.

Moore, Ralph. *How to Multiply your Church: The Most Effective Way to Grow*. Grand Rapids: Baker, 2009.

Moore, Ralph. *Making Disciples: Developing Lifelong Followers of Jesus*. Grand Rapids: Baker, 2012.

Moore, Ralph. *Starting a New Church*. Grand Rapids: Baker, 2002.

Morton, Scott. *Funding Your Ministry: Whether You're Gifted or Not, An In-depth, Biblical Guide for Successfully Raising Personal Support*. Colorado Springs: Dawson Media, 1999.

Murray, Iain H. *David Martyn Lloyd-Jones: The Fight of Faith 1939–1981*. Carlisle, PN: The Banner of Truth Trust, 1990.

Murray, Iain H. *David Martyn Lloyd-Jones: The First Forty Years 1899–1939*. Edinburgh, UK: The Banner of Truth Trust, 1983.

Murray, Iain H. *Wesley and Men Who Followed*. Edinburgh, UK. Banner of Truth, 2003.

Murray, Stuart. *Church Planting: Laying Foundations*. Scottdale, PA: Herald, 2001.

Nerger, Steve. *BiVo: Planters and Pastors, Mobilizing the Next Generation*. Alpharetta, GA: North American Mission Board, 2012.

Nickens, Brian. *The Little Church That Will: Crossing Over into the Coming Reformation.* Brian Nickens, Redding, CA: Self-published, 2011.

Nieuwhof, Carey. *Didn't See It Coming: Overcoming the 7 Greatest Challenges That No One Expects and Everyone Experiences.* New York: WaterBrook, 2018.

Niringiye, David Zac. *The Church: God's Pilgrim People.* Downers Grove, IL: IVP Academic, 2015.

Ollerton, David. *A New Mission to Wales: Seeing Churches Prosper across Wales in the Twenty-First Century.* Cardiff, Wales, UK: Waleswide, 2016.

Ollerton, David. *Ministry on the Move: New Testament Patterns of Apostles and Apostolic Teams for Supporting Church Plants and Existing Churches.* Llandysul, Wales, UK: Newid, 2008.

Ott, Craig, and Gene Wilson. *Global Church Planting: Biblical Principles and Best Practices for Multiplications.* Grand Rapids: Baker Academic, 2011.

Overstreet, Don. *Sent Out: The Calling, the Character, and the Challenge of the Apostle-Missionary.* Arlington, TX: Touch, 2015.

Paas, Stefan. *Church Planting in the Secular West: Learning from the European Experience.* Grand Rapids: Eerdmans, 2016.

Pamphilus, Eusebius. *The Ecclesiastical History of Eusebius Pamphilus: Bishop of Cesarea, in Palestine.* Grand Rapids: Baker, 1989.

Payne, J. D. *Apostolic Church Planting: Birthing New Churches from New Believers.* Downers Grove, IL: InterVarsity Press, 2015.

Payne, Jervis David. *Discovering Church Planting: An Introduction to the Whats, Whys, and Hows of Global Church Planting.* Downers Grove, IL: InterVarsity Press, 2009.

Peterson, David G. *The Acts of the Apostles.* Grand Rapids: Eerdmans, 2009.

Peterson, Jim. *Church Without Walls: Moving Beyond Traditional Boundaries.* Colorado Springs: NavPress, 1992.

Pfanz, Guy, and Monica Hoover. *Stacking the Deck: What Happens When We Believe God Wants It More Than We Do.* Muncie, IN: Small Voice, 2010.

Piper, John. *Tested by Fire: The Fruit of Suffering in the Lives of John Bunyan, William Cowper and David Brainerd.* Leicester, England: InterVarsity Press. 2001.

Piper, John. *The Roots of Endurance: Invincible Perseverance in the Lives of John Newton, Charles Simeon and William Wilberforce.* Nottingham, England: InterVarsity Press, 2002.

Plummer, Robert L., and John Mark Terry, eds. *Paul's Missionary Methods: In His Time and Ours.* Downers Grove, IL: IVP Academic, 2012.

Pollock, John. *The Apostle: A Life of Paul.* Wheaton, IL: Victor, 1985.

Rainer, Thom S., and Chuck Lawless, *The Challenge of the Great Commission.* Bemidji, MN: Pinnacle, 2005.

Rinehart, John. *Gospel Patrons: People Whose Generosity Changed the World.* Reclaimed, 2013.

Roxburgh, Alan J. *Structured for Mission: Renewing the Culture of the Church.* Downers Grove, IL: InterVarsity Pres, 2015.

Ryken, Leland. *Culture in Christian Perspective.* Portland, OR: Multnomah, 1986.

Sande, Ken, and Kevin Johnson. *Resolving Everyday Conflict.* Grand Rapids: Baker, 2011.

Sanders, Brian. *Microchurches: A Smaller Way.* Middletown, DE: Underground Media, 2019.

Sanders, Brian. *Underground Church: A Living Example of the Church in its Most Potent Form*. Grand Rapids: Zondervan, 2018.

Sanders, J. Oswald. *Spiritual Leadership*. Chicago: Moody, 1967.

Schnabel, Eckhard J. *Early Christian Mission: Jesus and the Twelve*. Downers Grove, IL: InterVarsity Press, 2004.

Schnabel, Eckhard J. *Early Christian Mission: Paul and the Early Church*. Downers Grove, IL: InterVarsity Press, 2004.

Schreiner, Thomas R. *Spiritual Gifts: What They Are & Why They Matter*. Nashville: Broadman & Holman, 2018.

Shaw, Ryan. *Spiritual Equipping for Missions: Thriving as God's Message Bearers*. Downers Grove, IL: InterVarsity Press, 2014.

Sills, M. David. *Changing World, Unchanging Mission: Responding to Global Challenges*. Downers Grove, IL: InterVarsity Press, 2015.

Sinclair, Daniel. *A Vision of the Possible: Pioneer Church Planting in Teams*. Downers Grove, IL: InterVarsity Press, 2005.

Slattery, Juli. *Rethinking Sexuality: God's Design and Why It Matters*. Colorado Springs: Multnomah, 2018.

Smith, T. Gordon. *Evangelical Sacramental & Pentecostal: Why the Church Should Be All Three*. Downers Grove, IL: InterVarsity Press, 2017.

Smith, James K. A., *Desiring the Kingdom*. Grand Rapids: Baker Academic, 2009.

Snyder, James L. *The Life of A.W. Tozer: In Pursuit of God*. Ventura, CA: Regal, 2009.

Sparks, Paul, Tim Soerens, and Dwight J. Friesen. *The New Parish: How Neighborhood Churches Are Transforming Mission Discipleship and Community*. Downers Grove, IL: InterVarsity Press, 2014.

Sproul, R. C. *Lifeviews: Make a Christian Impact on Culture and Society*. Grand Rapids: Revell, 2004.

Spurgeon, C. H. *Metropolitan Tabernacle Pulpit*. 1973.

Spurgeon, Charles H. *The Soul Winner*. Springdale, PA. Whitaker House. 1995.

Stetzer, Ed. *Planting New Churches in a Postmodern Age*. Nashville: Broadman & Holman, 2003.

Stetzer, Ed, and Daniel Im. *Planting Missional Churches: Your Guide to Starting Churches That Multiply*. Nashville: B&H Academic, 2016.

Stetzer, Ed, and Philip Nation. *Compelled: Living the Mission of God*. Birmingham, AL: New Hope, 2012.

Swindoll, Charles R. *Sanctity of Life: The Inescapable Issue*. Dallas: Word, 1990.

Tang, Leonard Jay, and Charles E. Cotherman. *Sent to Flourish: A Guide to Planting and Multiplying Churches*. Downers Grove, IL: InterVarsity Press, 2019.

Terry, John Mark, and J. D. Payne. *Developing a Strategy for Missions: A Biblical, Historical, and Cultural Introduction*. Grand Rapids: Baker, 2013.

Thomas, Bob. *Walt Disney: An American Original*. New York: Simon & Schuster, 1976.

Thomas, Gary. *The Sacred Search: What If It's Not About Who You Marry, But Why?* Colorado Springs: Cook, 2013.

Thompson, Edgar W. *Wesley: Apostolic Man*. Eugene, OR: Wipf & Stock, 2015.

Thune, Bob, and Will Walker. *The Gospel-Centered Life: A Nine-Lesson Study*. Greensboro, NC: New Growth, 2009.

Tozer. A. W. *Men Who Met God*. Camp Hill, PA: Christian Publications, 1986.

Tozer, A. W. *Out of the Rut, Into Revival: Dealing with Spiritual Stagnation*. London: Hodder & Stoughton, 1993.

Tyerman, Luke. *The Life of the Reverend George Whitefield, Volume I*. Azle, TX: Need of the Times Publishers, 1995.

Vaters, Karl. *Small Church Essentials: Field-Tested Principles for Leading a Healthy Congregation of Under 250*. Chicago: Moody, 2018.

Wagner, C. Peter. *Your Spiritual Gifts Can Help Your Church Grow: How to Find Your Gift and Use It*. Ventura, CA: Regal, 1979.

Walker, Matthew. *Why We Sleep: The New Science of Sleep and Dreams*. New York: Penguin Random House, 2017.

Wiersbe, Warren W. *Real Worship: It Will Transform Your Life*. Nashville: Thomas Nelson, 1986.

Wiersbe, Warren W. *Real Peace: Freedom and Conscience in the Christian Life*. Grand Rapids: Baker, 2003.

Williams, William. *The Experience Meeting: An Introduction to the Welsh Societies of the Evangelical Awakening*. Vancouver, Canada: Regent College Bookstore, 1995.

Wilson, Todd, and Dave Ferguson. *Becoming a Level Five Multiplying Church Field Guide*. Centreville, VA: Exponential, 2019.

Wilson, Todd. *Dream Big Plan Smart: Finding Your Pathway to Level Five Multiplication*. Centreville, VA: Exponential, 2016.

Wilson, Todd. *Multipliers: Leading Beyond Addition*. Centreville, VA: Exponential, 2017.

Witten, Robert R. *Pioneer Methodism; Or, Itinerant Life in Missouri*. Vernon, CA: Hannibal Print Company, 1881.

Woodward, J. R., and Dan White Jr. *The Church as Movement: Starting and Sustaining Missional-Incarnational Communities*. Downers Grove, IL: InterVarsity Press, 2016.

Wright, N. T. *Paul: A Biography*. New York: HarperCollins, 2018.

Wright, N. T., and Michael F Bird. *The New Testament in its World, An Introduction to the History, Literature, and Theology of the First Christians*. Grand Rapids: Zondervan Academic, 2019.

Yancey, Philip. *Rumors of Another World: What on Earth Are We Missing?* Grand Rapids: Zondervan, 2003.

Zodhiates, Spiros. *The Complete Word Study Dictionary: New Testament*. Chattanooga, TN: AMG, 1992.

SCRIPTURE INDEX

Romans

SUBJECT INDEX

Reaching the Unreached

Becoming Raiders of the Lost Art

Peyton Jones

Reaching the Unreached recounts the stories, struggles, and triumphs of individuals and churches that have reinvented themselves to meet the world where it is, working to reach the ones no one else is reaching. Author Peyton Jones teaches you how to awake the sleeping giant of Christ's church.

From accidentally planting a church in a Starbucks in Europe, to baptizing members of the Mexican mafia in Long Beach Harbor, Jones has been on the front lines of today's missional movement and has lived to tell the tale. In *Reaching the Unreached*, he teaches church planters, pastors, and church leaders how to convert pew jockeys into missionaries, one person at a time.

Today there are two types of churches: those who put their proverbial heads in the sand and those who champion first-century principles, meet the challenges head-on, and embrace the adventure of mission in community. Tomorrow, only one type of church will survive—those that accept the challenge to reach the unreached.

Available in stores and online!